ADVERTISEMENT.

NEW-YORK, *August* 1, 1864.

THE subscriber begs leave to present this edition of the New Tariff of Duties chargeable upon Importations into the Ports of the United States, thoroughly revised and corrected, in conformity with Act of Congress of March 2d, 1861, and Addendas of August 5, 1861, December 24, 1861, July 14, 1862, March 3, 1863, and **June 30, 1864**, by Mr. E. D. OGDEN, Chief Entry Clerk of the New-York Custom-House, so well known in connection with this work, having compiled the same for nearly thirty years, and with what accuracy is well known to the public, his being recognised as the only official copy published.

I would respectfully state, that owing to the enormous rise in the price of materials, labor, &c., &c., the expense attending this edition has been greater than any heretofore published, and I am compelled to ask a higher price for the work.

Mr. OGDEN, as well as the Publisher, have exercised great care to have this edition merit the same approbation of the public as former ones.

PHILIP E. BOGERT,
Late BOGERT, BOURNE & AUTEN,
Publisher,
STATIONER, PRINTER, LITHOGRAPHER AND BLANK BOOK MANUFACTURER,
174 *and* 176 *Pearl Street.*

TARIFF,

OR

RATES OF DUTIES

PAYABLE ON

Goods, Wares and Merchandise

IMPORTED INTO THE

UNITED STATES OF AMERICA,

IN CONFORMITY WITH THE ACT OF CONGRESS OF MARCH 2, 1861.

WITH ADDENDA OF

AUGUST 5, 1861, JULY 14, 1862,
DECEMBER 24, 1861, MARCH 3, 1863,
AND JUNE 30, 1864.

ALSO, CONTAINING ALL THE

Recent Circulars and Decisions of the Treasury Department

RELATING TO COMMERCE AND THE REVENUE.

TABLES OF FOREIGN WEIGHTS, MEASURES, CURRENCIES, ETC., REDUCED TO THE UNITED STATES STANDARD.

ARRANGED BY E. D. OGDEN,

CHIEF ENTRY CLERK, CUSTOM-HOUSE, PORT OF NEW-YORK.

New-York:

PUBLISHED BY PHILIP E. BOGERT,

STATIONER, PRINTER, LITHOGRAPHER, AND BLANK BOOK MANUFACTURER,

174 and 176 Pearl Street.

1864.

INDEX.

INDEX TO APPENDIX.

TREASURY DEPARTMENT,
December 26, 1861.

The act of Congress entitled "An act to increase the duties on tea, coffee, and sugar," approved December 24, 1861, is herewith transmitted for the information and government of officers of the customs and others concerned.

This act applies to all importations of the articles enumerated, whether in warehouse or imported on and after the 25th instant, on which day the act took effect.

S. P. CHASE,
Secretary of the Treasury.

[PUBLIC—No. 2.]

AN ACT to increase the duties on Tea, Coffee, and Sugar.

Be it enacted by the Senate and House of Representatives of the United States of America in Congress assembled, That from and after the date of the passage of this act, in lieu of the duties heretofore imposed by law on articles hereinafter mentioned, there shall be levied, collected, and paid, on the goods, wares, and merchandise herein enumerated and provided for, imported from foreign countries, the following duties and rates of duty, that is to say: First. On all teas, twenty cents per pound. Second. On coffee of all kinds, five cents per pound. Third. On raw sugar, commonly called Muscovada (Muscavado) or brown sugar, and on sugars not advanced above number twelve, Dutch standard, by claying, boiling, clarifying, or other process, and on syrup of sugar or of sugar cane, and concentrated molasses or concentrated melado, two cents and a half per pound; and on white and clayed sugar, when advanced beyond the raw state, above number twelve, Dutch standard, by clarifying or other process, and not yet refined, three cents per pound; on refined sugars, whether loaf, lump, crushed, or pulverized, five cents per pound; on sugars, after being refined, when they are tinctured, colored, or in any way adulterated, and on sugar candy, eight cents per pound; on molasses, six cents per gallon: *Provided,* That all syrups of sugar or of sugar cane, concentrated molasses or concentrated melado, entered under the name of molasses, or any other name than syrup of sugar or of sugar cane, concentrated molasses or concentrated melado, shall be liable to forfeiture to the United States, and the same shall be forfeited.

Approved December 24, [1861.]

DEPARTMENT OF STATE,
WASHINGTON, *December* 26, 1861.

I certify that the foregoing is a true copy from the original act on file in this department.

W. HUNTER, *Chief Clerk.*

CIRCULAR

TO

COLLECTORS AND OTHER OFFICERS OF THE CUSTOMS.

TREASURY DEPARTMENT,
August 7th, 1861.

The act of Congress of August 5th, 1861, entitled, "An Act to provide increased revenue from imports, to pay interest on the public debt, and for other purposes," so far as it relates to the duties on imports, goes into immediate effect, and I publish that portion of it for the information and government of officers of the customs and others concerned.

In executing the provision relating to drawback duties on the exportation of foreign imported merchandise, contained in the 5th section, collectors of the customs will, until otherwise instructed, be governed, in general, by the provisions of the collection act of March 2d, 1799, in regard to drawbacks. The right of drawback will attach only to merchandise imported under the provisions of the said act of August 5th, 1861, and exported in the original packages.

In allowing drawback of duties on the exportation of merchandise manufactured from imported raw material, as provided by the 4th section, collectors will be governed by the regulations of the 27th of March last, relating to drawback on cordage. Adequate proof of the quantity, quality, and value of raw material used in the manufacture, must, however, until otherwise directed, be submitted in each case for my decision as to the rate of drawback to be allowed. Full and detailed instructions will be prepared and issued as soon as practicable.

S. P. CHASE,
Secretary of the Treasury.

AN ACT to provide increased Revenue from Imports, to pay Interest on the Public Debt, and for other purposes.

Be it enacted by the Senate and House of Representatives of the United States of America in Congress assembled, That, from and after the date of the passage of this act, in lieu of the duties heretofore imposed by law on the articles hereinafter mentioned, and on such as may now be exempt from duty, there shall be levied, collected, and paid, on the goods, wares, and merchandise herein enumerated and provided for, imported from foreign countries, the following duties and rates of duty, that is to say: First. On raw sugar, commonly called muscovado or brown sugar, and on sugars not advanced above number twelve, Dutch standard, by claying, boiling, clarifying, or other process, and on syrup of sugar or of sugar cane and concentrated molasses, or concentrated melado, two cents per pound; and on white and clayed sugar, when advanced beyond the raw state, above number twelve, Dutch standard, by clarifying or other process, and not yet refined, two and a half cents per pound; on refined sugars, whether loaf, lump, crushed, or pulverized, four cents per pound; on sugars after being refined, when they are tinctured, colored, or in any way adulterated, and on sugar-candy, six cents per pound; on molasses, five cents per gallon; *Provided*, That all syrups of sugar or sugar-cane, concentrated molasses or melado, entered under the name of molasses, or any other name than syrup of sugar or of sugar-cane, concentrated molasses, or concentrated melado, shall be liable to forfeiture to the United States. On all teas, fifteen cents per pound; on almonds, four cents per pound; shelled almonds, six cents per pound; on brimstone, crude, three dollars per ton; on brimstone, in rolls, six dollars per ton; on coffee, of all kinds, four cents per pound; on cocoa, three cents per pound; on cocoa leaves and cocoa shells, two cents per pound; on cocoa prepared or manufactured, eight cents per pound; on chickory root, one cent per pound; and on chickory ground, two cents per pound; on chocolate, six cents per pound; on cassia, ten cents per pound; cassia buds, fifteen cents per pound; on cinnamon, twenty cents per pound; on cloves, eight cents per pound; on cayenne pepper, six cents per pound; on cayenne pepper, ground, eight cents per pound; on currents, five cents per pound, on argol, three cents per pound; on cream tartar, six cents per pound; on tartaric acid, tartar emetic, and rochelle salts, ten cents per pound; on dates, two cents per pound; on figs, five cents per pound; on ginger root, three cents per pound; on ginger, ground, five cents per pound; on liquorice paste and juice, five cents per pound; liquorice root, one cent per pound; on mace and nutmegs, twenty-five cents per pound; on nuts of all kinds, not otherwise provided for, two cents per pound; on pepper, six cents per pound; on pimento, six cents per pound; on plums, five cents per pound; prunes, five cents per pound; on raisins, five cents per pound; on unmanufactured Russia hemp, forty dollars per ton; on Manilla and other hemps of India, twenty-five dollars per ton; on lead, in pigs or bars, one dollar and fifty cents per one hundred pounds; in sheets, two dollars and twenty-five cents per one hundred pounds; on white lead, dry, or ground in oil, and red lead, two dollars and twenty-five cents per one hundred pounds; on salt, in sacks, eighteen cents per one hundred pounds; and in bulk, twelve cents per one hundred pounds; on soda ash, one-half cent per pound; on bicarbonate of soda, one cent per pound; on sal soda, one-half cent per pound; on caustic soda, one cent per pound; on chlorate of lime, thirty cents per one hundred pounds; on saltpetre, crude, one cent per pound; refined, or partially refined, two cents per pound; spirits of turpentine, ten cents per gallon; on oil of cloves, seventy cents per pound; on brandy, one dollar and twenty-five cents per gallon; on spirits distilled from grain, or other materials, fifty cents per gallon; on gum copal, and other gums or resinous substances used for the same or similar purposes as gum copal, ten cents per pound.

SEC. 2. *And be it further enacted,* That, from and after the day and year aforesaid, there shall be levied, collected, and paid, on the importation of the articles hereinafter mentioned, the following duties, that is to say: On arrowroot, twenty per centum ad valorum; on ginger, preserved or pickled, thirty per centum ad valorem; on limes, lemons, oranges, bananas, and plantains, twenty per centum ad valorem; on Peruvian bark, fifteen per centum ad valorem; on quinine, thirty per centum ad valorem; on rags, of whatever material, ten per centum ad valorem; on gunpowder, thirty per centum ad valorem; on feathers and downs, thirty per centum ad valorem; on hides, ten per centum ad valorem; on sole and bend leather, thirty per centum ad valorem; on India-rubber, raw or unmanufactured, ten per centum ad valorem; on India-rubber shoes and boots, thirty per centum ad valorem; on ivory, unmanufactured, and on vegetable ivory, ten per centum ad valorem; on wines of all kinds, fifty per centum ad valorem; on silk in the gum, not more advanced in the manufacture than single tram and thrown or organzine, twenty-five per centum ad valorem; on all silks valued at not over one dollar per square yard, thirty per centum ad valorem; on all silks valued over one dollar per square yard, forty per centum ad valorem; on all silk velvets, or velvets of which silk is the component material of chief value, valued at three dollars per square yard, or under, thirty per centum ad valorem; valued at over three dollars per square yard, forty per centum ad valorem; on floss silks, thirty per centum ad valorem; on silk ribbons, galloons, braids, fringes, laces, tassels, buttons, button-cloths, trimmings, and on silk twist, twist composed of mohair and silk, sewing silk in gum or purified, and all other manufactures of silk, or of which silk shall be the component material of chief value, not otherwise provided for, forty per centum ad valorem.

SEC. 3. *And be it further enacted,* That all articles, goods, wares and merchandise, imported from beyond the Cape of Good Hope in foreign vessels, not entitled by reciprocal treaties to be exempt from discriminating duties, tonnage, and other charges, and all other articles, goods, wares, and merchandise not imported direct from the place of their growth or production, or in foreign vessels, entitled by reciprocal treaties to be exempt from discriminating duties, tonnage, and other charges, shall be subject to pay, in addition to the duties imposed by this act, ten per centum ad valorem: *Provided,* That this rule shall not apply to goods, wares, and merchandise imported from beyond the Cape of Good Hope in American vessels.

SEC. 4. *And be it further enacted,* That from and after the passage of this act, there shall be allowed, on all articles wholly manufactured of materials imported, on which duties have been paid when exported, a drawback, equal in amount to the duty paid on such materials and no more, to be ascertained under such regulations as shall be prescribed by the Secretary of the Treasury: *Provided,* That ten per centum on the amount of all drawbacks, so allowed, shall be retained for the use of the United States by the collectors paying such drawbacks, respectively.

SEC. 5. *And be it further enacted*, That all goods, wares, and merchandise, actually on shipboard and bound to the United States, and all goods, wares, and merchandise, on deposit in warehouses or public stores at the date of the passage of this act, shall be subject to pay such duties as provided by law before and at the time of the passage of this act: *Provided*, That all goods deposited in public store or bonded warehouse after this act takes effect and goes into operation, if designed for consumption in the United States, must be withdrawn therefrom, or the duties thereon paid in three months after the same are deposited, and goods designed for exportation and consumption in foreign countries may be withdrawn by the owner at any time before the expiration of three years after the same are deposited, such goods, if not withdrawn in three years, to be regarded as abandoned to the Government, and sold under such regulations as the Secretary of the Treasury may prescribe, and the proceeds paid into the Treasury: *Provided*, That merchandise upon which the owner may have neglected to pay duties within three months from the time of its deposit may be withdrawn and entered for consumption at any time within two years of the time of its deposit, upon the payment of the legal duties, with an addition of twenty-five per centum thereto: *Provided, also*, That merchandise upon which duties have been paid, if exported to a foreign country, within three years shall be entitled to return duties, proper evidence of such merchandise having been landed abroad to be furnished to the collector by the importer, one per centum of said duties to be retained by the Government.

SEC. 6. *And be it further enacted*, That the act entitled "An Act to provide for the payment of outstanding Treasury Notes, to authorize a loan, to regulate and fix the duties on imports, and for other purposes," approved March two, eighteen hundred and sixty-one, be and the same is hereby amended, as follows: That is to say, First, in section six, article first, after the words "in cordials and," strike out "liquors," and insert "liqueurs;" Second, in the same section, after the word "represent," insert, "*Provided, also*, That no lower rate or amount of duty shall be levied, collected, and paid on brandy, spirits, and all other spirituous beverages, than that now fixed by law for the description of first proof, but shall be increased in proportion for any greater strength than the strength of first proof;" Third, in section seventh, clause fifth, the words, "on screws, washed or plated, and all other screws, of iron or any other metal," shall be stricken out, and the words "on screws, of any other metal than iron," shall be inserted; Fourth, section twelve, article first, after the words "eighteen cents," where the first occur, insert, "or less;" Fifth, section thirteen, article second, after the word "manufacturer," insert "except hosiery;" Sixth, in the same section, article third, strike out "wool" wherever it occurs, and insert in each place "worsted;" Seventh, in section fourteen, article first, after the words "ten per centum," insert "ad valorem;" Eighth, in section fifteen, before the word "yarns" insert "hemp;" in the same section, after the word "sheetings," insert "of flax or hemp;" and strike out "jute goods," and in lieu thereof insert "jute yarns;" Ninth, in section twenty-two, strike out the words "unwrought clay, three dollars per ton;" Tenth, in section nineteen, strike out "compositions of glass or paste, not set; intended for use by jewellers;" Eleventh, in section twenty-two, strike out "compositions of glass or paste, when set;" Twelfth, in section twenty-three, article sheathing metal, strike out "yard," and insert "foot."

SEC. 7. *And be it further enacted*, That all acts and parts of acts repugnant to the provisions of this act be and the same are hereby repealed: *Provided*, That the existing laws shall extend to, and be in force for, the collection of the duties imposed by this act, for the prosecution and punishment of all offences, and for the recovery, collection, distribution, and remission of all fines, penalties, and forfeitures, as fully and effectually as if every regulation, penalty, forfeiture, provision, clause, matter, and thing to that effect in the existing laws contained, had been inserted in and re-enacted by this act.

Approved August 5th, 1861.

TREASURY DEPARTMENT,
March 13, 1861.

The following act of Congress and joint resolution, approved March 2, 1861, the provisions of which relating to duties on imports go into effect on the 1st proximo, are published for the information and government of the officers of the customs at the several ports and others concerned.

SALMON P. CHASE,
Secretary of the Treasury.

[PUBLIC—No. 22.]

AN ACT to provide for the payment of outstanding Treasury Notes, to authorize a Loan, to regulate and fix the Duties on Imports, and for other purposes.

Be it enacted by the Senate and House of Representatives of the United States of America, in Congress assembled, That the President of the United States be, and hereby is authorized, at any time within twelve months from the passage of this act, to borrow, on the credit of the United States, a sum not exceeding ten millions of dollars, or so much thereof as, in his opinion, the exigencies of the public service may require, to be applied to the payment of appropriations made by law, and the balance of treasury notes now outstanding, and no other purposes, in addition to the money received, or which may be received, into the treasury from other sources: *Provided,* That no stipulation or contract shall be made to prevent the United States from reimbursing any sum borrowed under the authority of this act at any time after the expiration of ten years from the first day of July next, by the United States giving three months' notice, to be published in some newspaper published at the seat of government, of their readiness to do so; and no contract shall be made to prevent the redemption of the same at any time after the expiration of twenty years from the said first day of July next, without notice.

SEC. 2. *And be it further enacted,* That stock shall be issued for the amount so borrowed, bearing interest not exceeding six per centum per annum; and the Secretary of the Treasury be, and is hereby authorized, with the consent of the President, to cause certificates of stock to be prepared, which shall be signed by the Register and sealed with the seal of the Treasury Department, for the amount so borrowed, in favor of the parties lending the same, or their assigns, which certificates may be transferred on the books of the treasury, under such regulations as may be established by the Secretary of the Treasury: *Provided,* That no certificate shall be issued for a less sum than one thousand dollars: *And provided, also,* That whenever required, the Secretary of the Treasury may cause coupons of semiannual interest payable thereon to be attached to certificates issued under this act; and any certificate with such coupons of interest attached may be assigned and transferred by delivery of the same, instead of being transferred on the books of the treasury.

SEC. 3. *And be it further enacted,* That, before awarding any of said loan, the Secretary of the Treasury shall, as the exigencies of the public service require, cause to be inserted in two of the public newspapers of the city of Washington, and in one or more public newspapers in other cities of the United States, public notice that sealed proposals for so much of said loan as is required will be received until a certain day, to be specified in such notice, not less than thirty days from its first insertion in a Washington newspaper; and such notice shall state the amount of the loan, at what periods the money shall be paid, if by instalments, and at what places. Such sealed proposals shall be opened, on the day appointed in the notice, in the presence of such persons as may choose to attend, and the proposals decided on by the Secretary of the Treasury, who shall accept the most favorable offered by responsible bidders for said stock. And the said Secretary shall report to Congress, at the commencement of the next session, the amount of money borrowed under this act, and of whom and on what terms it shall have been obtained, with an abstract or brief statement of all the proposals submitted for the same, distinguishing between those accepted and those rejected, with a detailed statement of the expense of making such loans: *Provided,* That no stock shall be disposed of at less than its par value: *And provided, further,* That no part of the loan hereby authorized shall be applied to the service of the present fiscal year.

SEC. 4. *And be it further enacted,* That in case the proposals made for said loan, or for so much thereof as the exigencies of the public service shall require, shall not be satisfactory, the President of the United States shall be, and hereby is authorized, to decline to accept such offer if for less than the par value of the bonds constituting the said stock, and in lieu thereof, and to the extent and amount of the loan authorized to be made by this act, to issue treasury notes for sums not less than fifty dollars, bearing interest at the rate of six per centum per annum, payable semi-annually, on the first days of January and July in each year, at proper places of payment to be prescribed by the Secretary, with the approval of the President; and under the like circumstances and conditions, the President of the United States is hereby authorized to substitute treasury notes of equal amount for the whole or any part of any of the loans for which he is now by law authorized to contract and issue bonds. And the treasury notes so issued under the authority herein given shall be received in payment for all debts due to the United States when offered, and in like manner shall be given in payment for any sum due from the United States, when payment in that mode is requested by the person to whom payment is to be made, or for their par value in coin. And the faith of the United States is hereby pledged for the due payment of the interest and the redemption of the principal of the stock or treasury notes which may be issued under the authority of this act; and the sum of twenty thousand dollars is hereby appropriated, out of any money in the treasury not otherwise appropriated, to pay the expenses of preparing the certificates of stock or treasury notes herein authorized, to be done in the usual mode and under the restrictions as to employment and payment of officers contained in the laws authorizing former loans and issues of treasury notes; and it shall be at the option of holders of the treasury notes hereby authorized by this act, to exchange the same for the stock herein anthorized, at par, or for bonds, in lieu of which said treasury notes were issued: *Provided,* That no certificate shall be exchanged for treasury notes, or bonds, in sums less than five hundred dollars: *And provided, further,* That the authority to issue the said treasury notes, or give the same in payment for debts due from the United States, shall be limited to the thirtieth day of June, eighteen hundred and sixty-two; and that the same may be redeemable at the pleasure of the United States at any time within two years after the passage of this act; and that said notes shall cease to bear interest after they shall have been called in by the Secretary of the Treasury under the provisions of this act.

SEC. 5. *And be it further enacted,* That from and after the first day of April, Anno Domini eighteen hundred and sixty-one, in lieu of the duties heretofore imposed by law on the articles hereinafter mentioned, and on such as may now be exempt from duty, there shall be levied, collected, and paid, on the goods, wares, and merchandise herein enumerated and provided for, imported from foreign countries, the following duties and rates of duties, that is to say:

First. On raw sugar, commonly called Muscovada or brown sugar, not advanced beyond the raw state by claying or other process; and on syrup of sugar, or of sugar cane, and concentrated molasses, or concentrated melado, and on white and clayed sugars, when advanced beyond the raw state by claying, or other process, and not refined, three-fourths of one cent per pound; on refined sugars, whether loaf, lump, crushed, or pulverized, two cents per pound; on sugars, after being refined, when they are tinctured, colored, or in any way adulterated, and on sugar candy, four cents per pound: *Provided,* That all syrups of sugar, or of sugar cane, concentrated molasses or melado, entered under the name of molasses, or any other name than syrup of sugar or of sugar cane, concentrated molasses, or concentrated melado, shall be liable to forfeiture to the United States; on molasses, two cents per gallon; on confectionery of all kinds, not otherwise provided for, thirty per centum ad valorem.

SEC. 6. *And be it further enacted,* That from and after the day and year aforesaid there shall be levied, collected, and paid, on the importation of the articles hereinafter mentioned, the following duties, that is to say:

First. On brandy, for first proof, one dollar per gallon; on other spirits manufactured or distilled from grain, for first-proof, forty cents per gallon; on spirits from other materials, for first-proof, forty cents per gallon; on cordials and liquors of all kinds, fifty cents per gallon; on arrack, absynthe,

2

kirschenwasser, ratafia, and other similar spirituous beverages not otherwise provided for, fifty cents per gallon; on bay rum, twenty-five cents per gallon: *Provided*, That the duty upon brandy spirits, and all other spirituous beverages herein enumerated, shall be collected upon the basis of first-proof, and so in proportion for any greater strength than the strength of first-proof; on wines of all kinds, forty per centum ad valorem: *Provided*, That all imitations of brandy, or spirits, or of any of the said wines, and all wines imported by any names whatever, shall be subject to the duty provided for the genuine article which it is intended to represent: *Provided further*, That brandies or other spirituous liquors may be imported in bottles, when the package shall contain not less than one dozen, and all bottles shall pay a separate duty, according to the rate established by this act, whether containing wines, brandies, or other spirituous liquors, subject to duty as hereinbefore mentioned; on ale, porter, and beer, in bottles, twenty-five cents per gallon; otherwise than in bottles, fifteen cents per gallon; on all spirituous liquors not enumerated, thirty-three and one-third per centum ad valorem.

Second. On cigars of all kinds, valued at five dollars or under per thousand, twenty cents per pound; over five dollars and not over ten, forty cents per pound; and over ten dollars, sixty cents per pound, and in addition thereto ten per centum ad valorem; on snuff, ten cents per pound; on unmanufactured tobacco, in leaf, twenty-five per centum ad valorem; on all other manufactured or unmanufactured tobacco, thirty per centum ad valorem.

SEC. 7. *And be it further enacted*, That from and after the day and year aforesaid there shall be levied, collected, and paid on the importation of the articles hereinafter mentioned the following duties, that is to say:

First. On bar iron, rolled or hammered, comprising flats not less than one inch, or more than seven inches wide, nor less than one-quarter of an inch or more than two inches thick; rounds, not less than one-half an inch or more than four inches in diameter; and squares not less than one-half an inch, or more than four inches square, fifteen dollars per ton: *Provided*, That all iron in slabs, blooms, loops, or other forms, less finished than iron in bars, and more advanced than pig iron, except castings, shall be rated as iron in bars, and pay a duty accordingly: *And provided further*, That none of the above iron shall pay a less rate of duty than twenty per centum ad valorem; on all iron imported in bars for railroads or inclined planes, made to patterns and fitted to be laid down upon such roads or planes, without further manufacture, and not exceeding six inches high, twelve dollars per ton; on boiler plate iron, twenty dollars per ton; on iron wire drawn and finished, not more than one-fourth of one inch in diameter nor less than number sixteen wire gauge, seventy-five cents per one hundred pounds and fifteen per centum ad valorem; over number sixteen, and not over number twenty-five wire gauge, one dollar and fifty cents per one hundred pounds, and in addition fifteen per centum ad valorem; over or finer than number twenty-five wire gauge, two dollars per one hundred pounds, and in addition fifteen per centum ad valorem; on all other descriptions of rolled or hammered iron, not otherwise provided for, twenty dollars per ton.

Second, On iron in pigs, six dollars per ton; on vessels of cast iron, not otherwise provided for, and on sad irons, tailors' and hatters' irons, stoves and stove plates, one per cent per pound; on cast iron steam, gas, and water pipe, fifty cents per one hundred pounds ; on cast iron butts and hinges, two cents per pound; on hollow ware, glazed or tinned, two cents and a half per pound ; on all other castings of iron, not otherwise provided for, twenty-five per centum ad valorem.

Third. On old scrap iron, six dollars per ton: *Provided,* That nothing shall be deemed old iron that has not been in actual use, and fit only to be remanufactured.

Fourth. On band and hoop iron, slit rods not otherwise provided for, twenty dollars per ton; on cut nails and spikes, one cent per pound ; on iron cables or chains, or parts thereof, and anvils, one dollar and twenty-five cents per one hundred pounds ; on anchors, or parts thereof, one dollar and fifty cents per one hundred pounds; on wrought board nails, spikes, rivets, and bolts, two cents per pound; on bed screws and wrought hinges, one cent and a half per pound; on chains, trace chains, halter chains, and fence chains, made of wire or rods, one-half of one inch in diameter or over, one cent and a half per pound; under one-half of one inch in diameter, and not under one-fourth of one inch in diameter, two cents per pound; under one-fourth of one inch in diameter, and not under number nine wire gauge, two cents and a half per pound; under number nine wire gauge, twenty-five per centum ad valorem ; on blacksmiths' hammers and sledges, axles, or parts thereof, and malleable iron in castings, not otherwise provided for, two cents per pound; on horse-shoe nails, three cents and a half per pound; on steam gas, and water tubes and flues of wrought iron, two cents per pound; on wrought-iron railroad chairs, and on wrought-iron nuts and washers, ready punched, twenty-five dollars per ton; on cut tacks, brads, and sprigs, not exceeding sixteen ounces to the thousand, two cents per thousand; exceeding sixteen ounces to the thousand, two cents per pound.

Fifth. On smooth or polished sheet iron, by whatever name designated, two cents per pound; on other sheet iron, common or black, not thinner than number twenty wire gauge, twenty dollars per ton ; thinner than number twenty, and not thinner than number twenty-five wire gauge, twenty-five dollars per ton; thinner than number twenty-five wire gauge, thirty dollars per ton; on tin plates galvanized, galvanized iron, or iron coated with zinc, two cents per pound; on mill irons and mill cranks of wrought iron, and wrought iron for ships, locomotives, locomotive tire, or parts thereof, and steam engines, or parts thereof, weighing each twenty-five pounds or more, one cent and a half per pound; on screws commonly called wood screws, two inches or over in length, five cents per pound; less than two inches in length, eight cents per pound; on screws washed or plated, and all other screws of iron or any other metal, thirty per centum ad valorem; on all manufactures of iron not otherwise provided for, thirty per centum ad valorem.

Sixth. On all steel in ingots, bars, sheets, or wire, not less than one-fourth of one inch in diameter, valued at seven cents per pound or less, one and a half cent per pound; valued at above seven cents per pound, and not above eleven cents per pound, two cents per pound; steel in any form, not otherwise provided for, shall pay a duty of twenty per centum ad valorem; on steel wire less than one-fourth of an inch in diameter, and not less than number sixteen wire gauge, two dollars per one hundred pounds, and in addition thereto, fifteen per centum ad valorem; less or finer than number sixteen wire gauge, two dollars and fifty cents per one hundred pounds, and in addition thereto, fifteen per centum ad valorem; on cross-cut saws, eight cents per lineal foot; on mill, pit, and drag saws, not over nine inches wide, twelve and a half cents per lineal foot; over nine inches wide, twenty cents per lineal foot; on skates costing twenty cents or less per pair, six cents per pair; on those costing over twenty cents per pair, thirty per centum ad valorem; on all manufactures of steel, or of which steel shall be a component part, not otherwise provided for, thirty per centum ad valorem: *Provided,* That all articles partially manufactured, not otherwise provided for, shall pay the same rate of duty as if wholly manufactured.

Seventh. On bituminous coal, one dollar per ton of twenty-eight bushels, eighty pounds to the bushel; on all other coal, fifty cents per ton of twenty-eight bushels, eighty pounds to the bushel; on coke and culm of coal, twenty-five per centum ad valorem.

Sec. 8. *And be it further enacted,* That from and after the day and year aforesaid, there shall be levied, collected, and paid on the importation of the articles hereinafter mentioned the following duties, that is to say:

First. On lead in pigs and bars, one cent per pound; on old scrap lead, fit only to be remanufactured, one cent per pound; on lead in sheets, pipes, or shot, one cent and a half per pound; on pewter, when old and fit only to be remanufactured, one cent per pound.

Second. On copper in pigs, bars, or ingots, two cents per pound; on copper when old and fit only to be remanufactured, one cent and a half per pound; on sheathing copper, in sheets forty-eight inches long and fourteen inches wide, and weighing from fourteen to thirty-four ounces the square foot, two cents per pound; on copper rods, bolts, nails, spikes, copper bottoms, copper in sheets or plates, called braziers' copper, and other sheets of copper not otherwise provided for, twenty-five per centum ad valorem; on zinc, spelter, or teutenegue, manufactured in blocks or pigs, one dollar per one hundred pounds; on zinc, spelter, or teutenegue in sheets, one cent and a half per pound.

Sec. 9. *And be it further enacted,* That from and after the day and year aforesaid, there shall be levied, collected, and paid on the importation of the articles hereinafter mentioned the following duties, that is to say:

First. On white lead and oxide of zinc, dry or ground in oil, red lead, and litharge, one cent and a half per pound; on sugar of lead or acetate of lead and nitrate of lead, chromate and bichromate of potash, three cents per pound; on hydriodate, and prussiate of potash and chromic acid, and salts of iodine, and resublimed iodine, fifteen per centum ad valorem; on whiting, twenty-five cents per one hundred pounds; on Paris white, pipe clay, and ochres or ochrey earth, not otherwise provided for, when dry, thirty-five cents per one hundred pounds; when ground in oil, one dollar and thirty-five cents per one hundred pounds; on umber, fifty cents per one hundred pounds; on putty, one cent per pound; on linseed, flaxseed, hempseed, and rapeseed oil, twenty cents per gallon; on kerosine oil, and all other coal oils, ten cents per gallon; on alum, alum substitute, sulphate of alumina and aluminous cake, fifty cents per one hundred pounds; on copperas, green vitriol, or sulphate of iron, twenty-five cents per one hundred pounds; on bleaching powders, fifteen cents per one hundred pounds; on refined camphor, six cents per pound; on refined borax, three cents per pound; on tallow, one cent per pound; on tallow candles, two cents per pound; on spermaceti or wax candles and tapers, and on candles and tapers of spermaceti and wax combined, eight cents per pound; on stearine candles, and all other candles and tapers, four cents per ponnd; on spirits of turpentine, ten cents per gallon; on opium, one dollar per pound; on morphine and its salts, one dollar per ounce; on liquorice paste or juice, three cents per pound.

SEC. 10. *And be it further enacted*, That from and after the day and year aforesaid, there shall be levied, collected, and paid on the importation of the articles hereinafter mentioned the following duties, that is to say:

First. On salt, four cents per bushel of fifty-six pounds: *Provided*, That salt imported in bags, or not in bulk, shall pay a duty of six cents per bushel of fifty-six pounds; on bristles, four cents per pound; on honey, ten cents per gallon; on vinegar, six cents per gallon; on mackerel, two dollars per barrel; on herrings, pickled or salted, one dollar per barrel; on pickled salmon, three dollars per barrel; on all other fish pickled, in barrels, one dollar and fifty cents per barrel; on all other foreign caught fish imported otherwise than in barrels or half barrels, or whether fresh, smoked, or dried, salted or pickled, not otherwise provided for, fifty cents per one hundred pounds.

Second. On beef and pork, one cent per pound; on hams and bacon, two cents per pound; on cheese, four cents per pound; on wheat, twenty cents per bushel; on butter, four cents per pound; on lard, two cents per pound; on rye and barley, fifteen cents per bushel; on Indian corn or maize, ten cents per bushel; on oats, ten cents per bushel; on potatoes, ten cents per bushel; on cleaned rice, one cent per pound; on uncleaned rice, or paddy, fifty cents per one hundred pounds; on sago and sago flour, fifty cents per one hundred pounds; on flaxseed or linseed, sixteen cents per bushel of fifty-two pounds; on hemp and rapeseed, ten cents per bushel of fifty-two pounds; on raw hides and skins of all kinds, whether dried, salted, or pickled, not otherwise provided for, five per centum ad valorem.

SEC. 11. *And be it further enacted,* That from and after the day and year aforesaid, there shall be levied, collected, and paid on the importation of the articles hereinafter mentioned, the following duties, that is to say:

First. On cassia, four cents per pound; on cassia buds, eight cents per pound; on cloves, four cents per pound; on pepper, two cents per pound; on Cayenne pepper, three cents per pound; on ground Cayenne pepper, four cents per pound; on pimento, two cents per pound; on cinnamon, ten cents per pound; on mace and nutmegs, fifteen cents per pound; on prunes, two cents per pound; on plums, one cent per pound; on dates, one-half of one cent per pound; on currants, two cents per pound; on figs, three cents per pound; on sultana, muscatel, and bloom raisins, either in boxes or jars, two cents per pound; on all other raisins, one cent per pound; on almonds, two cents per pound; on shelled almonds, four cents per pound; on all nuts not otherwise provided for, except those used for dyeing, one cent per pound.

SEC. 12. *And be it futher enacted,* That from and after the day and year aforesaid, there shall be levied, collected, and paid, on the importation of the articles hereinafter mentioned, the following duties, that is to say:

First. On all wool unmanufactured, and all hair of the alpaca, goat, and other like animals, unmanufactured, the value whereof at the last port or place from whence exported to the United States shall be less than eighteen cents per pound, five per centum ad valorem; exceeding eighteen cents per pound, and not exceeding twenty-four cents per pound, there shall be levied, collected, and paid a duty of three cents per pound; exceeding twenty-four cents per pound, there shall be levied, collected, and paid a duty of nine cents per pound: *Provided,* That any wool of the sheep, or hair of the alpaca, the goat, and other like animals which shall be imported in any other than the ordinary condition, as now and heretofore practiced, or which shall be changed in its character or condition for the purpose of evading the duty, or which shall be reduced in value by the admixture of dirt or any foreign substance to eighteen cents per pound or less, shall be subject to pay a duty of nine cents per pound, anything in this act to the contrary notwithstanding: *Provided, also,* That when wool of different qualities is imported in the same bale, bag, or package, and the aggregate value of the contents of the bale, bag, or package shall be appraised by the appraisers at a rate exceeding twenty-four cents per pound, it shall be charged with a duty of nine cents per pound: *Provided further,* That if bales of different qualities are embraced in the same invoice, at the same price whereby the average price shall be lessened more than ten per centum, the value of the whole shall be appraised according to the value of the bale of the best quality, and no bale or bales shall be liable to a less rate of duty in consequence of being invoiced with wool of lower value: *Provided, also,* That sheep skins, raw or unmanufactured, imported with the wool on, washed or unwashed, shall be subject to a duty of fifteen per centum ad valorem.

SEC. 13. *And be it further enacted,* That from and after the day and year aforesaid, there shall be levied, collected, and paid, on the importation of the articles hereinafter mentioned, the following duties, that is to say:

First. On Wilton, Saxony, and Aubusson, Axminster patent velvet, Tournay velvet, and tapestry velvet carpets and carpeting, Brussels carpets wrought by the Jacquard machine, and all medallion or whole carpets, valued at one dollar and twenty-five cents or under per square yard, forty cents per square yard; valued at over one dollar and twenty-five cents per square yard, fifty cents per square yard: *Provided,* That no carpet or rugs of the above description shall pay a duty less than twenty-five per centum ad valorem; on Brussels and tapestry Brussels carpets and carpeting, printed on the warp or otherwise, thirty cents per square yard; on all treble-ingrain and worsted-chain Venetian carpets and carpeting, twenty-five cents per square yard; on hemp or jute carpeting, four cents per square yard; on druggets, bockings, and felt carpets and carpeting, printed, colored, or otherwise, twenty cents per square yard; on all other kinds of carpets and carpeting, of wool, flax, or cotton, or parts of either, or other material, not otherwise specified, a duty of thirty per centum ad valorem: *Provided,* That mats, rugs, screens, covers, hassocks, bedsides, and other portions of carpets or carpeting, shall pay the rate of duty herein imposed on carpets or carpeting of similar character; on all other mats, screens, hassocks, and rugs, a duty of thirty per centum ad valorem.

Second. On woollen cloths, woollen shawls, and all manufactures of wool of every description, made wholly or in part of wool, not otherwise provided for, a duty of twelve cents per pound, and in addition thereto twenty-five per centum ad valorem; on endless belts for paper, and blanketing for printing machines, twenty-five per centum ad valorem; on all flannels valued at thirty cents or less per square yard, twenty-five per centum ad valorem; valued above thirty cents per square yard, and on all flannels colored, printed, or plaided, and flannels composed in part of cotton or silk, thirty per centum ad valorem; on hats of wool, twenty per centum ad valorem; on woollen and worsted yarn, valued at fifty cents and not over one dollar per pound, twelve cents per pound, and in addition thereto, fifteen per centum ad valorem; on woollen and worsted yarn, valued at over one dollar per pound, twelve cents per pound, and in addition thereto, twenty-five per centum ad valorem; on woollen and worsted yarns, or yarns for carpets, valued under fifty cents per pound, and not exceeding in fineness number fourteen, twenty-five per centum ad valorem; exceeding number fourteen, thirty per centum ad valorem; on clothing ready-made, and wearing apparel of every description, composed wholly or in part of wool, made up or manufactured wholly or in part by the tailor, seamstress, or manufacturer, twelve cents per pound, and in addition thereto, twenty-five per centum ad valorem; on blankets of all kinds, made wholly or in part of wool, valued at not exceeding twenty-eight cents per pound, there shall be charged a duty of six cents per pound, and in addition thereto, ten per centum ad valorem; on all valued above twenty-eight cents per pound, but not exceeding forty cents per pound, there shall be charged a duty of six cents per pound, and in addition thereto, twenty-five per centum ad valorem; on all valued above forty cents per pound there shall be charged a duty of twelve cents per pound, and in addition thereto, twenty per centum ad valorem; on woollen shawls, or shawls of which wool shall be the chief component material, a duty of sixteen cents per pound, and in addition thereto, twenty per centum ad valorem.

Third. On all delaines, Cashmere delaines, muslin delaines, barege delaines, composed wholly or in part of wool, gray, or uncolored, and on all other gray or uncolored goods of similar description, twenty-five per centum ad valorem; on bunting, and on all stained, colored, or printed, and on all other manufactures of wool, or of which wool shall be a component material, not otherwise provided for, thirty per centum ad valorem.

Fourth. On oilcloth, for floors, stamped, painted, or printed, valued at fifty cents or less per square yard, twenty per centum ad valorem; valued at over fifty cents per square yard, and on all other oilcloth, thirty per centem ad valorem.

Sec. 14. *And be it further enacted,* That from and after the day and year aforesaid, there shall be levied, collected and paid on the importation of the articles hereinafter mentioned, the following duties, that is to say:

First. On all manufactures of cotton not bleached, colored, stained, painted, or printed, and not exceeding one hundred threads to the square inch, counting the warp and filling, and exceeding in weight five ounces per square yard, one cent per square yard; on finer or lighter goods of like description, not exceeding one hundred and forty threads to the square inch, counting the warp and filling, two cents per square yard; on goods of like description, exceeding one hundred and forty threads, and not exceeding two hundred threads to the square inch, counting the warp and filling, three cents per square yard; on like goods exceeding two hundred threads to the square inch, counting the warp and filling, four cents per square yard; on all goods embraced in the foregoing schedules, if bleached, there shall be levied, collected and paid, an additional duty of one-half of one cent per square yard; and if printed, painted, colored, or stained, there shall be levied, collected and paid, a duty of ten per centum in addition to the rates of duty provided in the foregoing schedules: *Provided,* That upon all plain woven cotton goods not included in the foregoing schedules, and upon cotton goods of every description, the value of which shall exceed sixteen cents per square yard, there shall be levied, collected and paid, a duty of twenty-five per centum ad valorem: *And provided further,* That no cotton goods having more than two hundred threads to the square inch, counting the warp and filling, shall be admitted to a less rate of duty than is provided for goods which are of that number of threads.

Second. On spool and other thread of cotton, thirty per centum ad valorem.

Third. On shirts and drawers, wove or made on frames, composed wholly of cotton and cotton velvet, twenty-five per centum ad valorem; and on all manufactures composed wholly of cotton, bleached, unbleached, printed, painted, or dyed, not otherwise provided for, thirty per centum ad valorem.

Fourth. On all brown or bleached linens, ducks, canvas paddings, cot-bottoms, burlaps, drills, coatings, brown Hollands, blay linens, damasks, diapers, crash, huckabacks, handkerchiefs, lawns, or other manufactures of flax, jute, or hemp, [or of which flax, jute, or hemp] shall be the component material of chief value, being of the value of thirty cents and under per square yard, twenty-five per centum ad valorem; valued above thirty cents per square yard, thirty per centum ad valorem; on flax or linen threads, twine and packthread, and all other manufactures of flax, or of which flax shall be the component material of chief value, and not otherwise provided for, thirty per centum ad valorem.

Sec. 15. *And be it further enacted,* That from and after the day and year aforesaid, there shall be levied, collected and paid on the importation of the articles hereinafter mentioned, the following duties, that is to say: *First.* On unmanufactured hemp, thirty-five dollars per ton; on Manilla, and other hemps of India, fifteen dollars per ton; on jute, Sisal grass, sun hemp, coir, and other vegetable substances not enumerated, used for cordage, ten dollars per ton; on jute butts, five dollars per ton; on codilla, or tow of hemp, ten dollars per ton; on tarred cables or cordage, two cents and a half per pound; on untarred Manilla cordage, two cents per pound; on all other untarred cordage, three cents per pound; on hemp yarns, four cents per pound; on coir yarn, one cent per pound; on seines, six cents per pound; on cotton bagging, or any other manufacture not otherwise provided for, suitable for the uses to which cotton bagging is applied, whether composed in whole or in part of hemp, jute, or flax, or any other material valued at less than ten cents per square yard, one cent and a half per pound; over ten cents per square yard, two cents per pound; on sail duck, twenty-five per centum ad valorem; on Russia and other sheetings, brown and white, twenty-five per centum ad valorem; and on all other manufactures of hemp, or of which hemp shall be a component part, not otherwise provided for, twenty per centum ad valorem; on unmanufactured flax, fifteen dollars per ton; on tow of flax, five dollars per ton; on grass cloth, twenty-five per centum ad valorem; on jute goods, fifteen per centum ad valorem; on all other manufactures of jute or Sisal grass, not otherwise provided for, twenty per centum ad valorem.

Sec. 16. *And be it further enacted,* That from and after the day and year aforesaid, there shall be levied, collected, and paid on the importation of the articles hereinafter mentioned, the following duties, that is to say:

First. On silk in the gum, not more advanced in manufacture than singles, tram, and thrown or organzine, fifteen per centum ad valorem; on all silks valued at not over one dollar per square yard, twenty per centum ad valorem; on all silks valued at over one dollar per square yard, thirty per centum ad valorem; on all silk velvets, or velvets of which silk is the component material of chief value, valued at three dollars per square yard, or under, twenty-five per centum ad valorem; valued at over three dollars per square yard, thirty per centum ad valorem; on floss silks, twenty per centum ad valorem; on silk ribbons, galloons, braids, fringes, laces, tassels, buttons, button cloths, trimmings, and on silk twist, twist composed of mohair and silk, sewing silk in the gum or purified, and all other manufactures of silk, or of which silk shall be the component material of chief value, not otherwise provided for, thirty per centum ad valorem.

SEC. 17. *And be it further enacted,* That from and after the day and year aforesaid, there shall be levied, collected, and paid on the importation of the articles hereinafter mentioned, the following duties, that is to say:

First. On rough plate, cylinder, or broad window glass, not exceeding ten by fifteen inches, one cent per square foot; above that, and not exceeding sixteen by twenty-four inches, one cent and a half per square foot; above that, and not exceeding twenty-four by thirty inches, two cents per square foot; all above that, and not exceeding in weight one pound per square foot, three cents per square foot: *Provided,* That all glass imported in sheets or tables, without reference to size or form, shall pay the highest duty herein imposed: *And provided, further,* That all rough plate cylinder, [or] broad glass, weighing over one hundred pounds per one hundred square feet, shall pay an additional duty on the excess; on crown, plate, or polished, and on all other window glass not exceeding ten by fifteen inches, one cent and a half per square foot; above that, and not exceeding sixteen by twenty-four inches, two cents and a half per square foot; above that, and not exceeding twenty-four by thirty inches, four cents per square foot; all above that, five cents per square foot: *Provided,* That all crown, plate, or polished, and all other window glass weighing over one hundred and fifty pounds per one hundred square feet, shall pay an additional duty on such excess of four cents per pound; on all plain and mould and press glassware, not cut, engraved, or painted, twenty-five per centum ad valorem; on all articles of glass, cut, engraved, painted, colored, printed, stained, silvered, or gilded, thirty per centum ad valorem; on porcelain and Bohemian glass, glass crystals for watches, paintings on glass or glasses, pebbles for spectacles, and all manufactures of glass, or of which glass shall be a component material, not otherwise provided for, and all glass bottles or jars filled with sweetmeats, preserves or other articles, thirty per centum ad valorem.

Second. On China and porcelain ware of all descriptions, thirty per centum ad valorem; on all brown earthen and common stone ware, twenty per centum ad valorem; on all other earthen, stone, or crockery ware, printed, white, glazed, edged, painted, dipped, or cream colored, composed of earthy or mineral substances, twenty-five per centum ad valorem.

SEC. 18. *And be it further enacted,* That from and after the day and year aforesaid, there shall be levied, collected and paid on the importation of the articles hereinafter mentioned, the following duties, that is to say:

On all books, periodicals and pamphlets, and all printed matter and illustrated books and papers, and on watches and parts of watches, and watch materials, and unfinished parts of watches, fifteen per centum ad valorem.

Sec. 19. *And be it further enacted*, That from and after the day and year aforesaid, there shall be levied, collected and paid, a duty of ten per centum on the importation of the articles hereinafter mentioned and embraced in this section; that is to say:

Acids, nitric, yellow and white, oxalic, and all other acids of every description used for medicinal purposes or in the fine arts not otherwise provided for; aloes, amber, ammonia, sal ammonia, muriate and carbonate of ammonia; anise seed; arrow root; assafœtida;

Bamboos; barks of all kinds not otherwise provided for; beeswax; black lead, or plumbago; borate of lime; brass, in pigs or bars, or when old and fit only to be remanufactured; Brazil paste; bronze liquor; building stones;

Cantharides; castor beans or seeds; chronometers, box or ship's, and parts thereof; cocculus indicus, compositions of glass or paste not set, intended for use by jewellers; cornmeal;

Diamonds, glaziers', set or not set; Dutch and bronze metal in leaf;

Engravings or plates, bound or unbound; ergot;

Flocks, waste or shoddy; fruit, green, ripe, or dried, not otherwise provided for; furs, dressed or undressed; when on the skin; furs, hatters', dressed or undressed, when not on the skin;

Gamboge; ginger, ground, preserved or pickled; glass plates or disks, unwrought, for optical instruments; goldbeaters' skin; green turtle; grindstones, wrought or finished; gum copal; gum substitute or burnt starch;

Hair of all kinds, cleaned, but unmanufactured, not otherwise provided for; hops, horns, horn-tips, bones, bone-tips, and teeth manufactured;

Iodine, crude; ipecacuanha; iron liquor;

Jalap; juniper berries;

Lemon and lime juice, lime;

Manganese, manna; marrow and all other grease, and soap stocks and soap stuffs; mineral kermes; moss, Iceland; music printed with lines bound or unbound;

Oatmeal; oils, palm, seal, and cocoa-nut; olive oil in casks, other than salad oil; oranges, lemons and limes; orange and lemon peel;

Paintings and statuary, not otherwise provided for; paving stones; pearl or hulled barley; Peruvian bark; plaster of Paris, when ground; Prussian blue;

Quicksilver;

Rhubarb; rye flour;

Saffron and saffron cake; saltpetre, or nitrate of soda, or potash, when refined, or partially refined; salts of tin; sarsaparilla; sepia; shaddock; sheathing paper; sponges; spunk; squills;

Tapioca; tagger's iron; teazels; terne tin in plates or sheets; tin foil; tin in plates or sheets;

Vanilla beans; vegetables, not otherwise provided for; verdigris;

Yams;

Sec. 20. *And be it further enacted*, That from and after the day and year aforesaid, there shall be levied, collected, and paid, a duty of twenty per centum on the importation of the articles hereinafter mentioned and embraced in this section, that is to say:

Antimony, tartrate of; acids, citric and tartaric;

Blank books, bound or unbound; blue or Roman vitriol, or sulphate of copper; boards, planks, laths, scantling, staves, spars, hewn and sawed timber, and timber used in building wharves; brick, fire-brick, and roofing and paving tile, not otherwise provided for; brimstone, in rolls; bronze powder; Burgundy pitch; burrstones, manufactured or bound up into millstones;

Calomel; castor oil; castorum; chicory root; chocolate; chromate of lead; corks; cotton laces, cotton insertings, cotton trimming laces, and cotton braids; cowhage down; cubebs;

Dried pulp;

Ether;

Feather beds, feathers for beds, and downs of all kinds; feldspar; fig blue; firewood; fish glue or isinglass; fish skins; flour of sulphur; Frankfort black; fulminates, or fulminating powders;

Glue; gold and silver leaf; grapes; gunpowder;

Hair, curled, moss, seaweed, and all other vegetable substances used for beds or mattresses; hat bodies made of wool, or of which wool is the component material of chief value; hatters' plush, composed of silk and cotton, but of which cotton is the component material of chief value;

Lampblack; leather, tanned, bend, or sole; leather, upper, of all kinds, except tanned calfskin, which shall pay twenty-five per centum ad valorem;

Magnesia; malt; mats of cocoa-nut; matting, China, and other floor matting, and mats made of flags, jute, or grass; mercurial preparations, not otherwise provided for; medicinal roots and leaves, and all other drugs and medicines in a crude state, not otherwise provided for; metals unmanufactured, not otherwise provided for; mineral and bituminous substances in a crude state not otherwise provided for; musical instruments of all kinds, and strings for musical instruments of whip gut, catgut, and all other strings of the same material; mustard ground or unmanufactured;

Needles of all kinds for sewing, darning and knitting;

Oils, neatsfoot and other animal oils, spermaceti, whale, and other fish oil, the produce of foreign fisheries; oils, volatile, essential or expressed, not otherwise provided for; osier or willow, prepared for basket-makers' use;

Paints, dry or ground in oil, not otherwise provided for; pitch; plaster of Paris calcined;

Quills;

Ratans and reeds manufactured or partially manufactured; red precipitate; Roman cement; rosin;

Sal soda, hyposulphate of soda, and all carbonates of soda by whatever name designated, not otherwise provided for; salts, Epsom, Glauber, Rochelle, and all other salts and preparations of salts not otherwise provided for; shoes or boots, and other articles, composed wholly of India-rubber, not otherwise provided for; skins, tanned, and dressed of all kinds; spices of all kinds, not otherwise provided for; spirits of turpentine; starch;

stereotype plates; still bottoms; strychnine; sulphate of barytes, crude or refined; sulphate of magnesia; sulphate of quinine;

Tar; thread laces and insertings; type metal; types, new;

Varnish of all kinds; Vandyke brown; Venetian red; vermilion;

Whalebone, the produce of foreign fisheries; white vitriol or sulphate of zinc; wood unmanufactured, not otherwise provided for; woollen listings;

SEC. 21. *And be it further enacted,* That from and after the day and year aforesaid there shall be levied, collected, and paid, on copper ore and diamonds, cameos, mosaics, gems, pearls, rubies, and other precious stones, when not set, a duty of five per centum ad valorem on the same; when set in gold, silver, or other metal, or on imitations thereof, and all other jewelry, twenty-five per centum ad valorem; on hair cloth and hair seatings, and all other manufactures of hair, not otherwise provided for, twenty-five per centum ad valorem.

SEC. 22. *And be it further enacted,* That from and after the day and year aforesaid there shall be levied, collected, and paid a duty of thirty per centum on the importation of the articles hereinafter mentioned and embraced in this section, that is to say:

Alabaster and spar ornaments;

Anchovies, sardines, and all other fish preserved in oil;

Argentine, alabatta, or German silver, manufactured or unmanufactured;

Articles embroidered with gold, silver, or other metal;

Articles worn by men, women, or children, of whatever material composed, made up, or made wholly or in part by hand, not otherwise provided for;

Asses' skins;

Balsams, cosmetics, essences, extracts, pastes, perfumes, and tinctures, used either for the toilet or for medicinal purposes;

Baskets, and all other articles composed of grass, ozier, palm leaf, straw, whalebone, or willow, not otherwise provided for;

Beads of amber, composition, or wax, and all beads;

Benzoates; Bologna sausages;

Bracelets, braids, chains, curls, or ringlets composed of hair, or of which hair is a component material;

Braces, suspenders, webbing, or other fabrics, composed wholly or in part of India rubber, not otherwise provided for;

Brooms and brushes of all kinds;

Buttons and button moulds of all kinds;

Canes and sticks for walking, finished or unfinished;

Capers, pickles, and sauces of all kinds, not otherwise provided for;

Caps, hats, muffs and tippets of fur, and all other manufactures of fur, or of which fur shall be a component material;

Caps, gloves, leggins, mits, socks, stockings, wove shirts and drawers, and all similar articles made on frames of whatever material composed, worn by men, women, or children, and not otherwise provided for;

Carbonate of magnesia;

Card-cases, pocket-books, shell boxes, souvenirs, and all similar articles, of whatever material composed;

Carriages and parts of carriages;

Clocks and parts of clocks;

Clothing, ready-made, and wearing apparel of every description, of whatever material composed, except wool, made up or manufactured wholly or in part by the tailor, seamstress, or manufacturer;

Coach and harness furniture of all kinds, saddlery, coach and harness hardware, silver plated, brass, brass plated or covered, common tinned, burnished or japanned, not otherwise provided for;

Combs of all kinds;

Compositions of glass or paste, when set;

Composition tops for tables, or other articles of furniture;

Comfits, sweetmeats, or fruits preserved in sugar, brandy or molasses, not otherwise provided for;

Coral, cut or manufactured;

Cotton cords, gimps and galloons;

Cotton laces, colored;

Court plaster;

Crayons of all kinds;

Cutlery of all kinds;

Dolls and toys of all kinds;

Encaustic tiles;

Epaulets, galloons, laces, knots, stars, tassels, tresses and wings of gold, silver, or other metal;

Fans and fire-screens of every description, of whatever material composed;

Feathers and flowers, artificial or ornamental, and parts thereof, of whatever material composed;

Flats, braids, plaits, sparterre and willow squares, used for making hats and bonnets;

Firecrackers;

Frames and sticks for umbrellas, parasols, and sunshades, finished or unfinished;

Furniture, cabinet and household;

Hair pencils;

Hat bodies of cotton;

Hats and bonnets, for men, women, and children, composed of straw, chip, grass, palm leaf, willow, or any other vegetable substance, or of hair, whalebone, or other material not otherwise provided for;

Human hair, cleansed or prepared for use;

Ink and ink powder;

Japanned, patent, or enamelled leather or skins of all kinds;

Japanned ware of all kinds, not otherwise provided for;

Jet and manufactures of jet, and imitations thereof;

Lead pencils;

Maccaroni, vermicelli, gelatine, jellies, and all similar preparations;

Manufactures of silk, or of which silk shall be a component material, not otherwise provided for;

Manufactures of the bark of the cork tree, except corks;

Manufactures of bone, shell, horn, ivory or vegetable ivory;

Manufactures, articles, vessels and wares not otherwise provided for, of brass, copper, gold, iron, lead, pewter, platina, silver, tin or other metal, or of which either of these metals or any other metal shall be the component material of chief value;

Manufactures, not otherwise provided for, composed of mixed materials, in part of cotton, silk, wool, or worsted, or flax;

Manufactures of cotton, linen, silk, wool, or worsted, if embroidered or tamboured, in the loom or otherwise, by machinery or with the needle, or other process, not otherwise provided for;

Manufactures of cedar wood, granadilla, ebony, mahogany, rosewood and satin wood;

Marble in the rough or blocks, manufactures of marble, marble paving tiles, and all marble sawed, squared, dressed, or polished;

Manufactures and articles of leather, or of which leather shall be a component part, not otherwise provided for;

Manufactures of paper, or of which paper is a component material, not otherwise provided for;

Manufactures, articles and wares, of papier mache;

Manufactures of goat's hair or mohair, or of which goat's hair or mohair shall be a component material, not otherwise provided for;

Manufactures of wood, or of which wood is the chief component part, not otherwise provided for;

Medicinal preparations, not otherwise provided for;

Metallic pens;

Mineral waters;

Muskets, rifles, and other fire-arms;

Oilcloth of every description, of whatever material composed, not otherwise provided for;

Olive salad oil;

Olives;

Paper boxes and all other fancy boxes;

Paper envelopes;

Paper hangings, and paper for screens or fire-boards; paper; antiquarian, demy, drawing, elephant, foolscap, imperial letter, and all other paper not otherwise provided for;

Parasols and sunshades;

Parchment;

Plated and gilt ware of all kinds;

Playing cards;

Prepared vegetables, meats, fish, poultry, and game, sealed or unsealed, in cans or otherwise;

Red chalk pencils;

Salmon, preserved;

Scagliola tops, for tables or other articles of furniture;

Sealingwax;

Side arms of every description;

Silver-plated metal, in sheets or other form;

Slates, roofing slates, slate pencils, slate chimney pieces, mantels, slabs for tables, and all other manufactures of slate;

Soap, Castile, perfumed, Windsor, and all other kinds;

Twines and packthread, of whatever material composed, not otherwise provided for;

Umbrellas;

Unwrought clay, three dollars per ton;

Vellum, velvet, when printed or painted; wafers; water colors;

Webbing, composed of wool, cotton, flax, or any other materials.

SEC. 23. *And be it further enacted*, That from and after the day and year aforesaid, the importation of the articles hereinafter mentioned and embraced in this section shall be exempt from duty, that is to say:

Acids, acetic, acetous, benzoic, boracic, muriatic, sulphuric, and pyroligneous, and all acids of every description used for chemical and manufacturing purposes, not otherwise provided for; alcornoque;

All books, maps, charts, mathematical, nautical instruments, philosophical apparatus, and all other articles whatever, imported for the use of the United States; all philosophical apparatus, instruments, books, maps, and charts, statues, statuary, busts and casts of marble, bronze, alabaster, or plaster of Paris; paintings and drawings, etchings, specimens of sculpture, cabinets of coins, medals, regalia, gems, and all collections of antiquities: *Provided*, The same be specially imported, in good faith, for the use of any society incorporated or established for philosophical, literary or religious purposes, or for the encouragement of the fine arts, or for the use or by the order of any college, academy, school, or seminary of learning in the United States;

Ambergris; annatto, roncou or Orleans; animal carbon (bone black;)

Animals, living, of all kinds;

Antimony, crude or regulus of;

Argol, or crude tartar; arsenic;

Articles in a crude state used in dyeing or tanning, not otherwise provided for; asphaltum;

Bananas;

Bark, Peruvian, or bark quilla;

Barilla, and soda ash;

Bells, old, and bell metal.

Berries, nuts, flowers, plants, and vegetables used exclusively in dyeing or in composing dyes; but no article shall be classed as such that has undergone any manufacture;

Birds, singing or other, and land and water fowls;

Bismuth; bitter apples;

Bolting cloths;

Bones, burnt, and bone-dust;

Books, maps, and charts, imported by authority of the Joint Library Committee of Congress for the use of the library of Congress: *Provided*, That, if, in any case, a contract shall have been made with any bookseller, importer, or other person aforesaid, shall have paid the duty or included the duty in said contract, in such case the duty shall be remitted;

Borax, crude, or tincal; boucho leaves;

Brazil wood, braziletto, and all other dye-woods, in sticks;

Breccia, in blocks or slabs;

Brimstone, crude, in bulk; brime;

Bullion, gold and silver;

Burrstones, wrought or unwrought, but unmanufactured, and not bound up into millstones;

Cabinets of coins, medals, and all other collections of antiquities;

Cadmium; calamine; camphor, crude;

Chalk, French chalk, and red chalk;

Cochineal; cobalt;

Cocoa, cocoa shells, cocoa leaves, and cocoa nuts;

Coffee and tea, when imported direct from the place of their growth or production, in American vessels, or in foreign vessels entitled by reciprocal treaties to be exempt from discriminating duties, tonnage, and other charges;

Coffee, the growth or production of the possessions of the Netherlands, imported from the Netherlands in the same manner;

Coins, gold, silver, and copper;

Copper, when imported for the United States mint;

Cotton; cork-tree bark, unmanufactured;

Cream of tartar; cudbear, vegetable, and orchil;

Divi-divi; dragon's blood;

Emery, in lump or pulverized;

Extract of indigo;

Extract of madder;

Extract and decoctions of logwood, and other dye-woods, not otherwise provided for;

Felt, adhesive, for sheathing vessels;

Fish, fresh caught, for daily consumption;

Flints; flint, ground;

Fullers' earth;

Ginger root; gum, Arabic, Barbary, East India, Jedda, Senegal, Tragacanth, Benjamine or Benzoin, myrrh, and all other gums and resins in a crude state, not otherwise provided for;

Guttapercha, unmanufactured;

Grindstones, rough or unfinished;

Garden seeds, and all other seeds for agricultural, horticultural, medicinal, and manufacturing purposes, not otherwise provided for;

Glass, when old, not in pieces which can be cut for use, and fit only to be remanufactured;

Goods, wares, and merchandise, the growth, production, or manufacture of the United States, exported to a foreign country, and brought back to the United States in the same condition as when exported, upon which no drawback or bounty has been allowed: *Provided,* That all regulations to ascertain the identity thereof, prescribed by existing laws, or which may be prescribed by the Secretary of the Treasury, shall be complied with;

Guano;

Household effects, old, and in use of persons or families from foreign countries, if used abroad by them and not intended for any other person or persons, or for sale;

Hair of all kinds, uncleaned and unmanufactured, and all long horse hair, used for weaving, cleaned or uncleaned, drawn or undrawn;

India rubber, in bottles, slabs, or sheets, unmanufactured; India rubber, milk of;

Indigo; ice; irridium; irris, orris root;

Ivory, unmanufactured; ivory nuts, or vegetable ivory;

Junk, old, and oakum;

Kelp;

Lac dye; lac spirits; lac sulphur;

Lastings, mohair cloth, silk, twist, or other manufactures of cloth, cut in strips or patterns of the size and shape for shoes, slippers, boots, bootees, gaiters, and buttons, exclusively, not combined with India rubber;

Leeches; liquorice root;

Madder, ground or prepared, and madder root;

Manuscripts; marine coral, unmanufactured;

Medals, of gold, silver, or copper;

Machinery, suitable for the manufacture of flax and linen goods only, and imported for that purpose solely, but not including that which may be used for any other manufactures;

Maps and charts; mineral blue;

Models of inventions, and other improvements in the arts: *Provided,* That no article or articles shall be deemed a model or improvement which can be fitted for use;

Munjeet, or India madder;

Natron; nickel; nutgalls; nux vomica;

Oil, spermaceti, whale, and other fish, of American fisheries, and all other articles the produce of such fisheries;

Orpiment, or sulphuret of arsenic;

Paintings and statuary, the production of American artists residing abroad: *Provided,* The same be imported in good faith as objects of taste, and not of merchandise;

Palm leaf, unmanufactured;

Pearl, mother of;

Personal and household effects, not merchandise, of citizens of the United States dying abroad;

Pine apples; plantains;

Plaster of Paris, or sulphate of lime, unground;

Platina, unmanufactured; platina vases or retorts;

Polishing stones; pumice and pumice stones;

Quassia-wood;

Rags of whatever material, except wool;

Ratans and reeds, unmanufactured;

Rottenstone;

Safflower; saltpetre, or nitrate of soda, or potash, when crude;

Sandalwood; seedlac;

Sheathing metal, or yellow metal, not wholly of copper, nor wholly or in part of iron, ungalvanized, in sheets forty-eight inches long and fourteen inches wide, and weighing from fourteen to thirty-four ounces per square yard;

Shellac; shingle bolts and stave bolts;

Silk, raw, or as reeled from the cocoon, not being doubled, twisted, or advanced in manufacture any way, and silk cocoons and silk waste;

Smalts; specimens of natural history, mineralogy, and botany;

Staves for pipes, hogsheads, or other casks;

Stoneware, not ornamented, above the capacity of ten gallons;

Substances expressly used for manure; sumac;

Terra japonica, catechu, or cutch;

Tin, in pigs, bars, or blocks;

Tortoise and other shell, unmanufactured;

Trees, shrubs, bulbs, plants, and roots not otherwise provided for;

Turmeric; types, old, and fit only to be remanufactured;

Wearing apparel in actual use, and other personal effects, (not merchandise,) professional books, implements, instruments, and tools of trade, occupation, or employment of persons arriving in the United States: *Provided,* That this exemption shall not be construed to include machinery, or other articles imported for use in any manufacturing establishment, or for sale;

Weld; woad or pastel;

Woods, namely: cedar, lignum vitæ, lancewood, ebony, box, granadilla, mahogany, rosewood, satinwood, and all cabinet woods, unmanufactured;

Wool, unmanufactured, and all hair of the goat, alpaca, and other like animals, unmanufactured, the value whereof at the last port or place from whence exported to the United States shall be eighteen cents, or under, per pound.

SEC. 24. *And be it further enacted,* That from and after the day and year aforesaid there shall be levied, collected, and paid on the importation of all raw or unmanufactured articles, not herein enumerated or provided for, a duty of ten per centum ad valorem; and on all articles manufactured in whole or in part, not herein enumerated or provided for, a duty of twenty per centum ad valorem.

SEC. 25. *And be it further enacted,* That all goods, wares, and merchandise which may be in the public stores on the day and year aforesaid, shall be subject to no other duty upon the entry thereof than if the same were imported respectively after that day.

SEC. 26. *And be it further enacted,* That whenever the word "ton" is used in this act, in reference to weight, it shall be deemed and taken to be twenty hundred weight, each hundred weight being one hundred and twelve pounds avoirdupois.

SEC. 27. *And be it further enacted,* That railroad iron, partially or wholly worn, may be imported into the United States without payment of duty, under bond to be withdrawn and exported after the said railroad iron shall have been repaired or remanufactured; and the Secretary of the Treasury is hereby authorized and directed to prescribe such rules and regulations as may be necessary to protect the revenue against fraud, and secure the identity, character, and weight of all such importations when again withdrawn and exported, restricting and limiting the export and withdrawal to the same port of entry where imported, and also limiting all bonds to a period of time of not more than six months from the date of the importation.

SEC. 28. *And be it further enacted,* That in all cases where the duty upon any imports of goods, wares, or merchandise shall be subject to be levied upon the true market value of such imports in the principal markets of the country from whence the importation shall have been made, or at the port of exportation, the duty shall be estimated and collected upon the value on the day of actual shipment whenever a bill of lading shall be presented showing the date of shipment, and which shall be certified by a certificate of the United States Consul, Commercial Agent, or other legally authorized deputy.

SEC. 29. *And be it further enacted,* That the annual statistical accounts of the commerce of the United States with foreign countries, required by existing laws, shall hereafter be made up and completed by the Register of the Treasury, under the direction of the Secretary of the Treasury, so as to comprehend and include, in tabular form, the quantity by weight or measure, as well as the amount of value, of the several articles of foreign commerce, whether dutiable or otherwise; and also a similar and separate statement of the commerce of the United States with the British Provinces, under the late, so-called, reciprocity treaty with Great Britain.

SEC. 30. *And be it further enacted,* That from and after the day and year aforesaid there shall be allowed a drawback on foreign hemp, manufactured into cordage in the United States and exported therefrom, equal in amount to the duty paid on the foreign hemp from which it shall be manufactured, to be ascertained under such regulations as shall be prescribed by the Secretary of the Treasury, and no more: *Provided,* That ten per centum on the amount of all drawbacks so allowed shall be retained for the use of the United States by the collectors paying such drawbacks respectively.

SEC. 31. *And be it further enacted,* That all acts and parts of acts repugnant to the provisions of this act be, and the same are hereby repealed: *Provided,* That the existing laws shall extend to, and be in force for, the collection of the duties imposed by this act; for the prosecution and punishment of all offences, and for the recovery, collection, distribution, and remission of all fines, penalties, and forfeitures, as fully and effectually as if every regulation, penalty, forfeiture, provision, clause, matter, and thing to that effect, in the existing laws contained, had been inserted in and re-enacted by this act.

SEC. 32. *And be it further enacted,* That when merchandise of the same material or description, but of different values, are invoiced at an average price, and not otherwise provided for, the duty shall be assessed upon the whole invoice at the rate the highest valued goods in such invoice are subject to under this act. The words value and valued, used in this act, shall be construed and understood as meaning the true market value of the goods, wares, and merchandise in the principal markets of the country from whence exported at the date of exportation.

SEC. 33. *And be it further enacted,* That all goods, wares, and merchandise actually on shipboard and bound to the United States, within fifteen days after the passage of this act, and all goods, wares, and merchandise in deposit in warehouse or public store on the first day of April, eighteen hundred and sixty-one, shall be subject to pay such duties as provided by law before and at the time of the passage of this act; and all goods in warehouse at the time this act takes effect, on which the duties are lessened by its provisions, may be withdrawn on payment of the duties herein provided.

Approved 2d March, 1861.

DEPARTMENT OF STATE,
WASHINGTON, *March* 13, 1861.

I do hereby certify that the foregoing is a true and accurate copy of the original on file in this department.

W. HUNTER, *Chief Clerk.*

[PUBLIC RESOLUTION 9.]

A RESOLUTION to correct certain errors in the Act entitled "An Act to provide for the payment of outstanding Treasury Notes, to authorize a Loan, to regulate and fix the duties on Imports and for other purposes," approved the second of March, eighteen hundred and sixty-one.

Resolved by the Senate and House of Representatives of the United States of America in Congress assembled, That the act entitled "An act to provide for the payment of outstanding treasury notes, to authorize a loan, to regulate and fix the duties on imports and for other purposes," approved the second March, eighteen hundred and sixty-one, shall be so far altered and corrected as to strike from said act the following words, that is to say, from the list of articles exempt from duty "wool, unmanufactured, and all hair of the goat, alpaca, and other like animals, unmanufactured, the value whereof, at the last port or place from whence exported to the United States shall be eighteen cents, or under, per pound," from section twenty-four, as follows:

SEC. 24. *And be it further enacted,* That all goods, wares, and merchandise, which may be in the public stores on the day and year aforesaid, shall be subject to no other duty upon entry thereof than if the same were imported respectively after that day; and from section thirteen, as follows: "On woollen shawls, or shawls of which wool shall be the chief component material, a duty of sixteen cents per pound, and in addition thereto, twenty per centum ad valorem."

Approved 2d March, 1861.

DEPARTMENT OF STATE,
Washington, March 13, 1861.

I do hereby certify that the foregoing is a true and accurate copy of the original on file in this department.

W. HUNTER, *Chief Clerk.*

TREASURY DEPARTMENT,
July 17, 1862.

The following act of Congress, approved July 14, 1862, the provisions of which relating to duties on imports go into effect from and after the 1st day of August, 1862, is published for the information and government of the Officers of the Customs at the several ports and of all others concerned.

S. P. CHASE,
Secretary of the Treasury.

[PUBLIC--No. 134.]

AN ACT increasing, temporarily, the duties on imports, and for other purposes.

Be it enacted by the Senate and House of Representatives of the United States of America in Congress assembled, That from and after the first day of August, Anno Domini, eighteen hundred and sixty-two, in lieu of the duties heretofore imposed by law on the articles hereinafter mentioned there shall be levied, collected, and paid, on the goods, wares and merchandise herein enumerated and provided for, imported from foreign countries, the following duties and rates of duty, that is to say:

On syrup of sugar, or of sugar cane, or concentrated molasses, or concentrated melado, two cents per pound;

On all sugar not above number twelve, Dutch standard in color, two and one-half cents per pound;

On all sugar above number twelve, and not above number fifteen, Dutch standard in color, three cents per pound;

On all sugar above number fifteen, not stove-dried, and not above number twenty, Dutch standard in color, three and one-half cents per pound;

On all refined sugar in form of loaf, lump, crushed, powdered, pulverized, or granulated, and all stove-dried or other sugar above number twenty, Dutch standard in color, four cents per pound: *Provided,* That the standards by which the color and grades of sugars are to be regulated shall be selected and furnished to the collectors of such ports of entry as may be necessary, by the Secretary of the Treasury, from time to time, and in such manner as he may deem expedient;

On sugar candy, not colored, six cents per pound; on all other confectionery, made wholly or in part of sugar, and on sugars, after being refined, when tinctured, colored, or in any way adulterated, ten cents per pound;

On molasses, six cents per gallon: *Provided,* That all syrups of sugar or sugar cane, concentrated molasses or concentrated melado, entered under the name of molasses, or any other name than syrup of sugar, or of sugar cane, concentrated molasses, or concentrated melado, shall be liable to forfeiture to the United States, and the same shall be forfeited.

On cigars of all kinds, valued at five dollars or less per thousand, thirty five cents per pound; valued at over five dollars and not over ten dollars per thousand, sixty cents per pound; valued at over ten and not over twenty dollars per thousand, eighty cents per pound; valued at over twenty dollars per thousand, one dollar per pound; and in addition thereto on all cigars valued at over ten dollars per thousand, ten per centum ad valorem: *Provided*, That paper cigars, or cigarettes, including wrappers, shall be subject to the same duties imposed on cigars;

On snuff, thirty-five cents per pound;

On tobacco, in leaf, unmanufactured and not stemmed, twenty-five cents per pound;

On stemmed, and tobacco manufactured of all descriptions, not otherwise provided for, thirty-five cents per pound.

SEC. 2. *And be it further enacted*, That from and after the day and year aforesaid, in addition to the duties heretofore imposed by law on the articles hereinafter mentioned and included in this section, there shall be levied, collected, and paid on the goods, wares, and merchandise herein enumerated and provided for, imported from foreign countries, the following duties and rates of duty, that is to say:

On brandy, for first proof, twenty-five cents per gallon;

On other spirits, manufactured or distilled from grain or other materials, for first proof, fifty cents per gallon;

On cordials and liqueurs of all kinds, and arrack, absynthe, kirschenwasser, ratafia, and other similar spirituous beverages not otherwise provided for, twenty-five cents per gallon;

On bay rum, twenty-five cents per gallon;

On ale, porter and beer, in bottles or otherwise, five cents per gallon;

On all spirituous liquors not otherwise enumerated, sixteen and two-thirds per centum ad valorem: *Provided*, That no lower rate or amount of duty shall be levied, collected and paid, on brandy, spirits, and all other spirituous beverages, than that fixed by law for the description of first proof, but shall be increased in proportion for any greater strength than the strength of first proof: *And provided further*, That bottles containing wines subject to ad valorem duties shall be liable to and pay the same rate of duty as that fixed upon the wines therein contained.

SEC. 3. *And be it further enacted*, That from and after the day and year aforesaid, in addition to the duties heretofore imposed by law on the articles hereinafter mentioned and included in this section, there shall be levied, collected, and paid, on the goods, wares, and merchandise herein enumerated and provided for, imported from foreign countries, the following duties and rates of duty, that is to say:

On bar iron, rolled or hammered, comprising flats not less than one inch or more than seven inches wide, nor less than one-quarter of an inch or more than two inches thick; rounds not less than one-half an inch nor more than four inches in diameter; and squares not less than one-half an inch nor more than four inches square, not exceeding in value the sum of fifty dollars per ton, two dollars per ton; exceeding in value the sum of fifty dollars per ton, three dollars per ton;

On bar iron, rolled or hammered, comprising flats less than one-quarter of an inch thick or more than seven inches wide, rounds less than one-half an inch or more than four inches in diameter, and squares less than one-half an inch or more than four inches square, five dollars per ton;

On all iron imported in bars for railroads and inclined planes made to patterns and fitted to be laid down on such roads or planes without further manufacture, one dollar and fifty cents per ton;

On boiler or other plate iron, five dollars per ton;

On iron wire, drawn and finished, not more than one-fourth of an inch in diameter nor less than number sixteen, wire gauge, one dollar per one hundred pounds; over number sixteen and not over number twenty-five, wire gauge, one dollar and fifty cents per one hundred pounds; over or finer than number twenty-five, wire gauge, two dollars per one hundred pounds: *Provided,* That wire covered with cotton, silk, or other material, shall pay five cents per pound in addition to the foregoing rates;

On hollow-ware, glazed or tinned, one-half cent per pound;

On sadirons, tailors' and hatters' irons, stoves, and stove plates, one-fourth of one cent per pound;

On band and hoop iron and slit rods, and all other descriptions of rolled or hammered iron, not otherwise provided for, five dollars per ton;

On cut nails and spikes, one-fourth of one cent per pound;

On iron cables or cable chains, or parts thereof, seventy-five cents per one hundred pounds: *Provided,* That no chains made of wire or rods of a diameter less than one-half of one inch shall be considered a chain cable;

On anvils, one dollar per one hundred pounds;

On anchors, or parts thereof, fifty cents per one hundred pounds;

On wrought board nails, spikes, rivets, bolts, bed-screws, and wrought hinges, one-fourth of one cent per pound;

On chains, trace chains, halter chains, and fence chains, made of wire or rods, not under one-fourth of one inch in diameter, one-fourth of one cent per pound; under one-fourth of one inch in diameter and not under number nine, wire gauge, one-half of one cent per pound; under number nine, wire gauge, five per centum ad valorem;

On blacksmiths' hammers, and sledges, and axles, or parts thereof, one-half of one cent per pound;

On horseshoe nails, one cent per pound;

On steam, gas, and water tubes, and flues of wrought iron, one-fourth of one cent per pound;

On wrought iron railroad chairs, and wrought iron nuts and washers, ready punched, five dollars per ton;

On smooth or polished sheet iron, by whatever name designated, one-half cent per pound;

On sheet iron, common or black, not thinner than number twenty, wire gauge, three dollars per ton; thinner than number twenty, and not thinner than number twenty-five, wire gauge, four dollars per ton; thinner than number twenty-five, wire gauge, five dollars per ton;

On tin plates galvanized, galvanized iron, or iron coated with any metal by electric batteries, one-half cent per pound;

On locomotive tire, or parts thereof, one cent per pound;

On mill-irons, and mill-cranks of wrought iron, and wrought iron for ships, steam-engines, and locomotives, or parts thereof, weighing each twenty-five pounds or more, one-fourth of one cent per pound;

On screws, commonly called wood-screws, one cent and a half per pound;

On screws, washed or plated, and all other screws of iron, except wood-screws, five per centum ad valorem;

On all manufactures of iron, not otherwise provided for, five per centum ad valorem;

On cast iron, steam, gas, and water pipes, twenty-five cents per one hundred pounds; on all other castings of iron, not otherwise provided for, nor exempted from duty, five per centum ad valorem: *Provided,* That the following descriptions of iron, manufactures of iron, and manufactures of steel, shall not be subject to any additional duty or rates of duty under the provisions of this act, that is to say: iron in pigs; cast iron butts and hinges; old scrap iron; malleable iron, and malleable iron castings, not otherwise provided for; cut-tacks, brads, and sprigs; cross-cut, mill, pit, and drag saws;

On steel in ingots, bars, sheets, or wire, not less than one-fourth of an inch in diameter, valued at seven cents per pound or less, one-fourth of one cent per pound; valued at above seven cents per pound and not above eleven cents per pound, one-half cent per pound; valued above eleven cents per pound, and on steel-wire and steel in any form, not otherwise provided for, five per centum ad valorem;

On skates valued at twenty cents or less per pair, two cents per pair; when valued at over twenty cents per pair, five per centum ad valorem.

On iron squares, marked on one side, two cents and a half per pound; on all other squares made of iron or steel, five cents per pound;

On files, rasps, and floats, of all descriptions, two cents per pound, and in addition thereto, five per centum ad valorem;

On all manufactures of steel, or of which steel shall be a component part, not otherwise provided for, five per centum ad valorem: *Provided,* That no allowance or reduction of duties for partial loss or damage shall be hereafter made in consequence of rust of iron or steel, or upon the manufactures of iron or steel, except on polished Russia sheet iron;

On bituminous coal, ten cents per ton of twenty-eight bushels, eighty pounds to the bushel; on all other coal, ten cents per ton of twenty-eight bushels, eighty pounds to the bushel;

On coke and culm of coal, five per centum ad valorem.

SEC. 4. *And be it further enacted,* That from and after the day and year aforesaid, in addition to the duties heretofore imposed by law on the articles hereinafter mentioned and included in this section, there shall be levied, collected, and paid on the goods, wares, and merchandise herein enumerated and provided for, imported from foreign countries, the following duties and rates of duty, that is to say:

On copper rods, bolts, nails, spikes, copper bottoms, copper in sheets or plates, called braziers' copper, and other sheets and manufactures of copper, not otherwise provided for, five per centum ad valorem;

On zinc, spelter, and teutenegue, unmanufactured, in blocks or pigs, twenty-five cents per one hundred pounds;

On zinc, spelter, and teutenegue, in sheets, one-half of one cent per pound;

On lead, in pipes and shot, three-fourths of one cent per pound;

On brass, in bars or pigs, and old brass, fit only to be remanufactured, five per centum ad valorem.

SEC. 5. *And be it further enacted,* That from and after the day and year aforesaid, in lieu of the duties heretofore imposed by law on the articles hereinafter mentioned, and on such as may now be exempt from duty, there shall be levied, collected, and paid on the goods, wares, and merchandise enumerated and provided for in this section, imported from foreign countries, the following duties and rates of duty, that is to say:

Acid, boracic, five cents per pound; citric, ten cents per pound; oxalic, four cents per pound; sulphuric, one cent per pound; tartaric, twenty cents per pound; gallic, fifty cents per pound; tannic, twenty-five cents per pound;

Alum, patent alum, alum substitute, sulphate of alumina, and aluminous cake, sixty cents per one hundred pounds;

Argols, or crude tartar, six cents per pound; cream tartar, ten cents per pound;

Asphaltum, three cents per pound;

Balsam copaiva, twenty cents per pound; Peruvian, fifty cents per pound; tolu, thirty cents per pound;

Blanc fixe, enamelled white, satin white, or any combination of barytes and acid, two cents and a half per pound;

Barytes and sulphate of barytes, five mills per pound;

Burning fluid, fifty cents per gallon;

Bitter apples, colocynth, or coloquintida, ten cents per pound;

Borax, crude, or tincal, five cents per pound; refined, ten cents per pound;

Borate of lime, five cents per pound;

Buchu leaves, ten cents per pound;

Camphor, crude, thirty cents per pound; refined, forty cents per pound;

Cantharides, fifty cents per pound;

Cloves, fifteen cents per pound; cassia, fifteen cents per pound; cassia buds, twenty cents per pound; cinnamon, twenty-five cents per pound;

Cayenne pepper, twelve cents per pound; ground, fifteen cents per pound; black pepper, twelve cents per pound; ground, fifteen cents per pound; white pepper, twelve cents per pound; ground, fifteen cents per pound;

Cocculus Indicus, ten cents per pound;

Cuttle-fish bone, five cents per pound;

Cubebs, ten cents per pound;

Dragon's blood, ten cents per pound;

Emery, ore or rock, six dollars per ton; manufactured, ground, or pulverized, one cent per pound;

Ergot, twenty cents per pound;

Epsom salts, one cent per pound; glauber salts, five mills per pound; Rochelle salts, fifteen cents per pound;

Fruit ethers, essences or oils of apple, pear, peach, apricot, strawberry, and raspberry, made of fusil oil or of fruit, or imitations thereof, two dollars and fifty cents per pound;

French green, Paris green, mineral green, carmine lake, wood lake, dry carmine, Venetian red, vermilion, mineral blue, Prussian blue, chrome yellow, rose pink, extract of resin or analine colors, Dutch pink, and paints and painters' colors, (except white and red lead and oxide of zinc,) dry or ground in oil, and moist water colors, used in the manufacture of paper-hangings and colored papers and cards, not otherwise provided for, twenty-five per centum ad valorem;

Ginger root, five cents per pound; ginger ground, eight cents per pound;

On gold leaf, one dollar and fifty cents per package of five hundred leaves; on silver leaf, seventy-five cents per package of five hundred leaves;

Gum aloes, six cents per pound; benzoin, ten cents per pound; sandarac, ten cents per pound; shellac, ten cents per pound; mastic, fifty cents per pound; copal, kowrie, damar, and all gums used for like purposes, ten cents per pound;

Honey, fifteen cents per gallon;

Iodine, crude, fifty cents per pound; resublimed, seventy-five cents per pound;

Ipecacuanha, or ipecac, fifty cents per pound;

Jalap, fifty cents per pound;

Licorice root, one cent per pound; paste or juice, five cents per pound;

Litharge, two and one-fourth cents per pound;

Magnesia, carbonate, six cents per pound; calcined, twelve cents per pound;

Manna, twenty-five cents per pound;

Nitrate of soda, one cent per pound;

Morphine and its salts, two dollars per ounce; mace and nutmeg, thirty cents per pound;

Ochres and ochrey earths, not otherwise provided for, when dry, fifty cents per one hundred pounds; when ground in oil, one dollar and fifty cents per one hundred pounds;

Oils, fixed or expressed, croton, fifty cents per pound; almonds, ten cents per pound; bay or laurel, twenty cents per pound; castor, fifty cents per gallon; mace, fifty cents per pound; olive, not salad, twenty-five cents per gallon; salad, fifty cents per gallon; mustard, not salad, twenty-five cents per gallon; salad, fifty cents per gallon;

Oils, essential or essence, anise, fifty cents per pound; almonds, one dollar and fifty cents per pound; amber, crude, ten cents per pound; rectified, twenty cents per pound; bay leaves, seventeen dollars and fifty cents per pound; bergamot, one dollar per pound; cajeput, twenty-five cents per pound; caraway, fifty cents per pound; cassia, one dollar per pound; cinnamon, two dollars per pound; cloves, one dollar per pound; citronella, fifty cents per pound; cognac or œnanthic ether, two dollars per ounce; cubebs, one dollar per pound; fennel, fifty cents per pound; juniper, twenty-five cents per pound; lemons, fifty cents per pound; orange, fifty cents per pound; origanum, or red thyme, twenty-five cents per pound; roses, or otto, one dollar and fifty cents per ounce; thyme, white, thirty cents per pound; valerian, one dollar and fifty cents per pound; all other essential oils, not otherwise provided for, fifty per centum ad valorem;

Opium, two dollars per pound;

Opium prepared for smoking, eighty per centum ad valorem;

Paraffine, ten cents per pound;

Paris white, when dry, sixty cents per one hundred pounds; when ground in oil, one dollar and fifty cents per one hundred pounds;

Pimento, twelve cents per pound; when ground, fifteen cents per pound;

Potash, bichromate, three cents per pound; hydriodate, iodate, iodide, and acetate, seventy-five cents per pound; prussiate, yellow, five cents per pound; prussiate, red, ten cents per pound; chlorate, six cents per pound;

Petroleum and coal illuminating oil, crude, ten cents per gallon; refined, or kerosene, produced from the distillation of coal, asphaltum, shale, peat, petroleum, or rock oil, or other bituminous substances, used for like purposes, twenty cents per gallon;

Putty, one dollar and fifty cents per one hundred pounds;

Quinine, sulphate of, and other salts of quinine, forty-five per centum ad valorem;

Rhubarb, fifty cents per pound;

Rose leaves, fifty cents per pound;

Rum essence or oil, and bay rum essence or oil, two dollars per ounce;

Saltpetre, or nitrate of potash, crude, two cents per pound; refined, three cents per pound;

Seeds, anise, five cents per pound; star anise, ten cents per pound; canary, one dollar per bushel of sixty pounds; caraway, three cents per pound; cardamom, fifty cents per pound; cummin, five cents per pound; coriander, three cents per pound; fennel, two cents per pound; fe[n]ugreek, two cents per pound; hemp, one-half cent per pound; mustard, brown, three cents per pound; white, three cents per pound; rape, one cent per pound; castor seeds or beans, thirty cents per bushel;

Sugar of lead, four cents per pound;

Tartar emetic, fifteen cents per pound;

Varnish, valued at one dollar and fifty cents or less per gallon, fifty cents per gallon, and twenty per centum ad valorem; valued at above one dollar and fifty cents per gallon, fifty cents per gallon, and twenty-five per centum ad valorem;

Vanilla beans, three dollars per pound;

Verdigris, six cents per pound;

Whiting, when dry, fifty cents per one hundred pounds; when ground in oil, one dollar and fifty cents per one hundred pounds;

Acetous, benzoic, muriatic, and pyroligneous acids, cutch or catechu, orchil and cudbear, safflower and sumac, ten per centum ad valorem;

Arsenic in all forms, ammonia, and sulphate and carbonate of ammonia; bark, cinchona, Peruvian, Lima, Calisaya, quilla, and all other medicinal barks, flowers, leaves, plants, roots, and seeds, not otherwise provided for; cobalt, and oxide of cobalt; gums, amber, Arabic, Jedda, Senegal, tragacanth, myrrh, and all other gums and gum resins not otherwise provided for; quassia wood; smalts; sarsaparilla; tapioca; tonqua beans and sponges, twenty per centum ad valorem; acetic acid, twenty-five per centum ad valorem;

Santonine and glycerine, thirty per centum ad valorem;

On all pills, powders, tinctures, troches or lozenges, syrups, cordials, bitters, anodynes, tonics, plasters, liniments, salves, ointments, pastes, drops, waters, essences, spirits, oils, or other medicinal preparations or compositions, recommended to the public as proprietary medicines, or prepared according to some private formula or secret art as remedies or specifics for any disease or diseases or affections whatever affecting the human or animal body, fifty per centum ad valorem;

On all essences, extracts, toilet waters, cosmetics, hair oils, pomades, hair dressings, hair restoratives, hair dyes, tooth washes, dentifrices, tooth pastes, aromatic cachous, or other perfumeries or cosmetics, by whatsoever name or names known, used or applied as perfumes or applications to the hair, mouth, or skin, fifty per centum ad valorem.

Sec. 6. *And be it further enacted*, That from and after the day and year aforesaid, in addition to the duties heretofore imposed by law on the articles hereinafter mentioned, and on such as may now be exempt from duty, there shall be levied, collected, and paid on the goods, wares, and merchandise enumerated and provided for in this section, imported from foreign countries, a duty of ten per centum ad valorem, that is to say:

Antimony, crude;

Assafœtida;

Beeswax;

Blacking of all descriptions;

Building stone of all descriptions not otherwise provided for;

Calomel;

Catsup;

Civet, oil of;

Cobalt ores;

Extract of indigo; extract of madder; extract and decoctions of logwood, and other dyewoods;

Flints and flint, ground;

Flocks, waste or shoddy;

Furs, dressed, when not on the skin;

Garancine;

Ginger, preserved or pickled;

Green turtle;

Grindstones, unwrought, or wrought or finished;

Gutta-percha, unmanufactured;

Isinglass or fish glue;

Japanned ware of all kinds not otherwise provided for;

Lastings, mohair cloth, silk, twist, or other manufacture of cloth woven or made in patterns of such size, shape and form, or cut in such manner as to be fit for shoes, slippers, boots, bootees, gaiters and buttons, exclusively, not combined with India-rubber.

Mats of cocoa-nut;

Matting, China, and other floor-matting, and mats made of flags, jute, or grass;

Manufactures of gutta-percha;

Milk of India-rubber; medicinal preparations not otherwise provided for;

Music, printed with lines, bound or unbound;

Musical instruments of all kinds, and strings for musical instruments of whipgut or catgut, and all other strings of the same material,

Nickel;

Osier or willow, prepared for basket-makers' use;

Philosophical apparatus and instruments;

Plaster of Paris, when ground;

Quills;

Strychnine;

Staves for pipes, hogsheads, or other casks;

Teeth, manufactured;

Thread lace and insertings;

Woollen listings.

SEC. 7. *And be it further enacted*, That, in addition to the duties heretofore imposed by law on the articles hereinafter mentioned and provided for in this section, there shall be levied, collected and paid, on the goods, wares and merchandise herein enumerated, imported from foreign countries, the following duties and rates of duty, that is to say:

On chocolate and cocoa prepared, one cent per pound;

On copperas, green vitriol, or sulphate of iron, one-fourth cent per pound;

On linseed, flax-seed, hemp-seed, and rape-seed oil, three cents per gallon;

On saleratus and bicarbonate of soda, one-half cent per pound;

On caustic soda, one-half cent per pound;

On salt, in sacks, barrels, other packages, or in bulk, six cents per one hundred pounds;

On soap, fancy, scented, honey, cream, transparent, and all descriptions of toilet and shaving soap, two cents per pound; all other soaps, five per centum ad valorem;

On spirits of turpentine, five cents per gallon;

On starch of all descriptions, one-half cent per pound;

On white and red lead, dry or ground in oil, fifteen cents per one hundred pounds;

On oxide of zinc, dry or ground in oil, twenty-five cents per one hundred pounds.

SEC. 8. *And be it further enacted,* That from and after the day and year aforesaid, in lieu of the duties heretofore imposed by law on the articles hereinafter mention[ed,] and on such as may now be exempt from duty, there shall be levied, collected, and paid on the goods, wares and merchandise enumerated and provided for in this section, imported from foreign countries, the following duties and rates of duty, that is to say:

On anchovies, preserved in salt, thirty per centum ad valorem;

On andirons, made of cast iron, one cent and one-fourth per pound;

On barley, pearl or hulled, one cent per pound;

On bonnets, hats, and hoods for men, women and children, composed of straw, chip, grass, palm-leaf, willow, or any other vegetable substance, or of silk, hair, whalebone, or other material not otherwise provided for, forty per centum ad valorem;

On braids, plaits, flats, laces, trimmings, sparterre, tissues, willow sheets and squares, used for making or ornamenting hats, bonnets, and hoods, composed of straw, chip, grass, palm-leaf, willow, or any other vegetable substance, or of hair, whalebone, or other material, not otherwise provided for, thirty per centum ad valorem;

On books, periodicals, pamphlets, blank-books, bound or unbound, and all printed matter, engravings, bound or unbound, illustrated books and papers, and maps and charts, twenty per centum ad valorem: *Provided,* That all imported cotton and linen rags for the manufacture of paper shall be free of duty;

On bristles, ten cents per pound;

On candles and tapers, stearine and adamantine, five cents per pound; on spermaceti, paraffine and wax candles and tapers, pure or mixed, eight cents per pound; on all other candles and tapers, two and one-half cents per pound;

On chicory root, two cents per pound; on chicory ground, burnt, or prepared, three cents per pound;

On acorn coffee and dandelion root, raw or prepared, and all other articles used or intended to be used as coffee, or a substitute for coffee, and not otherwise provided for, three cents per pound;

On coloring for brandy, fifty per centum ad valorem;

On cork wood, unmanufactured, thirty per centum ad valorem; on corks, fifty per centum ad valorem;

On cotton, one-half cent per pound;

On feathers and downs for beds or bedding, of all descriptions, thirty per centum ad valorem;

On ostrich, vulture, cock, and other ornamental feathers, crude or not dressed, colored or manufactured, twenty per centum ad valorem; when dressed, colored, or manufactured, forty per centum ad valorem;

On feathers and flowers, artificial and parts thereof, of whatever material composed, not otherwise provided for, forty per centum ad valorem;

On fire-crackers, fifty cents per box of forty packs, not exceeding eighty to each pack; and in the same proportion for a greater number;

On fruit, shade, lawn, and ornamental trees, shrubs, plants, and bulbous roots and flower seeds, not otherwise provided for, thirty per centum ad valorem;

On gloves, made of skins or leather, forty per centum ad valorem;

On gunpowder, and all explosive substances used for mining, blasting, artillery or sporting purposes, valued at less than twenty cents per pound, six cents per pound; valued at twenty cents or over per pound, six cents per pound, and twenty per centum ad valorem in addition thereto;

On garden seeds, and all other seeds for agricultural and horticultural purposes, not otherwise provided for, thirty per centum ad valorem;

On hides, raw, and skins of all kinds, whether dried, salted, or pickled, ten per centum ad valorem;

On hollow-ware and vessels of cast-iron, not otherwise provided for, one cent and one-fourth per pound;

On hops, five cents per pound;

On human hair, raw, uncleaned, and not drawn, twenty per centum ad valorem; when cleaned or drawn, but not manufactured, thirty per centum ad valorem; when manufactured, forty per centum ad valorem;

On lead ore, one dollar per one hundred pounds;

On marble, white statuary, in block, rough, or squared, seventy-five cents per cubic foot; veined marble, and marble of all other descriptions, not otherwise provided for, in block, rough, or squared, forty per centum ad valorem;

On all manufactures of marble, marble slabs, marble paving tiles, and marble sawed, dressed, or polished, fifty per centum ad valorem;

On manufactures of bladders, thirty per centum ad valorem;

On manufactures of India-rubber and silk, or of India-rubber and silk and other materials, fifty per centum ad valorem;

On mustard, ground, in bulk, twelve cents per pound; when enclosed in glass or tin, sixteen cents per pound;

On plates engraved, of steel, copper, wood, or any other material, twenty-five per centum ad valorem;

On plumbago or black lead, ten dollars per ton;

On potatoes, twenty-five cents per bushel;

On percussion caps, fulminates, fulminating powders, and all articles used for like purposes, not otherwise provided for, thirty per centum ad valorem;

On playing cards, valued at twenty-five cents or less per pack, fifteen cents per pack; valued above twenty-five cents per pack, twenty-five cents per pack;

On pens, metallic, ten cents per gross;

On pen-holder tips, metallic, ten cents per gross;

On pen-holders, complete, ten cents per dozen;

On lead pencils, one dollar per gross;

On rice, cleaned, one cent and a half per pound; paddy, three-quarters of one cent per pound; uncleaned rice, one cent per pound;

On sago and sago flour, one cent and a half per pound;

On sheathing copper, and sheathing metal or yellow metal not wholly of copper nor wholly or in part of iron, ungalvanized, in sheets forty-eight inches long and fourteen inches wide, and weighing from fourteen to thirty-four ounces per square foot, three cents per pound;

On tin in pigs, bars, or blocks, fifteen per centum ad valorem;

On tin in plates or sheets, terne, and tagger tin, twenty-five per centum ad valorem; on oxide, muriatic, and salts of tin and tin foil, thirty per centum ad valorem;

SEC. 9. *And be it further enacted*, That in addition to the duties heretofore imposed by law on the articles hereinafter mentioned and included in this section, there shall be levied, collected, and paid, on the goods, wares, and merchandise herein enumerated and provided for, imported from foreign countries, the following duties and rates of duty, that is to say:

On Wilton, Saxony and Aubusson, Axminister, patent velvet, Tournay velvet, and tapestry velvet carpets and carpeting, Brussels carpets wrought by the Jacquard machine, and all medallion or whole carpets, five cents per square yard; on Brussels and tapestry Brussels carpets and carpeting, printed on the warp or otherwise, three cents per square yard; on all treble-ingrain and worsted chain Venetian carpets and carpeting, three cents per square yard; on hemp or jute carpeting, two cents per square yard; on all other kinds of carpets and carpeting, of wool, flax, or cotton, or parts of either or other material, (except druggets, bockings, and felt carpets and carpetings,) not otherwise provided for, five per centum ad valorem: *Provided*, That mats, rugs, screens, covers, hassocks, bed-sides, and other portions of carpets or carpeting, shall pay the rate of duty herein imposed on carpets and carpeting of similar character; on all other mats, screens, hassocks and rugs, five per centum ad valorem;

On woollen cloths, woollen shawls, and all manufactures of wool, of every description, made wholly or in part of wool, not otherwise provided for, a duty of six cents per pound, and in addition thereto, five per centum ad valorem;

On goods of like description, when valued at over one dollar per square yard, or weighing less than twelve ounces per square yard, a duty of six cents per pound, and in addition thereto, ten per centum ad valorem;

On endless belts or felts for paper, and blanketing for printing machines, five per centum ad valorem;

On flannels, of all descriptions, five per centum ad valorem;

On hats of wool, ten per centum ad valorem;

On woollen and worsted yarn, of all descriptions, five per centum ad valorem;

On clothing ready made, and wearing apparel of every description, composed wholly or in part of wool, made up or manufactured wholly or in part by the tailor, seamstress, or manufacturer, six cents per pound, and in addition thereto, five per centum ad valorem: *Provided*, That Balmoral skirts, or goods of like description, or used for like purposes, made wholly or in part of wool, shall be subjected to the same duties that are levied upon ready-made clothing;

On blankets of all kinds, made wholly or in part of wool, five per centum ad valorem;

On all delaines, cashmere delaines, muslin delaines, barege delaines, composed wholly or in part of worsted, wool, mohair, or goats' hair, and on all goods of similar description, not exceeding in value forty cents per square yard, two cents per square yard;

On bunting, worsted yarns, and on all other manufactures of worsted, or of which worsted shall be a component material, not otherwise provided for, five per centum ad valorem;

On oil-cloth for floors, stamped or printed, of all descriptions, five per centum ad valorem;

On coir floor matting and carpeting, five per centum ad valorem.

SEC. 10. *And be it further enacted*, That from and after the day and year aforesaid, in addition to the duties heretofore imposed by law on the articles hereinafter mentioned and provided for in this section, there shall be levied, collected, and paid, on the goods, wares, and merchandise herein enumerated, imported from foreign countries, the following duties and rates of duty, that is to say:

First. On all manufactures of cotton, bleached or unbleached, and not colored, stained, painted, or printed, and not exceeding one hundred threads to the square inch, counting the warp and filling, and exceeding in weight five ounces per square yard, one-fourth of one cent per square yard; on finer or lighter goods of like description, not exceeding one hundred and forty threads to the square inch, counting the warp and filling, one-half cent per square yard; on goods of like description, exceeding one hundred and forty threads and not exceeding two hundred threads to the square inch, counting the warp and filling, three-fourths of one cent per square yard; on like goods, exceeding two hundred threads to the square inch, counting the warp and filling, one cent per square yard; on all goods embraced in the foregoing schedules, (except jeans, denimes, drillings, bedtickings, ginghams, plaids, cottonades, pantaloon stuffs, and goods of like description, not exceeding in value the sum of sixteen cents per square yard,) if printed, painted, colored, or stained, they shall be considered to have been bleached goods, and there shall be levied, collected, and paid a duty of one cent per square yard, in addition to the rates of duty provided for bleached goods: *Provided*, That upon all plain woven cotton goods not included in the foregoing schedules, and upon cotton goods of every description, the value of which shall exceed sixteen cents per square yard, there shall be levied, collected, and paid a duty of five per centum ad valorem: *And provided, further*, That no cotton goods having more than two hundred threads to the square inch, counting the warp and filling, shall be admitted to a less rate of duty than is provided for goods which are of that number of threads.

Second. On spool and other thread of cotton, ten per centum ad valorem.

Third. On shirts and drawers, wove or made on frames, composed wholly of cotton, and cotton velvet, five per centum ad valorem.

Fourth. On all cotton jeans, denimes, drillings, bedtickings, ginghams, plaids, cottonades, pantaloon stuffs, and goods of like description, not exceeding in value the sum of sixteen cents per square yard, two cents per square yard, and on all manufactures composed wholly of cotton, bleached, unbleached, printed, painted, or dyed, not otherwise provided for, five per centum ad valorem.

Fifth. On all brown or bleached linens, ducks, canvas paddings, cot-bottoms, burlaps, drills, coatings, brown hollands, blay linens, damasks, diapers, crash, huckabacks, handkerchiefs, lawns, or other manufactures of flax, jute, or hemp, (or of which flax, jute, or hemp shall be the component material of chief value,) five per centum ad valorem; on flax or linen threads, twine and packthread, and all other manufactures of flax, or of which flax shall be the component material of chief value, and not otherwise provided for, five per centum ad valorem.

SEC. 11. *And be it further enacted*, That from and after the day and year aforesaid, in addition to the duties heretofore imposed by law on the articles hereinafter mentioned and provided for in this section, there shall be levied, collected, and paid, on the goods, wares, and merchandise herein enumerated, imported from foreign countries, the following duties and rates of duty, that is to say:

On jute, Sisal grass, sun hemp, coir, and other vegetable substances not enumerated, (except flax, tow of flax, Russia and Manilla hemp, and codilla, or tow of hemp,) five dollars per ton;

On jute butts, one dollar per ton;

On tarred cables, or cordage, one-fourth of one cent per pound;

On untarred Manilla cordage, one-fourth of one cent per pound;

On all other untarred cordage, one-half cent per pound;

On hemp yarn, one cent per pound;

On coir yarn, one-half cent per pound;

On seines, one-half cent per pound;

On cotton bagging, or other manufactures not otherwise provided for, suitable for the uses to which cotton bagging is applied, whether composed in whole or in part of hemp, jute, or flax, or any other material valued at less than ten cents per square yard, three-fourths of one cent. per pound; over ten cents per square yard, one cent per pound;

On sail duck, five per centum ad valorem;

On Russia and other sheetings, made of flax or hemp, brown and white, five per centum ad valorem; and

On all other manufactures of hemp, or of which hemp shall be a component part, not otherwise provided for, five per centum ad valorem.

On grass cloth, five per centum ad valorem;

On jute yarns, five per centum ad valorem;

On all other manufactures of jute or Sisal grass, not otherwise provided for, five per centum ad valorem: *Provided*, That all hemp, or preparations of hemp used for naval purposes by the Government of the United States, shall be of American growth or manufacture: *Provided, further*, The same can be obtained of as good quality and at as low a price.

Sec. 12. *And be it further enacted*, That from and after the day and year aforesaid, in lieu of the duties heretofore imposed by law on the articles hereinafter mentioned, and on such as may now be exempt from duty, there shall be levied, collected, and paid, on the goods, wares, and merchandise enumerated and provided for in this section, imported from foreign countries, the following duties and rates of duty, that is to say:

On all brown earthenware and common stoneware, gas retorts, stoneware not ornamented, and stoneware above the capacity of ten gallons, twenty per centum ad valorem;

On China and porcelain ware, gilded, ornamented, or decorated in any manner, forty per centum ad valorem;

On China and porcelain ware, plain white, and not decorated in any manner, and all other earthen, stone, or crockery ware, white, glazed, edged, printed, painted, dipped, or cream colored, composed of earthy or mineral substances, and not otherwise provided for, thirty-five per centum ad valorem;

Slates, slate pencils, slate chimney pieces, mantels, slabs for tables, and all other manufactures of slate, forty per centum ad valorem;

On unwrought clay, pipe clay, fire clay, and kaoline, five dollars per ton;

On fuller's earth, three dollars per ton;

On white chalk, four dollars per ton; on red and French chalk, ten per centum ad valorem; on chalk of all descriptions, not otherwise provided for, twenty-five per centum ad valorem;

On all plain and mould and press glassware, not cut, engraved, or painted, thirty per centum ad valorem;

On all articles of glass, cut, engraved, painted, colored, printed, stained, silvered or gilded, not including plate-glass silvered, or looking-glass plates, thirty-five per centum ad valorem;

On fluted, rolled, or rough plate-glass, not including crown, cylinder, broad, or common window glass, not exceeding ten by fifteen inches, seventy-five cents per one hundred square feet; above that, and not exceeding sixteen by twenty-four inches, one cent per square foot; above that, and not exceeding twenty-four by thirty inches, one cent and a half per square foot; all above that, two cents per square foot: *Provided*, That all fluted, rolled, or rough plate-glass, weighing over one hundred pounds per one hundred square feet, shall pay an additional duty on the excess at the same rates herein imposed;

On all cast polished plate-glass, unsilvered, not exceeding ten by fifteen inches, three cents per square foot; above that, and not exceeding sixteen by twenty-four inches, five cents per square foot; above that, and not exceeding twenty-four by thirty inches, eight cents per square foot; above that, and not exceeding twenty-four by sixty inches, twenty-five cents per square foot; all above that, fifty cents per square foot;

On all cast polished plate-glass, silvered, or looking-glass plates, exceeding ten by fifteen inches, four cents per square foot; above that, and not exceeding sixteen by twenty-four inches, six cents per square foot; above that, and not exceeding twenty-four by thirty inches, ten cents per square foot; above that, and not exceeding twenty-four by sixty inches, thirty-five cents per square foot; all above that, sixty cents per square foot: *Provided*, That no looking-glass plates, or plate-glass silvered, when framed, shall pay a less rate of duty than that imposed upon similar glass, of like description, not framed, but shall be liable to pay, in addition thereto, thirty per centum ad valorem upon such frames;

On porcelain and Bohemian glass, glass crystals for watches, paintings on glass or glasses, pebbles for spectacles, and all manufactures of glass, or of which glass shall be a component material, except crown, cylinder, and other window glass, not otherwise provided for, and all glass bottles or jars filled with sweetmeats, preserves, thirty-five per centum ad valorem;

SEC. 13. *And be it further enacted*, That from and after the day and year aforesaid, in addition to the duties heretofore imposed by law on the articles hereinafter mentioned, there shall be levied, collected, and paid, on the goods, wares, and merchandise enumerated and provided for in this section, imported from foreign countries, a duty of five per centum ad valorem, that is to say:

Argentine, alabalta, or German silver, manufactured or unmanufactured;

Articles embroidered with gold, silver, or other metal;

Articles worn by men, women, or children, of whatever material composed, made up, or made wholly or in part by hand, not otherwise provided for;

Britannia ware;

Baskets, and all other articles composed of grass, ozier, palm-leaf, straw, whalebone, or willow, not otherwise provided for;

Bracelets, braids, chains, curls, or ringlets composed of hair, or of which hair is a component material;

Braces, suspenders, webbing, or other fabrics composed wholly or in part of India-rubber, not otherwise provided for;

Brooms and brushes of all kinds;

Canes and sticks for walking, finished or unfinished;

Capers, pickles, and sauces of all kinds, not otherwise provided for;

Caps, hats, muffs, and tippets of fur, and all other manufactures of fur, or of which fur shall be a component material;

Caps, gloves, leggins, mits, socks, stockings, wove shirts and drawers, and all similar articles made on frames, of whatever material composed, worn by men, women, and children, and not otherwise provided for;

Card cases, pocket books, shell boxes, souvenirs, and all similar articles, of whatever material composed;

Carriages and parts of carriages;

Clocks and parts of clocks;

Clothing, ready made, and wearing apparel of whatever description, of whatever material composed, except wool, made up or manufactured wholly or in part by the tailor, seamstress, or manufacturer;

Coach and harness furniture of all kinds, saddlery, coach and harness hardware, silver plated, brass plated, or covered, common tinned, burnished, or japanned, not otherwise provided for;

Combs of all kinds;

Compositions of glass or plate, when set;

Composition tops for tables, or other articles of furniture;

Comfits, sweetmeats, or fruits preserved in sugar, brandy, or molasses, not otherwise provided for;

Cotton cords, gimps, and galloons;

Cotton laces, cotton insertings, cotton trimming laces, and cotton braids, colored or uncolored;

Court-plaster;

Cutlery of all kinds;

Dolls and toys of all kinds;

Encaustic tiles;

Epaulets, galloons, laces, knots, stars, tassels, tresses, and wings, of gold, silver, or other metal;

Fans and fire-screens of every description, of whatever material composed;

Frames and sticks for umbrellas, parasols, and sunshades, finished or unfinished;

Furniture, cabinet and household;

Furs, dressed;

Hair pencils;

Hat bodies of cotton or wool, or of which wool is the component material of chief value;

Hair cloth, hair seatings, and all other manufactures of hair, not otherwise provided for;

Ink, printers' ink, and ink powder;

Japanned, patent or enamelled leather, or skins of all kinds;

Jet and manufactures of jet, and imitations thereof;

Leather, tanned, of all descriptions;

Maccaroni, vermicelli, gelatine, jellies, and all similar preparations;

Manufactures of bone, shell, horn, ivory or vegetable ivory;

Manufactures of paper, or of which paper is a component material, not otherwise provided for;

Manufactures of the bark of the cork tree, except corks;

Manufactures, articles, vessels and wares, not otherwise provided for, of gold, silver, copper, brass, iron, steel, lead, pewter, tin, or other metal, or of which either of these metals or any other metal shall be the component material of chief value;

Manufactures not otherwise provided for, composed of mixed materials, in part of cotton, silk, wool, or worsted, hemp, jute, or flax;

Manufactures of cotton, linen, silk, wool, or worsted, if embroidered or tamboured, in the loom or otherwise, by machinery or with the needle or other process, not otherwise provided for;

Manufactures of cedar wood, granadilla, ebony, mahogany, rosewood, and satin wood;

Manufactures and articles of leather, or of which leather shall be a component part, not otherwise provided for;

Manufactures, articles, and wares, of papier mache;

Manufactures of goats' hair or mohair, or of which goats' hair or mohair shall be a component material, not otherwise provided for;

Manufactures of wood, or of which wood is the chief component part, not otherwise provided for;

Morocco skins;

Muskets, rifles, and other fire-arms;

Needles, sewing, darning, knitting, and all other descriptions;

Oil-cloth of every description, of whatever material composed, not otherwise provided for;

Paper boxes, and all other fancy boxes;

Paper envelopes;

Paper-hangings, and paper for screens or fire-boards; paper, antiquarian, demy, drawing, elephant, foolscap, imperial, letter, and all other paper, not otherwise provided for;

Pins, solid head or other;

Plated and gilt ware of all kinds;

Prepared vegetables, meats, fish, poultry, and game, sealed or unsealed, in cans or otherwise;

Ratans and reeds, manufactured or partially manufactured;

Roofing slates;

Scagliola tops for tables or other articles of furniture;

Sealing-wax;

Side arms of every description;

Silver-plated metal, in sheets or other form;

Stereotype plates;

Still bottoms;

Twines and packthread, of whatever material composed, not otherwise provided for;

Type metal;

Types, new;

Umbrellas, parasols, and sunshades;

Velvet, when printed or painted;

Wafers;

Water-colors;

Watches and parts of watches, and watch materials, and unfinished parts of watches;

Webbing, composed of wool, cotton, flax, or any other materials, not otherwise provided for;

SEC. 14. *And be it further enacted*, That from and after the day and year aforesaid, there shall be levied, collected, and paid on all goods, wares, and merchandise of the growth or produce of countries beyond the Cape of Good Hope, when imported from places this side of the Cape of Good Hope, a duty of ten per cent ad valorem, and in addition to the duties imported on any such articles when imported directly from the place or places of their growth or production.

SEC. 15. *And be it further enacted*, That upon all ships, vessels, or steamers, which, after the thirty-first day of December, eighteen hundred and sixty-two, shall be entered at any custom-house in the United States from any foreign port or place, or from any port or place in the United States, whether ships or vessels of the United States, or belonging wholly or in part to subjects of foreign powers, there shall be paid a tax or tonnage duty of ten cents per ton of the measurement of said vessel, in addition to any tonnage duty now imposed by law. *Provided*, That the said tax or tonnage duty shall not be collected more than once in each year on any ship, vessel, or steamer having a license to trade between different districts of the United States, or to carry on the bank, whale, or other fisheries, whilst employed therein, or on any ship, vessel, or steamer, to or from any port or place in Mexico, the British provinces of North America, or any of the West India Islands: *Provided, also*, That nothing in this act contained shall be deemed in anywise to impair any rights and privileges which have been or may be acquired by any foreign nation under the laws and treaties of the United States relative to the duty on tonnage of vessels: *Provided, further*, That so much of the act of August eighteen, eighteen hundred and fifty-six, entitled "An Act to authorize protection to be given to citizens of the United States who may discover deposits of guano," as prohibits the export thereof, is hereby suspended for one year from and after the passage of this act.

SEC. 16. *And be it further enacted*, That from and after the passage of this act, in estimating the allowance for tare on all chests, boxes, cases, casks, bags, or other envelope or covering of all articles imported liable to pay any duty, where the original invoice is produced at the time of making entry thereof, and the tare shall be specified therein, it shall be lawful for the collector, if he shall see fit, or for the collector and naval officer, if such officer there be, if they shall see fit, with the consent of the consignees, to estimate the said tare according to such invoice; but in all other cases the real tare shall be allowed, and may be ascertained under such regulations as the Secretary of the Treasury may from time to time prescribe, but in no case shall there be any allowance for draft.

SEC. 17. *And be it further enacted,* That from and after the first day of November, eighteen hundred and sixty-two, no goods, wares, or merchandise subject to ad valorem or specific duty, whether belonging to a person or persons residing in the United States or otherwise, or whether acquired by the ordinary process of bargain and sale, or otherwise, shall be admitted to entry, unless the invoice of such goods, wares, or merchandise be verified by the oath of the owner, or one of the owners, or, in the absence of the owner, one of the party who is authorized by the owner to make the shipment and sign the invoice of the same, certifying that the invoice annexed contains a true and faithful account, if subject to ad valorem duty and obtained by purchase, of the actual cost thereof, and of all charges thereon, and that no discounts, bounties, or drawbacks are contained in the said invoice but such as have actually been allowed on the same; and when consigned or obtained in any manner other than by purchase, the actual market value thereof, and if subject to specific duty, of the actual quantity thereof; which said oath shall be administered by the consul or commercial agent of the United States in the district where the goods are manufactured, or from which they are sent; and if there be no consul or commercial agent of the United States in the said district, the verification hereby required shall be made by the consul or commercial agent of the United States at the nearest point, or at the port from which the goods are shipped, in which case the oath shall be administered by some public officer, duly authorized to administer oaths, and transmitted, with a copy of the invoice, to the consul or commercial agent, for his authentication; and this act shall be construed only to modify, and not repeal, the act of March first, eighteen hundred and twenty-three, entitled "An Act supplementary to, and to amend an act entitled 'An Act to regulate the collection of duties on imports and tonnage,' passed second March, one thousand seven hundred and ninety-nine, and for other purposes," and the forms of the oaths therein set forth shall be modified accordingly. And there shall be paid to the said consul, vice-consul, or commercial agent, by the person or persons by or in behalf of whom the said invoices are presented and deposited, one dollar for each and every invoice verified, which shall be accounted for by the officers receiving the same, in such manner as is now required by the laws regulating the fees and salaries of consuls and commercial agents: *Provided,* That nothing herein contained shall be construed to require for goods imported under the reciprocity treaty with Great Britain, signed June fifth, eighteen hundred and fifty-four, any other consular certificate than is now required by law: *And provided, further,* That the provisions of this section shall not apply to invoices of goods, wares, and merchandise, imported into the United States from beyond Cape Horn and the Cape of Good Hope, until the first day of April, one thousand eight hundred and sixty-three: *And provided further,* That the provisions of this section shall not apply to countries where there is no consul, vice-consul, or commercial agent of the United States.

SEC. 18. *And be it further enacted*, That, from and after the date aforesaid, it shall be the duty of consuls and commercial agents of the United States, having any knowledge or belief of any case or practice of any person or persons who obtain or should obtain verification of invoices as described in the preceding section, whereby the revenue of the United States is or may be defrauded, to report the facts to the collector of the port where the revenue is or may be defrauded, or to the Secretary of the Treasury of the United States.

SEC. 19. *And be it further enacted*, That, from and after the passage of this act, the act entitled "An act to provide for the payment of outstanding treasury notes, to authorize a loan, to regulate and fix the duties on imports, and for other purposes," approved March two, eighteen hundred and sixty-one, be, and the same is hereby amended as follows, that is to say: First, in section twelve, before the word "eighteen," where it first occurs, strike out "less than;" second, in section twenty-three, after the words, "artists residing abroad," strike out, "provided the same be imported in good faith as objects of taste and not of merchandise," and insert "provided the fact, as aforesaid, shall be certified by the artist, or by a consul of the United States;" and in the same section, before the word "orpiment," insert "ores of gold and silver."

SEC. 20. *And be it further enacted*, That the sixth section of an act entitled "An act to extend the warehousing system by establishing private bonded warehouses, and for other purposes," be, and the same is hereby amended so that the additional duty of one hundred per centum shall not apply to the invoice or appraised value of the merchandise withdrawn, but shall be so construed as to require for failure to transport and deliver within the time limited a duty to be levied and collected of double the amount which said goods, wares, and merchandise would be liable upon the original entry thereof.

SEC. 21. *And be it further enacted*, That all goods, wares, and merchandise, which may be in public stores or bonded warehouse on the first day of August, eighteen hundred and sixty-two, may be withdrawn for consumption upon payment of the duties now imposed thereon by law: *Provided*, The same shall be so withdrawn within three months from the date of original importation; but all goods, wares, and merchandise which shall remain in the public stores or bonded warehouse for more than three months from the date of original importation, if withdrawn for consumption, and all goods on shipboard on the first day of August, eighteen hundred and sixty-two, shall be subject to the duties prescribed by this act: *Provided*, That all goods which now are or may be deposited in public stores or bonded warehouse after this act takes effect and goes into operation, must be withdrawn therefrom, or the duties thereon paid within one year from the date of original importation, but may be withdrawn by the owner for exportation to foreign countries, or may be transhipped to any port of the Pacific or western coast of the United States at any time before the expiration of three years from the date of original importation; such goods on arrival at a Pacific or western port, as aforesaid, to be subject to the same rules and regulations as if originally imported there; any goods remaining in public store or bonded warehouse beyond three years shall be regarded as abandoned to the Government, and sold under such regulations as the Secretary of the Treasury may prescribe, and the proceeds paid into the treasury: *Provided, further*, That merchandise upon which duties have been paid may remain in warehouse in custody of the officers of the customs at the expense and risk of the owners of said merchandise, and if exported directly from said custody to a foreign country within three years, shall be entitled to return duties, proper evidence of such merchandise having been landed abroad to be furnished to the collector by the importer, one per centum of said duties to be retained by the Government: *And provided, further*, That all drugs, medicines, and chemical preparations, entered for exportation and deposited in warehouse or public store, may be exported by the owner or owners thereof in the original package, or otherwise, subject to such regulations as shall be prescribed by the Secretary of the Treasury: *And provided, further*, That the third or last proviso to the fifth section of an act entitled "An act to provide increased revenue from imports, to pay interest on the public debt, and for other purposes," approved the sixth day of August, eighteen hundred and sixty-one, be, and the same is hereby repealed; and no return of the duties shall be allowed on the export of any merchandise after it has been removed from the custody and control of the Government; but nothing herein contained shall be held to apply to or repeal section thirty of the act entitled "An act to provide for the payment of outstanding treasury notes, to authorize a loan, to regulate and fix the duties on imports, and for other purposes," approved March second, eighteen hundred and sixty-one, or section four of an act entitled "An act to provide increased revenue from imports, to pay interest on the public debt, and for other purposes," approved August fifth, eighteen hundred and sixty-one.

Sec. 22. *And be it further enacted*, That the privilege of purchasing supplies from the public warehouses, duty free, be extended under such regulations as the Secretary of the Treasury shall prescribe to the vessels-of-war of any nation in ports of the United States, which may reciprocate such privilege towards the vessels-of-war of the United States in its ports.

Sec. 23. *And be it further enacted*, That all acts and parts of acts repugnant to the provisions of this act be, and the same are hereby repealed: *Provided*, That the existing laws shall extend to, and be in force for, the collection of the duties imposed by this act, for the prosecution and punishment of all offences, and for the recovery, collection, distribution, and remission of all fines, penalties, and forfeitures, as fully and effectually as if every regulation, penalty, forfeiture, provision, clause, matter, and thing to that effect, in the existing laws contained, had been inserted in and re-enacted by this act.

Sec. 24. *And be it further enacted*, That in the ninety-fifth section of the act entitled "An act to provide internal revenue to support the Government and [to] pay interest on the public debt," approved July first, eighteen hundred and sixty-two, be so amended that no instrument, document, or paper, made, signed, or issued prior to the first day of January, eighteen hundred and sixty-three, without being duly stamped, or having thereon an adhesive stamp to denote the duty imposed thereon, shall for that cause be deemed invalid and of no effect: *Provided, however*, That no such instrument, document, or paper shall be admitted or used as evidence in any court until the same shall have been duly stamped, nor until the holder thereof shall have proved to the satisfaction of the court that he has paid to the collector or deputy collector of the district within which such court may be held the sum of five dollars, for the use of the United States.

SEC. 26. *And be it further enacted*, That no part of the act aforesaid, in relation to stamp duties, shall be held to take effect before the first day of September, eighteen hundred and sixty-two; and so much of said act as relates to the appointment of collectors and assessors shall be held to take effect on the twenty-first day of July, eighteen hundred and sixty-two, instead of from and after its approval by the President.

Approved July 14, 1862.

DEPARTMENT OF STATE,
WASHINGTON, *July* 16, 1862.

The foregoing, as corrected, is a true copy of the original act on file in this Department.

W. HUNTER,
Chief Clerk.

AN ACT to modify existing Laws imposing Duties on Imports, and for other Purposes.

Be it enacted by the Senate and House of Representatives of the United States of America in Congress assembled, That all goods, wares, and merchandise now in public stores or bonded warehouses, on which duties are unpaid, having been in bond more than one year and less than three years, when the act entitled "An act increasing temporarily the duties on imports, and for other purposes," approved July fourteenth, eighteen hundred and sixty-two, went into effect, may be entered for consumption and the bonds cancelled, at any time before the first day of June next, on payment of duties at the rates prescribed by the act aforesaid, and all acts, and parts of acts, inconsistent with the provisions of this act, are hereby repealed.

SEC. 2. *And be it further enacted,* That section fourteen of an act entitled "An act increasing temporarily the duties on imports, and for other purposes," approved July fourteenth, eighteen hundred and sixty-two, be, and the same hereby is, modified so as to allow cotton and raw silk as reeled from the cocoon, of the growth or produce of countries beyond the Cape of Good Hope, to be exempt from any additional duty when imported from places this side of the Cape of Good Hope, for two years from and after the passage of this act.

SEC. 3. *And be it further enacted,* That so much of an act entitled "An act to authorize protection to be given to citizens of the United States, who may discover deposits of guano," approved August eighteen, eighteen hundred and fifty-six, as prohibits the export thereof, is hereby suspended in relation to all persons who have complied with the provisions of section second of said act for two years from and after July fourteenth, eighteen hundred and sixty-three.

SEC. 4. *And be it further enacted,* That the proviso in section fifteen of an act entitled "An act increasing temporarily the duties on imports, and for other purposes," approved July fourteen, eighteen hundred and sixty-two, shall be construed to include any ship, vessel, or steamer to or from any port or place south of Mexico down to and including Aspinwall and Panama.

SEC. 5. *And be it further enacted,* That in lieu of the duties now imposed by law there shall be levied and collected upon printing paper unsized, used for books and newspapers exclusively, twenty per centum ad valorem; upon seedlac and sticklac the same duties now imposed upon gum shellac; upon polishing powders, of all descriptions, Frankfort black, and Berlin, Chinese, Fig and wash blue, twenty-five per centum ad valorem.

SEC. 6. *And be it further enacted,* That from and after the passage of this act, the duty on petroleum and coal illuminating oil, crude and not refined, when imported from foreign countries in a crude state, shall be twenty per centum ad valorem, and no more.

SEC. 7. *And be it further enacted,* That from and after the passage of this act, there shall be allowed a drawback on foreign saltpetre, manufactured into gunpowder in the United States and exported therefrom, equal in amount to the duty paid on the foreign saltpetre from which it shall be manufactured, to be ascertained under such regulations as shall be prescribed by the Secretary of the Treasury, and no more: *Provided*, That ten per centum on the amount of all drawbacks so allowed shall be retained for the use of the United States by the collectors paying such drawbacks respectively.

APPROVED, March 3, 1863.

[Public—No. 146.]

AN ACT to increase duties on imports and for other purposes.

Be it enacted by the Senate and House of Representatives of the United States of America, in Congress assembled, That on and after the first day of July, anno Domini eighteen hundred and sixty-four, in lieu of the duties heretofore imposed by law on the articles hereinafter mentioned, there shall be levied, collected, and paid, on goods, wares, and merchandise herein enumerated and provided for, imported from foreign countries, the following duties and rates of duty, that is to say:

First. On teas of all kinds, twenty-five cents per pound.

Second. On all sugar not above number twelve, Dutch standard in color, three cents per pound.

On all sugar above number twelve, and not above number fifteen, Dutch standard in color, three cents and a half per pound.

On all sugar above number fifteen, not stove-dried, and not above number twenty, Dutch standard in color, four cents per pound.

On all refined sugar in forms of loaf, lump, crushed, powdered, pulverized, or granulated, and all stove-dried or other sugar above number twenty, Dutch standard in color, five cents per pound: *Provided*, That the standard by which the color and grades of sugar are to be regulated, shall be selected and furnished to the collectors of such ports of entry as may be necessary by the Secretary of the Treasury, from time to time, and in such manner as he may deem expedient.

On sugar candy, not colored, ten cents per pound. On all other confectionery, not otherwise provided for, made wholly or in part of sugar, and on sugars after being refined, when tinctured, colored, or in any way adulterated, valued at thirty cents per pound or less, fifteen cents per pound. On all confectionery valued above thirty cents per pound, or when sold by the box, package, or otherwise than by the pound, fifty per centum ad valorem.

Third. On molasses from sugar-cane, eight cents per gallon. On sirup of sugar-cane juice, melado, concentrated melado, or concentrated molasses, two cents and a half per pound: *Provided*, That all sirups of sugar or sugar-cane, cane juice, concentrated molasses, or concentrated melado, entered under the name of molasses, or any other name than sirup of sugar, or of sugar-cane, cane juice, concentrated molasses, or concentrated melado, shall be liable to forfeiture to the United States, and the same shall be forfeited.

Sec. 2. *And be it further enacted*, That on and after the day and year aforesaid, in lieu of the duties heretofore imposed by law on the articles hereinafter mentioned, there shall be levied, collected, and paid, on the goods, wares, and merchandise enumerated and provided for in this section, imported from foreign countries, the following duties and rates of duty, that is to say:

First. On brandy, for first proof, two dollars and fifty cents per gallon.

On other spirits, manufactured or distilled from grain or other materials, for first proof, two dollars per gallon.

On cordials, and liqueurs of all kinds, and arrack, absynthe, kirschenwasser, ratafia, and other similar spirituous beverages, not otherwise provided for, two dollars per gallon.

On bay rum, one dollar and fifty cents per gallon.

On wines of all kinds, valued at not over fifty cents per gallon, twenty cents per gallon and twenty-five per centum ad valorem; valued at over fifty cents and not over one dollar per gallon, fifty cents per gallon and twenty-five per centum ad valorem; valued at over one dollar per gallon, one dollar per gallon and twenty-five per cent. ad valorem: *Provided*, That no champagne or sparkling wines, in bottles, shall pay a less rate of duty than six dollars per dozen bottles, each bottle containing not more than one quart and more than one pint, or six dollars per two dozen bottles, each bottle containing not more than one pint.

On all spirituous liquors, not otherwise enumerated, one hundred per centum ad valorem: *Provided*, That no lower rate or amount of duty shall be levied, collected, and paid, on brandy, spirits, and other spirituous beverages, than that fixed by law for the description of first proof, but shall be increased in proportion for any greater strength than the strength of first proof; and no brandy, spirits, or other spirituous beverages under first proof shall pay a less rate of duty than fifty per centum ad valorem: *Provided further*, That all imitations of brandy, or spirits, or of wines imported by any names whatever, shall be subject to the highest rate of duty provided for the genuine articles, respectively intended to be represented, and in no case less than one dollar per gallon: *And provided further*, That brandies, or other spirituous liquors, may be imported in bottles when the package shall contain not less than one dozen; and all bottles shall pay a separate duty of two cents each, whether containing wines, brandies, or other spirituous liquors subject to duty as hereinbefore mentioned.

Second. On ale, porter, and beer, in bottles, thirty-five cents per gallon; otherwise than in bottles, twenty cents per gallon.

Third. On cigars of all kinds, valued at fifteen dollars or less per thousand, seventy-five cents per pound and twenty per centum ad valorem; valued at over fifteen dollars and not over thirty dollars per thousand, one dollar and twenty-five cents per pound and thirty per centum ad valorem; valued at over thirty dollars and not over forty-five dollars per thousand, two dollars per pound and fifty per centum ad valorem; valued at over forty-five dollars per thousand, three dollars per pound and sixty per centum ad valorem: *Provided*, That paper cigars or cigarettes, including wrappers, shall be subject to the same duties imposed on cigars.

On snuff and snuff flour, manufactured of tobacco, ground, dry, or damp, and pickled, scented, or otherwise, of all descriptions, fifty cents per pound.

On tobacco in leaf, manufactured and not stemmed, thirty-five cents per pound.

On tobacco manufactured, of all descriptions, and stemmed tobacco not otherwise provided for, fifty cents per pound.

Sec. 3. *And be it further enacted*, That on and after the day and year aforesaid, in lieu of the duties heretofore imposed by law on the articles hereinafter mentioned, there shall be levied, collected, and paid, on the goods, wares, and merchandise herein enumerated and provided for, imported from foreign countries, the following duties and rates of duty, that is to say:

On bar iron, rolled or hammered, comprising flats not less than one inch or more than six inches wide, nor less than three-eighths of an inch or more than two inches thick; rounds not less than three-fourths of an inch nor more than two inches in diameter; and squares not less than three-fourths of an inch nor more than two inches square, one cent per pound. On bar iron, rolled or hammered, comprising flats less than three-eighths of an inch or more than two inches thick, or less than one inch or more than six inches wide; rounds less than three-fourths of an inch or more than two inches in diameter; and squares less than three-fourths of an inch or more than two inches square, one cent and one-half per pound: *Provided*, That all iron in slabs, blooms, loops, or other forms, less finished than iron in bars, and more advanced than pig iron, except castings, shall be rated as iron in bars, and pay a duty accordingly: *And provided further*, That none of the above iron shall pay a less rate of duty than thirty-five per centum ad valorem.

On all iron imported in bars for rail-roads and inclined planes, made to patterns, and fitted to be laid down on such roads or planes without further manufacture, sixty cents per one hundred pounds. On boiler or other plate iron not less than three-sixteenths of an inch in thickness, one cent and a half per pound. On iron wire, bright, coppered, or tinned, drawn and finished, not more than one-fourth of an inch in diameter, nor less than number sixteen, wire gauge, two dollars per one hundred pounds, and in addition thereto fifteen per centum ad valorem; over number sixteen and not over number twenty-five, wire gauge, three dollars and fifty cents per one hundred pounds, and in addition thereto fifteen per centum ad valorem: *Provided*, That wire covered with cotton, silk, or other material, shall pay five cents per pound in addition to the foregoing rates. On smooth or polished sheet iron, by whatever name designated, three cents per pound. On sheet iron, common or black, not thinner than number twenty, wire gauge, one cent and one-fourth of one cent per pound; thinner than number twenty, and not thinner than number twenty-five, wire gauge, one cent and a half per pound; thinner than number twenty-five, wire gauge, one cent and three-fourths of one cent per pound.

On tin plates, and iron galvanized or coated with any metal by electric batteries, or otherwise, two cents and a half per pound.

On all band, hoop, and scroll iron, from one-half to six inches in width, not thinner than one-eighth of an inch, one and one-fourth cent per pound.

On all band, hoop, and scroll iron, from one-half to six inches wide, under one-eighth of an inch in thickness, and not thinner than number twenty, wire gauge, one and one-half cent per pound.

On all band, hoop, and scroll iron, thinner than number twenty, wire gauge, one and three-fourths cent per pound.

On slit rods one cent and one-half per pound, and on all other descriptions of rolled or hammered iron not otherwise provided for, one cent and one-fourth per pound.

On locomotive tire, or parts thereof, three cents per pound.

On mill-irons and mill-cranks of wrought iron, and wrought iron for ships, steam-engines, and locomotives, or parts thereof, weighing each twenty-five pounds or more, two cents per pound.

On anvils and on iron cables, or cable chains, or parts thereof, two cents and a half per pound.

On chains, trace chains, halter chains, and fence chains, made of wire or rods, not less than one-fourth of one inch in diameter, two cents and a half per pound; less than one-fourth of one inch in diameter, and not under number nine, wire gauge, three cents per pound; under number nine, wire gauge, thirty-five per centum ad valorem.

On anchors, or parts thereof, two cents and one-fourth per pound.

On blacksmiths' hammers and sledges, axles, or parts thereof, and malleable iron in castings, not otherwise provided for, two cents and a half per pound.

On wrought-iron rail-road chairs, and wrought-iron nuts and washers, ready punched, two cents per pound.

On bed-screws and wrought-iron hinges, two cents and a half per pound.

On wrought-board nails, spikes, rivets and bolts, two and one-half cents per pound.

On cut nails and spikes, one and a half cent per pound.

On horseshoe nails, five cents per pound.

On cut tacks, brads or sprigs, not exceeding sixteen ounces to the thousand, two and one-half cents per thousand; exceeding sixteen ounces to the thousand, three cents per pound.

On steam, gas and water *tubs* [tubes] and flues, of wrought iron, two cents and a half per pound.

On screws, commonly called wood screws, two inches or over in length, eight cents per pound; less than two inches in length, eleven cents per pound.

On screws of any other metal than iron, and all other screws of iron, except wood screws, thirty-five per centum ad valorem.

On iron in pigs, nine dollars per ton.

On vessels of cast-iron, not otherwise provided for, and on andirons, sadirons, tailors' and hatters' irons, stoves and stove plates, of cast-iron, one and one-half cent per pound.

On cast-iron, steam, gas and water-pipe, one and one-half cent per pound.

On cast-iron butts and hinges, two and a half cents per pound.

On hollow ware, glazed or tinned, three and one-half cents per pound.

On all other castings of iron, not otherwise provided for, thirty per centum ad valorem.

On all manufactures of iron, not otherwise provided for, thirty-five per centum ad valorem.

On old scrap iron, eight dollars per ton: *Provided*, That nothing shall be deemed old iron that has not been in actual use, and fit only to be remanufactured.

On steel, ingots, bars, coils, sheets, and steel wire, not less than one-fourth of one inch in diameter, valued at seven cents per pound or less, two cents and one-fourth per pound; valued at above seven cents, and not above eleven cents per pound, three cents per pound; valued at above eleven cents per pound, three cents and a half per pound, and ten per centum ad valorem.

On steel wire less than one-fourth of an inch diameter, and not less than number sixteen, wire gauge, two and one-half cents per pound, and in addition thereto, twenty per centum ad valorem; less or finer than number sixteen, wire gauge, three cents per pound, and in addition thereto twenty per centum ad valorem.

On steel in any form, not otherwise provided for, thirty per centum ad valorem.

On skates costing twenty cents or less per pair, eight cents per pair; costing over twenty cents per pair, thirty-five per centum ad valorem.

On cross-cut saws, ten cents per lineal foot.

On mill, pit, and drag saws, not over nine inches wide, twelve and a half cents per lineal foot.

On all hand-saws not over twenty-four inches in length, seventy-five cents per dozen, and in addition thereto thirty per centum ad valorem; over twenty-four inches in length, one dollar per dozen, and in addition thereto thirty per centum ad valorem.

On all back-saws not over ten inches in length, seventy-five cents per dozen, and in addition thereto thirty per centum ad valorem; over ten inches in length, one dollar per dozen, and in addition thereto thirty per centum ad valorem.

On files, file blanks, rasps, and floats of all descriptions, not exceeding ten inches in length, ten cents per pound, and in addition thereto thirty per centum ad valorem; exceeding ten inches in length, six cents per pound, and in addition thereto thirty per centum ad valorem.

On pen knives, jack knives, and pocket knives of all kinds, fifty per centum ad valorem.

On needles for knitting or sewing machines, one dollar per thousand, and in addition thereto thirty-five per centum ad valorem.

On iron squares marked on one side, three cents per pound, and in addition thereto thirty per centum ad valorem; on all other squares of iron or steel, six cents per pound, and thirty per centum ad valorem.

On all manufactures of steel, or of which steel shall be a component part, not otherwise provided for, forty-five per centum ad valorem: *Provided*, That all articles of steel partially manufactured, or of which steel shall be a component part, not otherwise provided for, shall pay the same rate of duty as if wholly manufactured.

On bituminous coal, and shale, one dollar and twenty-five cents for a ton of twenty-eight bushels, eighty pounds to the bushel; on all other coal, forty cents per ton of twenty-eight bushels, eighty pounds to the bushel.

On coke and culm of coal, twenty-five per centum ad valorem.

On lead, in pigs and bars, two cents per pound.

On old scrap lead, fit only to be re-manufactured, one cent and one half per pound.

On lead in sheets, pipes, or shot, two and three quarter cents per pound.

On pewter, when old and fit only to be re-manufactured, two cents per pound.

On lead ore, one and a half cent per pound.

On copper in pigs, bars, or ingots, two and a half cents per pound.

On sheathing copper, in sheets forty-eight inches long and fourteen inches wide, weighing from fourteen to thirty-four ounces per square foot, three and a half cents per pound.

On copper rods, bolts, nails, spikes, copper bottoms, copper in sheets or plates, called braziers' copper, and other sheets of copper not otherwise provided for, thirty-five per centum ad valorem.

On zinc, spelter, or teutenegue, manufactured in blocks or pigs, one and a half cent per pound.

On zinc, spelter, or teutenegue in sheets, two and one-quarter cents per pound.

On diamonds, cameos, mosaics, gems, pearls, rubies, and other precious stones, when not set, a duty of ten per centum ad valorem.

SEC. 4. *And be it further enacted*, That on and after the day and year aforesaid, there shall be levied, collected, and paid, on the importation of the articles hereinafter mentioned, the following duties, that is to say: On all wool, unmanufactured, and all hair of the alpaca, goat, and other like animals, unmanufactured, the value whereof at the last port or place from whence exported to the United States, exclusive of charges in such ports, shall be twelve cents or less per pound, three cents per pound; exceeding twelve cents and not exceeding twenty-four cents per pound, six cents per pound; exceeding twenty-four cents per pound, and not exceeding thirty-two cents, ten cents per pound, and in addition thereto ten per centum ad valorem; exceeding thirty-two cents per pound, twelve cents per pound, and in addition thereto ten per centum ad valorem: *Provided*, That any wool of the sheep, or hair of the alpaca, the goat, and other like animals, which shall be imported in any other than the ordinary condition, as now and heretofore practiced, or which shall be changed in its character or condition for the purpose of evading the duty, or which shall be reduced in value by the admixture of dirt or of any foreign substance, shall be subject to pay a duty of twelve cents per pound and ten per centum ad valorem, any thing in this act to the contrary notwithstanding: *Provided, further*, That when wool of different qualities is imported in the same bale, bag or package, and the aggregate value of the contents of the bale, bag or package shall be appraised by the appraisers at a rate exceeding twenty-four cents per pound, it shall be charged with a duty of ten cents per pound and ten per centum ad valorem; and when bales of different qualities are embraced in the same invoice at the same price, whereby the average price shall be lessened more than ten per centum, the value of the whole shall be appraised according to the value of the bale of the best quality; and no bale, bag, or package shall be liable to a less rate of duty in consequence of being invoiced with wool of lower value: *And provided, further*, That wool which shall be imported scoured, shall pay, in lieu of the duties herein provided, three times the amount of such duties.

Second. On sheepskins, raw or unmanufactured, imported with the wool on, washed or unwashed, shall be subject to a duty of twenty per centum ad valorem; and on flocks, waste or shoddy, three cents per pound.

SEC. 5. *And be it further enacted*, That on and after the day and year aforesaid, there shall be levied, collected, and paid, on the importation of the articles hereinafter mentioned, the following duties, that is to say:

First. On Wilton, Saxony, and Aubusson, Axminster, patent velvet, Tournay velvet, and tapestry velvet carpets and carpeting, Brussels carpets wrought by the Jacquard machine, and all medallion or whole carpets, valued at one dollar and twenty-five cents or under per square yard, seventy cents per square yard; valued at over one dollar and twenty-five cents per square yard, eighty cents per square yard: *Provided*, That no carpeting, carpets, or rugs, of the foregoing description, shall pay a duty of less than fifty per centum ad valorem. On Brussels and tapestry Brussels carpets and carpetings, printed on the warp or otherwise, fifty cents per square yard. On all treble ingrain, three-ply and worsted chain Venetian carpets and carpeting, forty cents per square yard. On yarn Venetian and two-ply ingrain carpets and carpeting, thirty-five cents per square yard. On hemp or jute carpeting, six and a half cents per square yard. On druggets, bockings, and felt carpets and carpeting, printed, colored, or otherwise, twenty-five cents per square yard. On carpets and carpeting of wool, flax or cotton, or parts of either, or other material not otherwise specified, forty per centum ad valorem: *Provided*, That mats, rugs, screens, covers, hassocks, bedsides, and other portions of carpets or carpetings, shall be subject to the rate of duty herein imposed on carpets or carpeting of like character or description, and on all other mats, screens, hassocks and rugs, forty-five per centum ad valorem.

Second. On woollen cloths, woollen shawls, and all manufactures of wool of every description, made wholly or in part of wool, not otherwise provided for, twenty-four cents per pound, and in addition thereto forty per centum ad valorem. On goods of like description, when valued at over two dollars per square yard, a duty, in addition to the foregoing rates, of five per centum ad valorem: *Provided*, That goods of like description, composed of worsted, the hair of the alpaca, goat, or other like animals, and weighing over eight ounces to the square yard, shall be subject to pay the same duty and rates of duty herein provided for woollen cloths. On endless belts or felts for paper, and blanketing for printing machines, twenty cents per pound, and in addition thereto thirty-five per centum ad valorem. On flannels, uncolored, valued at thirty cents or less per square yard, twenty-four cents per pound, and thirty per centum ad valorem; valued at above thirty cents per square yard, and on all flannels, colored, printed or plaided, not otherwise provided for, and flannels composed in part of cotton, twenty-four cents per pound, and thirty-five per centum ad valorem. On flannels composed in part of silk, fifty per centum ad valorem. On hats of wool, twenty-four [cents] per pound, and in addition thereto thirty-five per centum ad valorem. On woollen and worsted yarn, valued at fifty cents and not over one dollar per pound, twenty cents per pound, and in addition thereto twenty-five per centum ad valorem; valued at over one dollar per pound, twenty-four cents per pound, and in addition thereto thirty per centum ad valorem. On woollen and worsted yarn valued at less than fifty cents per pound, and not exceeding in fineness number fourteen, sixteen cents per pound, and in addition thereto twenty-five per centum ad valorem. On clothing, ready made, and wearing apparel of every description, composed wholly or in part of wool, made up or manufactured wholly or in part by the tailor, seamstress or manufacturer, except hosiery, twenty-four cents per pound, and in addition thereto forty per centum ad valorem. On blankets of all kinds, made wholly or in part of wool, valued at not exceeding twenty-eight cents per pound, twelve cents per pound, and in addition thereto twenty per centum ad valorem; valued at above twenty-eight cents and not exceeding forty cents per pound, twenty-four cents per pound and twenty-five per centum ad valorem; valued above forty cents per pound, twenty-four cents per pound and thirty per centum ad valorem. On Balmorals, and goods of a similar description, or used for like purposes, composed of wool, worsted or any other material, twenty-four cents per pound, and in addition thereto thirty-five per centum ad valorem.

On women's and children's dress goods, composed wholly or in part of wool, worsted, mohair, alpaca or goats' hair, gray or uncolored, not exceeding in value the sum of thirty cents per square yard, four cents per square yard, and in addition thereto twenty-five per centum ad valorem; exceeding in value thirty cents per square yard, six cents per square yard, and in addition thereto thirty per centum ad valorem.

On all goods of the last mentioned description, if stained, colored or printed, not exceeding in value the sum of thirty cents per square yard, four cents per square yard, and thirty per centum ad valorem; exceeding in value thirty cents per square yard, six cents per square yard, and in addition thereto thirty-five per centum ad valorem.

On shirts, drawers, and hosiery, of wool, or of which wool shall be a component material, not otherwise provided for, twenty cents per pound, and in addition thereto thirty per centum ad valorem.

On bunting, and on all other manufactures of worsted, mohair, alpaca, or goats' hair, or of which worsted, mohair, alpaca, or goats' hair shall be a component material, not otherwise provided for, fifty per centum ad valorem.

On lastings, mohair cloth, silk, twist, or other manufacture of cloth, woven or made, in patterns of such size, shape and form, or cut in such manner as to be fit for shoes, slippers, boots, bootees, gaiters and buttons, exclusively, not combined with India rubber, ten per centum ad valorem.

On oil cloths for floors, stamped, painted or printed, valued at fifty cents or less per square yard, thirty per centum ad valorem; valued at over fifty cents per square yard, and on all other oil-cloth, except silk oil-cloth, forty per centum ad valorem.

SEC. 6. *And be it further enacted*, That on and after the day and year aforesaid there shall be levied, collected, and paid, on the importation of the articles hereinafter mentioned, the following duties, that is to say:

First. On cotton, raw or unmanufactured, two cents per pound.

Second. On all manufactures of cotton, (except jeans, denims, drillings, bed tickings, ginghams, plaids, cottonades, pantaloon stuffs and goods of like description,) not bleached, colored, stained, painted or printed, and not exceeding one hundred threads to the square inch, counting the warp and filling, and exceeding in weight five ounces per square yard, five cents per square yard; if bleached, five cents and a half per square yard; if colored, stained, painted or printed, five cents and a half per square yard, and in addition thereto ten per centum ad valorem. On finer and lighter goods of like description, exceeding one hundred threads and not exceeding two hundred threads to the square inch, counting the warp and filling, unbleached, five cents per square yard; if bleached, five and a half cents per square yard; if colored, stained, painted or printed, five and a half cents per square yard, and in addition thereto twenty per centum ad valorem. On goods of like description, exceeding two hundred threads to the square inch, counting the warp and filling, unbleached, five cents per square yard; if bleached, five and a half cents per square yard; if colored, stained, painted or printed, five and a half cents per square yard, and in addition thereto twenty per centum ad valorem.

Third. On all cotton jeans, denims, drillings, bed tickings, ginghams, plaids, cottonades, pantaloon stuffs and goods of like description, or for similar use, if unbleached, and not exceeding one hundred threads to the square inch, counting the warp and filling, and exceeding five ounces to the square yard, six cents per square yard; if bleached, six cents and a half per square yard; if colored, stained, painted or printed, six cents and a half per square yard, and in addition thereto ten per centum ad valorem. On finer or lighter goods of like description, exceeding one hundred threads and not exceeding two hundred threads to the square inch, counting the warp and filling, if unbleached, six cents per square yard; if bleached, six and a half cents per square yard; if colored, stained, painted or printed, six and a half cents per square yard, and in addition thereto fifteen per centum ad valorem. On goods of like description, exceeding two hundred threads to the square inch, counting the warp and filling, if unbleached, seven cents per square yard; if bleached, seven and a half cents per square yard; if colored, stained, painted or printed, seven and a half cents per square yard, and in addition thereto fifteen per centum ad valorem: *Provided*, That upon all plain woven cotton goods, not included in the foregoing schedules, unbleached, valued at over sixteen cents per square yard, bleached, valued at over twenty cents per square yard, colored, valued at over twenty-five cents per square yard, and cotton jeans, denims and drillings, unbleached, valued at over twenty cents per square yard, and all other cotton goods, of every description, the value of which shall exceed twenty-five cents per square yard, there shall be levied, collected, and paid, a duty of thirty-five per centum ad valorem: *And provided, further*, That no cotton goods having more than two hundred threads to the square inch, counting the warp and filling, shall be admitted to a less rate of duty than is provided for goods which are of that number of threads.

Fourth. On spool thread of cotton, six cents per dozen spools, containing on each spool not exceeding one hundred yards of thread, and in addition thereto thirty per centum ad valorem; exceeding one hundred yards, for every additional hundred yards of thread on each spool, or fractional part thereof in excess of one hundred yards, six cents per dozen, and thirty per centum ad valorem.

On cotton shirts and drawers, woven or made on frames, and on all cotton hosiery, thirty-five per centum ad valorem.

On cotton velvet, thirty-five per centum ad valorem.

On cotton braids, insertings, lace, trimming or bobbinet, and all other manufactures of cotton, not otherwise provided for, thirty-five per centum ad valorem.

SEC. 7. *And be it further enacted*, That on and after the day and year aforesaid, in lieu of the duties heretofore imposed by law on the articles hereinafter mentioned, there shall be levied, collected, and paid, on the goods, wares, and merchandise enumerated and provided for in this section, imported from foreign countries, the following duties and rates of duty, that is to say:

First. On brown and bleached linens, ducks, canvas, paddings, cotton bottoms, burlaps, diapers, crash, huckabacks, handkerchiefs, lawns, or other manufactures of flax, jute or hemp, or of which flax, jute or hemp shall be the component material of chief value, not otherwise provided for, valued at thirty cents or less per square yard, thirty-five per centum ad valorem; valued at above thirty cents per square yard, forty per centum ad valorem. On flax or linen yarn for carpets, not exceeding number eight Lea, and valued at twenty-four cents or less per pound, thirty per centum ad valorem. On flax or linen yarns valued at above twenty-four cents per pound, thirty-five per centum ad valorem. On flax or linen thread, twine and pack thread, and all other manufactures of flax, or of which flax shall be the component material of chief value, not otherwise provided for, forty per centum ad valorem.

Second. On tarred cables or cordage, three cents per pound. On untarred Manilla cordage, two and a half cents per pound. On all other untarred cordage, three and a half cents per pound. On hemp yarns, five cents per pound. On coir yarn, one and a half cent per pound. On seines, six and half cents per pound.

Third. On gunny cloth, gunny bags, and cotton bagging, or other manufactures not otherwise provided for, suitable for the uses to which cotton bagging is applied, composed in whole or in part of hemp, jute, flax or other material, valued at ten cents or less per square yard, three cents per pound; over ten cents per square yard, four cents per pound. On sail duck or canvas for sails, thirty per centum ad valorem. On Russia and other sheetings of flax or hemp, brown and white, thirty-five per centum ad valorem. On all other manufactures of hemp, or of which hemp shall be the component material of chief value, not otherwise provided for, thirty per centum ad valorem. On grass cloth, thirty per centum ad valorem. On jute yarns, twenty-five per centum ad valorem. On all other manufactures of jute or Sisal grass, not otherwise provided for, thirty per centum ad valorem.

SEC. 8. *And be it further enacted,* That on and after the day and year aforesaid, in lieu of the duties heretofore imposed by law on the articles hereinafter mentioned, there shall be levied, collected, and paid, on the goods, wares and merchandise enumerated and provided for in this section, imported from foreign countries, the following duties and rates of duty, that is to say:

On spun silk for filling in skeins or cops, twenty-five per centum ad valorem. On silk in the gum not more advanced than singles, tram, and thrown or organzine, thirty-five per centum ad valorem. On floss silks, thirty-five per centum ad valorem. On sewing silk in the gum, or purified, forty per centum ad valorem. On all dress and piece silks, ribbons, and silk velvets, or velvets of which silk is the component material of chief value, sixty per centum ad valorem. On silk vestings, pongees, shawls, scarfs, mantillas, pelerines, handkerchiefs, veils, laces, shirts, drawers, bonnets, hats, caps, turbans, chemisettes, hose, mitts, aprons, stockings, gloves, suspenders, watch chains, webbing, braids, fringes, galloons, tassels, cords, and trimmings, sixty per centum ad valorem.

On all manufactures of silk, or of which silk is the component material of chief value, not otherwise provided for, fifty per centum ad valorem.

SEC. 9. *And be it further enacted,* That on and after the day and year aforesaid, in lieu of the duties heretofore imposed by law on the articles hereinafter mentioned, there shall be levied, collected, and paid, on the goods, wares, and merchandise enumerated and provided for in this section, imported from foreign countries, the following duties and rates of duty, that is to say:

On all brown earthenware and common stoneware, gas retorts, stoneware not ornamented, twenty-five per centum ad valorem.

On China, porcelain, and Parian ware, gilded, ornamented, or decorated in any manner, fifty per centum ad valorem.

On China, porcelain, and Parian ware, plain white, and not decorated in any manner, forty-five per centum ad valorem; on all other earthen, stone, or crockery ware, white, glazed, edged, printed, painted, dipped, or cream-colored, composed of earthy or mineral substances, and not otherwise provided for, forty per centum ad valorem.

On slates, slate pencils, slate chimney pieces, mantels, slabs for tables, and all other manufactures of slate, forty per centum ad valorem.

On unwrought clay, pipe clay, fire clay, and kaoline, five dollars per ton.

On fullers' earth, three dollars per ton.

On white chalk and cliff stone, ten dollars per ton. On red and French chalk, twenty per centum ad valorem. On chalk of all descriptions, not otherwise provided for, twenty-five per centum ad valorem.

On whiting and Paris white, one cent per pound.

On whiting ground in oil, two cents per pound.

On all plain and mould and press glass not cut, engraved, or painted, thirty-five per centum ad valorem.

On all articles of glass cut, engraved, painted, colored, printed, stained, silvered, or gilded, not including plate-glass silvered, or looking-glass plates, forty per centum ad valorem.

On all unpolished cylinder, crown, and common window glass, not exceeding ten by fifteen inches square, one cent and a half per pound; above that, and not exceeding sixteen by twenty-four inches square, two cents [per] pound; above that, and exceeding twenty-four by thirty inches square, two cents and a half per pound; all above that, three cents per pound.

On cylinder and crown glass, polished, not exceeding ten by fifteen inches square, two and one-half cents per square foot; above that, and not exceeding sixteen by twenty-four inches square, four cents per square foot; above that, and not exceeding twenty-four by thirty inches square, six cents per square foot; above that, and not exceeding twenty-four by sixty inches, twenty cents per square foot; all above that, forty cents per square foot.

On fluted, rolled, or rough plate glass, not including crown, cylinder, or common window glass, not exceeding ten by fifteen inches square, seventy-five cents per one hundred square feet; above that, and not exceeding sixteen by twenty-four inches square, one cent per square foot; above that, and not exceeding twenty-four by thirty inches square, one cent and a half per square foot; all above that, two cents per square foot: *Provided*, That all fluted, rolled, or rough plate glass, weighing over one hundred pounds per one hundred square feet, shall pay an additional duty on the excess at the same rates herein imposed.

On all cast polished plate glass, unsilvered, not exceeding ten by fifteen inches square, three cents per square foot; above that, and not exceeding sixteen by twenty-four inches square, five cents per square foot; above that, and not exceeding twenty-four by thirty inches square, eight cents per square foot; above that, and not exceeding twenty-four by sixty inches square, twenty-five cents per square foot; all above that, fifty cents per square foot.

On all cast polished plate glass, silvered, or looking-glass plates not exceeding ten by fifteen inches square, four cents per square foot; above that, and not exceeding sixteen by twenty-four inches square, six cents per square foot; above that, and not exceeding twenty-four by thirty inches square, ten cents per square foot; above that, and not exceeding twenty-four by sixty inches square, thirty-five cents per square foot; all above that, sixty cents per square foot: *Provided*, That no looking-glass plates or plate glass, silvered, when framed, shall pay a less rate of duty than that imposed upon similar glass of like description not framed, but shall be liable to pay in addition thereto thirty per centum ad valorem upon such frames.

On porcelain and Bohemian glass, glass crystals for watches, paintings on glass or glasses, pebbles for spectacles, and all manufactures of glass, or of which glass shall be a component material, not otherwise provided for, and all glass bottles or jars filled with sweetmeats or preserves, not otherwise provided for, forty per centum ad valorem.

SEC. 10. *And be it further enacted*, That on and after the day and year aforesaid, in lieu of the duties heretofore imposed by law on the articles hereinafter mentioned, and on such as may now be exempt from duty, there shall be levied, collected, and paid, on the goods, wares and merchandise enumerated and provided for in this section, imported from foreign countries, the following duties and rate of duties, that is to say:

First. On annatto seed, extract of annatto, nitrate of barytes, carmined indigo, crude tica, extract of safflower, finishing powder, gold size and patent size, cobalt, oxide of cobalt, smalt, zaffre, and terra alba, twenty per centum ad valorem; on nickel, fifteen per centum ad valorem.

Second. On albumen, asbestos, asphaltum, crocus colcottra, blue or Roman vitriol or sulphate of copper, bone or ivory drop black, murexide, ultramarine, Indian red, and Spanish brown, twenty-five per centum ad valorem.

SEC. 11. *And be it further enacted*, That on and after the day and year aforesaid, in lieu of the duties heretofore imposed by law on the articles hereinafter mentioned, there shall be levied, collected, and paid, on goods, wares, and merchandise enumerated and provided for in this section, imported from foreign countries, the following duties and rates of duty, that is to say:

On acetic acid, acetous or concentrated vinegar, or pyroligneous acid, exceeding the specific gravity of 1.040, eighty cents per pound; not exceeding the specific gravity of 1.040, known as number eight, twenty-five cents per pound.

On acetate or pyrolignite of ammonia, seventy cents per pound; of baryta, forty cents per pound; of iron, strontia, and zinc, fifty cents per pound; of lead, twenty cents per pound; of magnesia and soda, fifty cents per pound; of lime, twenty-five per centum ad valorem.

On analine dyes, one dollar per pound and thirty-five per centum ad valorem.

On blancfixe, enamelled white, satin white, lime white, and all combinations of barytes with acids or water, three cents per pound; on carmine lake, dry or liquid, thirty-five per centum ad valorem; on French green, Paris green, mineral green, mineral blue, and Prussian blue, dry or moist, thirty per centum ad valorem.

On almonds, six cents per pound; shelled, ten cents per pound.

On articles not otherwise provided for, made of gold, silver, German silver, or platina, or of which either of these metals shall be a component part, forty per centum ad valorem.

On antimony, crude, and regulus of antimony, ten per centum ad valorem.

On opium, two dollars and fifty cents per pound.

On opium prepared for smoking, and the extract of opium, one hundred per centum ad valorem.

On morphine and its salts, two dollars and fifty cents per ounce.

On arrowroot, thirty per centum ad valorem.

On brimstone, crude, six dollars per ton.

On brimstone, in rolls, or refined, ten dollars per ton.

On castor beans or seeds, per bushel of fifty pounds, sixty cents.

On chicory root, four cents per pound; ground, burnt, or prepared, five cents per pound.

On cassia, twenty cents per pound.

On cassia buds and ground cassia, twenty-five cents per pound.

On cinnamon, thirty cents per pound.

On chloroform, one dollar per pound.

On collodion and ethers of all kinds, not otherwise provided for, and etherial preparations or extracts, fluid, one dollar per pound.

On cologne water and other perfumery, of which alcohol forms the principal ingredient, three dollars per gallon, and fifty per centum ad valorem.

On cloves, twenty cents per pound; on clove stems, ten cents per pound.

On fusel oil, or amylic alcohol, two dollars per gallon.

On Hoffman's anodyne and spirits of nitric ether, fifty cents per pound.

On bristles, fifteen cents per pound; on hogs' hair, one cent per pound; on istle or Tampico fibre, one cent per pound.

On brushes of all kinds, forty per centum ad valorem.

On honey, twenty cents per gallon.

On lead, white or red, and litharge, dry or ground in oil, three cents per pound.

On percussion caps, forty per centum ad valorem.

On lemons, oranges, pine apples, plantains, cocoa-nuts, and fruits preserved in their own juice, and fruit juice, twenty-five per centum ad valorem.

On liquorice root, two cents per pound; on liquorice paste or liquorice in rolls, ten cents per pound.

On nutmegs, fifty cents per pound.

On mace, forty cents per pound.

On oils, croton, one dollar per pound; olive, in flasks or bottles, and salad, one dollar per gallon; castor, one dollar per gallon; cloves, two dollars per pound; cognac or œnanthic ether, four dollars per ounce.

On peanuts, or ground beans, one cent per pound; shelled, one and a half cent per pound.

On filberts and walnuts, of all kinds, three cents per pound.

On petroleum and coal illuminating oil, crude, ten cents per gallon. On illuminating oil and naphtha, benzine, and benzole, refined or produced from the distillation of coal, asphaltum, shale, peat, petroleum, or rock oil, or other bituminous substances used for like purposes, thirty cents per gallon.

On pimento, and black, white, and red or cayenne pepper, fifteen cents per pound; on ground pimento and pepper of all kinds, eighteen cents per pound.

On spirits of turpentine, thirty cents per gallon.

On sulphur, flour of, twenty dollars per ton and fifteen per cent. ad valorem.

On tannin, tannic acid, two dollars per pound; on gallic acid, one dollar and fifty cents per pound.

On santonine, five dollars per pound.

On salt in sacks, barrels, and other packages, twenty-four cents per one hundred pounds; on salt in bulk, eighteen cents per one hundred pounds.

On crude saltpetre, two and one-half cents per pound.

On strychnine and its salts, one dollar and one-half per ounce.

On taggar's iron, thirty per centum ad valorem.

On vinegar, ten cents per gallon.

On watches, gold or silver, twenty-five per centum ad valorem.

On wood pencils, filled with lead or other materials, fifty cents per gross, and in addition thereto thirty per centum ad valorem.

On ostrich, vulture, cock and other ornamental feathers, crude or not dressed, colored or manufactured, twenty-five per centum ad valorem; when dressed, colored or manufactured, fifty per centum ad valorem.

On playing cards, costing not over twenty-five cents per pack, twenty-five cents per pack; costing over twenty-five cents per pack, thirty-five cents per pack.

SEC. 12. *And be it further enacted*, That on and after the day and year aforesaid, there shall be levied, collected, and paid, a duty of fifty per centum ad valorem on the importation of the articles hereinafter mentioned and embraced in this section, that is to say:

Anchovies and sardines, preserved in oil or otherwise.

Artificial and ornamental feathers and flowers, or parts thereof, of whatever material composed, not otherwise provided for, beads and bead ornaments.

Billiard chalk.

Ginger, preserved or pickled.

Ivory or bone dice, draughts, chess men, chess balls and bagatelle balls.

Jellies of all kinds.

On kid or other leather gloves of all descriptions, for men's, women's or children's wear.

On wooden and other toys for children.

SEC. 13. *And be it further enacted*, That on and after the day and year aforesaid, in lieu of the duties heretofore imposed by law on the articles hereinafter mentioned, there shall be levied, collected, and paid, on the goods, wares, and merchandise enumerated and provided for in this section, imported from foreign countries, the following duties and rates of duty, that is to say:

On books, periodicals, pamphlets, blank books, bound or unbound, and all printed matter, engravings, bound or unbound, illustrated books and papers, and maps and charts, twenty-five per centum ad valorem.

On cork, bark or wood, unmanufactured, thirty per centum ad valorem.

On cork and cork bark, manufactured, fifty per centum ad valorem.

On hatters' furs, not on the skin, and dressed furs on the skin, twenty per centum ad valorem. Furs on the skin, undressed, ten per centum ad valorem.

On fire-crackers, one dollar per box of forty packs, not exceeding eighty to each pack, and in the same proportion for any greater number.

On gutta-percha, manufactured, forty per centum ad valorem.

On gunpowder, and all explosive substances used for mining, blasting, artillery, or sporting purposes, when valued at twenty cents or less per pound, a duty of six cents per pound, and in addition thereto twenty per centum ad valorem; valued above twenty cents per pound, a duty of ten cents per pound, and in addition thereto twenty per centum ad valorem.

On marble, white statuary, brocatella, sienna and verd-antique, in block, rough or squared, one dollar per cubic foot, and in addition thereto twenty-five per centum ad valorem. On veined marble and marble of all other descriptions, not otherwise provided for, in block, rough or squared, fifty cents per cubic foot, and in addition thereto twenty per centum ad valorem.

On mineral or medicinal waters, or waters from springs impregnated with minerals, for each bottle or jug containing not more than one quart, three cents, and in addition thereto twenty-five per centum ad valorem; containing more than one quart, three cents for each additional quart, or fractional part thereof, and in addition thereto twenty-five per centum ad valorem.

On palm-leaf fans, one cent each.

On pipes, clay, common or white, thirty-five per centum ad valorem.

On meerschaum, wood, porcelain, lava, and all other tobacco-smoking pipes and pipe-bowls, not herein otherwise provided for, one dollar and fifty cents per gross, and in addition thereto seventy-five per centum ad valorem.

On pipe cases, pipe stems, tips, mouth-pieces and metallic mountings for pipes, and all parts of pipes or pipe fixtures, and all smoker's articles, seventy-five per centum ad valorem.

On pen-tips and pen-holders, or parts thereof, thirty-five per centum ad valorem.

On pens, metallic, ten cents per gross, and in addition thereto twenty-five per centum ad valorem.

On soap, fancy, perfumed, honey, transparent, and all descriptions of toilet and shaving soap, ten cents per pound, and in addition thereto twenty-five per centum ad valorem.

On all soap not otherwise provided for, one cent per pound, and in addition thereto thirty per centum ad valorem.

On starch, made of potatoes or corn, one cent per pound, and twenty per centum ad valorem.

On starch, made of rice, or any other material, three cents per pound, and twenty per centum ad valorem.

On rice, cleaned, two and a half cents per pound; on uncleaned, two cents per pound.

On paddy, one cent and a half per pound.

Sec. 14. *And be it further enacted*, That on the entry of any vessel, or of any goods, wares, or merchandise, the decision of the collector of customs at the port of importation and entry, as to the rate and amount of duties to be paid on the tonnage of such vessel, or on such goods, wares or merchandise, and the dutiable costs and charges thereon, shall be final and conclusive against all persons interested therein, unless the owner, master, commander or consignee of such vessel, in the case of duties levied on tonnage, or the owner, importer, consignee or agent of the merchandise, in the case of duties levied on goods, wares, or merchandise, or the costs and charges thereon, shall, within ten days after the ascertainment and liquidation of the duties by the proper officers of the customs, as well in cases of merchandise entered in bond, as for consumption, give notice in writing to the collector on each entry, if dissatisfied with his decision, setting forth therein, distinctly and specifically, the grounds of his objection thereto, and shall, within thirty days after the date of such ascertainment and liquidation, appeal therefrom to the Secretary of the Treasury, whose decision on such appeal shall be final and conclusive; and such vessel, goods, wares, or merchandise, or costs and charges, shall be liable to duty accordingly, any act of Congress to the contrary notwithstanding, unless suit shall be brought within ninety days after the decision of the Secretary of the Treasury on such appeal for any duties which shall have been paid before the date of such decision on such vessel, or on such goods, wares, or merchandise, or costs or charges, or within ninety days after the payment of duties paid after the decision of the Secretary. And no suit shall be maintained in any court for the recovery of any duties alleged to have been erroneously or illegally exacted, until the decision of the Secretary of the Treasury shall have been first had on such appeal, unless said decision of the Secretary shall be delayed more than ninety days from the date of such appeal in case of an entry at any port east of the Rocky Mountains, or more than five months in case of an entry west of those mountains.

Sec. 15. *And be it further enacted*, That the decision of the respective collectors of customs as to all fees, charges, and exactions of whatever character, other than those mentioned in the next preceding section, claimed by them, or by any of the officers under them, in the performance of their official duty, shall be final and conclusive against all persons interested in such fees, charges, or exactions, unless the like notice that an appeal will be taken from such decision to the Secretary of the Treasury shall be given within ten days from the making of such decision, and unless such appeal shall actually be taken within thirty days from the making of such decision; and the decision of the Secretary of the Treasury shall be final and conclusive upon the matter so appealed, unless suit shall be brought for the recovery of such fees, charges, or exactions, within the period as provided for in the next preceding section in regard to duties. And no suit shall be maintained in any court for the recovery of any such fees, costs and charges, alleged to have been erroneously or illegally exacted, until the decision of the Secretary of the Treasury shall have been first had on such appeal, unless such decision of the Secretary shall be delayed more than ninety days from the date of such appeal in case of an entry at any port east of the Rocky Mountains, nor more than five months in case of an entry west of those mountains.

Sec. 16. *And be it further enacted*, That whenever it shall be shown to the satisfaction of the Secretary of the Treasury that, in any case of unascertained duties, or duties or other moneys paid under protest and appeal, as hereinbefore provided, more money has been paid to the collector, or person acting as such, than the law requires should have been paid, it shall be the duty of the Secretary of the Treasury to draw his warrant upon the Treasury in favor of the person or persons entitled to the over-payment, directing the said Treasurer to refund the same out of any money in the Treasury not otherwise appropriated.

Sec. 17. *And be it further enacted*, That a discriminating duty of ten per centum ad valorem, in addition to the duties imposed by law, shall be levied, collected, and paid, on all goods, wares, and merchandise, which, on and after the day this act shall take effect, shall be imported in ships or vessels not of the United States: *Provided*, That this discriminating duty shall not apply to goods, wares, and merchandise which shall be imported, on and after the day this act takes effect, in ships or vessels not of the United States, entitled, by treaty or any act or acts of Congress, to be entered in the ports of the United States on payment of the same duties as shall then be paid on goods, wares, and merchandise imported in ships or vessels of the United States.

Sec. 18. *And be it further enacted*, That on and after the day and year this act shall take effect there shall be levied, collected, and paid, on all goods, wares, and merchandise of the growth or produce of countries east of the Cape of Good Hope, (except raw cotton,) when imported from places west of the Cape of Good Hope, a duty of ten per centum ad valorem, in addition to the duties imposed on any such articles when imported directly from the place or places of their growth or production: *Provided*, That section three of the act approved August five, eighteen hundred and sixty-one, entitled "An act to provide increased revenue from imports, to pay interest on the public debt, and for other purposes," and section fourteen of the act approved July fourteen, eighteen hundred and sixty-two, entitled "An act increasing temporarily the rates of duties on imports, and for other purposes," be and the same are hereby repealed.

Sec. 19. *And be it further enacted*, That all goods, wares, and merchandise which may be in the public stores or bonded warehouses on the day and year this act shall take effect, shall be subjected to no other duty upon the entry thereof for consumption than if the same were imported respectively after that day; and so much of the act of August sixth, eighteen hundred and forty-six, or any other act, as requires the sale of fire-crackers, or prohibits their deposit in bonded warehouse, is hereby repealed.

Sec. 20. *And be it further enacted*, That the joint resolution "to increase temporarily the duties on imports," approved April twenty-ninth, eighteen hundred and sixty-four, shall not be deemed to have taken effect until after the thirtieth day of April, eighteen hundred and sixty-four, and shall be and remain in force until and including the thirtieth day of June, eighteen hundred and sixty-four; and any duties which shall have been exacted and received, contrary to the provisions of this section, shall be refunded by the Secretary of the Treasury.

Sec. 21. *And be it further enacted*, That during the period of one year from the passage of this act, there may be imported into the United States, free of duty, any machinery designed for and adapted to the manufacture of woven fabrics from the fibre of flax or hemp, including all the preliminary processes requisite therefor; and that steam agricultural machinery and implements may be imported free from duty for one year from the passage of this act.

Sec. 22. *And be it further enacted*, That all acts and parts of acts repugnant to the provisions of this act be and the same are hereby repealed: *Provided*, That the existing laws shall extend to and be in force for the collection of the duties imposed by this act for the prosecution and punishment of all offences, and for the recovery, collection, distribution and remission of all fines, penalties and forfeitures, as fully and effectually as if every regulation, penalty, forfeiture, provision, clause, matter, and thing to that effect in the existing laws contained, had been inserted in, and re-enacted by this act: *And provided further*, That the duties upon all goods, wares, and merchandise imported from foreign countries not provided for in this act, shall be and remain as they were, according to existing laws prior to the twenty-ninth of April, eighteen hundred and sixty-four.

SEC. 23. *And be it further enacted*, That on and after the day and year this act shall take effect, it shall be lawful for the owner, consignee, or agent of any goods, wares, or merchandise, which shall have been actually purchased, or procured otherwise than by purchase, at the time when he shall produce his original invoice, or invoices, to the collector, and make and verify his written entry of his goods, wares, and merchandise, as provided by section thirty-six of the act of March two, seventeen hundred and ninety-nine, entitled "An act to regulate the collection of duties on imports and tonnage, and not afterwards, to make such addition in the entry to the cost or value given in the invoice as, in his opinion, may raise the same to the true market value of such goods, wares, or merchandise, in the principal markets of the country whence they shall have been imported, and to add thereto all costs and charges which, under existing laws, would form part of the true value at the port where the same may be entered, upon which the duties should be assessed. And it shall be the duty of the collector, within whose district the same may be imported, or entered, to cause the dutiable value of such goods, wares, and merchandise to be appraised, estimated, and ascertained, in accordance with the provisions of existing laws. And if the appraised value thereof shall exceed, by ten per centum, or more, the value so declared on the entry, then, in addition to the duties imposed by law on the same, there shall be levied, collected, and paid, a duty of twenty per centum ad valorem on such appraised value: *Provided*, That the duty shall not be assessed upon an amount less than the invoice or entered value, any law of Congress to the contrary notwithstanding: *And provided further*, That on and after the day and year aforesaid, the eighth section of the act, entitled "An act reducing the duty on imports, and for other purposes," approved July thirty, eighteen hundred and forty-six, and the act amendatory thereof, approved March three, eighteen hundred and fifty-seven, be, and the same are hereby repealed.

SEC. 24. *And be it further enacted*, That in determining the valuation of goods imported into the United States from foreign countries, except as hereinbefore provided, upon which duties imposed by any existing laws are to be assessed, the actual value of such goods on shipboard at the last place of shipment to the United States shall be deemed the dutiable value. And such value shall be ascertained by adding to the value of such goods at the place of growth, production or manufacture, the cost of transportation, shipment and transhipment, with all the expenses included, from the place of growth, production or manufacture, whether by land or water, to the vessel in which shipment is made to the United States, the value of the sack, box, or covering of any kind, in which such goods are contained, commission at the usual rate, in no case less than two and one-half per centum, brokerage, and all export duties, together with all costs and charges, paid or incurred for placing said goods on shipboard, and all other proper charges specified by law.

SEC. 25. *And be it further enacted*, That so much of section twenty-three of the act entitled "An act to provide for the payment of outstanding Treasury notes, to authorize a loan, to regulate and fix the duties on imports, and for other purposes," approved March two, eighteen hundred and sixty-one, as exempts from duty all philosophical apparatus and instruments imported for the use of any society incorporated for philosophical, literary, or religious purposes, or for the encouragement of the fine arts, or for the use, or by the order of any college, academy, school, or seminary of learning in the United States, is hereby repealed. And the same shall be subject to a duty of fifteen per centum ad valorem.

SEC. 26. *And be it further enacted*, That when any cask, barrel, carboy, or other vessel of American manufacture, exported or sent out of the country, filled with the products of the United States, shall be returned to the United States empty, the same shall be admitted free of duty, under such rules and regulations as may be prescribed by the Secretary of the Treasury.

SEC. 27. *And be it further enacted*, That on and after January first, eighteen hundred and sixty-five, the invoices of all goods, wares, and merchandise, imported into the United States, shall be made out in the weights or measures of the country or place from which the importations shall be made, and shall contain a true statement of the actual weights or measures of such goods, wares, and merchandise, without any respect to the weights or measures of the United States.

SEC. 28. *And be it further enacted*, That in all cases where officers of the customs or other salaried officers of the United States shall be, or shall have been, appointed by the Secretary of the Treasury, to carry into effect the licenses, rules, and regulations provided for by the fifth section of the act of the thirteenth of July, eighteen hundred and sixty-one, entitled "An act further to provide for the collection of duties on imports, and for other purposes," such officer of the United States shall be entitled to receive one thousand dollars per annum for his services, under the act aforesaid, in addition to his salary or compensation under any other law: *Provided*, That the aggregate compensation of any such officer shall not exceed the sum of five thousand dollars in any one year.

SEC. 29. *And be it further enacted*, That any baggage or personal effects arriving in the United States in transit to any foreign country, may be delivered by the parties having it in charge to the collector of customs, to be by him retained, without the payment or exaction of any import duty, and to be delivered to such parties on their departure for their foreign destination, under such rules, regulations, and fees as the Secretary of the Treasury may prescribe.

Approved, June 30, 1864.

[Public, No. 58.]

AN ACT

Amendatory of certain acts imposing duties upon foreign importations.

Be it enacted by the Senate and House of Representatives of the United States of America in Congress assembled, That section six of an act entitled "An act to increase the duties on imports, and for other purposes," approved June thirty, eighteen hundred and sixty-four, be amended, so that paragraphs second, third, and fourth, of section six of said act, shall read as follows:

Second. On all manufactures of cotton (except jeans, denims, drillings, bed-tickings, ginghams, plaids, cottonades, pantaloon stuff, and goods of like description) not bleached, colored, stained, painted, or printed, and not exceeding one hundred threads to the square inch, counting the warp and filling, and exceeding in weight five ounces per square yard, five cents per square yard; if bleached, five cents and a half per square yard; if colored, stained, painted, or printed, five cents and a half per square yard, and, in addition thereto, ten per centum ad valorem. On finer and lighter goods of like description, not exceeding two hundred threads to the square inch, counting the warp and filling, unbleached, five cents per square yard; if bleached, five and a half cents per square yard; if colored, stained, painted, or printed, five and a half cents per square yard, and, in addition thereto, twenty per centum ad valorem. On goods of like description, exceeding two hundred threads to the square inch, counting the warp and filling, unbleached, five cents per square yard; if bleached, five and a half cents per square yard; if colored, stained, painted, or printed, five and a half cents per square yard, and, in addition thereto, twenty per centum ad valorem.

Third. On all cotton jeans, denims, drillings, bed-tickings, ginghams, plaids, cottonades, pantaloon stuffs, and goods of like description, or for similar use, if unbleached, and not exceeding one hundred threads to the square inch, counting the warp and filling, and exceeding five ounces to the square yard, six cents per square yard; if bleached, six cents and a half per square yard; if colored, stained, painted, or printed, six cents and a half per square yard, and, in addition thereto, ten per centum ad valorem. On finer or lighter goods of like description, not exceeding two hundred threads to the square inch, counting the warp and filling, if unbleached, six cents per square yard; if bleached, six and a half cents per square yard; if colored, stained, painted, or printed, six and a half cents per square yard, and, in addition thereto, fifteen per centum ad valorem. On goods of lighter description, exceeding two hundred threads to the square inch, counting the warp and filling, if unbleached, seven cents per square yard; if bleached, seven and a half cents per square yard; if colored, stained, painted, or printed, seven and a half cents per square yard, and, in addition thereto, fifteen per centum ad valorem: *Provided,* That upon all plain woven cotton goods, not included in the foregoing schedule, unbleached, valued at over sixteen cents per square yard, bleached, valued at over twenty cents per square yard, colored, valued at over twenty-five cents per square yard, and cotton jeans, denims, and drillings, unbleached, valued at over twenty cents per square yard, and all other cotton goods of every description, the value of which shall exceed twenty-five cents per square yard, there shall be levied, collected, and paid a duty of thirty-five per centum ad valorem: *And provided further*, That no cotton goods having more than two hundred threads to the square inch, counting the warp and filling, shall be admitted to a less rate of duty than is provided for goods which are of that number of threads.

Fourth. On spool thread of cotton, six cents per dozen spools, containing on each spool not exceeding one hundred yards of thread, and, in addition thereto, thirty per centum ad valorem; exceeding one hundred yards, for every additional hundred yards of thread on each spool or fractional part thereof, in excess of one hundred yards, six cents per dozen, and thirty-five per centum ad valorem. On cotton thread or yarn when advanced beyond single yarn, by twisting two or more strands together, if not wound upon spools, four (4) cents per skein or hank of eight hundred and forty (840) yards, and thirty per cent. ad valorem.

SEC. 2. *And be it further enacted*, That from and after the day when this act takes effect, in addition to the duties heretofore imposed by law on the importation of the articles mentioned in this section, there shall be levied, collected, and paid the following duties and rates of duty, that is to say: On brandy, rum, gin, and whiskey, and on cordials, liquors, arrack, absynthe, and all other spirituous liquors and spirituous beverages, fifty cents per gallon, of first proof and less strength, and shall be increased in proportion for any greater strength than the strength of first proof. On spun silk for filling in skins or cops, ten per centum ad valorem. On iron bars for railroads or inclined planes, ten cents per one hundred pounds. On wrought-iron tubes, one cent per pound.

SEC. 3. *And be it further enacted*, That from and after this act takes effect, in lieu of the duties heretofore imposed by law on the importation of the articles mentioned in this section, there shall be levied, collected, and paid the following duties and rates of duty, that is to say: On cotton, five cents per pound. On illuminating oil and naphtha, benzine, and benzole, refined or produced from the distillation of coal, asphaltum, shale, peat, petroleum, or rock oil, or other bituminous substances used for like purposes, forty cents per gallon. On crude petroleum, or rock oil, twenty cents per gallon; on crude coal oil, fifteen cents per gallon. On tobacco stems, fifteen cents per pound. On ready-made clothing of silk, or of which silk shall be a component material of chief value, sixty per centum ad valorem. On quicksilver, fifteen per centum ad valorem.

SEC. 4. *And be it further enacted*, That section fifteen of an act entitled "An act increasing temporarily the duties on imports, and for other purposes," approved July fourteen, eighteen hundred and sixty-two, be, and the same hereby is, amended so as to impose a tax or tonnage duty of thirty cents per ton, in lieu of "ten cents," as therein mentioned: *Provided*, That the receipts of vessels paying tonnage duty shall not be subject to the tax provided in section one hundred and three of "An act to provide internal revenue to support the government, to pay interest on the public debt, and for other purposes," approved June thirtieth, eighteen hundred and sixty-four, nor by any act amendatory thereof: *Provided further*, That no ship, vessel, or steamer, having a license to trade between different districts of the United States, or to carry on the bank, whale, or other fisheries, or on any ship, vessel, or steamer to or from any port or place in Mexico, the British provinces of North America, or any of the West India islands, or in all these trades, shall be required to pay the tonnage duty, contemplated by this act, more than once a year.

SEC. 5. *And be it further enacted*, That the term "statuary," as used in the laws now in force imposing duties on foreign importations, shall be understood to include professional productions of a statuary or of a sculptor only.

SEC. 6. *And be it further enacted*, That there shall be hereafter collected and paid on all goods, wares, and merchandise of the growth or produce of countries [east] of the Cape of Good Hope, (except raw cotton and raw silk, as reeled from the cocoon, or not further advanced than tram, thrown, or organzine,) when imported from places west of the Cape of Good Hope, a duty of ten per centum ad valorem, in addition to the duties imposed on any such article when imported directly from the place or places of their growth or production.

SEC. 7. *And be it further enacted,* That in all cases where there is or shall be imposed any ad valorem rate of duty on any goods, wares, or merchandise imported into the United States, and in all cases where the duty imposed by law shall be regulated by, or directed to be estimated or based upon, the value of the square yard, or of any specified quantity or parcel of such goods, wares, or merchandise, it shall be the duty of the collector, within whose district the same shall be imported or entered, to cause the actual market value, or wholesale price thereof, at the period of the exportation to the United States, in the principal markets of the country from which the same shall have been imported into the United States, to be appraised, and such appraised value shall be considered the value upon which duty shall be assessed. That it shall be lawful for the owner, consignee, or agent of any goods, wares, or merchandise, which shall have been actually purchased, or procured otherwise than by purchase, at the time, and not afterwards, when he shall produce his original invoice, or invoices, to the collector and make and verify his written entry of his goods, wares, or merchandise, as provided by section thirty-six of the act of March two, seventeen hundred and ninety-nine, entitled "An act to regulate the collection of duties on imports and tonnage," to make such addition in the entry to the cost or value given in the invoice as in his opinion may raise the same to the actual market value or wholesale price of such goods, wares, or merchandise, at the period of exportation to the United States, in the principal markets of the country from which the same shall have been imported; and it shall be the duty of the collector, within whose district the same may be imported or entered, to cause such actual market value or wholesale price to be appraised in accordance with the provisions of existing laws, and if such appraised value shall exceed by ten per centum or more the value so declared in the entry, then, in addition to the duties imposed by law on the same, there shall be levied, collected, and paid a duty of twenty per centum ad valorem on such appraised value: *Provided,* That the duty shall not be assessed upon an amount less than the invoice or entered value, any act of Congress to the contrary notwithstanding: *And provided further,* That the sections twenty-third and twenty-fourth of the act approved June thirtieth, eighteen hundred and sixty-four, entitled "An act to increase duties on imports, and for other purposes," and all acts and parts of acts requiring duties to be assessed upon commissions, brokerage, costs of transportation, shipment, transhipment, and other like costs and charges incurred in placing any goods, wares, or merchandise on shipboard, and all acts or parts of acts inconsistent with the provisions of this act, are hereby repealed.

SEC. 8. *And be it further enacted,* That so much of an act entitled "An act to authorize protection to be given to citizens of the United States who may discover deposits of guano," approved August eighteen, eighteen hundred and fifty-six, as prohibits the export thereof, is hereby suspended in relation to all persons who have complied with the provisions of section second of said act for two years from and after July fourteenth, eighteen hundred and sixty-five.

SEC. 9. *And be it further enacted,* That this act shall take effect on and after the first day [of] April, eighteen hundred and sixty-five.

SEC. 10. *And be it further enacted,* That so much of sections thirty-nine, forty, forty-one, forty-two, forty-three, and forty-four of the act entitled "An act to regulate the duties on imports and tonnage," approved March second, seventeen hundred and ninety-nine, as requires the branding or marking and certifying of casks, chests, vessels, and cases containing distilled spirits, or teas, be and the same is hereby revived, to be executed under such rules and regulations as shall be prescribed by the Secretary of the Treasury.

SEC. 11. *And be it further enacted,* That flax and hemp machinery and steam agricultural machinery, as designated in section 21 of the act "to increase duties on imports, and for other purposes," approved June thirtieth, eighteen hundred and sixty-four, may be imported free from duty for one year from the passage of this act.

SEC. 12. *And be it further enacted,* That in all proceedings brought by the United States in any court for due recovery as well of duties upon imports alone as of penalties for the non-payment thereof, the judgment shall recite that the same is rendered for duties, and such judgment, interest, and costs shall be payable in the coin by law receivable for duties, and the execution issued on such judgment shall set forth that the recovery is for duties, and shall require the marshal to satisfy the same in the coin by law receivable for duties; and in case of levy upon and sale of the property of the judgment debtor, the marshal shall refuse payment from any purchaser at such sale in any other money than that specified in the execution.

SEC. 13. *And be it further enacted,* That the eighth section of the act of March twenty-third, eighteen hundred and fifty-four, "to extend the warehousing system by establishing private bonded warehouses, and for other purposes," which authorized the Secretary of the Treasury, in case of the actual injury or destruction of goods, wares, or merchandise by accidental fire or other casualty, while in warehouse under bond, &c., to abate or refund the duties paid or accruing thereon, be extended so as to include goods, wares, or merchandise injured or destroyed in like manner while in the custody of the officers of the customs, and not in bond, and also to goods, wares, and merchandise so injured or destroyed after their arrival within the limits of any port of entry of the United States, and before the same have been *bonded* [landed] under the *suspension* [supervision] of the officers of the customs: *Provided,* That this act shall apply only to cases arising from and after its passage, and to cases where the duties have not already been paid.

Approved, March 3, 1865.

TARIFF:

OR,

RATES OF DUTIES

Imposed by the Act of Congress of March 2, 1861,

WITH ADDENDA OF

August 5, 1861, December 24, 1861, July 14, 1862, and March 3, 1863,

AND

JUNE 30, 1864,

On all Goods, Wares and Merchandise

IMPORTED INTO THE UNITED STATES OF AMERICA.

A.

	DUTY.
ABSYNTH, 50° and under	$2 00 ℔ gal.
————, 51	2 04 "
————, 52	2 08 "
————, 53	2 12 "
————, 54	2 13 "
————, 55	2 20 "
————, 56	2 24 "
————, 57	2 28 "
————, 58	2 32 "
————, 59	2 36 "
————, 60	2 40 "
————, 61	2 44 "
————, 62	2 48 "
————, 63	2 52 "
————, 64	2 56 "
————, 65	2 60 "
————, 66	2 64 "
————, 67	2 68 "
————, 68	2 72 "
————, 69	2 76 "
————, 70	2 80 "
————, 71	2 84 "
————, 72	2 88 "
————, 73	2 92 "
————, 74	2 96 "
————, 75	3 00 "

	DUTY.
Absynth, all under 50° and costing over $4 00 per gallon	50 ℔ cent.
Absynth, oil of, or wormwood	50 "
Acacia, or gum arabic	20 "
Accordions	30 "
Acid, chromic	15 "
Acetate of lead, or sugar of lead	4 c. ℔ lb.
——— of potasse	75 "
——— of baryta	40 "
——— of iron	50 "
——— of strontian	50 "
——— of zinc	50 "
——— of lead	20 "
——— of magnesia	50 "
——— of soda	50 "
——— of lime	25 ℔ cent.
——— of quicksilver	10 "
Acid, acetic, acetous or concentrated vinegar, or pyroligneous, exceeding the specific gravity of 1040°	80c. ℔ lb.
As above, not over 1040°, called No. 8	25 "
Acid, benzoic	10 "
——, boracic	5 c. ℔ lb.
——, citric, white or yellow	10 "
——, gallic (med.)	$1 50 "
——, muriatic	10 ℔ cent.
——, nitric, or nitric fort	10 "

	DUTY.
Acid, oxalic	4 c. ℘ lb.
——, tannic	$2 "
——, tartaric, in crystals or powder	20 c. "
——, sulphuric, or oil of vitriol	1 "
Acorns	10 ℘ cent.
Acorn coffee and dandelion root, raw or prepared, and other articles for similar use, not provided for	3 c. ℘ lb.
Acids, all kinds of, used for chemical or manufacturing purposes, not otherwise provided for	free.
Acids used in the fine arts, not otherwise provided for	10 ℘ cent.
Adhesive felt, for covering ships' bottoms	free.
Adhesive plaster, salve	40 ℘ cent.
Adianthum (a veg. sub.)	10 ℘ ct. & $5 ℘ ton.
Adzes	45 ℘ cent.
Agaric (a fungus)	10 "
Agates	10 "
———, bookbinders'	20 "
Alabata, in sheets	35 "
Alabaster and spar ornaments	30 "
Alba, canella	20 "
Albumen, prepared white of an egg	25 "
Ale, in bottles	35c. ℘ gal.
Ale, in casks	20 "
Ale, otherwise than in bottles	20 "
Alkanet root	20 ℘ cent.
Alkermes	20 "
Aluminum, a crude metal	20 "
Alspice, oil of	50 "
Almonds	6 cts. ℘ lb.
———, shelled	10 "
———, paste	50 ℘ cent.
Aloës	6 cts. ℘ ℔.
Alum	60 cts. ℘ 100 ℔s.
Alum, patent	60 cts. ℘ 100 lbs.
——substitute	60 cts. ℘ 100 lbs.
Alumina, sulphate of	60 cts. ℘ 100 ℔s.
Aluminous cake	60 cts. ℘ 100 lbs.
Alzarine (extract of madder)	10 ℘ cent.
Amber, gum	20 "
——, beads	50 "

	DUTY.
Amber, oil of, crude	10 cts. ℘ lb.
Ambergris	free.
Amylic alcohol	$2 ℘ gal.
Amethyst	10 ℘ cent.
Ammonia	20 "
——— acetate, or pyroligneate of	70 c. ℘ lb.
———, sulphate of	20 ℘ cent.
———, salts	20 "
———, carb.	20 "
———, muriate of	20 "
———, refined	20 "
Analine, dyes	$1 ℘ ℔. and 35 "
———,	20 "
Anatomical preparations. (According to materials of which composed.)	
Anchovies (in oil)	50 ℘ cent.
——— (in salt)	50 "
Angelica root	20 "
Angora goats' wool or hair, (see hair.)	
Animals, all alive	free.
Animal oil, not otherwise enumerated	20 ℘ cent.
Animal carbon	free.
Annatto	free.
Annatto extract	20 ℘ cent.
Annatto seed	20 "
Annealed iron wire to pay duty as other iron wire.	
Anise seed	5 cts. ℘ ℔.
———, star	10 "
Anise seed, oil of	50 "
Anthos, oil of	50 ℘ cent.
Antimony, crude, or regulus of	10 "
Antique oil	50 "
Antiquities, specially imported	free.
Anvils,	2½ cts. ℘ ℔.
Any goods, wares, or merchandise of the growth, produce, or manufacture of the United States, or of its fisheries, upon which no drawback, bounty, or allowance have been paid	free.

ERRATA.

The Articles below should read—

'age	85,	Acetate of lead, or sugar of,	20 cents per pound.
"	89,	Benzoates,	30 per cent.
"	95,	Chapapote, (Asphaltum,)	25 "
"	100,	Dominoes, bone or ivory, (if not toys,)	35 "
"	100,	do. do. do. (if any metal,)	35 "
"	100,	Crucibles, sand,	25 "
"	101,	Epaulets, worsted,	50 "
"	110,	Hobby-horses,	50 "
"	115,	Lead, sugar of,	20 cents per pound.
"	120,	Merino shawls, made of combed wool, (as shawls, worsted.)	
"	121,	Needles, crochet, of steel,	45 per cent.
"	121,	do. do. of iron,	35 "
"	121,	do. do. of bone or ivory,	35 "
"	128,	Porcelain slates,	45 "
"	133,	Shawls, camel's hair, (as shawls, worsted.)	
"	133,	Shawls, worsted, under 8 ounces per square yd.,	35 per cent.
"	133,	Shawls, Thibet, (as shawls, worsted.)	
"	134,	Shuttle-cock and battle-doors, (if toys,)	50 per cent.
"	137,	Spoke shaves,	45 "
"	139,	Super acetate of lead, or sugar of lead,	20 cents per pound.

DUTY.

Apothecaries' vials and bottles exceeding the capacity of six, and not exceeding the capacity of 16 ounces each, not cut............35 ⅌ cent.
————————, cut............40 "
Apparatus, philosophical, or instruments, books, maps, charts, statues, statuary, busts, casts of marble, bronze, alabaster or plaster of Paris, paintings, drawings, etchings, specimens of sculpture, cabinets of coins, medals, regalia, gems, and all collections of antiquities imported by order and for the use of any Society incorporated for philosophical, literary, or religious purposes, or for the encouragement of the fine arts, or by order and for the use of any seminary of learning, school or college within the United States or the territories thereof ....free.
Apparatus, philosophical, or instruments, are exempt from the above schedule, and under act July, 1864, will pay ....15 ⅌ cent.
Apparatus, philosophical, not specially imported,................40 "
Apparel, wearing, and other personal baggage in actual use...........free.
Aprons, silk......................60 ⅌ cent.
Aqua ammonia, or hartshorn ......40 "
Aqua fortis......................10 "
—— mellis, or honey water ......50 "
Argentophile (prep. for cleaning brass) ....20 "
Arrack, 50 degrees ....$2 00 ⅌ gal.
———, 51 " ....2 04 "
———, 52 " ....2 08 "
———, 53 " ....2 12 "
———, 54 " ....2 16 "
———, 55 " ....2 20 "
———, 56 " ....2 24 "
———, 57 " ....2 28 "

DUTY.

Arrack, 58 degrees ....$2 32 ⅌ gal.
———, 59 " ....2 36 "
———, 60 " ....2 40 "
———, 61 " ....2 44 "
———, 62 " ....2 48 "
———, 63 " ....2 52 "
———, 64 " ....2 56 "
———, 65 " ....2 60 "
———, 66 " ....2 64 "
———, 67 " ....2 68 "
———, 68 " ....2 72 "
———, 69 " ....2 76 "
———, 70 " ....2 80 "
———, under 50 degrees in strength, and value over $4 per gallon, ...50 ⅌ cent.
———, all imitations to pay same as genuine.
Armenian, bole ....50 ⅌ cent.
Armenian, stone ....10 "
Archelia, archil, or orchelia ....10 "
———— if a vegetable dye ....10 "
Argent, vivum, or quicksilver......10 ⅌ cent.
Argentine.......................35 "
Argol, or crude tartar.............6c. ⅌ lb.
——, partially refined, as brown tartar 6c. ⅌ lb.
Arms, fire.......................35 ⅌ cent.
——, side ....35 "
Arrow root ....30 "
Arsenic ....20 "
———, sulphate of................20 "
Articles embroidered with gold, silver, or metal ....35 "
Articles of the growth, produce, or manufacture of the United States, or its territories, brought back in the same condition as when exported, and on which no drawback was allowed...................free.
Articles, all, composed wholly or in part of gold, silver, or platina, not otherwise provided for..........40 ⅌ cent.
Articles in a crude state, used in dyeing or tanning, not otherwise provided for...................free.

DUTY.

Articles not in a crude state, used in dyeing or tanning, not otherwise provided for....................20 ℔ cent.
Articles, all manufactures of, and not subject to any other rate of duty ....20 ℔ cent.
Articles, raw or unmanufactured, not provided for.....................10 "
Articles manufactured from copper, or of which copper is the material of chief value, not combined with gold, silver, German silver. platina or steel, not otherwise specified...35 "
Articles worn by men, women, or children, of whatever materials composed, made up in whole or in part by hand, not otherwise provided for ....35 "
Articles, all, imported for the use of the United States ....free.
Artificial feathers and parts........50 ℔ cent.
Artificial flowers, or parts thereof..50 "
Asbestos, a crude mineral substance.25 "
Asphaltum........................25 "
Assafœtida.......................20 "
Asses' skin (or parchment)........30 "
———, imitation of, or parchment ....30 "
Ava root ....20 "
Aubusson carpetings (see carpeting).
Augers ....45 "
Auripigmentum, or orpiment, sulphate of arsenic................20 "
Awl hafts ....35 "
Awls ....45 "
Axes ....45 "
Axletrees, iron ....2½ cts. ℔ lb.
Ayr-stones ....10 ℔ cent.

B.

BACON........................2 cts. ℔ lb.
Baggage, personal, in actual use....free.
Bagging, called cotton bagging, (see cotton bagging.)

DUTY.

Bags, bead, made in part by hand..50 ℔ cent.
——, grass ....30 "
——, gunny, (see cotton bagging.)
——, woolen.....24 cts. ℔ lb. and 40 "
——, worsted.....................50 "
——, flax ....40 "
——, hemp.......................30 "
——, silk ....50 "
——, carpet, worsted.............50 "
——, carpet, combed wool, or worsted, and leather.................50 "
Baizes ....25 cts. ℔ sq. yd.
Balls, billiard ....35 ℔ cent.
——, wash.......10 cts. ℔ lb. and 25 "
Balmorals, and goods of similar description, or used for like purposes, of wool, worsted, or other materials,..........24 cts. ℔ lb. and 35 "
Balm of Gilead ....40 "
Balsam copaiva..................20 cts. ℔ lb.
——— of Tulu ....30 " "
——— Peruvian...................50 " "
———, medicinal, not otherwise provided for.......................30 ℔ cent.
———, all kinds of cosmetic ......50 "
Bamboos, unmanufactured ....10 "
Bananas ....25 "
Bangups, a cotton stuff or cord, (see cottons.)
Bark of cork trees, unmanufactured..........................30 "
——, Peruvian ....20 "
——, flat cararaya (Peruvian) .....20 "
——, all not specially mentioned...10 "
——, all medicinal ....20 "
Barrege, cotton, (see cottons.)
———, wool, (see woolens.)
———, worsted, or silk and worsted, not provided for ....50 "
Barley ....15 cts. ℔ bush.
———, pearl, or hulled ....1 ct. ℔ lb.
Barytes, sulphate of, crude or refined..........................½ ct. ℔ lb.
Barytes, nitrate of ....20 ℔ cen

DUTY.

Barytes and acid combined.........3 cts. ⅌ lb.
Bar iron, when manufactured in whole or in part by rolling, (see iron.)
Bar iron, not manufactured in whole or in part by rolling, (see iron.)
Barwood (a dye wood)............free.
Barilla..........................free.
Bass (the inner bark of a tree).....20 ⅌ cent.
Bassoons........................30 "
Baskets, wood or osier............35 "
———, palm leaf.................35 "
———, straw...................35 "
———, grass or whalebone.......35 "
Battledores.....................35 "
Bay Rum, essence of..............$2 ⅌ oz.
Bay water, or bay rum.........$1 50 ⅌ gal.
—— wax, or myrtle wax..........20 ⅌ cent.
Bayonets........................45 "
Bdellium, if crude...............20 "
————, refined.................20 "
Beads, of precious stones..........50 "
———, gold and silver..........50 "
———, all not otherwise enumerated.50 "
Bead ornaments..................50 "
Beans, tonqua...................20 "
———, vanilla..................$3 ⅌ lb.
———, all other not specially mentioned..........................10 ⅌ cent.
Beaver, fur undressed on the skins..10 "
Beam knives.....................45 "
Beams, scale....................35 "
Bed feathers....................30 "
—— ticking, linen (see flax.)
—— ticking, cotton, (see cotton.)
—— caps........................35 "
—— screws...................$2\frac{1}{2}$ cts. ⅌ lb.
—— sides, as carpeting, (see mats.)
Beef..........................1 ct. ⅌ lb.
Beer, in bottles................35 cts. ⅌ gal.
——, casks...................20 "
——, otherwise than in bottles..20 "
Beeswax.......................20 ⅌ cent.
Bellows pipes...................35 "

DUTY.

Bells, old, and bell metal..........free.
Bell cranks, of iron...............35 ⅌ cent.
—— levers, of iron...............35 "
—— pulls, of iron................35 "
Bellows.........................35 "
Belts, sword leather..............35 "
Benzine, or benzole oil, refined...30 cts. ⅌ gal.
Benzoates.......................30 "
Benzoic acid.....................10 "
Benzoin (a gum)..............10 cts. ⅌ lb.
Beds, feather....................20 ⅌ cent.
Bed spreads, or covers, made of the scraps or waste ends of printed calicoes, sewed together........35 "
Bells, of bell metal, fit only to be remanufactured.................free.
Bell metal, manufactured.........35 ⅌ cent.
Bells, silver or gold..............40 "
Berlin blue.....................25 "
Bergamot, essence of............$1 ⅌ lb.
Berries, used for dyeing, all exclusively, in a crude state..........free.
Berries, not otherwise provided for.10 ⅌ cent.
Bezoar stones....................10 "
Bichromate of potash............3 cts. ⅌ lb.
Bicarbonate of soda, or saleratus...$1\frac{1}{2}$ "
Bick irons......................35 ⅌ cent.
Binding, carpet, if worsted........50 "
————, cotton.................35 "
————, worsted...............50 "
————, silk..................60 "
————, leather,...............35 "
————, linen.................40 "
————, quality,...............50 "
Bird's eye stuff, linen (see flax.)
Birds..........................free.
Bismuth........................free.
————, oxyde of..............20 ⅌ cent.
Bitts, carpenters'................45 "
Bitter apple....................10c. ⅌ lb.
Bitumen........................20 ⅌ cent.
Black, ivory...................25 "
———, lamp...................20 "
——— lead.....................$10 ⅌ to

DUTY.

Black, lead pots....................35 ⅌ cent.
——— glass bottles, not exceeding the capacity of one quart ....35 ⅌ cent.
Black glass bottles, exceeding one quart ....35 "
Black lead powder ....20 "
Blacking........................30 "
Bladders........................20 "
Blacksmiths' hammers ....2½c. ⅌ lb.
—————, sledges ....2½ "
Black frankfort.................25 ⅌ cent.
Blanc fixe......................3 c. ⅌ lb.
Blankets, all, wholly or in part of wool, value not over 28 cts. ⅌ lb., 12 cts. ⅌ lb. and...............20 ⅌ cent.
Blankets, all, wholly or in part of wool, value over 28 cts. and not over 40 cts. ⅌ lb. 24 cts. ⅌ lb. and.25 "
Blankets, all, wholly or in part of wool, value over 40 cts. ⅌ lb., 24 cts. ⅌ lb. and..................30 "
Bleaching powders ....30 cts. ⅌ 100 lbs.
Blue, Prussian ....30 ⅌ cent.
——, vitriol.....................25 "
——, guineas (see cottons.)
——, guinet.....................20 "
Blue gall ....free.
Blooms, iron in, subject to the same duty as iron in bolts or bars. (See iron.)
Boards, planed ....20 ⅌ cent.
———, rough ....20 "
Bobinet lace, (cotton)...........35 "
Bobbin or braid cotton............35 "
——— wire, covered with cotton as wire.
Bocking, all..................25 c. ⅌ sq. yd.
Bodkins, ivory...................35 ⅌ cent.
———, bone ....35 "
———, silver.................. 40 "
———, gold.....................40 "
———, plated...................35 "
———, gilt ....35 "
———, iron.....................35 "

DUTY.

Bodkins, steel ....45 ⅌ cent.
———, brass.....................35 "
———, copper ....35 "
Bologna sausages ....30 "
Bolting cloths....................free.
Bolts, iron, for fastenings ....35 ⅌ cent.
——, brass, for fastenings ....35 "
——, copper ....35 "
Bolts, composition................35 "
Bolt rope, as cordage (tarred.) ..... 3c. ⅌ ℔.
—— rope, as cordage, not Manilla, (untarred)......................3½ c. ⅌ lb.
Bole, Armenian...................50 ⅌ cent.
Bone, black ....25 "
——, dust, ...free.
Bones, burnt.....................free.
Bone, dice, draughts, chessmen, chess and bagatelle balls............50 ⅌ cent.
Bonnets, Leghorn ....40 "
———, chip ....40 "
———, grass.....................40 "
———, fur leather...............35 "
———, straw.....................40 "
———, muslin ....40 "
Bonnets, silk or satin.............60 "
Bonnet wire, covered with silk, same as wire.
——— wire, covered with cotton thread, if wire of chief value, same as wire.
Boucho leaves ....10 c. ⅌ lb.
Bone alphabets ....35 ⅌ cent.
——, chessmen ....50 "
——, whale, rosettes ....35 "
——, tip and bones ....10 "
——, whale, other manufactures of.35 "
——, whale, not of the American fisheries ....10 "
Boots...........................35 "
——, lace, silk or satin, for children.35 "
Bootees, for women or men, silk ...35 "
Boots and bootees, men's, of leather.35 "
——————, women's, of leather.35 "
——————, children's, of leather 35 "

DUTY.

Bookbinders' agates ferrulea ......20 ⅌ cent.

Books, maps, and charts, imported for the use of Congressional library, by authority, provided the price paid importer does not include duty ....free.

Books, blank, when bound.......

Books, blank, when unbound ....

Books, periodicals, and other works in the course of printing and republication in the United States.

Books, printed magazines, pamphlets, periodicals, and illustrated newspapers, bound or unbound, not otherwise provided for.....

Books, Hebrew, or of which that language forms the text, when bound ....

Books, do. do. unbound ...

——, all in foreign languages, except Latin, Greek, and Hebrew, bound or in boards .... } 25 ⅌ cent.

Books, do. do. in sheets or pamphlets ....

Books, editions of works in Hebrew, Greek, Latin, or English, which have been printed 40 years prior to date of importation ....

Books, all reports of Legislative Committees appointed under foreign governments ....

Books, Polyglots, Lexicons, and Dictionaries ....

Books, periodicals, pamphlets....

———, illustrated ....

Books of engravings, bound or unbound ....

Books and instruments, professional, of persons arriving in the U. S...free.

Books, specially imported for the use of schools, &c ....free.

Boot web, linen..................40 ⅌ cent.

Borate of lime ....5 cts. ⅌ lb.

Borax, or tincal, crude...........5 " "

DUTY.

Borax, or tincal, refined.........10 cts. ⅌ lb.

Botany, specimens in.............free.

Bottles, apothecaries', exceeding the capacity of 6, and not exceeding the capacity of 16 ounces each...35 ⅌ cent.

Bottles, black glass, not exceeding 1 quart ....35 "

Bottles, black glass, exceeding one quart ....35 "

Bottles, perfumery and fancy, not exceeding the capacity of 4 ounces each (cut).....................40 "

Bottles, perfumery and fancy, exceeding 4 ounces, and not exceeding 16 ounces (cut)...................40 "

Bottles (containing wine or spirituous liquors) ....2 cts. each.

Bougies.........................35 ⅌ cent.

Boucho leaves..................10 cts. ⅌ ℔.

Boxes, gold or silver.............40 ⅌ cent.

———, musical..................30 "

———, japanned dressing.........40 "

———, cedar, granadilla, ebony, rose, and satin..........35 "

———, all other wood...........35 "

———, sand, of tin..............35 "

———, shell, not otherwise enumerated................35 "

———, if paper only ....35 "

———, fancy, not otherwise specified ....35 "

Box boards, paper................35 "

Bracelets, gold or set.............25 "

————, gilt....................25 "

————, hair....................35 "

Braces, carpenters', without bitts....35 "

Braces and bitts, carpenters'........45 "

Brace bitts.......................45 "

Braces or suspenders, silk ....60 "

Braces or suspenders, cotton.......35 "

Braces or suspenders, all leather ...35 "

———, all other..................35 "

———, India rubber ....35 "

Brackets.........................35 "

	DUTY.
Brads, cut, not exceeding 16 ounces to the 1000	2½ c. ℔ M.
Brads, cut, exceeding 16 ounces to the 1000	3 c. ℔ lb.
Braids, cotton	35 ℔ cent.
——, in ornaments, for head-dresses	35 "
Braids, hair, not made up for head-dresses	35 "
Braids, hair, made up for head-dresses	35 "
Braids, straw, for making bonnets or hats	30 "
Brandy, 50 degrees	$2 50 ℔ gal.
——, 51 "	2 55 "
——, 52 "	2 60 "
——, 53 "	2 65 "
——, 54 "	2 70 "
——, 55 "	2 75 "
——, 56 "	2 80 "
——, 57 "	2 85 "
——, 58 "	2 90 "
——, 59 "	2 95 "
——, 60 "	3 00 "
——, 61 "	3 05 "
——, 62 "	3 10 "
——, 63 "	3 15 "
——, 64 "	3 20 "
——, 65 "	3 25 "
——, 66 "	3 30 "
——, 67 "	3 35 "
——, 68 "	3 40 "
——, 69 "	3 45 "
——, 70 "	3 50 "
Brandy, all imitations of, to pay same as genuine.	
Brandies, and imitations of, under 50 degrees, value over $5.00 ℔ gall.	50 ℔ cent.
Brass, manufactures of, not otherwise enumerated	35 "
Brass, in plates or sheets	35 "
——, in bars	15 "
——, in pigs	15 "
——, old, only fit to be remanufactured	15 "

	DUTY.
Brass wire	35 ℔ cent.
——, rolled	35 "
——, battery	35 "
——, studs	35 "
——, screws	35 "
Brazil paste, or pasta de Brazil	10 "
—— wood	free.
—— pebbles, prepared for spectacles	40 ℔ cent.
Bread baskets, japanned	40 "
——, plated	35 "
——, silver	40 "
Breccia, in blocks or slabs	free.
Bricks, fire or roofing	20 ℔ cent.
Britannia ware	35 "
Bridle bitts (see saddlery)	35 "
Bridles	35 "
Brimstone, crude	$6 ℔ ton.
Brimstone, in rolls	$10 ℔ ton.
Brime	free.
Bristol stones	10 ℔ cent.
—— boards	35 "
—— ——, perforated	35 "
Bristles	15 cts. ℔ lb.
Brodequins, leather	35 ℔ cent.
Bronze casts	35 "
Bronze, all manufactures of	35 "
Bronze metal in leaf	10 "
Bronze powder	20 "
Bronze powder, pale, yellow, white, and red	20 "
——, liquid, gold, or bronze color	10 "
Brown, rolls, linen, (see linens.)	
——, Spanish dry	25 "
——, Spanish, in oil	25 "
—— smalts	20 "
Brooms, all kinds	35 "
Brucine (medical prep.)	40 "
Brushes of all kinds	40 "
Buckles of copper, brass, iron, pewter, tin, lead, or of which either of these articles is a component material	35 "
Buckles, of gold or silver	40 "

	DUTY.
Buckrams, (see linens.)	
Bugles, musical instruments	30 ₰ cent.
———, glass, if cut	40 "
———, glass, if not cut	35 "
Building stones, not provided for	20 "
Ballets	35 "
Bullrushes	10 "
Bulbs, or bulbous roots	30 "
Bullion	free.
Bunting	50 ₰ cent.
Burlaps, (see linens.)	
Burning fluid	50 cts. ₰ gallon.
Burr stones, unwrought	free.
————, bound up in mill stones	20 ₰ cent.
Burgundy pitch	20 "
Busts, lead	35 "
Buttons, all except silk	30 "
Button moulds, of whatever material	30 "
Buttons with links	30 "
Butter	4 cts. ₰ lb.
Butchers' knives	35 ₰ cent.

C.

CABINETS of coins, medals, gems, and all other collections of antiquities	free.
Cabinet wares	35 ₰ cent.
Cables, tarred	3 cts. ₰ lb.
———, untarred	3½ "
———, made of grass	3½ "
———, untarred Manilla	2½ "
Cadmium	free.
Cajeput, or cajeputa, oil of	25 cts. ₰ lb.
Cakes, linseed	20 ₰ cent.
Calamine	free.
Calx (lime)	10 ₰ cent.
Calcined magnesia	12 cts. ₰ lb.
Calisaya bark	20 ₰ cent.
Calfskins, raw	10 "
Calfskins, salted, in a raw state	10 "
————, tanned	30 "
Calomel,	30 "
ameos, real	10 "

	DUTY.
Cameos, imitation of	40 ₰ cent.
———, real, set	25 "
———, imitation, set	30 "
Camel's hair	free.
——— ——, pencils, in quill	35 ₰ cent.
——— —— ———, other	35 "
Camomile flowers	20 "
Camphor, refined	40 cts. ₰ lb.
————, crude	30 " "
Camwood	free.
Canary seed	$1 ₰ bushel.
Canella, alba	20 ₰ cent.
Candlesticks, alabaster	30 "
————, bone	35 "
————, earthenware, white or colored	40 "
Candlesticks, brass	35 "
————, bronze	35 "
————, gilt	35 "
————, gold	40 "
————, glass, cut	40 "
————, not cut	35 "
————, iron	35 "
————, japanned	40 "
————, marble	50 "
————, plated	35 "
————, pewter	35 "
————, porcelain, not ornamented	45 "
————, silver	40 "
————, spa	30 "
————, stone ware, common	25 "
————, tin	35 "
————, washed	35 "
Candles, adamantine	5 cts. ₰ lb.
———, tallow	2½ "
———, wax, pure or mixed	8 "
———, spermaceti, pure or mixed	8 "
———, stearine	5 "
———, paraffine, pure or mixed	8 "
———, all others	2½ "
Candy, sugar, colored, value over 30 cts. ₰ lb., or when sold by the box, package, or not by the pound	50 ₰ cent.

	DUTY.
Candy, sugar, colored, valued at 30 cts. ℘ lb. or less	15 cts. ℘ ℔.
Candy, sugar, not colored	10 "
Canes, walking, finished or not	35 ℘ cent.
Cannon, brass	35 "
——, iron	35 "
Cantharides	50 cts. ℘ lb.
Canton crapes (see silks.)	
Canvas, for floor cloths or wearing apparel, linen (see flax.)	
Caoutchouc gums, India rubber	10 ℘ cent.
Capers	35 "
Caps of chip	40 "
——, cotton wove	35 "
—— of cotton, if jointly made by hand	35 "
Caps of fur	35 "
—— of lace, trimmed, (cotton)	35 "
—— of lace, not trimmed, "	35 "
—— of leather	35 "
—— of linen	35 "
—— of silk	60 "
—— of wool, wove	20 cts. ℘ ℔. and 30 "
—— of worsted, wove	35 "
Caps, &c., unbleached cottons	35 "
Cap pieces, for stills	35 "
Caps, lace, sewed	35 "
Caps, gloves, leggings, mits, socks, stockings, wove shirts and drawers, and all similar articles made in frames, and worn by men, women, or children, and not otherwise provided for	35 "
Caps, lace, not sewed, (cotton)	35 "
Capsules	40 "
Carbines or carabines	35 "
Carbon, animal	free.
Carbonate of magnesia	6 cts. ℘ lb.
——, of ammonia	20 ℘ cent.
Carboys, of the capacity of half a gal.	35 "
Carboys, above half, and not above 3 gals.	35 "
Carboys, exceeding three gals. and not exceeding ten gallons	35 "

	DUTY.
Carbuncles	10 ℘ cent.
Cardamom seed	50 cts. ℘ lb.
Card cases, of whatever material composed	35 ℘ cent.
Cards, playing, value 25 cts. or less ℘ pack	25 cts. ℘ pk.
Cards, playing, over 25 cts. ℘ pk.	35 cts. ℘ pk.
——, visiting	35 ℘ cent.
Cards, blank	35 "
——, wool,	45 "
——, cotton	45 "
Carmine, a water color	35 "
——, lake, drug or liquid	35 "
——, dry	35 "
——, a liquid dye	20 "
Carpet binding	50 "
Carpeting, Wilton; ——, Saxony; ——, Aubusson; ——, Axminster; ——, patent velvet; ——, Tournay; ——, tapestry; ——, Brussels, wrought by Jacquard machine; Carpeting, medallion, or whole carpet — Value $1 25 ℘ sq. yd. or under	70c. ℘ sq. yd.
Carpeting, as above, value over $1.25 per sq. yd.	80 cts. ℘ sq. yd.
Provided that none of the above carpeting shall pay a less duty than 50 ℘ cent.	
Carpeting, Brussels, printed on warp or otherwise	50c. ℘ sq. yd.
Carpeting, Brussels tapestry, printed on warp or otherwise	.50 " "
Carpeting, treble ingrain, three ply	40 " "
Carpeting, Venetian worsted chain	40 " "
Carpeting, yarn, Venetian, and two ply ingrain	35 " "
Carpeting, hemp	6½ " "
——, jute	6½ " "
——, felt, all	25 " "

	DUTY.
Carpeting, all other, of whatever material	40 ℔ cent.
Carriages of all descriptions, and parts thereof	35 "
Caraway seed	3 c. ℔ lb.
Carui, or caraway, oil of	50 "
Carvers	35 ℔ cent.
Cascarilla bark	20 "
Casement rods, iron for (see iron.)	
Cassimere, woolen (see woolen.)	
———, cotton, wool being a component part, chief value, (see wool.)	
Casks, empty	35 "
Cassada, or meal of	20 "
Cassia, Chinese, Calcutta, and Sumatra	20 cts. ℔ lb.
Cassia, ground	25 "
——— buds	25 "
——— fistula	20 ℔ cent.
Castanas, or castinai	2 cts. ℔ lb.
Castings of plaster	35 ℔ cent.
Castor beans or seeds, 50 lbs. to bush	60c. ℔ bushel.
Castor oil	$1 ℔ gal.
Castors, brass or iron	35 ℔ cent.
———, wood	35 "
Castors or cruets, silver, without glasses	40 "
Castors or cruets, plated, do. do.	35 "
———, wood, do. do.	35 "
Castor glasses, not in the frames, or cruets, cut	40 "
Castor glasses, not in the frames, or cruets, not cut	35 "
Castorum	20 "
Cast-iron vessels, not otherwise specified (see iron.)	
Catches, brass, copper, or iron	35 "
Catechu, as cutch	10 "
Catgut	30 "
Catsup	40 "
Caulking mallets	35 "
Caustic soda	1½ ct. ℔ lb.
Cayenne pepper	15 cts. ℔ lb.
Cayenne pepper, ground	18 "
Cedar wood	free.
Cement, Roman	20 ℔ cent.
Chafing dishes, copper	35 "
Chafing dishes, iron or tin	35 "
Chain cables	2½cts. ℔ lb.
Chain breeching, iron, (see iron.)	
——— curbs, gilt	35 ℔ cent.
Chains, hair	35 "
———, iron, (see iron.)	
Chains, brass	35 "
———, copper	35 "
———, gold or silver, not jewelry	40 "
———, gold or silver, if jewelry	25 "
———, gilt, if jewelry	25 "
———, plated	35 "
———, steel	45 "
———, tinned, (on iron)	35 "
———, washed, (on iron)	35 "
———, dog	35 "
———, ox (see iron.)	
———, trace (see iron.)	
Chairs, sitting	35 "
Chalk, billiard	50 "
———, red	20 "
———, French	20 "
———, white	$10 ℔ ton.
———, all not otherwise provided for	25 ℔ cent.
Chamomile flowers	20 "
Chandeliers, brass	35 "
———, glass, cut	40 "
Chapapote	3 c. ℔ lb.
Charts	25 ℔ cent.
Charts, books of, not connected with any work of which they form a vol	25 "
When so connected, will pay the same as the other volumes	25 "
Checks, cotton, (see cottons.)	
———, linen, (see flax.)	
Cheese	4 cts. ℔ lb.

DUTY.

Chemical preparations, not otherwise enumerated .... 20 ℘ cent.
Chemical salts, not otherwise enumerated .... 20 "
Chenille, cords or trimmings of, cotton .... 35 "
Cheroots, India segars (see segars.)
Chessmen, bone, ivory, ... 50 "
———, wood .... 35 "
Chest handles .... 35 "
Chickory root .... 4 cts. ℘ lb.
Chickory root, ground, burnt, or prepared .... 5 cts. ℘ lb.
Chili peppers .... 15 c. per lb.
China ware, plain white .... 45 ℘ cent.
———, ornamented in any manner .. 50 "
——— root .... 20 "
Chincona bark .... 20 "
Chiacona root .... 20 "
Chinchilla skins, undressed .... 10 "
———, dressed .... 20 "
Chinese blue .... 25 "
Chip hats or bonnets .... 40 "
Chisels .... 45 "
Chloride of lime .... 30 cts. per 100 lbs.
Chlorometers, glass .... 40 ℘ cent.
Chloroform (medic) .... $1 ℘ ℔.
Chocolate .... 7 c. per lb.
Choppa romals and bandanna handkerchiefs, silk, (see silks.)
Chowdagary, a manufacture of cotton, (see cotton.)
Chromate of potash .... 3 c. per lb.
——— lead .... 25 ℘ cent.
Chromic, yellow .... 25 "
———, acid .... 15 "
Chronometers, and parts of box or ship .... 10 "
Chrysolites .... 20 "
Cicuta .... 20 "
Cinchona, Peruvian .... 20 "
Cinchonine bark (Peruvian) .... 20 "
Cinnabar, prep. of mercury .... 20 "
Cinnamon .... 30 c. per lb.

DUTY.

Cinnamon, oil of .... $2 ℘ ℔.
Circingle webb (woolen) .... 35 ℘ cent.
Citrate of lime .... 20 "
Citric acid .... 10 cts. ℘ ℔.
Citron, in its natural state .... 10 ℘ cent.
———, preserved .... 35 "
Citron, oil of .... 50 "
Civit, oil of .... 30 "
Clasps, brass .... 35 "
———, gold or silver .... 40 "
———, gilt or plated .... 35 "
———, steel .... 45 "
———, set, gold or silver .... 40 "
———, iron .... 35 "
Clay, ground or prepared .... $5 ℘ ton.
———, unwrought, pipe and fire clay .... $5 "
Cliff stone, ... $10 "
Cloaks, if wool or silk, not part .... 35 ℘ cent.
Cloak pins, gilt or plated .... 35 "
———, steel .... 45 "
Clocks, and parts of .... 35 "
Cloth, India rubber .... 35 "
Cloth, India rubber, linen being a component part .... 35 "
Cloth, woolen, (see woolens.)
———, leopard spot, (see woolens.)
———, bolting .... free.
———, all oil, for floors, pat. stamped, printed or painted, (see oil cloth.)
Cloth, oil, not denominated patent floor cloth .... 40 ℘ cent.
Clothing, ready-made, or wearing apparel of every kind, in whole or part of wool ... 24 cts. ℘ lb. and 40 "
Clothing, all articles worn by men, women, or children, not otherwise specified, of whatever material composed, made wholly or in part by hand, not otherwise provided for, ... 35 "
Cloves .... 20 cts. per lb.
Clove stems, ... "
———, oil of .... $2 per lb.

DUTY.

Clum of coal ....25 ℔ cent.
Coaches, or parts thereof..........35 "
Coach furniture, of all descriptions.35 "
—— lace, according to material composed of.
Coal, bituminous, 28 bush. to the ton, 80 lbs. per bush...............$1.25 ℔ ton.
——, all other, " 40 cts. "
Coal hods, copper ....35 ℔ cent.
————, iron ....35 "
Cobalt, and oxide of ....20 "
———, ores ....10 "
Cochineal ....free.
Cocculus indicus................10 cts. ℔ lb.
Cocks..........................35 ℔ cent.
Cocoa.........................3 cts. per lb.
Cocoa leaves.....................2 cts. "
———, prepared or manufactured.9 cts. "
——— matting ....30 ℔ cent.
——— shells.....................2 cts. ℔ lb.
Cocoanuts.......................25 per cent.
Codilla, or tow of hemp or flax...$10 per ton.
Coir, unmanufactured...........$15 "
—— matting ....30 ℔ cent.
Codfish, dry.....................½ ct. per lb.
Coffee, when imported in American vessels from the place of its growth.....................5 cts. per lb.
Coffee, the growth or production of the possessions of the Netherlands, imported from the Netherlands in foreign vessels, entitled so to do by treaty.............5 cts. per lb.
Coffee, all other................5 " "
Coffee-mills ....35 ℔ cent.
Coins, gold or silver..............free.
——, specially imported..........free.
——, cabinets of, not specially imported, and of copper...........free.
Coins, copper....................free.
Coir ....$15 per ton.
Coke ....25 ℔ cent.
Colcodium, and ether of all kinds, not otherwise provided for, fluid.$1 per lb.

DUTY.

Colcother, dry (oxide of iron)....20 ℔ cent.
Cold cream......................50 "
Colocynth.....................10 cts. ℔ lb.
Cologne water, n d other perfumery of which alcohol is the principal ingredient......$3 per gal. and 50 per cent.
Colombo root...................20 "
Coloquintida...................10 cts. ℔ lb.
Coloring for brandy, if containing spirits ....100 ℔ cent.
Coloring for brandy ....100 "
Colors, water...................35 "
Colts' foot.......................20 "
Cols, sanglier, cravat stiffeners.....35 "
Combs, curry ....35 "
———, all, for the hair, of whatever material ....35 "
Commode handles...............35 "
———— knobs ....35 "
Comforters, made of worsted ......50 "
Compasses, brass or iron,..........35 "
————, of steel ....45 "
————, mariners' ....35 "
————, wood................35 "
Composition table tops............35 "
—————, of glass or paste, set ..30 "
—————, for jewelers, not set...40 "
Confectionery, all valued at 30 cents per lb., or less................15 cts. ℔ lb.
Confectionery, all not otherwise provided for, of sugar, valued over 30 cents per lb., or sold by the box, package, or not by the lb....50 ℔ cent.
Contrayema root 20
Copper, in plates or sheets, called braziers' copper, and other in sheets, not otherwise provided for...........................35 "
Copper bottoms..................35 "
Copper still bottoms, and parts thereof.........................35 "
Copper plates, engraved ....25 "
———, manufactures of, not otherwise specified ....35 "

	DUTY.
Copper wire	35 ℔ cent.
——— vessels	35 "
——— for the use of the mint	free.
——— sheathing, 48 inches long, 14 inches wide, weight from 14 to 34 ounces per square foot	3½ cts. ℔ lb.
Copper rods	35 ℔ cent.
Copper bottoms	35 "
——— bolts	35 "
——— spikes	35 "
——— nails	35 "
——— sheets, called braziers' copper	35 "
Copper plates, called braziers' copper	35 "
Copper sheets, all other, not otherwise provided for	35 "
Copper, pigs	2½ cts. ℔ lb.
——— ingots	2½ "
——— bars	2½ "
———, old, fit only to be remanufactured	1½ "
Copper ore	5 ℔ cent.
Copperas	½ ct. ℔ lb.
Copper, chafing dishes	35 ℔ cent.
Coral	free.
——, cut or manufactured	30 ℔ cent.
Cordage, tarred	3 cts. ℔ lb.
———, untarred	3½ "
———, manilla, untarred	2½ "
———, all other	3½ "
Cordials, of all kinds, sweet	$2 ℔ gal.
Coriander seed	3 c. ℔ lb.
Corks	50 ℔ cent.
Cork, manufactures of	50 "
Cork tree, bark of, unmanufactured	30 "
Cornelian stone	10 "
——— rings	20 "
Corn fans	35 "
Corn, Indian, or maize	10 cts. ℔ bush.
Corn meal	10 ℔ cent.
Corrosive sublimate (mercurial)	20 "
Corsets	35 "

	DUTY.
Cosmetics	50 ℔ cent.
Cotton, easy embroidery, or floss	40 "
Cotton	2c. per lb.
——— braids	35 ℔ cent.
——— cord, gimps and galloons	35 "
——— braces, or suspenders	35 "
Cottons, (except jeans, denims, drillings, bed-tickings, ginghams, plaids, cottonades, pantaloon stuff and goods of like description,) not bleached, colored, stained, painted or printed, and not exceeding 100 threads to the square inch, counting the warp and filling, and exceeding in weight five ounces per square yard	5c.℔sq.yd.
Cotton, as above, if bleached	5½ "
Cotton, as above, if colored, stained, painted or printed	5½c. per sq. yd. and 10 ℔ ct.
Cotton, unbleached, over 100 and not over 200 threads to the square inch, counting the warp and filling	5c.℔sq.yd.
Cotton, as above, bleached	5½ "
Cotton, as above, colored, stained, painted or printed	5½c. per sq. yd. and 20 ℔ ct.
Cotton, unbleached, over 200 threads to the square inch, counting the warp and filling	5c.℔sq.yd.
Cotton, as above, if bleached	5½ "
Cotton, as above, if colored, stained, painted or printed	5½c. per sq. yd. and 20 ℔ ct.
Cottons, jeans, denims, drillings, bed-tickings, ginghams, plaids, cottonades, pantaloon stuffs and goods of like description, or for similar use, not over 100 threads to the square inch, counting the warp and filling, and exceeding five ounces to the square yard, if unbleached,	6c.℔sq.yd.
Cottons, as above, if bleached	6½ "
Cottons, as above, if colored, stained, painted or printed	6½c. per sq. yd. and 10 ℔ cent.

	DUTY.
Cottons, over 100 but not over 200 threads to the square inch, counting the warp and filling, if unbleached	6c. ℔ sq. yd.
Cottons, above, if bleached........	6½ "
Cottons, as above, if colored, stained, painted or printed	6½c. per sq. yd. and 15 ℔ ct.
Cottons, as above, over 200 threads to the square inch, counting the warp and filling, unbleached	7c. ℔ sq. yd.
Cottons, as above, if bleached.....	7½ "
Cottons, as above, if colored, stained, painted or printed	7½c. per sq. yd. and 15 ℔ ct.
Provided, that no cotton goods, having more than 200 threads to the square inch, counting the warp and filling, shall be admitted to a less rate of duty than is provided for goods which are of that number of threads.	
Cottons, provided, on all plain woven cotton goods, not included in the foregoing schedules, over 16 cents per square yard, unbleached, shall pay........................	35 ℔ cent.
Cottons, as above, if bleached, and valued over 20 cts. per sq. yard..	35 "
Cottons, as above, if colored, valued over 25 cts. per square yard.....	35 "
Cottons, or cotton jeans, denims and drillings, valued over 20 cts. per square yard, unbleached........	35 "
Cottons, on all other cotton goods, valued over 25 cts. per sq. yard..	35 "
Cotton shirts, woven, or made on frames........................	35 "
Cotton drawers, woven, or made on frames........................	35 "
Cotton spool, containing each not over 100 yds...	6 cts. per doz. and 30 "
Cotton spool, over 100 yds., in addition for every 100 yds. or fractional part thereof..	6 cts. per doz. and 30 "
Cotton thread, other.............	40 "
——— velvet	35 "
Cotton bagging, or other manufactures, not otherwise provided for, suitable for the uses to which cotton bagging is applied, composed in whole or in part of hemp, jute, flax, gunny bags, gunny cloth, or other material, and valued less than 10 cts. per sq. yard........	3 cts. ℔ lb.
Cotton, as above, valued over 10 cents per square yard...........	4 "
Cotton caps, gloves, leggings, mitts, socks, stockings, made on frames, bleached or colored	35 ℔ cent.
Cotton hose, unbleached	35 "
——— mitts, bleached or colored..	35 "
——— gloves, bleached or colored.	35 "
——— insertings................	35 "
Cotton lace, known as trimming or bobbinet......................	35 "
Cotton lace, colored..............	35 "
——— stockings.................	35 "
Counters—bone, ivory, or rice......	35 "
————, gold or silver..........	40 "
————, pearl.................	20 "
Counting-house boxes, entirely paper	35 "
——————, with brass rings	35 "
Court-plaster....................	35 "
Cow-hides, raw	10 "
—— ——, tanned................	35 "
Cowage or cowitch...............	20 "
Cowries (shells).......	free.
Crapes, silk (see silks.)	
Crash (see linens.)	
Cravats, in pieces or single, unmade, according to their material.	
Cravats........................	35 ℔ cent.
Cravat stiffeners.................	35 "
Crayons	30 "
Creas, cotton, (see cottons.)	
——, linen, (see linens.)	
Cream of tartar.................	10 cts. ℔ lb.
Cremnitz, white, (as white lead.)	
Crocus Colcottra	25 ℔ cent.
Crocus powder..................	20 "

	DUTY.
Crome yellow	25 ℔ cent.
Crowns, Leghorn hat	40 "
Crucibles, black lead	30 "
———, sand	25 "
Crystals, watch	40 "
———, glass, for seals (see glass.)	
———, of tin	20 "
———, orange, (see glass.)	
Cubebs	10 cts. ℔ lb.
Cudbear	10 ℔ cent.
Cummin seed	5 cts. ℔ lb.
Cupboard turns	35 ℔ cent.
Curls, hair	35 "
Curriers' knives	45 "
Currants	5 cts. ℔ lb.
Curtain rings	35 ℔ cent.
Custas, as manufactures of cottons.	
Cutch	10 "
Cutting knives	45 "
Cuttle-fish bone (sepia)	5 cts. ℔ lb.
Cut glassware, not otherwise specified	40 ℔ cent.
Cutlasses	35 "
Cutlery, of all kinds, except pocket, pen and jack-knives,	35 "

D.

	DUTY.
DAGGERS	35 ℔ cent.
Daguerreotype plates	35 "
Dates—green, ripe, or dried	2 cts. ℔ lb.
Dates, preserved in sugar or molasses	35 ℔ cent.
Decanters, cut glass	40 "
———, plain do	35 "
Demijohns, of half gallon or less	35 "
———, over half and not over three	35 "
Demijohns, over three	35 "
Dentifrice	50 "
Devonshire kerseys, (see wool.)	
Dextrine (comp. of farina and acids.	20 "
Diamonds	10 "
Diamonds, set	25 ℔ cent.
———, glaziers'	10 "
Diaper linen (see linens.)	
Diapers, cotton, (see cotton.)	
Dice, ivory or bone	50 "
Dimities and dimity muslin (see cottons.)	
Dimity furniture, dimity cambrics, and all other dimity (see cottons.)	
Directions for patent medicines	25 "
Dirks	35 "
Dishes, chafing, copper	35 "
———, ———, iron or tin	35 "
Distilled vinegar, medicinal	40 "
Dividers, brass, iron	35 "
———, silver	40 "
———, wood	35 "
Divi divi (a vegetable substance in a crude state, used for dyeing and tanning)	free.
Dog chains (see iron.)	
Dolls, of every description	35 ℔ cent.
Domets, a flannel (see flannels.)	
Dominoes, bone or ivory	50 "
———, bone or ivory, if any metal	50 "
Dowlas, (see linens.)	
Doyleys, cotton (see cottons.)	
———, linen (see linens.)	
———, woolen (see woolens.)	
Down, all kinds	30 "
Dragons' blood	10 cts. ℔ lb.
Drawing pencils, black lead	50 cts. per gross, and 30 ℔ cent.
——— ———, not black lead,	50 cts. per gross, and 30 "
Drawings	20 "
Draw knobs, of brass, iron, washed, gilt, or plated	35 "
Draw knobs, of brass and glass	40 "
———, entirely of cut glass	40 "
———, entirely of plain glass	35 "
———, ivory	35 "
———, bone	35 "

DUTY.

Drawing knives.................45 ℔ cent.
Drawers, Guernsey, worsted.......35 "
———, knit, without needle-work.35 "
———, silk, wove...............60 "
———, cotton, wove, bleached or colored.....................35 "
Dress goods, for women and children, in whole or part of wool, worsted, mohair, alpaca or goat's hair, gray or uncolored, value not over 30 cents per square yard,
4 cts. ℔ sq. yd. and 25 ℔ cent.
Dress goods, as above, over 30 cents per square yd..6 cts. ℔ sq.yd. and 30 "
Dress goods, as above, if stained, colored or printed, value not over 30 cents per square yard,
4 cts. ℔ sq. yd. and 30 "
Dress goods, as above, value over 30 cents per square yard,
6 cts. ℔ sq. yd. and 35 "
Dried pulp......................20 "
Drillings, linen (see linens.)
———, if cotton be a component material, subject to the regulations respecting cotton cloths.
Druggets, all.............. 25 cts. per sq. yd.
Drugs, dyeing, not otherwise enumerated, not crude ....20 ℔ cent.
Drugs, in a crude state, used in tanning or dyeing ....free.
Drugs, medicinal, not otherwise enumerated, in a crude state ....20 ℔ cent.
Duck sail, of cotton ....30 "
——, ravens, of hemp ....30 "
——, ———, of flax.............30 "
Dulce (seaweed.) ....10 ℔ ct. & $5 ℔ ton.
Dutch metal, in leaf.............10 ℔ cent.
Dust pans......................35 "
Dutch pink ....25 "
Dye woods ....free.
Dyeing drugs, and materials for composing dyes, crude, not otherwise enumerated ....free.

E.

DUTY.

EARTH, in oil ....$1 50 ℔ 100 lbs.
Earth, brown, red, blue, yellow, dry, as ochre.............. 50 c. "
Earthenware, (brown or common)..25 ℔ cent.
———, stone or crockery ware, all other, white, glazed, edged, printed, painted, dipped, cream color ....40 "
Ebony, unmanufactured...........free.
———, manufactures of...........35 ℔ cent.
———, green (or dyewood)........free.
Elastic garters, made of elastic wire, covered with leather, with metal clasps ....35 ℔ cent.
Elephants' teeth..................10 "
Elecampane ....20 "
Embroideries, all in gold or silver, fine or half fine, or other metal...35 "
Embroidery, if done by hand with a needle, and with thread of gold...35 "
Emeralds ....10 "
Emery, ore or rock................$6 ℔ ton.
———, manufactured, ground or pulverized........................1 ct. ℔ ℔.
Emery cloth, cotton...............35 ℔ cent.
Emetic, tartar, medicinal.........15 cts. ℔ ℔.
Enameled white................. 3 "
Engraved plates of steel, copper, wood, or other material..........25 ℔ cent.
Encaustic tiles ....35 "
Engravers' copper, prepared or polished..........................35 "
Engravers' scrapers................45 "
——— burnishers ....45 "
——— or lined apothecaries' glass measures, (see glass.)
Engravings, books of, bound or not.25 "
Epaulets, plated..................35 "
———, gilt, mi fin. ....35 "
———, worsted ....35 "
———, cotton..................35 "

DUTY.

Epaulets, of gold and silver ....35 ℔ cent.
Ergot.........................20 cts. ℔ ℔.
Escutcheons, silver ....40 ℔ cent.
——, brass, iron, gilt, or plated 35 "
Escutcheon pins...................35 "
Essence of almonds ....$1.50 ℔ ℔.
Essence of aspic, or d'aspic ....50 ℔ cent.
—— bergamot...............$1.00 ℔ ℔.
—— juniper.................25 cts. "
—— cajeput ....25 c. "
—— cloves ....$2.00 "
—— caraway.................50c. "
—— cassia ....$1.00 "
—— cinnamon.............$2.00 "
—— citronella ....50 "
—— cognac...............$4.00 ℔ oz.
—— cubebs...............$1.00 ℔ lb.
—— fennel ....50 "
—— valerian ....$1.50 "
—— fruit ....$2.50 "
—— lavender..............50 ℔ cent.
—— lemons ....50 c. ℔ ℔.
—— muscade, or nutmegs...50 ℔ cent.
—— mustard salad........$1.00 ℔ gal.
—— oranges..............50 cts. ℔ ℔.
—— origanum, or thyme, red.25 "
—— rosemary ....50 ℔ cent.
—— rose.................$1.50 ℔ oz.
—— rue....................50 ℔ cent
—— sabine................50 "
—— spruce................50 "
—— tyre...................50 "
—— ginger................50 "
—— peppermint............50 "
—— thyme, white ....30c. ℔ ℔.
Essences, extracts, toilet waters, cosmetics, hair oils, pomades, hair restoratives, hair dressings, hair dyes, tooth washes, dentifrices, tooth pastes, aromatic cachous, or other perfumes, cosmetics, by whatever name or names known, used, or applied as perfumes or applications to the hair, mouth, or skin ..50 ℔ cent.

DUTY.

Estopillas, linen (see flax.)
Etchings or engravings............20 ℔ cent.
Ethers, preparations or extracts, fluid, all not provided for.............$1 ℔ ℔.
Etoile, or stars for ornaments, gold, or mi fin........................35 ℔ cent.
Extract of belladonna.............40 "
—— Campeachy wood.......10 "
—— cicutæ.................40 "
—— colocynth..............40 "
—— elaterium..............40 "
—— gentian.................40 "
—— hyoscyamus ....40 "
—— indigo ....10 "
—— logwood ....10 "
—— annux vomica ....40 "
—— madder ....10 "
—— opium..................40 "
—— rhatania ....40 "
—— rhubarb ....40 "
—— stramonium............40 "
Extracts and decoctions of dyewoods, not otherwise provided for. 10 "
Extract, all other medicinal ...... 40 "
Eyes and rods for stairs...........35 "
——, bull's, a bean...............10 "
——, ——, glass ....35 "

F.

FALSE COLLARS...............35 ℔ cent.
Fans, palm leaf..................1c. each.
——, all others ....35 ℔ cent.
Fancy or perfumed shaving soaps, including Windsor soap and wash-balls..........10 cts. ℔ ℔. and 25 "
Fastenings, shutter or other, of copper, iron, brass, gilt, plated .....35 "
Fastenings of steel ....45 "
——, japanned..............40 "
Fearnought cloth, (see woolens.)
Feathers, ostrich, vulture, cock, or oth er feathers, ornamental, manufactured........................50 "

DUTY.

Feathers, ornamental, crude.......25 ℘ cent.
———, for beds................30 "
Feather beds....................20 "
Felt, patent adhesive, for ships' bottoms.........................free.
Felt, roofing.....................20 ℘ cent.
Felts, or hat bodies, made in whole or in part of wool, (see woolens.)
Feldspar........................20 "
Felting, hatters', (see wool.)
Fennel, essence of................50 c. ℘ lb.
Ferrets, cotton...................35 ℘ cent.
Ferri, rubigo.....................20 "
Fiddles..........................30 "
Fids............................30 "
Fifes, bone......................30 "
——, ivory......................30 "
——, of wood...................30 "
Figures, alabaster............ 10 "
———, brass................ 10 "
———, bronze............. 10 "
———, (such as used in churches)...................... 10 "
Figures, gold or silver........ 10 "
———, gilt or plated........ 10 "
———, marble.............. 10 "
———, plaster, if baked...... 10 "
———, ———, cast......... 10 "
(Statuary.)
Figs, green, ripe, or dried........5 cts. ℘ lb.
——, preserved in sugar or molasses.35 ℘ cent.
Fig blue.........................25 "
Filberts.........................3 cts. ℘ lb.
Files and file blanks, all not over 10 inches long.....10 cts. ℘ ℔. and 30 ℘ cent.
Files and file blanks, over 10 inches long...........6 cts. ℘ ℔. and 30 "
Filtering stones..................20 "
—————, unmanufactured...10 "
Finishing powders................20 "
Firearms, other than muskets and rifles..........................35 "
Fire crackers, per box of 40 packs, 80 to each pack, (and in same proportion for greater numbers)....$1 ℘ box.

DUTY.

Fire irons........................35 ℘ cent.
—— screens.....................35 "
—— wood.......................20 "
Fish, mackerel...................$2 ℘ bbl.
——, herring, pickled or salted.....$1 "
——, salmon.....................$3 "
——, all other, pickled, in bbls.....$1 50 "
——, all not in bbls., and not otherwise provided for...............½ ct. ℘ lb.
Fish, fresh, for daily consumption, foreign........................free.
Fish, all, in oil, not otherwise provided for........................30 ℘ cent.
—— glue, called isinglass.........30 "
—— hooks......................45 "
—— sauce......................35 "
—— skins, raw..................20 "
Fisheries of the United States and their territories, all products of..free.
Fishing lines, silk................50 ℘ cent.
Flageolets, wood.................30 "
————, bone or ivory.........30 "
Flannels, uncolored, all valued at 30 cts. per sq. yd. or less, 24 cts. ℘ ℔. and 30 "
Flannels, all valued above 30 cts. per sq. yd......24 cts. ℘ ℔. and 35 "
Flannels, all colored, printed, or plaided........24 cts. ℘ ℔. and 35 "
Flannels, all composed in part of silk..........................50 "
Flannels, composed in part of cotton...........24 cts. per ℔. and 35 "
Flasks, or bottles that come in gin cases..........................35 "
Flasks, powder, brass, copper, if no steel..........................35 "
Flasks, horn, entirely of..........35 "
Flat irons.......................1½ ct. ℘ lb.
Flats, for making hats or bonnets..30 ℘ cent.
Flax, manufactures of, or of which flax is a component part of chief value; valued not over 30 cts. per sq. yd..........................35 "

DUTY.

Flax, manufactures of, or of which flax is a component part of chief value; value over 30 cents per sq. yd. .... 40 ℘ cent.
Flax, manufactures of, or of which flax is a component part of chief value, not otherwise provided for. 40 "
Flax, thread .... 40 "
——, packed thread .... 40 "
—— twine .... 40 "
——, unmanufactured .... $15 ℘ ton.
——, tow of .... $5 "
Flaxseed (52 lbs. per bush.).... 16 cts. ℘ bush.
——— oil.......... 23 cts. ℘ gall.
Fleams .... 35 ℘ cent.
Fleshers' (knives) .... 45 "
Flies, Spanish, or cantharides .... 50 cts. ℘ ℔.
Flints .... 10 ℘ cent.
——, stone .... 10 "
——, ground.......... 10 "
Float files, not over 10 inches long, 10 cts. ℘ ℔. and 30 "
————, over 10 inches long, 6 cts. ℘ ℔. and 30 "
Flocks .... 3 cts. ℘ ℔.
Flor benzoin.......... 10 ℘ cent.
Florentine buttons, covered with bombazette over a metal form ... 30 "
Floss silk, and other similar silks, purified from the gum.......... 35 "
Floss cotton (see cotton thread).... 40 "
Flour, of wheat .... 20 "
——, of rye.......... 10 "
——, sago .... 1½ ct. ℘ lb.
Flower water, orange, (see Cologne water) .... 50 ℘ cent.
Flowers, artificial .... 50 "
———, crude, used exclusively in dyeing .... free.
Flowers, all medicinal .... 20 ℘ cent.
———, all not otherwise provided for.......... 10 "
Flutes, of wood .... 30 "
———, ivory or bone entirely ..... 30 "

DUTY.

Flushings, (see woolens.)
Foils, fencing, steel .... 45 ℘ cent.
Foil, copper .... 35 "
——, silver .... 40 "
——, tin .... 30 "
Fol. digitalis.......... 20 "
Forks, of gold or silver .... 40 "
Forks, wood .... 35 "
———, ivory, turtle shell, mother of pearl, deer horn, or bone handles, and iron or steel blades .... 35 "
Fossils .... 10 "
Fox-glove .... 20 "
Frames, or sticks for umbrellas or parasols, finished or not.......... 35 "
Frames, plated cruet.......... 35 "
———, quadrant .... 35 "
———, silver cruet .... 40 "
Frankfort black .... 25 "
Frankincense, a gum.......... 20 "
French green .... 30 "
Fringes, cotton.......... 35 "
———, wool .... 24 cts. per lb. and 40 "
———, merino .... 50 "
Frize, or ratteens, of wool, (see wool.)
Frizettes, (curls) hair .... 35 "
———, silk .... 50 "
Frosts, (glass).......... 20 "
Fruit ethers .... $2 50 ℘ ℔.
—— juice,.......... 25 ℘ cent.
Fruits, preserved in brandy or sugar. 35 "
——, preserved in their own juice. 25 "
——, pickled .... 35 "
——, green, ripe, or dried, not otherwise provided for.......... 10 "
Frying pans.......... 35 "
Fullers' boards.......... 35 "
——— earth .... $3 ℘ ton.
Fulminates, or fulminating powders. 30 ℘ cent.
Furniture, coach and harness ...... 35 "
Furniture, household, not otherwise specified.......... 35 "
Furs, undressed, all kinds of, on the skin .... 10 "

DUTY.

Fur, dressed, all on the skin........20 ℔ cent.
—— hats, or caps of..............35 "
—— hat bodies, or felts...........35 "
Furs, hatters,' not on the skin......20 "
Fusil oil, or amylic alcohol........$2 ℔ gal.
Fustic ....free.
Fur muffs or tippets, or other manufactures, not specified...........35 ℔ cent.

G.

GALANGA ....20 ℔ cent.
Gallengal, or gallengal root ....20 "
Galloons, gold or silver, fine or half fine ....35 "
Galls, nut........................free.
Gambia ....10 ℔ cent.
Gamboge, medicinal gum..........10 "
Gamboge, refined ....10 "
Game bags, leather...............35 "
—— ——, twine ....35 "
Garance, or madder, prepared......free.
Garancene (extract of madder).....10 ℔ cent.
Garnets, glass, (see glass.)
———, a precious stone..........10 "
———, imitation of, a composition.40 "
———, hardware................35 "
Garden seeds, not otherwise specified ....30 "
Garters, elastic, made of wire, covered with leather, with or without metal clasps ....35 "
Garters, India rubber, with clasps..35 "
Gas retorts, of common earthen or stoneware, not ornamented ......25 "
Gauze, cotton, (see cottons.)
Gelatine.........................35 "
Gems ....10 "
——, set.........................25 "
Gentian, or gentian root..........20 "
German silver, manufactured......40 "
Gig hames (see saddlery)..........35 "
—— springs ....35 "
—— handles (see saddlery) ....35 "
Gilt bases ....35 "

DUTY.

Gilt capitals.....................35 ℔ cent.
—— chains ....35 "
—— ———, if mock jewelry ......25 "
—— ear-rings....................25 "
—— paper........................35 "
—— pins ....35 "
—— ——, if mock jewelry.........25 "
—— rings ....35 "
—— ——, if mock jewelry ....25 "
—— ware, silver or gold..........40 "
—— ware, of other metals.........35 "
—— wire..........................35 "
—— watch chains ....25 "
—— watch seals ....25 "
—— watch keys..................35 "
—— wood.........................35 "
Gilt studs, if mock jewelry ....25 "
Gimlets ....45 "
Gimps, cotton....................35 "
———, silk......... ....50 "
———, thread, linen..............40 "
———, wire, being a component part of chief value...................35 "
Gin, 50 degrees.............$2 00 ℔ gallon.
——, 51 " .... 2 04 "
——, 52 " .... 2 08 "
——, 53 " .... 2 12 "
——, 54 " .... 2 16 "
——, 55 " .... 2 20 "
——, 56 " .... 2 24 "
——, 57 " .... 2 28 "
——, 58 " .... 2 32 "
——, 59 " .... 2 36 "
——, 60 " .... 2 40 "
——, 61 " .... 2 44 "
——, 62 " .... 2 48 "
——, 63 " .... 2 52 "
——, 64 " .... 2 56 "
——, 65 " .... 2 60 "
——, 66 " .... 2 64 "
——, 67 " .... 2 68 "
——, 68 " .... 2 72 "
——, 69 " .... 2 76 "
——, 70 " .... 2 80 "

DUTY.

Gin, if under 50 degrees in strength, and value over $4 per gallon....50 ℔ cent.
Gin, all imitations of, to pay as genuine.
Ginger, ground ....8 cts. ℔ lb.
———, preserved and pickled.....50 ℔ cent.
———, roots....................5 cts. ℔ lb.
———, essence of ....50 ℔ cent.
Gin cases, with bottles in them, the cases pay......................35 "
and the bottles.................35 "
Ginghams, as cottons .... "
Ginseng.........................20 "
Girandoles.......................40 "
Glass, of antimony................20 "
———, old broken, fit only to be remanufactured..................free.
Glass wares, of cut glass...........40 ℔ cent.
Do. do. all others not specially mentioned, not cut ....35 "
Glass, apothecaries' vials and bottles, not exceeding the capacity of six ounces each ....35 "
Glass, apothecaries' vials, above six ounces, and not exceeding sixteen ounces each....................35 "
Glass bottles, black, not filled......35 "
——— ———, filled with preserves..40 "
——— buttons, cut, entirely of.....30 "
——— jars, filled with preserves.....40 "
——— ———, plain, not filled.........35 "
———, all fluted, rolled, or rough plate glass, not including crown, cylinder, broad or common window glass, not over 10 by 15 inches..................$\frac{3}{4}$ ct. ℔ squ. foot.
Glass, as above, over 10 by 15 and not over 16 by 24 in ..1 ct. "
Glass, as above, over 16 by 24 inches, and not over 24 by 30 inches ....$1\frac{1}{2}$ ct. "
Glass, as above, above 24 by 30 inches ....2 cts. "
Provided, that all as above, weighing over one pound per square foot, shall pay an additional duty on the excess at the same rates herein imposed.

DUTY.

Glass, all cast polished plate glass, unsilvered, not over 10 by 15 inches...........3 cts. ℔ squ. foot.
Glass, as above, over 10 by 15 but not over 16 by 24 in ..5 cts. "
Glass, as above, over 16 by 24 but not over 24 by 30 inch.8 cts. "
Glass, as above, above 24 by 30 but not over 24 by 60 in.25 cts. "
Glass, as above, above 24 by 60 inches................50 cts. "
Glass, all cast polished plate glass, silvered, or looking glass plates, not over 10 by 15 inches................4 cts. "
Glass, as above, over 10 by 15 but not over 16 by 24 inch.6 cts. "
Glass, as above, over 16 by 24 but not over 24 by 30 inch.10 cts. "
Glass, as above, over 24 by 30 but not over 24 by 60 inch.35 cts. "
Glass, as above, over 24 by 60 inches.................60 cts. "
Provided, that no looking glass plates, or plate glass silvered when framed, shall pay a less rate of duty than that imposed on similar glass of like description not framed, but shall pay in addition thereto 30 ℔ cent. for the frames.
Glasses, hour ....35 ℔ cent.
———, looking, with paper and wood frames, (see glass plate, silvered.)
Glass, paintings on, not otherwise specified........................40 "
Glass plates, or disks, unwrought, for optical instruments..........10 "
Glass shades, for time-pieces or mantel ornaments...................35 "
Glass, cut, all wares of............40 "

	DUTY.
Glass, all articles of, not specified, plain or moulded	35 ℔ cent.
Glass, plain or moulded, weighing under 8 ounces, except tumblers	35 "
Glass, cut, ornaments for chandeliers, &c	40 "
Glass tumblers, plain and moulded	35 "
—— articles, plain or moulded	35 "
——, watch, or watch crystals	40 "
——, pressed	35 "
——, colored	40 "
——, engraved	40 "
——, painted	40 "
——, printed	40 "
——, gilt	40 "
——, stained	40 "
——, silvered	40 "
——, Bohemian	40 "
——, porcelain	40 "
Glass spectacles	40 "
—— pebbles, for spectacles	40 "
——, all manufactures of, or of which glass is a component material, not otherwise provided for	40 "
Glass bottles, filled with preserves	40 "
——, jars, filled with preserves	40 "
——, all articles not specified, connected with other materials so as to prevent its being weighed	40 "
Glaziers' diamonds	10 "
Globes	35 "
Gloves, angora	35 "
———, worsted	35 "
———, cotton	35 "
———, linen	35 "
———, men's leather	50 "
———, women's leather habit	50 "
———, children's leather habit	50 "
———, women's leather, extra demi length	50 "
Gloves, children's, extra demi length	50 "
———, hair	30 "
Glue, isinglass	30 "
Glue	20 "

	DUTY.
Glycerine (med. prep.)	30 ℔ cent.
Goats' skins, raw	10 "
——— skins, tanned	25 "
Goncallo wood	20 "
Gold epaulets	35 "
——, all articles composed wholly or part of, not otherwise specified	40 "
Gold beaters' brine	free.
———— moulds	10 ℔ cent.
———— skins	10 "
—— coin or bullion	free.
—— dust	free.
—— embroideries	35 ℔ cent.
—— or silver lace, even if mi fin.	35 "
Gold leaf, and per package of 500 leaves	$1 50 ℔ package.
——, muriate of, (chem. prep.)	20 ℔ cent.
—— ornaments, made by spreading gold leaf on very thin paper	40 "
Gold, oxide of	20 "
——— paper, in sheets, strips, or other forms	40 "
Gold size	20 "
—— shell, for painting	35 "
—— studs	25 "
Golo shoes, or clogs, wood	35 "
—— shoes, or clogs, leather	35 "
Gouges	45 "
Gowns	35 "
Gown patterns, wool being a component part (see wool.)	
Grains tawed or tanned (see leather)	25 "
——— of Paradise	20 "
Grain tin	20 "
Granella, or grana, cochineal	free.
Granulated tin	20 ℔ cent.
Granza, or madder	free.
Grapes	20 ℔ cent.
Grass bags	30 "
——— cable or cordage, untarred	3½ cts. ℔ lb.
——— cloth	30 ℔ cent.
——— and cotton cloth	35 "
Grass flats, braids or plaits, for making hats or bonnets	30 "

	DUTY.
Grass hats or bonnets	40 ℔ cent.
Grasshopper springs	35 "
Grass, Sisal	$15 ℔ ton.
—— mats, of flags (see mats.)	
—— rope, untarred	$3\frac{1}{2}$ cts. ℔ lb.
Grease	10 ℔ cent.
Green turtle	20 "
Green vitriol	$\frac{1}{2}$ c. ℔ lb.
Gridirons	35 ℔ cent.
Grindstones, finished	20 "
————, rough or unfinished	10 "
Guava jelly, or paste	50 "
Gunny bags and cloth, (see cotton bagging.)	
Guano	free.
——— imitation of	free.
Guinea grains	20 ℔ cent.
Guitars	30 "
Guitar strings, gut	30 "
Guimauve, or camomile	20 "
Gum aloes	6 c. ℔ lb.
Gum benzoin, or Benjamin	10 "
——, Senegal, Arabic, tragacanth, Barbary, East India, Jedda, amber	20 ℔ cent.
Gum mastic	50 c. ℔ lb.
Gum copal, and other gums and resinous substances, used for the same or similar purposes as copal	10 "
Gum shellac	10 "
Gum, all other resinous substances not specified, in a crude state	20 ℔ cent.
Gum, do. do. not do	20 "
Gum substitute, burnt flour and starch	20 "
Gum sandrac, kowrie and damar	10 cts. ℔ lb.
Gum elastic bougies	35 ℔ cent.
———— catheters	35 "
———— injection bags	35 "
———— nipple shields	35 "
———— pessaries	35 "
———— setons	35 "
———— stomach tubes	35 "
Guns	35 "
Gun locks	45 ℔ cent.
Gunpowder, value less than 20 cts. per pound	6 cts. ℔ lb. and 20 "
Gunpowder, value over 20 cts. per pound	10 cts. per pound, and 20 "
Gun wadding of paper	35 "
Gutta percha, manufactured	40 "
Gutta percha, unmanufactured	10 "
Guts, sheeps', salted	20 "
Gypsum, or plaster of Paris	free.

H.

	DUTY.
HACKLES, flax	45 ℔ cent.
————, hemp	45 "
Hair of alpaca, goat, or other like animals, unmanufactured, value at the last place of shipment, exclusive of charges at such port, 12c. per pound or less	3 cts. ℔ lb.
Hair of alpaca, goat, or other like animals, unmanufactured, value as above, over 12 and not over 24c. per pound	6 "
Hair of alpaca, goat, or other like animals, unmanufactured, value, as above, over 24c. per pound, and not over 32c. per pound,	10c. ℔ lb. and 10 ℔ cent.
Hair, as above, value over 32c. per pound	12c. ℔ lb. and 10 "
Hair of alpaca, goat, or other like animals, unmanufactured, imported in such state, by the admixture of dirt, etc., as to reduce it in value. (See proviso in wool.)	
Hair, all other manufactures of, not provided for	30 "
Hair, made up for head-dresses	40 "
——, prepared for head-dresses	35 "
—— nets	40 "
—— cloth	30 "
—— curled, for beds	20 "

	DUTY.
Hair braids, for the head	35 ℘ cent.
—— belts	35 "
—— brooms	35 "
—— bracelets, chains, ringlets, and curls	35 "
Hair, hogs	1c. ℘ ℔.
Hair, human, prepared for use	30 ℘ cent.
——, ——, manufactured	40 "
—— gloves	30 "
——, unmanufactured, human	20 "
——, cleaned, not otherwise provided for	30 "
Hair, horse, cleaned	10 "
——, horse, long, used for weaving, cleansed or not	free.
Hair pins	35 ℘ cent.
—— powder, perfumed, all others not specified	50 "
Hair powder, not perfumed	50 "
—— seating	30 "
Hair, other, raw	free.
Hair pencils	35 ℘ cent.
Halter chains (see iron.)	
—— rings (see saddlery)	35 "
Hames, wood	35 "
Hammers, blacksmiths'	2½ c. ℘ ℔.
——, all others, if no steel	35 ℘ cent.
Hams, bacon	2 c. ℘ ℔.
Handkerchiefs, linen, (see linens.)	
——, bandanna and choppa (see silks.)	
Handkerchiefs, silk (see silks.)	
——, cotton (see cottons.)	
——, Madras (see cottons.)	
Handles for chests	35 ℘ cent.
Hangers	35 "
Hangings, paper	35 "
Hares' hair or fur	20 "
Hare skins, undressed	10 "
—— skins, dressed	20 "
Harlaem oil	50 "
Harness	35 "
—— furniture	35 "
Harp strings, gut	30 "

	DUTY.
Harp strings, wire	35 ℘ cent.
Harps and harpsichords	30 "
Hartshorn, spirits of	40 "
Hatchets	45 "
Hat bodies, cotton	35 "
——, in whole or in part wool, and wool of chief value	25 "
Hats, Leghorn	40 "
Hat linings, cotton, as cottons	"
Hats of chip, straw, or grass	40 "
——, cotton cloth, complete with the exception of the lining and band	40 "
Hats of wool......24 cts. ℘ ℔. and	35 "
Hats, fur	35 "
——, leather	40 "
——, palm leaf	40 "
——, rattan	40 "
——, japanned	40 "
——, silk, men's	60 "
Hats, Panama, Manilla, Leghorn, Naples, or elsewhere, composed of satin-straw, chip, grass, rattan, willow, or any vegetable substance, hair or whalebone, or any other material not specified	40 "
Hautboys	30 "
Havresacks, of leather	35 "
Hay knives	45 "
Head-dresses, ornaments for	35 "
Head matter, if fisheries of the United States	free.
Head pieces, for stills	35 ℘ cent.
Hearth rugs, all (see mats.)	
Hellebore root	20 "
Hemlock	20 "
Hemp seed	½ ct. ℘ ℔.
—— —— oil	23c. ℘ gal.
——, manufactures of, or of which hemp is a component part of chief value, valued not over 30c. per square yard	35 ℘ cent.
Hemp, manufactures of, or of which hemp is a component part of chief value, value over 30c. per sq. yd.	40 "

DUTY.

Hemp, unmanufactured..........$40 ℘ ton.
——, Manilla, unmanufactured...$25 "
——, sun, " ...$15 "
——, Indian, " ...$25 "
——, manufactures all of, or of which hemp is a component material of chief value, not otherwise provided for..................30 ℘ cent.
Hemp, codilla, or tow of hemp ....$10 ℘ ton.
——, Indian, (crude drug)........20 ℘ cent.
Henbane........................20 "
Herrings, pickled, in barrels.......$1 ℘ bbl.
————, pickled, in kegs.........$1 "
————, smoked or dry............½c. ℘ ℔.
Hides, raw........................10 ℘ cent.
——, salted or pickled...........10 "
——, tanned (sole leather).......35 "
Hinges, brass, copper.............35 "
———, silver or gold............40 "
Hobby horses, wood..............35 "
——— ———, paper.............35 "
Hods, coal, iron...................35 "
——— ——, copper...............35 "
Hoes, if any steel..................45 "
Hoffman's anodyne...............50 cts. ℘ ℔.
Hones...........................20 ℘ cent.
Honey..........................20c. ℘ gal.
——— water....................50 ℘ cent.
Hooks, fish......................45 "
——— and eyes, all...............35 "
———, reaping..................45 "
Hoops, iron, fit for use............35 "
Hops...........................5 cts. ℘ ℔.
Horn combs.....................35 ℘ cent.
—— tips.........................10 "
—— plates, for lanterns..........10 "
Horns...........................10 "
Hose, cotton, bleached or colored..35 "
——, worsted....................35 "
——, silk, sewed.................60 "
——, leather....................35 "
——, linen thread...............35 "
Hosiery, wool....20 cts. ℘ ℔. and 30 "
Household effects, old, and in use of persons or families from foreign countries, if used abroad by them, and not intended for any other person, or for sale.............free.
Household furniture.............35 ℘ cent.
——— ——— of cedar, granadilla, ebony, mahogany, rose and satin wood....................35 "
Hungary water (cosmetic).........50 "
Hyacinth roots...................30 "
Hydriodate of potash...........75 cts. ℘ ℔.
Hydrometers, of glass.............35 ℘ cent.
It is understood that those which come from France have no metal connected with them.
And that those which come from England have brass as a component part: this being so, they will be subject to a duty of...........35 "

I.

ICE............................free.
Imitation of precious stones, glass..40 ℘ cent.
Implements of trade of persons arriving in the United States......free.
India rubber in bottles, or sheets, or otherwise unmanufactured......10 ℘ cent.
India rubber, milk of............20 "
———— oil cloth or other manufactured articles, composed wholly or in part of India rubber, not otherwise provided for......35 "
India rubber cloth...............35 "
———— and silk, or silk and other material combined........50 "
India rubber shoes and boots......35 "
———— suspenders, (see suspenders)......................35 "
India rubber webbing............35 "
Indian meal.....................10 "
——— hemp, (crude drug)........20 "
Indian red.......................25 "

	DUTY.
Indigo	free.
——, carmined	20 ℘ cent.
Indispensables, or bags, leather	35 "
——, cotton	35 "
——, merino stuff	50 "
——, silk	50 "
——, bead	50 "
——, bead, with clasps	50 "
Ink	35 "
Ink powder	35 "
Ink stands, leather	35 "
——, paper, with glass	40 "
——, silver	40 "
——, wood	35 "
——, metal, (iron)	35 "
——, glass, plain	30 "
——, glass, cut	35 "
Instruments, philosophical	40 "
——, musical	30 "
——, philosophical, not specially imported, duty according to the materials they are composed of.	
Instruments, musical, brass	30 "
Inventions, models of (under restriction)	free.
Iodine (crude)	50 cts. ℘ ℔.
——, salts of	15 ℘ cent.
——, resublimed	75 cts. ℘ ℔.
Ipecac, ipecacuanha	50 "
Iridium	free.
Iris root	free.
Iron andirons, cast	1½ cts. ℘ ℔.
—— anvils	2½ "
—— anchors, and parts of	2¼ "
—— axles, "	2½ "
——, band, hoop and scroll, from ½ to 6 inches wide, and not less than ⅛ inch thick	1¼ "
Iron, as above, from ½ to 6 inches wide, under ⅛ inch thick, and not under No. 20 wire gauge	1½ "
Iron, as above, thinner than No. 20 wire gauge	1¾ "
Iron bars, rolled or hammered, comprising flats, not less than one or more than six inches wide, nor less than ⅝ or more than 2 inches thick	1 ct. ℘ ℔.
Iron, round, not less than ¾ or more than 2 inches in diameter	1 "
Iron, square, not less than ¾ or more than 2 inches square	1 "
Iron bars, rolled, or hammered, comprising flats, less than ⅝ or more than 2 inches thick, or less than 1 inch or more than 6 inches wide	1½ "
Iron, round, less than ¾ or more than 2 inches in diameter	1½ "
Iron, square, less than ¾ or more than 2 inches square	1½ "
Provided, that all iron in slabs, blooms, loops, or other forms, less finished than bars and more advanced than pig iron, except castings, shall pay as iron in bars.	
Provided, that none of the above iron shall pay a less rate of duty than	35 ℘ cent.
Iron bars, for railroads, or inclined planes, made to pattern, ready to lay down	60c. ℘ 100 lbs.
Iron boiler plates or other plate iron, not less than 3-16 inch thick	1½c. ℘ ℔.
Iron butts, cast	2½ "
—— bolts, wrought	2½ "
—— bed-screws	2½ "
—— brads, cut, not over 16 ounces per thousand	2½ cts. per M.
Iron brads, cut, over 16 ounces per thousand	3 cts. ℘ lb.
Iron cables, or chains, or parts of	2½ "
Iron castings, all not enumerated	30 ℘ cent.
Iron chains.. / —— trace... / —— halter.. / —— fence.. } of wire, or rods' not less than ¼ in. in diameter.	2½ cts. ℘ ℔.
—— chains, as above, less than one-quarter of an inch in diameter, and not under No. 9 wire guage,	3 "

	DUTY.
Iron chains, as above, under No. 9 wire gauge	35 ⅌ cent.
Iron, coated with zinc or any metal by electric batteries	2½ cts. ⅌ lb.
Iron flues, wrought	2½ "
—— gas pipe, cast	1½ "
—— gas tubes, wrought	2½ "
——, galvanized	2½ "
——, hatters'	1½ "
—— hinges, cast	2½ "
—— hollow ware, glazed	3½ "
————, tinned	3½ "
Iron, cast	1½ "
—— hinges, wrought	2½ "
—— hammers, blacksmith	2½ "
——, malleable, casting, not otherwise provided for	2½ "
Iron, malleable	2½ "
——, mill wrought	2 "
——, crank wrought	2 "
—— manufactures of all kinds, not otherwise enumerated	35 ⅌ cent.
Iron nails, cut	1½ ct. ⅌ lb.
————, wrought	2½ "
————, horse-shoe	5 "
Iron nuts, wrought	2 "
——, old scrap, fit only to be remanufactured	$8 ⅌ ton.
Iron, pig	$9 "
—— rivets, wrought	2½ c. ⅌ lb.
—— railroad chairs, wrought	2 "
—— sad	1½ "
—— stoves	1½ "
—— stove plates	1½ "
—— steam pipes, cast	1½ "
—— slit rods, not otherwise provided for	1½ "
Iron spikes, cut	1½ "
————, wrought	2½ "
Iron sledges	2½ "
—— steam tubes, wrought	2½ "
—— sprigs, cut, not over 16 ounces per thousand	2½ cts. ⅌ M
Iron sprigs, cut, over 16 oz. per M.	3c. ⅌ lb.
Iron sheets, smoothed or polished	3 cts. ⅌ lb.
————, common or black, not thinner than No. 20 wire gauge	1¼ "
Iron sheets, common or black, less than 20, not less than No. 25 wire gauge	1½ "
Iron sheets, common or black, less than No. 25 wire gauge	1¾ "
Iron screws, wood, 2 inches or over in length	8 "
Iron screws, wood, less than two inches in length	11 "
Iron screws, except wood	35 ⅌ cent.
——, tailors' irons	1½ cts. ⅌ lb.
—— tacks, cut, not over 16 ounces per thousand	2½ cts. ⅌ M.
Iron tacks, cut, over 16 ounces per thousand	3 cts. ⅌ lb.
Iron vessels, cast, not otherwise provided for	1½ "
Iron wire, bright, coppered or tinned, drawn and finished, not more than ¼ inch in diameter, nor less than No. 16 wire gauge,	2 cts. ⅌ lb. & 15 ⅌ cent.
Iron wire, as above, over 16 and not over 25 wire gauge,	3½ cts. ⅌ lb. and 15 "
Iron wire, over 25 wire gauge,	4 cts. ⅌ lb. and 15 "
Provided wire, covered with cotton, silk, or other material, shall pay 5 cts. ⅌ lb. in addition.	
Iron water pipe, cast	1½ ct. ⅌ lb.
———— tubes, wrought	2½ "
Iron washers, wrought, ready punched	2 "
Iron, wrought, for ships' (weight) of each 25 pounds or more	2 "
Iron, wrought, for locomotive tire, parts of	3 "
Iron, wrought, for steam engine and parts of, each 25 pounds or more	2 "

DUTY.

Iron, all rolled or hammered, not otherwise provided for.........1¼ cts. ℔ lb.
Iron castors ....35 ℔ cent.
—— combs, curry................35 "
—— cutting knives, for cutting hay or straw......................35 "
Iron cutting knives, if any steel....45 "
Iron ferrules, piano...............35 "
—— filings ....35 "
—— hoops, made fit for use ....35 "
—— liquor ....10 "
—— nails.........................35 "
——, manufactures of, partly finished, pay the same rate of duty as if entirely finished..............35 "
Iron scythes, part steel............45 "
—— shot..........................30 "
—— shovels, part steel............45 "
—— sickles, part steel ....45 "
—— spades, part steel ....45 "
—— squares, marked on one side, 3 cts. ℔ lb. and ....30 "
Iron squares, all other . 30 ℔ cent. and..........................6 cts. ℔ lb.
Iron square wire, used for the manufacture of stretchers for umbrellas, and cut in pieces not exceeding the length used therefor .....35 ℔ cent.
Iron, taggers'....................30 "
——, sulphate of ....½ ct. ℔ lb.
—— wire, annealed, to pay duty the same as other iron wire.
Iron, manufactures of, not otherwise provided for..................35 ℔ cent.
Isinglass ....30 "
Issue peas ....40 "
—— plaster ....40 "
Istle, or tampico fibre, ...1 ct. ℔ lb.
Ivory ....10 ℔ cent.
—— chessmen, dice, draughts, chess and bagatelle balls.............50 "
—— combs ....35 "
——, manufactured, not provided for 35 "
——, unmanufactured ....10 "

DUTY.

Ivory black......................25 ℔ cent.
—— parallel rules, (not mounted). 35 "
—— protractors.................35 "
—— scales......................35 "
—— sectors.....................35 "
—— nuts ....10 "
——, vegetable, manufactures of....35 "

J.

JACKS, a part of piano-fortes .....35 ℔ cent.
——, clothiers'...............35 "
Jalap ....50 c. ℔ lb.
Japanned wares, of all kinds, not provided for...................40 ℔ cent.
Jars, black glass, not exceeding one quart ....35 "
Jars, black glass, exceeding one qt. 35 "
Jessamine, or jasmine, oil of.......50 "
Jellies, and all other similar preparations ....50 "
Jerk beef........................1 ct. ℔ lb.
Jet, real.........................35 ℔ cent.
——, if composition ....35 "
—— stones.......................35 "
Jet bead ....50 "
Jewelry ....25 "
——, false, so called...........25 "
Joints, India ....35 "
Jostic, or jos light ....20 "
Juglandium, oil of................50 "
Juice of limes....................10 "
—— of lemons ....10 "
—— of oranges ....20 "
Juniper berries ....10 "
—— plants ....30 "
Junk, old.......................free.
Jute, manufactured, or of which jute is a component material of chief value, value 30 cents per square yard or less..................35 ℔ cent.
Jute, manufactured, or of which jute is a component material of chief value, value over 30 cts. per sq. yd. 40 "

	DUTY.
Jute, butts	$6 ℔ ton.
——, manufactures of, not otherwise provided for	30 ℔ cent.
Jute, unmanufactured	$15 ℔ ton.
——, carpeting	6½c. ℔ sq. yd.

K.

KALEIDOSCOPES	35 ℔ cent.
Kaoline	$5 ℔ ton.
Kelp	free.
Kentledge, (see iron.)	
Kermes (mineral)	10 ℔ cent.
Kersey ratteen, woolen cloth (see wool.)	
Kettles, brass, in nests	35 "
———, cast iron	1½ c. ℔ lb.
———, copper	35 ℔ cent.
Keys, watch, of gold	25 "
——, ——, of silver	25 "
——, all other, of iron, brass, or copper	35 "
Keys, all other, of gold or silver	40 "
Kilmarnock caps, worsted	50 "
King's yellow	25 "
Kirschenwasser (see arrack.)	
Knitting needles	25 "
Knives, cutting (meaning those for hay or straw)	45 "
Knives, curriers'	45 "
———, drawing	45 "
———, flesh	45 "
———, silver or gold	40 "
———, pen, jack, and pocket	50 "
Knobs, brass, gilt, plated, or washed, iron, or copper	35 "
Knobs, cut glass	40 "
———, glass, not cut	35 "
———, ——, with brass, iron, or composition shanks	40 "
Knockers	35 "
Knots and stars, of gold and silver, fine or half fine	35 "
Krems white, or white lead	3 cts. ℔ lb.
Kreosote	20 ℔ cent.

L.

	DUTY.
LABELS, printed	25 ℔ cent.
Labels, decanter or other, gilt or plated	35 "
Labels, decanter or other, gold or silver	40 "
Lac dye	free.
— marine (artificial gum)	20 ℔ cent.
— spirits, prepared dye	free.
— sulphur	free.
Lace, bobbinet	35 ℔ cent.
——, coach (cotton)	35 "
——, —— (worsted)	50 "
——, gold	35 "
——, plated, or mi fin	35 "
——, silver	35 "
——, silk	60 "
—— shawls, if sewed, (cotton)	35 "
—— edgings, cotton	35 "
—— insertings, cotton	35 "
—— gimp, cotton	35 "
—— quillings, cotton	35 "
—— tatting, cotton	35 "
—— purling, cotton	35 "
—— bobbinet veils, cotton (Cotton.)	35 "
—— chemisettes, not trimmed (Cotton.)	35 "
—— collars, not trimmed (Cotton.)	35 "
—— pelerines, not trimmed (Cotton.)	35 "
—— collarettes, not trimmed (Cotton.)	35 "
—— canezous, not trimmed (Cotton.)	35 "
—— handkerchiefs (Cotton.)	35 "
—— caps, not trimmed (Cotton.)	35 "
—— ——, made up and trimmed (Cotton.)	35 "
Lace collars, trimmed (Cotton.)	35 "
—— collarettes, trimmed (Cotton.)	35 "
—— pelerines, trimmed (Cotton.)	35 "
—— chemisettes, trimmed (Cotton.)	35 "
—— cazenous, trimmed (Cotton.)	35 "
—— handkerchiefs, trimmed (Cotton.)	35 "
—— collars and capes, ready to wear (Cotton.)	35 "
Lace pelerines (Cotton.)	35 "

DUTY.

Lace veils, cotton................35 ℔ cent.
Laces, all thread.................30 "
Lace, thread insertings...........30 "
Laces, gold and silver, invoiced fin, mi fin, argent fin, and argent mi fin.........................35 "
Laced boots or bootees...........35 "
Lacets, or lacings, silk............50 "
————, if cotton.......35 "
Lacquered ware..................35 "
Ladies' worked caps, trimmed, cotton............................35 "
Ladles, gilt on copper............35 "
———, gilt on silver.............40 "
———, gold or silver............40 "
———, iron, tin, Britannia, brass or copper........................35 "
Ladle heads.....................35 "
Lake (water colors)..............35 "
——, drop, " ....35 "
—— paints......................25 "
Lampblack......................20 "
Lamp hooks.....................35 "
—— pulleys, brass, copper, or iron...........................35 "
—— pulleys, wood..............35 "
Lamps, brass, copper, or tin.......35 "
———, entirely of plain glass.....35 "
———, cut glass.................40 "
———, with brass pillars.........35 "
Lancets.........................35 "
Lancet cases, shagreen paper......35 "
———— leather.....35 "
Lantern leaves, or horn plates.....10 "
Lanterns, tin, gilt, plated, brass, pewter, or copper..................35 "
Lapis, calaminaris, (calamine)......free.
———, infernalis, preparations.....20 ℔ cent.
———, tutia, oxide of zinc........$1\frac{3}{4}$ cts. ℔ lb.
Lard............................2 "
Larding pins....................35 ℔ cent.
Lasting, woven or madé in patterns, of such size and shape and form, and cut in such manner as to be fit for buttons, shoes, or bootees excusively, and not combined with India rubber...................10 ℔ cent.
Latches, iron, brass, gilt, plated, washed, or copper..............35 "
Lath............................20 "
Latten, brass...................35 "
Laudanum.......................40 "
Laurel, oil of...................20 cts. ℔ lb.
Lavender, essence of, double or single distilled....................50 ℔ cent.
Lavender, dry, flower of..........20 "
———, flower...................20 "
———, oil of....................50 "
——— water..................50 "
Lawn, cotton, (see cotton.)
———, linen, (see linen.)
———, or long lawn, linen, (see linen.)
Lead, all manufactures of, not otherwise specified.................35 "
Lead casts......................35 "
——, in bars....................2 cts. ℔ lb.
——, black.....................$10 ℔ ton.
——, powder of black............20 ℔ cent.
Lead combs.....................35 "
—— pots, black.................35 "
——, in pigs,....................2 ct. ℔ lb.
——, old, fit only to be remanufactured........................$1\frac{1}{2}$ "
Lead, sugar of...................4 "
——, red, dry or ground in oil.....3 "
——, nitrate of..................3 "
——, red........................3 "
Lead in sheets...................$2\frac{3}{4}$ "
—— shot.......................$2\frac{3}{4}$ "
——, toys.......................50 ℔ cent.
——, acetate....................20 cts. ℔ lb.
——, white, dry or ground in oil...3 "
—— pipes.......................$2\frac{3}{4}$ "
—— ore.........................$1\frac{1}{2}$ "
—— in any other form not specified.35 ℔ cent.
Leaders, leather..................35 "
———, worsted.................50 "
Leaf, Dutch metal................10 "

DUTY.

Leaf, gold, per package of 500 leaves ....$1 50 ℘ package.
Leaves, medicinal, in a crude state . 20 ℘ cent.
———, silver, of 500 leaves per package................75 cts. ℘ package.
Leather bracelets, elastic..........35 ℘ cent.
——— mitts ....50 "
——— garters, elastic ....35 "
———, and all manufactures thereof, or of which it is the material of chief value, not otherwise specified 35 "
Leather, bend....................35 "
———, caps of..................35 "
———, hats of..................40 "
——— bottles..................35 "
——— braces or suspenders......35 "
———, sole....................35 "
———, upper, (tanned calfskins)..30 "
———, ———, not otherwise specified ....25 "
Leather, patent (or japanned) or enameled ....35 "
Leaves for dyeing, in a crude state. free.
——— not used in dyeing, not otherwise provided for.............20 ℘ cent.
Leaves, boucho.................10 cts. ℘ ℔.
———, palm ....free.
———, medicinal ....20 ℘ cent.
Leeches ....free.
Lees, wine, crystallized, or crude tartar, or argols ....6 cts. ℘ ℔.
Leghorn hats or bonnets, and all hats or bonnets of straw, chip or grass, 40 ℘ cent.
Leghorn flats ....30 "
——— braids ....30 "
——— crowns or brims.........30 "
——— plaits...................30 "
Lemons, in bulk ....25 "
———, in boxes, barrels, or casks. 25 "
Lemon juice.....................10 "
———, oil of..................50 cts. ℘ ℔.
——— peel ....10 ℘ cent.
Lemon, essence of...............50 cts. ℘ ℔.
Leno, linen (see flax.)

DUTY.

Leno, muslin (see cottons.)
Leopard skins, raw...............10 ℘ cent.
———, dressed............20 "
Lima bark.......................20 "
Lime ....10 "
———, borate of..................5 cts. ℘ ℔.
———, chloride of ....30 cts. ℘ 100 lbs.
———, white ....3 cts. ℘ ℔.
Limes...........................25 ℘ cent.
Lime juice.......................10 "
Limets, oil of...................50 "
Lime, acetate of.................25 "
———, citrate....................20 "
Lines, fishing, a twine ....40 "
———, fishing, complete...........40 "
———, worsted ....50 "
Linen thread ....40 "
——— twine......................40 "
——— pack thread ....40 "
Linens, all manufactures of, not otherwise specified ....40 "
Linen bags ....40 "
——— canvas, black, woven, or made in form or patterns, of such size and shape exclusively for buttons, shoes, or bootees ....10 "
Linen mitts, wove on frames.......35 "
——— tape.......................40 "

Value 30 cents, or under, per square yard. 35 "

Linens, brown..............
———, bleached ....
———, burlaps.............
———, brown Hollands ......
———, blay ....
———, canvas padding ......
———, cot bottom..........
———, coatings ....
———, crash...............
———, ducks ....
———, drills...............
———, damask.............
———, diaper..............
———, huckabucks ....
———, handkerchiefs ....
———, lawns ....

DUTY.

Linens, as above, value over 30 cts. per square yard .... 40 ℔ cent.

Linen, all manufactures of, or of which flax, jute or hemp shall be component material of chief value, valued at over 40 cts. per square yard, not otherwise provided for . 40 "

Links, coat .... 35 "

Linseed .... 16 c. ℔ bush.

Linseed cakes .... 20 ℔ cent.

——— meal .... 20 "

——— oil .... 23 cts. ℔ gal.

Lint, linen .... 40 ℔ cent.

——, cotton .... 35 "

Liqueurs or cordials, all sweet ..... $2 ℔ gal.

Liquor, iron .... 10 ℔ cent.

———, purple .... 20 "

———, red .... 20 "

———, tin .... 20 "

———, cases .... 35 "

———, bottles, if cut .... 40 "

———, bottles, if not cut .... 35 "

Liquorice paste .... 10 c. ℔ lb.

——— root .... 2 "

———, in rolls, ... 10 "

Litharge .... 3 "

Lithographic stones .... 20 ℔ cent.

Lithontriptons .... 35 "

Litmus .... 20 "

Loadstones .... 20 "

Lotions, all cosmetic .... 50 "

Lozenges, all medicinal .... 50 "

Locks, brass .... 35 "

——, wood and iron .... 35 "

——, wood and steel .... 45 "

——, gun .... 45 "

Logwood .... free.

———, extracts of .... 10 ℔ cent.

Long cloths, liable to the regulations respecting manufactures of cotton.

Looking-glass plates, if silvered (see glass.)

——— frames, if gilt on metal .... 35 "

DUTY.

Looking-glass frames, if wood, or gilt on wood .... 35 ℔ cent.

Looking-glass frames, if metal ..... 35 "

Lunar caustic .... 40 "

Lustres, glass, cut .... 40 "

———, brass and glass .... 40 "

Lutes .... 30 "

Lye, soda .... 20 "

M.

MACARONI .... 35 ℔ cent.

Mace .... 40 c. ℔ lb.

Macassar oil .... 50 ℔ cent.

Machinery, models of, and other inventions .... free.

Machinery, including all the preliminary processes requisite therefor, exclusively designed or expressly imported for the manufacture of flax and linen goods .... free.

Machinery, steam, agricultural and implements .... free.

Mackerel, pickled .... $2 ℔ bbl.

Madder .... free.

Madder root .... free.

Madder, ground or prepared ...... free.

Magic lanterns, and similar articles, composed of tin, glass, wood, brass, copper, &c .... 35 ℔ cent.

Magnesia, calcined .... 12 cts. ℔ lb.

———, carbonate of .... 6 "

———, sulphate of, or epsom salts .... 1 ct. "

Mahogany .... free.

Mails, an iron article used in weaving .... 35 ℔ cent.

Mails, iron .... 35 "

——, steel .... 45 "

Mallets, wood .... 35 "

Malt .... 20 "

Manganese .... 10 "

Mangoes .... 10 "

	DUTY.
Mangroves, or shells of	20 ℔ cent.
Manilla grass (or hemp)	$25 ℔ ton.
Manna (med. gum)	25 cts. ℔ lb.
Mantillas, silk	60 ℔ cent.
Manufactured tobacco not otherwise provided for	50 cts. ℔. lb.
Manufactures of the United States and its territories	free.
Manufactures, all, of the United States, brought back	free.
Manufactures of articles, vessels and wares, not otherwise provided for, of brass, copper, iron, lead, pewter, tin, or of which either metal is of chief value	35 ℔ cent.
Manufactures of bark of cork tree, except corks	50 "
Manufactures of bladders	30 "
Manufactures of bone, shell, horn, ivory, and vegetable ivory	35 "
Manufactures of cotton, if tamboured or embroidered	35 "
Manufactures of cotton, wholly unbleached, (see cottons.)	
Manufactures of cotton and linen, not otherwise enumerated, flax chief value	40 "
Manufactures of cotton and silk, not otherwise enumerated, silk not chief value	60 "
Manufactures of cotton and worsted, not otherwise enumerated	50 "
Manufactures of cotton, embroidered or tamboured, not otherwise provided for	35 "
Manufactures not otherwise provided for, composed of mixed materials, in part of cotton, silk, wool, or worsted, flax, hemp or jute, not otherwise provided for	35 "
Manufactures of flax, or of which flax is a component part of chief value, not otherwise provided for	40 "
Manufactures of fur, or of which fur is a component material	35 ℔ cent.
Manufactures of gold, silver, German silver, platina, or of which either is a component part, not otherwise provided for	40 "
Manufactures of glass articles, vessels, and wares, not otherwise provided for, not cut	35 "
Manufactures of gutta percha	40 "
Manufactures of hemp, or of which it is a component material of chief value, not otherwise provided for	30 "
Manufactures of hair, not otherwise provided for	30 "
Manufactures of India-rubber and silk, or of silk and other materials	50 "
Manufactures of jute, or Sisal grass, not otherwise provided for	30 "
Manufactures of linen, if embroidered or tamboured, not otherwise provided for	35 "
Manufactures of leather, not otherwise provided for, of which leather is a component part	35 "
Manufactures of marble, more advanced than slabs or blocks, (rough)	50 "
Manufactures of mohair, alpaca, or goats' hair, of which they shall be a component part, not otherwise provided for	50 "
Manufactures of mohair cloth, silk twist, and other cloth woven or made in patterns of such size and form, or cut in such manner as to be fit for shoes, boots, bootees, and buttons, exclusively, and not combined with India rubber	10 "
Manufactures of paper, of which paper is a component part, not otherwise provided for	35 "

DUTY.

Manufactures of papier mache, not otherwise provided for..........35 ℔ cent.
Manufactures of silk, embroidered or tamboured, not otherwise provided for..........................35 "
Manufactures of silk, or of which silk shall be a component material, not otherwise provided for ...50 "
Manufactures of steel, or of which steel shall be a component part, not otherwise provided for ......45 "
Manufactures of tobacco, all not otherwise provided for.........50 cts. ℔ lb.
Manufactures of wood, viz.: cedar, granadilla, ebony, mahogany, rose, and satin......................35 ℔ cent.
Manufactures of wood, of which wood is a chief component part, not otherwise provided for.............35 "
Manufactures of wool, embroidered or tamboured, not otherwise provided for.....................35 "
Manufactures of wool, or of which wool is a component part of chief value, not otherwise provided for, 24 cts. per lb. and 40 "
As above, if value over $2 ℔ sq. yd. 24 cts. ℔ yd. and 45 "
Manufactures of combed wool or worsted, embroidered or tamboured, not otherwise provided for 35 "
Manufactures of combed wool, called worsted, mohair, alpaca or goats' hair, or of which it is a component part, not otherwise provided for..50 "
Manuscripts ....free.
Maps.............................25 ℔ cent.
Marble, manufactures of ....50 "
——— busts ....10 "
Marbles, for children's play, (baked) 50 "
Marble table tops ....50 "
———, white statuary, brocatella, sienna and antique, in slab or block, rough or squared. $1 ℔ cub. ft. and 25 "

DUTY.

Marble, all other, in slab or block, rough or square, 50 cts. ℔ cubic foot and 20 ℔ cent.
Marine coral.....................free.
Marmalade, a sweetmeat ....35 ℔ cent.
Marrow ....10 "
Mascate, essence of...............50 "
Marsh mallows, med. root..........20 "
Mastic, crude.....................50 cts. ℔ lb.
———, refined ....50 "
Matches, for pocket lights ....35 ℔ cent.
Mathematical instruments, especially imported for any college, academy, school, or seminary........15 "
Mathematical instruments, of brass. 35 "
———————, all of bone..........................35 "
Mathematical instruments, of gold..40 "
———————, gilt or plated.........................35 "
Mathematical instruments, of iron..35 "
———————, all of ivory 35 "
Mathematical instruments, of silver.40 "
———————, of wood. 35 "
Matico (medicinal leaf) ....20 "
Mats, cocoanut...................30 "
——, rugs, screen, covers, hossacks, bedside, and other portions of carpets, to pay the same duty as carpeting of similar character.
Mats, screen, hassocks and rugs, all other..........................45 "
Mats, straw, tow..................35 "
——, table, wood ....35 "
——, of flag, jute, or grass.........30 "
——, sheepskins ....35 "
Matting, cocoanut ....30 "
———, all floor, of flags, jute, or grass..........................30 "
Meal, cassada ....20 "
——, linseed ....20 "
——, oat ....10 "
Measures, glass, engraved ....40 "
Meats, prepared..................35 "

	DUTY.
Medals, gold, silver, and copper ...	free.
——, and other collections of antiquities ...	free.
Medicinal preparations or patent medicines ...	50 ℔ cent.
Medicinal preparations, not otherwise specified ...	40 "
Medicinal roots and leaves, barks, flowers, plants, seeds, not otherwise specified ...	20 "
Melado, concentrated ...	2½ cts. ℔ lb.
Metal, plated ...	35 ℔ cent.
Metallic slates, paper ...	35 "
——, tin ...	35 "
Metals, unmanufactured, not otherwise provided for ...	20 "
Melting pots, if earthen ...	25 "
—— or glue pots ...	35 "
Mercury, or quicksilver ...	10 "
——, all preparations of ...	20 "
Merino shawls, (so called,) body worsted or combed wool, not otherwise provided for ...	35 "
Merino cloth, entirely of combed wool, (see dress goods.)	
Merino fringe, worsted ...	50 "
—— trimmings, worsted ...	50 "
—— shawls, made of combed wool	35 "
—— cloth, worsted stuff, not otherwise provided for ...	50 "
Manilla hemp ...	$25 ℔ ton.
Mica, isinglass ...	30 ℔ cent.
Milk of roses ...	50 "
Millinery of all kinds, not otherwise provided for ...	35 "
Millepedes ...	20 "
Mill saws (see iron.)	
Mills, coffee ...	35 "
Miniature cases, ivory ...	35 "
—— sheets, ivory ...	35 "
Miniatures ...	10 "
Mineral and bituminous substances in a crude state, not otherwise provided for ...	20 "

	DUTY.
Mineral green ...	30 ℔ cent.
—— kermes ...	10 "
—— blue ...	30 "
—— or medicinal water, in bottles or jugs, containing not over one quart ...	3 cts. each and 25 "
—— as above, 3 cts. for each additional quart or part of, and	25 "
Mirrors, (see glass.)	
Mirror glasses, silvered, (see glass.)	
—— ——, not silvered, (see glass.)	
Mitts, cotton, bleached or colored ...	35 "
——, silk ...	60 "
——, woolen ...	20 cts. ℔ lb. and 30 "
——, leather ...	35 "
——, linen ...	35 "
Mock jewelry ...	25 "
—— pearls ...	40 "
Modeling, specially imported ...	free.
Modeling, not specially imported, according to the materials of which they are composed.	
Models of invention, or improvements, none so that can be fitted for use ...	free.
Mohair in strips or patterns of the size exclusively for buttons ...	10 ℔ cent.
Molasses ...	8 cts. ℔ gal.
——, concentrated ...	2½c. ℔ lb.
Moon seed (poppy seed) ...	20 ℔ cent.
Mops ...	35 "
Morocco skins ...	25 "
Morphine ...	$2.50 ℔ oz.
——, salts of ...	$2.50 "
Mortars, brass ...	35 ℔ cent.
——, marble ...	50 "
——, composition ...	35 "
Moss, Iceland ...	10 "
——, for beds ...	20 "
Mosaics, real, not set ...	10 "
——, ——, set ...	25 "
Mother of pearl shells ...	free.

DUTY.

Mother of pearl, articles made of, not otherwise enumerated...........20 ℔ cent.
Mother of pearl studs.............30 "
——— buttons, with metal eyes or shanks.................30 "
Mould buttons (see buttons).......30 "
Mouse traps, wood or wire........35 "
Muffs, of fur......................35 "
Munjeet (Indian madder)..........free.
Murexide........................25 "
Muriate of barytes............... 20 "
——— gold...................20 "
——— tin.....................30 "
——— strontium..............20 "
Muriatic acid....................10 "
Music in sheets, as pamphlets......20 "
———, bound, as books...........20 "
Musical instruments,...............30 "
———, brass........30 "
Musical instrument strings, of gut...30 "
———, part of metal.........................35 "
Mushrooms, prepared.............35 "
Mushroom sauce...................35 "
Musk..............................50 "
———, crude.......................20 "
Muskets..........................35 "
Musket bayonets.................45 "
——— barrels, if any steel........45 "
——— bullets....................35 "
——— rods.......................35 "
——— stocks....................35 "
Muslin handkerchiefs, (see cottons.)
——— chemisettes...............35 "
——— collars.....................35 "
——— bands......................35 "
——— canezous..................35 "
Mustard, ground, in glass or tin...16 cts. ℔ ℔.
———, ground, in bulk.........12 "
——— seed oil, not salad....25 cts. ℔ gall.
——— oil salad............$1 00 ℔ gall.
Myrrh, gum, crude...............20 ℔ cent.
———, ———, refined...............20 "
Myrobalan (a nut for dyeing)......free.

N.

DUTY.

NAILS, brass....................35 ℔ cent.
———, copper.................35 "
———, composition.............35 "
———, iron, cut...............$1\frac{1}{2}$ ct. ℔ ℔.
———, ———, wrought...........$2\frac{1}{2}$ "
———, ornamental, with brass, gilt, or polished heads..............35 ℔ cent.
Nail plates........................35 "
Nails, zinc.......................35 "
Nankeens, imported directly from China (as cottons.)
Nankeens, not imported direct from China, subject to the regulations on manufactures of cotton.
Nankeen shoes....................35 "
——— slippers................35 "
Napkins, cotton, as cottons.
Naphtha, refined.................30c. ℔ gal.
Naples soap.......10 cts. ℔ ℔. and 25 ℔ cent.
Narcotine (medc.)................40 "
Natron..........................$\frac{1}{2}$ ct. ℔ ℔.
Needles.........................25 ℔ cent.
———, crochet.................25 "
Needles for knitting or sewing machines.............$1 ℔ M. and 35 "
Nests, brass kettles in.............35 "
———, birds'......................20 "
Nets, fishing, seines.............$6\frac{1}{2}$ cts. ℔ ℔.
———, fishing, dip or scoop nets.....35 ℔ cent.
Nickel...........................15 "
Nippers, (iron)..................35 "
Nitrate of barytes................20 "
——— potash or saltpetre, unrefined.........................$2\frac{1}{2}$ cts. ℔ ℔.
Nitrate of potash or saltpetre, refined..........................3 "
Nitrate of potash, partially refined..3 "
——— iron.....................20 ℔ cent.
——— silver,..................40 "
——— strontium..............20 "
Nitrate of tin.....................20 "
——— lead..................3 cts. ℔ ℔.

DUTY.

Nitre, mur. tin .... 20 ⅌ cent.

——, refined soda................ 1 ct. ⅌ ℔.

——, unrefined soda.............. 1 "

Nitric ether, spirits of............. 50 "

Nitrous acid .... 10 ⅌ cent.

Nobs or knobs, glass, with shanks or rivets .... 40 "

Nobs or knobs, steel .... 45 "

Norfolk latches.................... 35 "

Noyeau .... $2 ⅌ gal.

Nutria skins, if undressed .... 10 ⅌ cent.

Nut-galls .... free.

Nutmegs .... 50 cts. ⅌ ℔.

Nuts, all not otherwise provided for 2 "

Nuts used in dyeing, specially in a crude state .... free.

Newspapers .... 25 ⅌ cent.

Nux vomica...................... 20 "

Nyansooks (as cottons.)

O.

OAKUM and junk................ free.

Oats .... 10 cts. ⅌ bush.

Oatmeal......................... 10 ⅌ cent.

Ochres, or ochrey earths, dry, not otherwise provided for .... 50 cts. ⅌ 100 ℔s.

Ochres, or ochrey earths, ground in oil...................... $1 50 ⅌ 100 lbs.

Ochres, all, or ochrey earths, in oil.................... $1 50 "

Brown, blue, red, and yellow earth, to be considered as ochre................ 50 cts. "

Odors or perfumes................ 50 ⅌ cent.

Oil cakes........................ 20 "

— cloth, table mats.............. 40 "

— ——, table mats, lined with woolen......................... 40 "

Oil cloth, silk.................... 50 "

Oil cloths, such as hat covers, over garments, not silk, are usually made of .... 40 "

DUTY.

Oil cloth, floor, stamped, painted or printed, value 50 cts. or under per square yard.................... 30 ⅌ cent.

Oil cloth, floor, stamped, painted, value over 50 cts. per square yard .. 40 "

Oil cloth, all other, except silk..... 40 "

————, furniture, other .... 40 "

————, medicated, not silk ...... 40 "

———— aprons .... 50 "

Oil, Harlæm .... 50 "

—, allspice .... 50 "

— absynthe, or wormwood....... 50 "

— of almonds, fixed or expressed . 10 c. ⅌ lb.

— of almonds, essential or essence of............................ $1.50 ⅌ lb.

Oil of amber or ambre, crude...... 10 c. ⅌ lb.

— of amber, rectified .... 20 "

— animali .... 20 ⅌ cent.

— of aniseed, essential or essence of........................... 50 c. ⅌ ℔.

Oil, bears'....................... 50 ⅌ cent.

—, bay, fixed or expressed .... 20 c. ⅌ ℔.

—, cajaput, or cajaputa .... 25 "

— chamomile................... 50 ⅌ cent.

Oil of cassia .... $1 ⅌ ℔.

— caryophil (oil of cloves) .... $2 "

Oil of caraway..................... 50c. "

——— cinnamon.................... $2 "

——— cloves....................... $2 "

——— cocoanuts.................. 10 ⅌ cent.

——— croton, fixed or expressed..... $1 ⅌ lb.

——— citronella.................. 50 "

Oils, all essential, not otherwise provided for....................... 50 ⅌ cent.

Oil of cogniacs, or ananthic ether .. $4 ⅌ oz.

——— cubebs .... $1 ⅌ lb.

——— fennel .... 50c. "

——— hartshorn .... 50 ⅌ cent.

——— juglandium .... 50 "

——— juniper .... 25 c. ⅌ lb.

——— laurel, fixed or expressed.... 20 "

——— mace, fixed or expressed..... 50 "

——— minth or mint .... 50 ⅌ cent.

——— nuts....................... 50 "

	DUTY.
Oil of palm bean	10 ℔ cent.
—— palm	10 "
—— poppies	50 "
—— petroleum, crude	10c. ℔ gal.
—— ——, refined	30 "
—— rue	50 ℔ cent.
—— sage	50 "
—— savin	50 "
—— sassafras	50 "
—— spruce	50 "
—— spike	50 "
—— spurge	50 "
—— valerian	$1.50 ℔ lb.
Oil, seal	10 ℔ cent.
— of allspice	50 "
—, succini (drug)	50 "
Oil of ambergris	50 "
—— almonds, essential	$1.50 ℔ lb.
—— anthos, or rosemary	50 ℔ cent.
—— bay leaves	$17.50 ℔ lb.
—— bergamot	$1 ℔ lb.
—— cedrat	50 ℔ cent.
Oils of apple, pear, peach, apricot, strawberry and raspberry	$2.50 ℔ lb.
Oil of jasmine, or jessamin	50 ℔ cent.
Oil of lavender	50 ℔ cent.
—— lemon	50 c. ℔ lb.
—— limets, limette	50 ℔ cent.
—— macassar	50 "
—— neats' foot	20 "
—— nerol, or orange flower	50 "
—— nutmegs	50 "
—— oranges	50 c. ℔ lb.
—— origanum, or thyme, red	25 "
—— pimento	50 ℔ cent.
—— rhodium	50 "
—— roses, or otto of roses	$1.50 ℔ oz.
—— rosemary, or anthos	50 ℔ cent.
—— sweet marjorum	50 "
—— thyme, or origanum, white	30 c. ℔ lb.
—— tuberos	50 ℔ cent.
—— vanilla beans	50 "
—— violets	50 "
—— ricini, or palma christi	$1 ℔ gal.

	DUTY.
Oil, coal, crude	10c. ℔ gal.
——, refined	30 "
Oil, castor	$1 "
—, olive, in casks, not salad	25 "
—, ——, in bottles or flasks	$1 "
—, flaxseed	23 "
—, hempseed	23 "
—, illuminating, from coal, shale, &c.	30 "
—, kerosene	30 "
—, linseed	23 "
—, rapeseed	23 "
—, salad	$1 "
—, spermaceti, of foreign fishing	20 ℔ cent.
—, fish, and all other of American fisheries, all articles the production of said fisheries	free.
Oil of vitriol	1 ct. ℔ lb.
—, whale and other (not sperm,) of foreign fishing	20 ℔ cent.
Old brass, fit only to be remanufactured	15 "
Old lead	1½ ct. ℔ lb.
Old copper, fit only to be remanufactured	1½ "
Old pewter, fit only to be remanufactured	2 "
Old silver, fit only to be remanufactured	free.
Olives	30 ℔ cent.
——, in oil or salt	30 "
Onions	10 "
Opium	$2.50 ℔ lb.
——, prepared for smoking	100 ℔ cent.
——, extract of	100 "
Orange crystals	20 "
—— flowers	10 "
Oranges	25 "
——, in boxes, barrels, or casks	25 "
Orange bitters	100 "
—— peel	10 "
—— issue peas	40 "
—— flower water	50 "
Orchilli, or orchello	10 "

DUTY.

Ore, specimens of, not otherwise provided for .... 10 ℘ cent.
Ore, copper .... 5 "
——, silver and gold .... free.
Organs .... 30 ℘ cent.
Ornaments, gilt wood .... 35 "
————, gold paper .... 40 "
————, for ladies' head-dresses, silk .... 50 "
Ornaments, cut glass, for mounting chandeliers .... 40 "
Ornaments, not for head-dresses, of metal, to pay duty according to metal of which composed.
Ornamental feathers, manufactured. 50 "
Orpiment .... 20 "
Orris root, or iris root .... free.
Osier, for basket makers' use ...... 30 ℘ cent.
Ostrich plumes and feathers, manufactured .... 50 "
Ostrich plumes and feathers, unmanufactured or raw .... 25 "
Otto, or oil of roses .... $1 50 ℘ oz.
Oxalic acid .... 4 cts. ℘ ℔.
Oxide of bismuth .... 20 ℘ cent.
Oxymuriate of lime .... 20 "
———— or chlorate of potasse, or potash .... 6 cts. ℘ ℔.
Oysters .... free.
Osnaburgs, (see flax.)

P.

PACK thread .... 40 ℘ cent.
Padding, wool, (see wool.)
Paddy .... $1\frac{1}{2}$ ct. ℘ ℔.
Pad screws (see saddlery) .... 35 ℘ cent.
Paint brushes .... 40 "
Painted floor cloths, oil, (see oil cloths.)
Painting brushes .... 40 "
Paintings.—To constitute a painting in the meaning of the law, it must be an object of taste or vertu, and not paintings on plates, goblets, vases, or any utensil for use, or capable of being converted to breastpins, ear-drops, or other ornaments to be worn .... 10 ℘ cent.
Paintings, the productions of American artists residing abroad, provided it shall be so certified by the artist or consul .... free.
Paintings, other, provided the same be imported in good faith as objects of taste, and not as merchandise .... 10 ℘ cent.
Paintings on glass .... 10 "
———— porcelain .... 10 "
———— canvas .... 10 "
Paintings, all, not otherwise provided for .... 10 "
Paints, dry or ground in oil, not otherwise provided for .... 25 "
Paints, (water colors) .... 35 "
———, water colors for paper hangings .... 25 "
Painters' colors, all not otherwise provided for .... 25 "

	If not water colors.	DUTY
Paints, Dutch pink		25 "
———, desenna		25 "
———, Frankford black		25 "
———, French green		30 "
———, ivory black		25 "
———, king's yellow		25 "
———, lake		25 "
———, lamp black		25 "
———, mineral green		30 "
———, olympian green		25 "
———, patent yellow		25 "
———, chalk		25 "
———, rose pink		25 "

———, Spanish brown, dry .... 25 "
———, ————, in oil ...... 25 "
———, terra umbra .... 50 cts. ℘ 100 lbs.
———, white lead .... 3 cts. ℘ ℔.
Palm leaves, unmanufactured ...... free.
—— leaf hats .... 40 ℘ cent.
—— leaf baskets .... 35 "

	DUTY.
Palm oil	10 ℔ cent.
Pamphlets	25 "
Pannel saws	45 "
Papers, illustrated	25 "
Paper, antiquarian, double elephant, atlas, columbier, elephant, imperial, super-royal, royal, medium, demy, foolscap, drawing and writing	35 "
Paper, bank folio and quarto post of all kinds, letter and bank note	35 "
Paper, copperplate, blotting, copying, colored for labels and needles, marble, and fancy colored	35 "
Paper, glass, morocco, sand, and tissue	35 "
Paper, pot and pith	35 "
——, pasteboard, pressing boards, and gold and silver paper in sheets or strips	35 "
Paper, colored, copper-plate, printing, and stainers'	35 "
Paper, binders' boards, box boards, mill boards, and paper makers' boards	35 "
Paper, wrapping and cartridge	35 "
Paper, envelopes and fancy note	35 "
——, music, with lines, in sheets	35 "
——, ——, ————, bound	35 "
Paper, printing, unsized, used for books and newspapers exclusively	20 "
Paper, for screens or fireboards	35 "
——, all other not enumerated	35 "
——, counting-house boxes	35 "
Paper boxes, fancy	35 "
—— hangings	35 "
—— labels	35 "
—— pill boxes	35 "
—— pin cases	35 "
—— segars, (see segars.)	
—— snuff boxes	35 "
Paper wadding	35 "
Paraffine	10 cts. ℔ lb.
Parasols, silk	50 ℔ cent.
Parasol sticks or frames	35 "
Parallel rules, ivory (not mounted)	35 ℔ cent.
————, (mounted)	35 "
Paving tiles	20 "
Parchment	30 "
Paris white, in oil	$1 50 ℔ 100 lbs.
————, dry	$1 "
Paris green	30 ℔ cent.
Parts of stills, viz.: Sheets made by rolling, intended for the sides; globes and heads, made by hammering thick sheet copper; and shoulders, made out of sheet copper, by hammering	35 "
Pasteboard	35 "
Paste giggers	35 "
Paste, almond	50 "
——, perfumed	50 "
——, or pasta de Brazil (ground Nicaragua wood, a dye)	10 "
Paste work that is set in gold or silver jewelry	30 "
Paste, imitation of precious stones	40 "
Pastel, or woad	free.
Patent floor cloth, oil, (see oil cloth.)	
—— yellow	25 ℔ cent.
Paving stones	10 "
Pearl, mother of	free.
Pearls, set	25 ℔ cent.
——, all, not set	10 "
——, composition, set	30 "
——, mock pearls	40 "
Peas	10 "
Peanuts (or ground beans)	1 ct. ℔ lb.
——, shelled	1½ "
Pellitory root	20 ℔ cent.
Pelts, salted	10 "
Pencils, wood, filled with lead or other material ....50 cts. per gross and	30 "
——, camels' hair	35 "
——, chalk ..50 cts. ℔ gross and	35 "
——, slate	40 "
Pencil cases, gold	40 "
————, silver	40 "
————, gilt or plated	35 "

DUTY.

Penknives, jack and pocket, all....50 ℔ cent.
Pen holders......................35 "
Pens, metallic....10 cts. ℔ gro. and 25 "
Pen holder tips, and parts of.......35 "
——," quills......................30 "
Pepper, black..................15 cts. ℔ lb.
———, ——, ground...........18 "
———, white..................15 "
———, ——, ground...........18 "
———, Cayenne...............15 "
———, Cayenne, ground........18 "
———, red....................15 "
Perfumery vials and bottles, uncut, not exceeding the capacity of 4 ounces each....................35 ℔ cent.
Perfumery vials and bottles, uncut, exceeding 4 ounces, and not exceeding 16 ounces each..........35 "
Percussion caps..................40 "
Perfumes.........................50 "
Perfumery, of which alcohol forms the principal ingredient, $3 ℔ gall. and 50 "
Perry (see arrack.)
Persian berries (a dye)...........free.
Personal and household effects, not merchandise, of citizens of the United States dying abroad.........free.
Peruvian bark.....................20 ℔ cent.
Pestles and mortars, composition...35 "
————————, of marble.....50 "
————————, of stone......35 "
Petershams, woolen cloth (see woolen.)
Petticoats, cotton patterns for, as cottons.
Petticoats, ready made, if no wool..35 "
Pewter, old, fit only to be remanufactured.......................2 ct. ℔ lb.
Pewter, articles of, not enumerated, manufactured from, or of which pewter is a component part......35 ℔ cent.
Phosphate of lime................20 "
——— —— soda................20 "

DUTY.

Philosophical books, maps, charts, statues, statuary, busts and casts, marble, bronze and alabaster, or plaster of Paris, specially imported for the use of Colleges, &c.....free.
Philosophical apparatus and instruments..........................40 ℔ cent.
Phosphorus lights, in glass bottles, with paper cases................35 "
Phosphorus.......................20 "
Phosphuret of lime...............20 "
Piano fortes.....................30 "
—— forte ferrules, (iron,)........35 "
Pickled fish, other than mackerel and salmon, in barrel............$1 50 ℔ bbl.
Pickled herring, in barrel.........$1 "
——— herring, in kegs..........$1 "
——— mackerel.................$2 "
——— salmon..................$3 "
Pickles..........................35 ℔ cent.
Picrotoxine, an extract............40 "
Picture glass (see window glass.)
Pills, powders, tinctures, troches or lozenges, syrups, cordials, bitters, anodynes, tonics, plasters, liniments, salves, ointments, pastes, drops, waters, essences, spirits, oils, or other medicinal preparations or compositions, recommended to the public as proprietary medicines, or prepared according to some private formula or secret art, as remedies or specifics for any disease or diseases, or affections whatever, affecting the human or animal body.................50 "
Pimento........................15 cts. ℔ lb.
———, ground..................18 c. ℔ lb.
Pin or needle cases of bone........35 ℔ cent.
———————— enamel.....35 "
———————— gold........40 "
———————— ivory.......35 "
———————— leather.....35 "
———————— iron........35 "

DUTY.

Pin or needle cases of mother of pearl .... 20 ℘ cent.
Pin or needle cases of paper .... 35 "
—————— set with pearl 35 "
—————— set with precious stones .... 35 "
Pin or needle cases of shell .... 35 "
—————— silver .... 40 "
—————— paper mounted .... 35 "
Pin or needle cases of wood .... 35 "
Pin cushions, silk .... 50 "
————, cotton .... 35 "
Pincers, (of iron) .... 35 "
Pine apples .... 25 "
Pink, Dutch .... 25 "
——, rose .... 25 "
—— root .... 20 "
—— saucers .... 40 "
Pins .... 35 "
——, rest, (iron, for inside of pianos.) 35 "
——, silver jewelry .... 25 "
——, iron .... 35 "
——, pound .... 35 "
Piperine, an extract .... 40 "
Pipe clay, unwrought .... $5 ℘ ton.
Pipes, clay, smoking .... 35 ℘ cent.
Pipes, meerschaums and other tobacco smoking and pipe bowls, not otherwise provided for, $1 50 per gross, and 75 "
Pipe cases, stems, mountings and all parts of pipes and pipe fixtures, and all smokers' articles .... 75 "
Pistols .... 35 "
Pitch, Burgundy .... 20 "
Pitch .... 20 "
Plaids, cotton (see cotton.)
Plantain, or Manilla grass, or Manilla hemp .... $25 ℘ ton.
Plaits, for making hats or bonnets .. 30 ℘ cent.
Plaster of Paris, calcined .... 20 "
————, unground .... free.
————, ground .... 20 ℘ cent.

DUTY.

Plaster, busts of .... 10 ℘ cent.
———, casts of .... 40 "
——— statues .... 10 "
——— castings .... 40 "
——— ornaments .... 40 "
Plaitings of straw for hats or bonnets. 30 "
Planks, wrought .... 20 "
———, rough .... 20 "
Plants, medicinal .... 20 "
———, other .... 30 "
Plantains .... 25 "
Plaintain bark, (Manilla grass) .... $25 ℘ ton.
Plane irons .... 45 ℘ cent.
Planes .... 45 "
Plata pina .... free.
Plate, silver .... 40 ℘ cent.
Plated carriage and harness furniture .... 35 "
Plated epaulets .... 35 "
——— metal, of copper .... 35 "
——— moulding .... 35 "
——— saddlery .... 35 "
——— slides .... 35 "
——— wire .... 35 "
——— wares of all kinds, not otherwise specified .... 35 "
Plaits for making hats or bonnets .. 30 "
Plates, copper, suitable for sheathing ships, that is, 14 by 48 inches, and weighing from 14 to 34 ounces per square foot .... 3 c. ℘ ℔.
Plates, nail (see iron.) .... 35 ℘ cent.
———, copper, engraved .... 25 "
———, ———, prepared for engravers, steel .... 45 "
Platillas, linen (see flax.)
Platina, unmanufactured .... free.
———, manufactures of, not otherwise provided for .... 40 ℘ cent.
Platina vases, or retorts .... free.
Playing cards, value 25 cts. or less per pack .... 25 cts. ℘ pack.
Playing cards, value over 25 cts. per pack .... 35 "

DUTY.

Pliers, (iron)....................35 ₰ cent.
Ploughs, (iron)....................35 "
Ploughs (a plane)....................45 "
Plumbago....................$10 ₰ ton.
Plums....................5 cts. ₰ lb.
Plumes, ornamental, manufactured .50 ₰ cent.
Plush or shag, worsted....................50 "
——, cotton, (see cottons.)
——, hair....................30 "
Plush, mohair, or goats' hair, not otherwise provided for....................50 "
——, wool, not otherwise provided for....................24 cts. ₰ lb. and 40 "
Pocket books, leather, or if leather is the article of chief value....................35 "
Pocket books, paper....................35 "
—— lights, phosphorus....................35 "
Pole caps....................35 "
—— carriage hooks....................35 "
Polishing powders....................25 "
—— stones....................free.
Polished or scraped brass....................35 ₰ cent.
Polypodium....................20 "
Pomatum....................50 "
Pomegranates....................10 "
Pomegranate peel....................20 "
Pongees, white (see silks.)
Poplins, stuff, (see dress goods.)
Poppy heads....................20 "
—— oil....................50 "
—— seed....................20 "
Porcelain and Parian ware, not ornamented....................45 "
Porcelain and Parian ware, ornamented....................50 "
—— glass....................40 "
—— slates....................35 "
Pork....................1 ct. ₰ lb.
Porphyry....................45 ₰ cent.
Portable desks....................35 "
Porter, in bottles....................35 cts. ₰ gal.
——, in casks....................20 "
——, imported, otherwise than in bottles....................20 "

DUTY.

Potasse, or potash, prussiate of, red. 10 cts. ₰ lb.
Potassium....................15 "
Potash, bichromate of....................3 "
——, chromate of....................3 "
——, chlorate of....................6 "
——, hydriodate of....................75 "
——, prussiate of, yellow....................5 "
——, pure....................15 ₰ cent.
——, iodate of....................75 cts. ₰ lb.
——, iodide of....................75 "
——, acetate of....................75 "
Potatoes....................25 cts. ₰ bush.
Pots, black lead....................35 ₰ cent.
——, cast iron....................1½ ct. ₰ lb.
Pots, melting earthen, common.....25 ₰ cent.
Poultry or game, prepared....................35 "
Pounce....................20 "
Pound ribbon, if silk....................60 "
Powder, black lead....................20 "
——, blue....................20 "
——, of brass....................20 "
——, of bronze....................20 "
——, gun, and all explosive substances for blasting, and of value less than 20 cts. ₰ lb.. 6 cts. ₰ lb. and 20 "
Powder, gun, and all explosive substances for blasting, and of value over 20 cts. ₰ lb.. 10 cts. ₰ lb. and 20 "
——, hair, plain or not perfumed.50 "
——, ——, perfumed....................50 "
——, ink....................35 "
——, puffs....................35 "
——, subtil, for the skin....................50 "
——, tooth....................50 "
Powders, pastes, balls, balsams, ointments, oils, waters, washes, tinctures, essences, or other preparations, or compositions, commonly called sweet scents, odors, perfumes, or cosmetics; and all powders and preparations for the teeth or gums....................50 "
Powdered sugar (see sugar.)
Precious stones, set....................25 "

DUTY.

Precious stones, of all kinds, not set. 10 ℔ cent.
——, glass, imitation of, set 30 "
——, imitations of ...... 40 "
Prepared clay .... $5 ℔ ton.
Pressing boards .... 35 ℔ cent.
Prepared vegetables, meats, poultry, game and fish, all, in any form ... 35 "
Preparations, anatomical, (according to material.)
Preparations, chemical, not otherwise enumerated .... 20 "
Preserves, in molasses, and all others except ginger .... 35 "
Preserved ginger .... 50 "
Prints or engravings .... 25 "
Prisms, cut glass .... 40 "
——, of cut glass and metal ...... 40 "
Produce, of the growth, manufacture, or fisheries of the United States and its territories .... free.
Professional books of persons arriving in the United States .... free.
Produce or growth of the United States, not otherwise mentioned, brought back .... free.
Protractors, ivory, mounted .... 35 ℔ cent.
Prunella .... 50 "
Prunella, and similar fabrics, woven or made in patterns of such size and shape, or cut in such manner as to be fit for shoes, bootees, and buttons .... 10 "
Prunes .... 5 cts. ℔ ℔.
Prussian blue .... 30 ℔ cent.
Prussiate of potash, or potasse, red .. 10c. ℔ lb.
Pucheri .... 20 ℔ cent.
Pulleys, iron, brass, or copper ..... 35 "
——, wood .... 35 "
Pumice .... free.
Pumpkins .... 10 ℔ cent.
Pumps, stomach .... 35 "
Punches, shoe, part steel .... 45 "
Punjums, Madras, cottons (see cottons.)

DUTY.

Purple brown .... 25 ℔ cent.
—— tin liquor .... 20 "
Putty .... $1\frac{1}{2}$ ct. ℔ ℔.
Pyroligneous acid, (see acid, pyroligneous.)

Q.

QUADRANTS and sextants .... 35 ℔ cent.
Quadrant frames .... 35 "
Quality binding, worsted .... 50 "
Quassia wood .... 20 "
Quicksilver .... 10 "
Quill baskets .... 30 "
Quilla bark .... 20 "
Quills, prepared or manufactured ... 30 "
——, unprepared .... 30 "
Quiltings, or bed-quilts, cotton ..... 35 "
Quinine .... 45 "
Quinine, sulphate of .... 45 "
——, salts of .... 45 "

R.

RADIX, or angelica root .. .. 20 ℔ cent.
Rancon, or Orleans, ... free.
Rag stones .... 10 ℔ cent.
Rags, of cotton or linen, for making paper .... free.
Rags, wool .... 10 ℔ cent.
Raisins, sultana, in boxes or jars ... 5 c. ℔ ℔.
——, Muscatelle, " " ... 5 "
——, bloom, " " ... 5 "
——, all other .... 5 "
Rakes, iron .... 35 ℔ cent.
——, steel .... 45 "
——, wood .... 35 "
Rape of grapes .... 20 "
—— seed .... 1 ct. ℔ lb.
—— —— oil .... 23 c. ℔ gal.
Rappers, brass .... 35 ℔ cent.
——, iron .... 35 "
Rass, cornu cervi .... 20 "

DUTY.

Rasps, not over 10 inches long, 10 cts. ℘ ℔. and 30 ℘ cent.

——, over 10 inches long, 6 cts. per ℔. and 30 "

Ratafia (see arrack.)

Rattans, unmanufactured .... free.

————, split or manufactured..... 25 ℘ cent.

Rattles, wood .... 35 "

———, ivory, with bells .... 35 "

———, coral, with bells........... 35 "

———, with silver bells........... 40 "

Ravens duck, if hemp............. 30 "

——— ——, if flax............... 30 "

Raw skins, that is, undressed....... 10 "

—— silk, as reeled from the cocoon, not advanced in manufacture at all free.

Raw silk, not more advanced in manufactures than singles, tram, thrown, or organzine............ 35 "

Razors .... 35 "

———, in boxes or cases.......... 35 "

Razor cases, leather............... 35 "

—— ——, metal................ 35 "

—— ——, paper .... 35 "

—— ——, wood .... 35 "

—— strops, leather.............. 35 "

—— ——, wood .... 35 "

Reaping-hooks, iron .... 35 "

——————, steel .... 45 "

Red chromate of potash........... 3 cts. ℘ ℔.

—— sanders .... free.

—— or crude tartar, or wine lees... 6 c. ℘ ℔.

—— liquor....................... 20 ℘ cent.

—— precipitate .... 20 "

—— wood, and red sanders wood... free.

—— wool, or fur for hatters, unmanufactured...................... 20 ℘ cent.

Reeds, unmanufactured........... free.

——, manufactured.............. 25 ℘ cent.

——, weavers'.................. 35 "

Reeves' colors .... 35 "

Regulus of antimony.............. 10 "

Reindeer skins, dressed............ 20 "

———— ——, undressed .... 10 "

DUTY.

Reindeer skins, tanned............ 25 ℘ cent.

———— tongues.................. 20 "

Reps, natural silk and cotton ...... 50 "

——, silk, (see silk.)

Resin .... 20 "

—— of jalap (med. prep.) .... 40 "

——, nux vomica (med. prep.) .... 40 "

Returned cargo, of American growth or manufacture................. free.

Returned cargo, of foreign growth or manufacture, according to the material of which it is composed, and is liable to the same duty as on its first importation.

Rhodium, oil of .... 50 ℘ cent.

Rhubarb .... 50 c. ℘ ℔.

Ribbon wire, or canetille, if covered with cotton thread. (See iron wire.)

Ribbon wire, covered with silk. (See iron wire.)

Ribbons, silk..................... 60 ℘ cent.

————, cotton .... 35 "

————, Bordeloux, silk and cotton 50 "

————, pound, if cotton.......... 35 "

Rice, clean...................... 2½ct. ℘ ℔.

——, unclean.................... 2 "

Rifles .... 35 ℘ cent.

Rings, brass .... 35 "

——, gilt...................... 35 "

——, gold, set or not set, as jewelry 25 "

——, hair, horse................. 30 "

——, hair, human................ 40 "

——, iron .... 35 "

——, plated or washed........... 35 "

——, pewter.................... 35 "

——, of precious stones, set....... 25 "

——, silver, as jewelry........... 25 "

——, silver-plated, for saddlery... 35 "

Rivets, brass..................... 35 "

———, iron..................... 2½ct. ℘ ℔.

———, steel .... 45 ℘ cent.

Robes, made up, if no wool........ 35 "

Robe patterns, according to the material of which they are composed.

DUTY.

Rock moss.......... 10 ⅌ cent.
Rancon.......... free.
Rods and eyes of brass, for stairs ... 35 ⅌ cent.
Rods and eyes, all other, of metal, except steel, for stairs.......... 35 "
Rods, wood.......... 35 "
——, copper.......... 30 "
——, composition.......... 35 "
——, steel.......... 45 "
Rolled brass.......... 35 "
Rolls, brown or white linen, (see linen.)
Roller buckles, as saddlery.......... 35 "
Romals, cotton goods, (see cottons.)
Roman cement.......... 20 "
—— vitriol.......... 25 "
Rope, made of hides cut in strips... 20 "
—— or cordage of cocoanut hulls. 3½ cts. ⅌ ℔.
Roofing slates.......... 40 ⅌ cent.
Roots, arrow.......... 30 "
——, madder.......... free.
——, medicinal, not specially mentioned, in a crude state.......... 20 ⅌ cent.
Roots, all bulbous not otherwise enumerated.......... 30 "
Rope, made of grass or bark...... 3½ cts. ⅌ ℔.
——, ciar or coiar.......... 3½ "
Rose leaves.......... 50 c. ⅌ ℔.
Rose pink (whiting and logwood) .. 25 ⅌ cent.
—— water.......... 50 "
—— wood.......... free.
Rosin.......... 20 ⅌ cent.
Rosolio, a cordial.......... $2 ⅌ gal.
Rotten stone.......... free.
Rouens, linen, (see flax.)
Rouge.......... 50 ⅌ cent.
Rubigo ferri.......... 20 "
Rubrum, bark acer.......... 20 "
Rubies.......... 10 "
——, set.......... 25 "
Rue, essence of.......... 50 "
Rugs, for bed covering, cotton..... 35 "
——, woolen, 24 cts. ⅌ ℔. and 40 "

DUTY.

Rugs, hearth, all, (see mats.)
——, for horses, (linen).......... 40 ⅌ cent.
Rules, of bone.......... 35 "
——, of brass.......... 35 "
——, of iron.......... 35 "
——, of ivory.......... 35 "
——, of wood.......... 35 "
——, of bone or ivory, with brass joints and slides.......... 35 "
Rules, wood, with brass.......... 35 "
Rum, (see gin.)
——, essence or oil of.......... $2 ⅌ oz.
——, bay, or bay water.......... $1 50 ⅌ gal.
——, bay, essence or oil of.......... $2 ⅌ oz.
——, cherry, a cordial.......... $2 ⅌ gallon.
Russia crash (see linens.)
—— duck (see linens.)
—— diaper (see linens.)
—— linen (see linens.)
—— sheetings, brown or white... 30 ⅌ cent.
Rust of iron.......... 20 "
Rye.......... 15 cts. ⅌ bush.
Rye flour.......... 10 ⅌ cent.

S.

SABRES.......... 35 ⅌ cent.
Saccharum saturni, S. of L.......... 20 cts. ⅌ ℔.
Sacking, linen (see flax.)
Saddlery, all not otherwise specified. 35 ⅌ cent.
——, silver-plated.......... 35 "
——, brass.......... 35 "
——, steel.......... 35 "
——, tinned.......... 35 "
——, japanned.......... 35 "
——, common.......... 35 "
Saddle hooks, silver.......... 35 "
—— ——, other.......... 35 "
Saddles.......... 35 "
Saddle-trees.......... 35 "
Safflour.......... 10 "
——, extract of.......... 20 "
Saffron.......... 10 "
—— cake.......... 10 "

	DUTY.
Sago	1½ ct. ℔ lb.
——, flour	1½ "
Salacine, a medicinal preparation	40 ℔ cent.
Sail duck	30 "
Sal ammoniac	20 "
—— diuretic	20 "
—— nitre, or saltpetre, or nitrate of potash, crude	2½ cts. ℔ lb.
Sal nitre, or saltpetre, refined	3 "
—— ——, partially refined	3 "
—— succinie	20 ℔ cent.
Salad oil	$1 ℔ gal.
Salempores, cottons (see cottons.)	
Salep	20 ℔ cent.
Salmon, preserved	35 "
——, —— in oil	30 "
——, pickled, in barrels	$3 ℔ bbl.
——, dry or smoked	½ ct. ℔ lb.
Saleratus	1½ cts. ℔ lb.
Salt	18 cts. ℔ 100 lbs.
——, not in bulk	24 " "
——, crude mineral, in bulk	18 " "
——, fossil, mineral, "	18 " "
Salts, brown	20 ℔ cent.
——, Epsom	1 ct. ℔ lb.
——, glauber	½ "
——, Rochelle	15 "
——, all other chemical salts not enumerated	20 ℔ cent.
Salted skivers	10 "
—— roans	10 "
—— pelts	10 "
Saltpetre, or sal nitre, or nitrate of potash, crude	2½ ct. ℔ lb.
Saltpetre, refined	3 "
——, partially refined	3 "
Sandarach, refined	10 "
Sanders wood	free.
—— red	free.
Sandal wood	free.
Sand stones	10 ℔ cent.
Sannas, cottons (see cottons.)	
Santonin	$5 ℔ lb.
Sarcocolla, crude	20 ℔ cent.
Sardines, in barrels (in salt)	50 ℔ cent.
——, in kegs, "	50 "
Sarsaparilla	20 "
Sarsnets, silk (see silks.)	
——, cotton (see cottons.)	
Sash fasteners, (iron)	35 "
Sassafras	20 "
——, oil of	50 "
Satin, Denmark, (see dress goods.)	
——, ——, if any cotton	50 "
——, gauze (see silk.)	
——, silk (see silk.)	
—— wood	free.
——, white	3 cts. ℔ lb.
Satins, figured, when in shape and size exclusively for buttons	10 ℔ cent.
Sauces, all kinds not otherwise enumerated	35 "
Saucepans, copper	35 "
——, iron	35 "
——, tin	35 "
Sausages	35 "
Saws, cross-cut	10 cts. ℔ lineal foot.
——, mill pit, not over 9 inches wide	12½ " "
Saws, drag, not over 9 inches wide	12½ " "
——, mill pit, over 9 inches wide	20 " "
Saws, drag, over 9 inches wide	20 " "
Saws, hand, not over 24 inches long,	75 cts. ℔ doz. and 30 ℔ cent.
——, ——, over 24 inches long,	$1 ℔ doz. and 30 "
——, back, not over 10 inches long,	75 cts. ℔ doz. and 30 "
——, ——, over 10 inches long,	$1 ℔ doz. and 30 "
—— sets, (steel)	45 "
Sawns, cottons (see cotton.)	
Scagliola tables, or slabs	35 "
Scale beams	35 "
Scales, bone	35 "

DUTY.

Scales, ivory, with steel joints......45 𝔓 cent.
———, ———, entirely of ....35 "
Scammoniate (med. gum)..........20 "
Scantling.......................20 "
——— and sawed timber, not planed or wrought into shape for use..20 "
Scilla, or squills..................10 "
Scissors ....35 "
Scoop nets.......................35 "
Scrapers, if any steel,.............45 "
Scrap lead, if old, fit only to be remanufactured ....1½ ct. 𝔓 ℔.
Screws, brass ....35 𝔓 cent.
———, washed or plated, not wood.35 "
Scythes ....45 "
Sealing wax ....35 "
Seaweed, and all other vegetable substances used for beds or mattresses ....20 "
Seeds, anise.................... 5 cts. 𝔓 ℔.
———, anise, star.................10 "
———, canary, 60 ℔s. to bush......$1 𝔓 bush.
———, caraway .... 3 cts. 𝔓 ℔.
———, cardamom..................50 "
———, cummin.................. 5 "
———, coriander .... 3 "
———, fennel.................... 2 "
———, fenugreek................ 2 "
———, hemp..................... ½ "
———, mustard, (brown or white,). 3 "
———, rape..................... 1 "
———, castor, 50 ℔s. to bush......60c. 𝔓 bush.
———, garden...................30 𝔓 cent.
———, for agricultural purposes...30 "
———, for horticultural purposes..30 "
———, medicinal.................20 "
Seed and stick lac...............10 cts. 𝔓 ℔.
Seines ....6½ " "
Segars, valued at $15 or less per M., 75 cts. 𝔓 ℔. and 20 𝔓 cent.
———, ——— over $15 but not over $30 per M., $1 25 𝔓 ℔. and 30 "
———, valued over $30 but not over $45 𝔓 M., $2 𝔓 lb. and 50 "

DUTY.

Segars, valued over $45 per M., $3 𝔓 ℔. and 60 𝔓 cent.
———, paper segarettes, including wrappers, as other segars.
Seneca, or radix root ....20 𝔓 cent.
Senna...........................20 "
Sepia (or cuttle fish).............. 5 cts. 𝔓 ℔.
Serge, woolen (see woolens.)
Sewing silk......................40 𝔓 cent.
Sextants.........................35 "
Shades, lace, sewed...............35 "
Shaddocks.......................10 "
Shale, per ton, of 28 bush., 80 ℔s. to bush.........................$1.25 𝔓 ton.
Shawls, cotton ....35 𝔓 cent.
———, Cashmere, silk ....60 "
———, camels' hair..............35 "
———, lace......................35 "
———, ———, sewed ....35 "
———, worsted, costing under $2 per sq. yard, weight over 8 ounces per sq. yard ....24 cts. 𝔓 ℔. and 40 "
Shawls, worsted, costing over $2 per sq. yard, and weight over 8 ounces per sq. yard.....24 cts. 𝔓 ℔. and 45 "
Shawls, silk ....60 "
———, Thibet....................35 "
Shears ....35 "
Sheathing copper, that is, in sheets of 14 by 48 inches, weighing 14 to 34 ounces per square foot.......3½ cts. 𝔓 ℔.
Sheathing metal, patent, composed in part of copper, not in part iron, ungalvanized, in sheets of 14 by 48 inches, weighing from 14 to 34 oz. 𝔓 square foot..................3 "
Sheathing paper..................10 𝔓 cent.
Sheep skins, in the wool...........20 "
——— shears ....45 "
Sheet brass ....35 "
Sheets, willow, principally used in making hats ....30 "
Sheetings, Russia, brown or white..35 "
———, linen ....35 "

	DUTY.
Sheetings, hemp	35 ℔ cent.
———, porter, flax	35 "
———, Russia, brown or white, flax	35 "
Sheetings, Russia, hemp	35 "
Shell, gold, for painting	40 "
—— silver, for painting	40 "
——, boxes, not otherwise enumerated	35 "
Shell baskets	35 "
——, turtle or tortoise	free.
Shellac	10 cts. ℔ lb.
Shells, cocoa	2 "
——, all other	free.
Shingles	35 ℔ cent.
Shingle bolts	free.
Shirtings, cotton, bleached (see cottons.)	
Shirtings, linen (see flax.)	
Shirts, other	35 ℔ cent.
——, woolen, wove on frames,	20c. ℔ lb. and 30 "
——, silk	60 "
Shoe binding, cotton	35 "
—— ——, silk	60 "
—— ——, woolen. 24 cents ℔ lb. and	40 "
Shoe horns	35 "
—— knives	35 "
—— thread	40 "
Shoes, horse	35 "
—— or slippers for children	35 "
——— for grown persons, of silk	35 "
Shoes or slippers of leather for men	35 "
——— of prunella, stuff, or other materials, except silk, for women	35 "
Shoes, i. e. double-soled pumps and welts, women's leather	35 "
Shoes, India rubber	35 "
Shot bags, leather mounted	35 "
—— ——, if the leather be of the most value	35 "
Shot belts, mounted	35 ℔ cent.
Shot belts, if the leather be of the most value	35 "
Shovels, (iron or brass, for the hearth)	35 "
Shovels, and with or without handles, iron and steel, to dig with	45 "
Shovels, wood	35 "
——— and tongs, or fire irons (iron)	35 "
Shrubs	30 "
Shumac, or sumac	10 "
Shuttle-cocks and battle-doors	35 "
Sickles, iron	35 "
———, steel	45 "
Side-arms	35 "
Sieves, lawn	35 "
———, cypress	35 "
———, wire	35 "
———, hair	35 "
Silks in the gum, not more advanced than singles, tram, or organzine	35 "
Silk, spun, for filling in skeins or cops,	25 "
——, floss	35 "
——, sewing, in the gum or purified	40 "
——, all dress and piece	60 "
——, velvet, or of which silk is chief value	60 "
Silk aprons	60 "
—— bonnets	60 "
—— braids	60 "
—— caps	60 "
—— chemisettes	60 "
—— cords	60 "
—— drawers	60 "
—— fringes	60 "
—— gloves	60 "
—— galloons	60 "
—— handkerchiefs	60 "
—— hats	60 "
—— hose	60 "
—— laces	60 "
—— mantillas	60 "
—— mits	60 "
—— pongees	60 "
—— pelerines	60 "

	DUTY.
Silk ribbons	60 ℔ cent.
—— shawls	60 "
—— scarfs	60 "
—— shirts	60 "
—— stockings	60 "
—— suspenders	60 "
—— turbans	60 "
—— tassels	60 "
—— trimmings	60 "
—— vestings	60 "
—— veils	60 "
—— watch chains	60 "
—— webbing	60 "
—— buttons	40 "
—— button cloth	40 "
——, manufactures all of, or of which silk shall be a component material of chief value, not otherwise provided for	50 "
Silks, all manufactures of, not otherwise specified	50 "
Silk cocoons	free.
——, raw, or as reeled from the cocoon, not advanced in manufacture at all	free.
Silk waste	free.
Silk and worsted Valencias, silk chief of value	50 ℔ cent.
Silk and worsted toilet nets	50 "
Silk and worsted	50 "
—————— shawls, hemmed	35 "
Silk and cotton vesting	50 "
—— bolting cloths	free.
—— bobbin	50 ℔ cent.
—— garters, with wire and clasps	35 "
—— hat bands	50 "
Silk ornaments for head dresses	50 "
—— oil cloth	50 "
—— stocks	35 "
——, all other articles, not otherwise specified, made up by hand in whole or part, if no wool, to be worn	50 "
Silver bullion and coin	free.
Silver epaulettes and wings	35 ℔ cent.
——, leaf, of 500 leaves ℔ pkge	75 cts. ℔ pkge.
——, nitrate of	40 ℔ cent.
——, all manufactures of, not otherwise specified	40 "
Silver, German, in sheets	35 "
——, German, manufactures of	40 "
Silvered wire	35 "
Sisal grass, unmanufactured	$15 ℔ ton.
—— ——, manufactures of, not provided for	30 ℔ cent.
Size, gold and patent	20 "
Skates, costing 20 cents per pair and under	8 cts. ℔ pair.
Skates, costing over 20 cts. per pair	35 ℔ cent.
Skeletons	20 "
Skivers, tanned, not otherwise provided	25 "
———, pickled	10 "
Skins, pickled, in casks	10 "
——, of all kinds in the hair, dried, raw, or unmanufactured	10 "
Skins, calf, tanned and dressed	30 "
——, glazed, as patent leather	35 "
——, fish, for saddlers, &c	20 "
——, fur, raw or undressed	10 "
——, —, dressed	20 "
——, white, for druggists	25 "
——, dressed with alum only	25 "
——, sheep, tanned or dressed	25 "
——, goat or morocco, tanned and dressed	25 "
Skins, kid, tanned and dressed	25 "
——, goat and sheep, tanned and not dressed	25 "
Skins, kid and lamb, tanned and not dressed	25 "
Skins, tanned and dressed, otherwise than in colors, viz.: fawn, kid, and lamb, known as chamois	25 "
Skins with wool upon them	20 "
Slates of all kinds	40 "
Slate pencils	40 "
——, all manufactures of	40 "

	DUTY.
Sledges, blacksmiths'	2½ cts. ⅌ lb.
——, other	2½ "
Slippers for children	35 ⅌ cent.
—— not for children, leather	35 "
——, prunella	35 "
——, silk	35 "
——, stuff	35 "
——, other material	35 "
Slippers, nankeen	35 "
Slit iron, in nail or spike rods (see iron.)	
Slit iron, for band iron (see iron.)	
——, for scroll iron (see iron.)	
——, for casement rods (see iron.)	
Smalts	20 "
Snails	10 "
Snake root	20 "
Snaps, a clasp or ketch	35 "
——, or snap bits, for bridles	35 "
Snuff and snuff flour, all	50 cts. ⅌ lb.
Snuffers, silver or gold	40 ⅌ cent.
——, all other, (of iron)	35 "
——, trays, silver and gold	40 "
Snuffer trays, all other, (of iron)	35 "
Soap, Castile	1 ct. ⅌ ℔. and 30 "
——, fancy, all,	10 cts. ⅌ ℔. and 25 "
——, hard, all other	1 ct. ⅌ ℔. and 30 "
——, Naples,	10 cts. ⅌ ℔. and 25 "
——, perfumed, all	10 cts. ⅌ ℔. and 25 "
——, shaving	10 cts. ⅌ ℔. and 25 "
——, soft, all	1 ct. ⅌ ℔. and 30 "
——, turpentine, or common,	1 ct. ⅌ ℔. and 30 "
——, wash-balls	10 cts. ⅌ ℔. and 25 "
——, Windsor	10 cts. ⅌ ℔. and 25 "
—— pans, cast iron, whole or in parts	30 "
Soap stocks and stuffs	10 "
Socket chisels	45 "
Socks, cotton (unbleached)	35 "
——, silk	60 "
——, linen or thread	35 "
——, wool	20 cts. ⅌ ℔. and 30 "

	DUTY.
Socks, worsted, including those for children	35 ⅌ cent.
Soda, ash	½ ct. ⅌ ℔.
——, bi-carbonate of	1½ "
——, carbonate of	½ "
——, iodate of	20 ⅌ cent.
——, caustic	1½ ct. ⅌ lb.
——, hydriodate of	20 ⅌ cent.
——, hyposulphate of	20 "
—— lye	20 "
—— powders	20 "
——, sal	½ ct. ⅌ lb.
——, salts of	½ "
——, all carbonate of, except soda ash, barilla, and kelp	20 ⅌ cent.
Solanine (med. prep.)	40 "
Soles, cork	50 "
Sooty romals, cotton (see cottons.)	
Souvenirs	35 "
Soy	35 "
Spades of iron, with or without handles	35 "
Spades of steel, with or without handles	45 "
Spanish brown, dry	25 "
——, ground in oil	25 "
Spanish flies, or cantharides	50 cts. ⅌ ℔.
Spars	20 ⅌ cent.
Spartaria, or sparterie, or willow sheets, for hats	30 "
Spatulas	35 "
Spartateen, or coral	10 "
Spa, or spaware	30 "
Specimens anatomical preparations	35 "
—— in botany	free.
—— in mineralogy	free.
—— in natural history	free.
—— of, in sculpture	free.
Spectacle cases, gold	40 ⅌ cent.
——, iron	35 "
——, leather	35 "
——, paper	35 "
——, silver	40 "
——, steel	45 "

	DUTY.
Spectacle glasses, not set	40 ⅌ cent.
————, pebbles, not set	40 "
Spectacles, brass mounted	35 "
————, iron mounted	35 "
————, plated	35 "
————, steel	45 "
————, gold mounted	40 "
————, silver mounted	40 "
————, turtle shell, mounted	35 "
————, turtle shell and silver	40 "
Spelter, manufactures of	35 "
———, in pigs or blocks	$1\frac{1}{2}$ c. ⅌ lb.
———, in sheets	$2\frac{1}{4}$ "
Spermaceti oil, of foreign fisheries	20 ⅌ cent.
Spider net (as cotton cloth.)	
Spices of all kinds, not otherwise provided for	20 "
Spikes, copper	35 "
———, composition	35 "
———, iron, wrought	$2\frac{1}{2}$ c. ⅌ lb.
———, cut	$1\frac{1}{2}$ "
Spike rods (see iron.)	
Spirituous liquors, not otherwise provided for	100 ⅌ cent.
Spirits, lac	free.
———, yellow	20 ⅌ cent.
———, distilled or manufactured from grain (see gin.)	
Spirits of turpentine	30 cts. ⅌ gal.
——— distilled from other materials than grain (see gin.)	
Spoke shaves	35 ⅌ cent.
Spokes	35 "
Sponges	20 "
Spoons, gold and silver	40 "
———, horn	35 "
———, all other	35 "
Spunk	10 "
Spurs, gold and silver	40 "
——, all other	35 "
Springs for wigs, (steel)	45 "
——— of brass wire, used in the making of wigs	35 "
Spy-glasses	35 "

	DUTY.
Squares, brass	35 ⅌ cent.
———, marked on one side,	3 cents ⅌ ℔. and 30 "
———, iron, other	6 cts. ⅌ ℔. and 30 "
———, steel	6 cts. ⅌ ℔. and 30 "
Square wire, used for the manufacture of stretchers for umbrellas, and cut in pieces not exceeding the length used therefor	35 "
Squares, wood	35 "
Squills, or scilla	10 "
Stamped floor cloths, oil (see oil cloths.)	
Starch, made of potatoes or corn,	1 ct. ⅌ ℔. and 20 "
———, other	3 cts. ⅌ ℔. and 20 "
Stars of gold, fine and half fine	35 "
Statuary, all, the production of American artists abroad, provided it shall be so certified by the artist or consul	free.
Statuary, not otherwise provided for	10 ⅌ cent.
Statues, and specimens of statuary specially imported in good faith as objects of taste, and not merchandise	10 "
Statues and specimens of statuary, not specially imported, viz.:	
Statues of alabaster	10 "
——— of brass or bronze	10 "
——— of marble	10 "
——— of metal	10 "
——— of plaster, cast	10 "
——— of wood	10 "
Staves, for pipes, hogsheads, and casks	10 "
Staves, other	20 "
Stave bolts	free.
Stavesacre	20 ⅌ cent.

Steel, in bars	value 7c. or less ⅌ lb.	$2\frac{1}{4}$ ct. ⅌ lb.
—— ingots		
—— sheets		
—— coils		

DUTY.

Steel, in bars .. / —— ingots ... / —— sheets ... / —— coils .... — value over 7 cts. and not over 11 cts. ℘ lb .. — 3 cts. ℘ ℔.

Steel, in bars .. / —— ingots ... / —— sheets ... / —— coils .... — value over 11 cts. ℘ ℔. — 3½ cts. ℘ ℔. and 10 ℘ cent.

—— wire, not less than a quarter inch in diameter, and value 7 c. per lb. or less.................. 2¼ c. ℘ ℔.

Steel wire, not less than ¼ inch in diameter, and value over 7c. per lb. and not over 11c. per lb......... 3 "

Steel wire, as above, value over 11 cts. per ℔....... 3½ cts. ℘ ℔. and 10 ℘ cent.

Steel wire, less than a quarter inch diameter and not less than No. 16 wire gauge...... 2½ cts. ℘ lb. and 20 "

Steel wire, less than No. 16 wire gauge .... 3 cts. ℘ lb. and 20 "

Steel, in any form not otherwise provided for .... 30 "

Steel plates, engraved............. 25 "

Steel manufactures, all of, in whole or part, not otherwise provided for 45 "

Steel chains...................... 45 "

—— cutting knives, scythes, sickles, reaping hooks, spades and shovels.. 45 "

Steel, all articles not enumerated, manufactured from steel, or of which steel is a component part.. 45 "

Steelyards .... 35 "

Stereotype plates................ 25 "

Sticks, walking, finished or not..... 35 "

———, or frames for umbrellas or parasols .... 35 "

Stiffeners for cravats............. 35 "

Stilettoes (daggers).............. 35 "

————, ivory .... 35 "

Still bottoms.................... 35 "

Still worms .... 35 "

Stirrup irons..................... 35 "

Stock locks, if any steel .... 45 "

DUTY.

Stockings and half stockings, worsted 35 ℘ cent.

Stockings, silk .... 60 "

Stomach pumps .... 35 "

Stoneware, common .... 25 "

————, all other, composed of earth or mineral substances, whether gilt, painted, printed or glazed 40 "

Stoneware, exceeding the capacity of 10 gallons, not ornamented ...... 25 "

Stoneware gas retorts not ornamented .... 25 "

Stones, Bristol .... 10 "

———, polishing................. free.

———, burr, unwrought .... free.

———, burr, wrought .... free.

———, building .... 20 ℘ cent.

———, cornelian................. 10 "

———, garnet .... 10 "

———, grind .... 10 "

———, lithographic .... 20 "

———, load .... 20 "

———, marbles .... 50 "

———, mill, (burr,) bound up ..... 20 "

———, mill, fit for immediate use.. 20 "

———, not merchantable, for ballast 10 "

———, oil....................... 20 "

———, paving................... 10 "

———, pumice.................. free.

———, precious .... 10 ℘ cent.

———, rotten.................... free.

———, rag and sand .... 10 ℘ cent.

———, touch .... 20 "

———, whet..................... 20 "

Storax or styrax, a balsam......... 30 "

Straw baskets.................... 35 "

——— for hats, in its natural state.. 10 "

——— knives, iron, for cutting straw. 35 "

——— ———, steel, for cutting straw 45 "

Stretchers for umbrellas and parasols. 35 "

Strings of musical instruments, if gut 30 "

———, bow, if gut .... 30 "

———, hatters', if gut............. 30 "

Strontian .... 20 "

————, muriate of............. 20 "

DUTY.

Strontian, nitrate of .... 20 ⅌ cent.
Strychnine and its salts .... $1.50 ⅌ oz.
Studs, gold, as jewelry .... 25 ⅌ cent.
——, silver, " .... 25 "
——, gilt, " .... 25 "
——, ivory .... 35 "
——, mother of pearl .... 30 "
——, plated .... 35 "
——, brass .... 35 "
——, copper .... 35 "
Stump joints, iron .... 35 "
————, steel .... 45 "
Sublimate, corrosive (mercurial) ... 20 "
Substances expressly used for manures .... free.
Succory root .... 4 cts. ⅌ lb.
———— ground, burnt, or prepared .... 5 "
Sugars, all not above No. 12 Dutch standard in color .... 3 "
Sugars, all above No. 12 Dutch standard, and not above No. 15 Dutch standard in color .... 3½ "
Sugars, all above No. 15, not stove dried, and not above No. 20 Dutch standard in color .... 4 "
Sugars, all refined in form of loaf, lump, crushed, powdered, pulverized, or granulated .... 5 "
Sugars, all stove dried, or other sugars above No. 20 Dutch standard in color .... 5 "
Provided the standard by which the color and grades of sugars are to be regulated shall be selected and furnished to the collectors of such port of entry as may be necessary by the Secretary of the Treasury, from time to time, and in such manner as he may deem expedient.
Sugars, refined, when tinctured, colored, or adulterated, valued at 30 cts. ⅌ ℔. or less .... 15 cts. ⅌ ℔.

DUTY.

Sugars, as above, valued over 30 cts. ⅌ ℔. (see candy) .... 50 ⅌ cent.
Sugars, syrup of .... 2½ cts. ⅌ ℔.
——, syrup of cane .... 2½ "
Sugar tongs, gold and silver .... 40 ⅌ cent.
—— ——, plated .... 35 "
Sulphate of ammonia .... 20 "
———— of lime .... 10 "
———— of quinine .... 45 "
———— of rhubarb .... 20 "
———— of zinc .... 20 "
———— of magnesia, epsom salts .. 1 ct. ⅌ ℔.
———— of iron .... ½ "
Sulph. mur. tin .... 20 ⅌ cent.
Sulphur, flor, flour of sulph. $20 ⅌ ton and .... 15 "
Sulphurate of arsenic .... 20 "
Sulphuric acid, or oil of vitriol ..... 1 ct. ⅌ ℔.
Sulphuric ether .... $1 "
Sumac .... 10 ⅌ cent.
Super acetate of lead, or sugar of lead .... 4 cts. ⅌ lb.
Surgeons' instruments, ivory ...... 35 ⅌ cent.
———— ————, silver ...... 40 "
———— ————, steel, not otherwise provided for .... 45 "
Surplice pins .... 35 "
Suspenders or braces, cotton .... 35 "
——————, linen .... 35 "
——————, leather ...... 35 "
——————, silk .... 60 "
——————, leather ends only .... 35 "
Suspenders, India rubber .... 35 "
Suspender webbing, India rubber .. 35 "
———— webbing, silk .... 60 "
———— ends .... 35 "
Swans, down of .... 30 "
Swans' skins, undressed .... 20 "
—— ——, dressed .... 20 "
Sweetmeats, all not otherwise provided for .... 35 "
Sword blades .... 45 "
—— ——, for canes .... 45 "

DUTY.

Sword knots, lace ... 35 ⅌ cent.

——— ———, gold and silver, fine and half fine ... 35 "

Sword knots, silk ... 50 "

——— ———, worsted ... 50 "

Swords ... 35 "

T.

TABLE CLOTHS, cotton (see cotton.)

Table linen (see flax.)

Table covers, woolen (see woolens.)

——— ———, oil cloths (see oil cloth)

——— fasteners ... 35 ⅌ cent.

——— knives and forks ... 35 "

——— mats, oil or floor cloth (see mats.)

——— tops, composition ... 35 "

Tables, with marble tops, slabs, or ornaments ... 35 "

Table tops, scagliola ... 35 "

Tables, wood ... 35 "

Tacks, brads, or sprigs, not exceeding 16 ounces per 1,000 ... 2½ cts. ⅌ M.

Tacks, brads, or sprigs, exceeding do. 3 cts. ⅌ lb.

———, steel ... 45 ⅌ cent.

———, tinned ... 35 "

Taggers' iron ... 30 "

Talc, a mineral ... 10 "

Tallow ... 1 ct. ⅌ lb.

——— candles ... 2½ "

Tamarinds, preserved in sugar or brandy ... 35 ⅌ cent.

Tamarinds ... 10 "

Tamboreens ... 30 "

Tannin and tannic acid ... $2 ⅌ ℔.

Tapers, paper, with cotton wick ... 35 ⅌ cent.

Tapers, adamantine ... 5 cts. ⅌ ℔.

———, spermaceti, pure or mixed .. 8 "

———, stearine ... 5 "

———, wax, pure or mixed ... 8 "

Tapers, paraffine, pure or mixed ... 8 "

———, all other ... 2½ "

Tapes, cotton ... 35 ⅌ cent.

DUTY.

Tapes, Harlæm ... 35 ⅌ cent.

———, leather ... 35 "

———, linen ... 40 "

———, silk ... 50 "

———, measuring, linen ... 40 "

———, ———, leather ... 35 "

———, tailors' ... 35 "

———, ———, in silver cases ... 40 "

Tapioca ... 20 "

Tares ... 10 "

Tar, Barbadoes, crude ... 20 "

———, coal ... 20 "

Tarpaulings ... 20 "

Tartaric acid ... 20 cts. ⅌ lb.

Tartareous acid ... 20 "

Tartar, crude (argol) ... 6 "

——— emetic ... 15 "

Tartrite of antimony, or tart.-emetic. 15 "

Tasters, cheese ... 35 ⅌ cent.

Tassels, cords, and trimmings, commonly used by upholsterers, coachmakers, and saddlers, if entirely silk ... 60 "

Tassels, if cotton and silk ... 50 "

———, if gold or silver, fine or half fine ... 35 "

Teas, of all kinds, imported direct from China or other places of their growth, in vessels entitled so to do ... 25 cts. ⅌ ℔.

Teas, other ... 25 "

Teapots, Britannia ... 35 ⅌ cent.

———, China, plain white ... 45 "

———, earthen, common brown .. 25 "

———, ———, other ... 40 "

———, gold ... 40 "

———, gilt ... 35 "

———, japanned ... 40 "

———, plated ... 35 "

———, silver ... 40 "

Teazles ... 10 "

Teeth, elephants' ... 10 "

———, manufactured ... 20 "

Telescopes ... 35 "

DUTY.

Terraglis, a kind of coral..........10 ℘ cent.
Terra alba.......................20 "
Terra-japonica, or japanica ....10 "
Terra de sienna, dry ....50 cts. ℘ 100 lbs.
————, in oil.........$1.50 "
Terra umbra ....50 cts. "
Terrets, all kinds of, as saddlery....
Terne, tin plates or sheets ....25 ℘ cent.
Teutenague, in sheets.............2¼ cts. ℘ lb.
————, in blocks ....1½ "
————, in pigs ....1½ "
———— boxes................35 ℘ cent.
————, unmanufactured, in blocks or pigs.................1½ ct. ℘ lb.
Thermometers, telescopes, magic and other lanterns, and similar articles, composed of tin, glass, wood, brass, or copper.......................35 ℘ cent.
Thimbles, brass ....35 "
————, bone...................35 "
————, gold ....40 "
————, ivory ....35 "
————, plated ....35 "
————, silver ....40 "
————, steel ....45 "
Thor marine, a small fish ....½ ct. ℘ lb.
Thread, escutcheons...............35 ℘ cent.
————, flax......................40 "
———— insertings ....30 "
————, lace ....30 "
————, pack.....................40 "
————, shoe (linen) ....40 "
———— stockings.................35 "
———— buttons, (flax)............30 "
Thridace ....20 "
Tica, (crude)......................20 "
Ticks, cotton (see cotton.)
————, flax (see flax.)
————, —— or linen, colored (see flax.)
————, linen, bleached or unbleached (see flax.)
Tiles, encaustic...................35 "
——, marble.....................50 "
——, paving and roofing ....20 "

DUTY.

Timber, hewn or sawed...........20 ℘ cent.
————, for wharves ....20 "
Timepieces ....35 "
Tin, in bars.......................15 "
——, banca.......................15 "
——, block ....15 "
——, boxes.......................30 "
——, crystals of...................30 "
—— foil ....30 "
——, granulated ....20 "
——, grain ....20 "
——, liquor.......................20 "
——, muriate of...................30 "
——, oxide of.....................30 "
——, in pigs ....15 "
——, in plates ....25 "
——, ————, galvanized by electric batteries.....................2½ cts. ℘ lb.
——, in sheets ....25 ℘ cent.
——, salts of.....................30 "
——, tagger ....25 "
——, all manufactures of, not enumerated, or of which tin is a component part.....................35 "
Tincal, or borax, crude ....5 cts. ℘ lb.
Tinctures, odoriferous.............50 ℘ cent.
————, bark, and other medicinal ....40 "
Tips of horns ....10 "
—— of bone......................10 "
—— and runners for parasols and umbrellas, metal................35 "
Tippets, if so made as to be classed as millinery....................35 "
Tippets, fur......................35 "
————, silk....................35 "
————, wool......24 cts. ℘ lb. and 40 "
Toasters, cheese..................35 "
Tobacco, manufactured, not provided for.......................50 c. ℘ lb.
Tobacco leaves, unmanufactured, and not stemmed...................35 "
Tobacco leaves, stemmed...........50 "
———— stems ....30 ℘ cent.

DUTY.

Toilet vials or bottles, not exceeding the capacity of 4 ounces each, cut. 40 ℔ cent.
Toilet vials or bottles, exceeding 4 ounces and not exceeding 16 ounces each, cut. . . . . 40 "
Tongues, reindeer . . . . 20 "
———, sounds (fish) . . . . 20 "
———, neats, smoked . . . . 20 "
Tongs, (shovels and tongs,) iron. . . . 35 "
Tonca, tonga, tongua, or tonqua beans . . . . 20 "
Tools and implements of trade of persons arriving in the United States does not include machinery, or articles imported for manufacturing establishments, or on sale . . free.
Tooth brushes. 40 ℔ cent.
——— powder . . . . 50 "
Toothpicks, bone . . . . 35 "
———, ivory . . . . 35 "
———, metal or wood . . . . 35 "
———, quills . . . . 30 "
———, shell . . . . 35 "
———, silver and gold. . . . . 40 "
Topaz, real . . . . 10 "
———, imitation . . . . 40 "
Tortoise shell . . . . free.
Touchstones . . . . 20 ℔ cent.
Tow of hemp . . . . $10 ℔ ton.
——— of flax . . . . $5 "
Toys, of every description . . . . 50 ℔ cent.
———, paper . . . . 50 "
———, wood. . . . . 50 "
Trace chains, iron, (see iron.)
Traces, leather. . . . . 35 "
Tragacanth, gum . . . . 20 "
Traps, iron . . . . 35 "
———, steel . . . . 45 "
———, wire . . . . 35 "
———, wood . . . . 35 "
Trays and waiters, gold or silver . . . 40 "
———, gilt . . . . 35 "
———, japanned . . . . 40 "
———, plated . . . . 35 "
Trays and waiters, wood . . . . 35 ℔ cent.
Treacle, molasses. . . . . 8 cts. ℔ gal.
Tresses, lace, even if mi fin . . . . 35 ℔ cent.
Trees, all. . . . . 30 "
Tripoli . . . . 25 "
Trowels . . . . 45 "
Truffles (vegetable) preserved . . . . . 35 "
———, earthen, common. . . . . 25 "
Trunk handles . . . . 35 "
Trusses with iron or steel springs of more value than the leather. . . . . . 45 "
Trusses, if leather and iron be the material. . . . . 35 "
Tubes, bone . . . . 35 "
———, ivory. . . . . 35 "
———, metal, iron or brass . . . . 35 "
———, silver . . . . 40 "
Tug buckles, as saddlery. . . . . 35 "
Tumblers, if cut glass. . . . . 40 "
———, if plain glass . . . . 35 "
Turmeric . . . . free.
Turquoises . . . . 10 ℔ cent.
Turpentine, spirits of . . . . 30 cts. ℔ gal.
Turtles. . . . . 20 ℔ cent.
Turtle shell. . . . . free.
Tweezers, steel. . . . . 45 ℔ cent.
———, gold and silver. . . . . 40 "
Twine, flax or linen,. . . . . 40 "
———, colored, for quills, cotton,. . . 35 "
Twist, cotton . . . . 40 "
———, silk. . . . . 40 "
———, mohair and silk. . . . . 40 "
———, worsted, lines. . . . . 50 "
Types, new . . . . 25 "
———, metal . . . . 25 "
———, old, if only fit to be remanufactured . . . . free.

U.

ULTRA MARINE. . . . . 25 ℔ cent.
Umber . . . . ½ ct. ℔ lb.
Umbrellas, (not silk). . . . . 35 ℔ cent.
———, silk . . . . 50 "

DUTY.

Umbrellas, sticks or frames for.....35 ℔ cent.

———, brass tips, runners, &c., for.........................35 "

Umbrella, square wire, used in the manufacture of stretchers, if cut in the usual lengths for............35 "

Umbrella furniture, silver for......40 "

———, bone or ivory..35 "

United States—all articles of the growth, produce, or manufacture of the United States, on which no allowance for bounty or drawback has been made on exportation....free.

United States—all articles imported for the use of, according to the material of which composed.

V.

VANDYKE, brown...............20 ℔ cent.

Valencias, wool (see wool.)

Valenciennes (thread lace) ....30 "

Valonia, or valeni, a nut, for dyeing.free.

Vanilla, plants of................30 ℔ cent.

——— beans ....$3 ℔ lb.

Varnishes of all kinds, value not over $1.50 ℔ gall..50 cts. ℔ gall. and 20 ℔ cent.

Varnishes of all kinds, value over $1.50 ℔ gall..50 cts. ℔ gall. and 25 "

Vases, porcelain, ornamented, containing flowers, with stands and shades.........................50 "

Vegetable substances, unmanufactured, used for beds ....20 "

Vegetable substances, unmanufactured, used for cordage ....$15 ℔ ton.

Vegetables, prepared ....35 ℔ cent.

———, used in dyeing, or in composing dyes exclusively, in a crude state.....................free.

Vegetables, not otherwise provided for..........................10 ℔ cent.

Vegetable substances, not otherwise provided for........10 ℔ ct. and $5 ℔ ton.

DUTY.

Vellum.........................30 ℔ cent.

Velvet, cotton ....35 "

———, printed or painted.........35 "

———, silk and cotton, silk not chief value ....50 "

Velvet, silk (see silks.)

———, binding, cotton............35 "

Velvet binding, silk...............60 "

Velveteens, cotton (see cottons.)

Veneering rods...................35 "

Venetian red, dry ....25 "

———, in oil...............25 "

Venison hams....................2 cts. ℔ lb.

Veratrine (medical prep.) ....40 ℔ cent.

Verdigris.........................6 cts. ℔ lb.

Verditure ....20 ℔ cent.

Vermicelli.......................35 "

Vermilion ....25 "

Vermuth (wine bitters) ....100 "

Vessels, cast iron, not otherwise specified.........................1½ ct. ℔ lb.

Vessels, copper...................35 ℔ cent.

Vestings, cotton (see cotton.)

———, silk and cotton ....50 "

———, silk (see silks)...........60 "

———, silk and wool, wool chief value, not otherwise provided for........24 cts. ℔ lb. & 40 "

Vestings, woolen, not otherwise provided for.........24 cts. ℔ lb. & 40 "

Vests, if no wool ....35 "

Vials, all perfumery and fancy, not cut, not exceeding the capacity of four ounces each ....35 "

Vials, perfumery and fancy, not cut, when exceeding four ounces, and not exceeding sixteen ounces each.35 "

Vials, all perfumery and fancy, cut .40 "

———, apothecaries', above six ounces, and not exceeding sixteen ounces ....35 "

Vices (iron).......................35 "

Vinegar ....10 cts. ℔ gal.

———, concentrated, (see acid acetous.)

	DUTY.
Violins	30 ⅌ cent.
Violin strings, gut	30 "
——— ———, wire	35 "
Vitriol, oil of, sulphuric acid	1 ct. ⅌ ℔.
———, blue or Roman, or sulphate of copper	25 ⅌ cent.
Vitriol, green	½ ct. ⅌ ℔.
———, white, or sulphate of zinc	20 ⅌ cent.

W.

	DUTY.
WADDING, paper	35 ⅌ cent.
Wafers	35 "
Wagon boxes	35 "
Waiters, gold or silver	40 "
———, gilt	35 "
———, japanned	40 "
———, ——— paper	40 "
———, plated	35 "
———, wood	35 "
———, leather	35 "
Walnuts, all	3 cts. ⅌ ℔.
Walking sticks or canes, mounted	35 ⅌ cent.
————————, unmounted	35 "
Warming pans, brass	35 "
—————, copper	35 "
Wash blue	25 "
Washes, cosmetic or dentifrice	50 "
Wash balls	10 cts. ⅌ lb. and 25 "
Waste or shoddy	3 cts. ⅌ ℔.
Watches, gold and silver	25 ⅌ cent.
————, and parts of other	20 "
Watch crystals	40 "
——— materials and unfinished parts of	20 "
Water, aqua mellis, or honey	50 "
——, bay, commonly called bay rum	$1 50 ⅌ gall.
Water, Hungary	50 ⅌ cent.
——, lavender	50 "
——, orange flower	50 "
——, rose	50 "
—— colors	35 "
Wax beads	50 "
Wax, bees, bleached or unbleached	20 ⅌ cent.
Wax, sealing	35 "
——, shoemakers'	20 "
—— tapers	8 cts. ⅌ ℔.
Wearing apparel of persons arriving in the United States in actual use, and personal effects, not merchandise	free.
Web, or webbing, boot, of cotton	35 ⅌ cent.
————————, of flax	35 "
————————, of silk	60 "
————————, of worsted	35 "
————————, of wool	35 "
Webbing, India rubber	35 "
Wedgewood ware (white)	40 "
Weights, brass	35 "
Weights, cast iron, without rings of wrought iron affixed to them	35 "
Weights, copper	35 "
Weights, lead	35 "
Weld	free.
Wet blue	25 ⅌ cent.
Whalebone, the product of foreign fishing	20 "
Whalebone, of American fishing	free.
Whale oil, of foreign fishing	20 ⅌ cent.
————, of American fishing, and all other articles the produce of said fisheries	free.
Wheat	20 cts. ⅌ bush.
——— flour	20 ⅌ cent.
Whetstones	20 "
Whips	35 "
Whiskey (see gin.)	
White vitriol	20 "
Whiting, dry	1 ct. ⅌ lb.
————, ground in oil	2 "
Wick, cottons,	35 ⅌ cent.
Wigs	35 "
Willow sheets, for hats	30 "
———, for making baskets or covering demijohns	30 "
Willows, coopers' split	20 "

	DUTY.
Window glass, crown and common cylinder, unpolished, not above 10 by 15 inches	1½ cts. ℔ lb.
Window glass, as above, over 10 by 15, and not over 16 by 24	2 "
Window glass, as above, 16 by 24, but not over 24 by 30	2½ "
Window glass, as above, all above 24 by 30 inches	3 "
Window glass, polished, cylinder and crown, not over 10 by 15 inches	2½ c. ℔ sq. ft.
Window glass, as above, over 10 by 15 inches, but not over 16 by 24	4 "
Window glass, as above, over 16 by 24, and not over 24 by 30 inches	6 "
Window glass, as above, all over 24 by 30 inches, but not above 24 by 60 inches	20 "
Window glass, as above, and over 24 by 60 inches	40 "

Wine, Burgundy, in bottles ....
——, ————, in casks..........
——, Canary, in casks or bottles...
——, Champagne, in bottles or casks.
——, Claret, in bottles............
——, ——, in casks............
——, Madeira, in bottles..........
——, ———, in casks...........
——, ———, imitation of, in bottles or casks...................
Wine, Oporto, in bottles..........
——, ———, in casks............
——, Port, imitations of, in bottles.
——, ——, ————, in casks..
——, Sherry, in casks or bottles...
——, St. Lucar, in casks or bottles..........................
——, Sicily Madeira, in casks or bottles..........................
Wine, all other of Sicily, in casks or bottles.......................

Valued not over 50 cts. ℔ gallon..20 cts. ℔ gallon and 25 ℔ cent.
Valued over 50 cts. and not over $1 ℔ gall...50 cts. ℔ gall. and 25 ℔ cent.
Valued over $1 ℔ gallon..$1 ℔ gallon and 25 ℔ cent.

Wine, Teneriffe, in casks or bottles.
Wines of all countries, in bottles, unless specially enumerated........
Wines of all countries, in casks, unless specially enumerated........
Wines, white, in casks, not enumerated, of France, Prussia, Sardinia, and of Portugal and its possessions.........................
Wines, of Austria and Prussia, in bottles.......................
Wines, white, in bottles, not enumerated, of France, Sardinia, and of Portugal and its possessions.....
Wines, all other, not otherwise provided for.....................

Valued not over 50c. ℔ gall...20c. ℔ gall. and 25 ℔ cent.
Valued over 50c. and not over $1 ℔ gall...$1 ℔ gall. and 25 ℔ cent.
Valued over $1 ℔ gall...$1 ℔ gall. and 25 ℔ cent.

Provided, that no champagne or sparkling wines, in bottles, shall pay a less rate of duty than $6 per doz. bottles, each bottle containing not more than one quart and more than one pint, or $6 per two doz. bottles, each bottle containing not more than one pint.

	DUTY.
Wine lees, liquid	20 ℔ cent.
—— bottles containing wine	2 cts. each.
—— lees, crystallized, or crude tartar	6 cts. ℔ lb.
Wings and epaulets, fin, mi fin	35 ℔ cent.
——, gold or silver	35 "
——, plated, fin, mi fin	35 "
Winter bark, or cannella alba	20 "
Wire, brass	35 "
——, covered with silk or cotton, same as other wire, duty according to number of wire, and 5 cents per pound in addition.	
Wire, copper	35 "
——, gilt	35 "
——, gold or silver	40 "
——, hat, covered, if cotton, same as wire, and 5 cents per pound in addition.	
Wire, iron (see iron.)	

DUTY.

Wire, plated......................35 ⅌ cent.
——, ribbon......................35 "
——, silvered......................35 "
——, steel (see steel.)
——, wove......................35 "
——, square, used for the manufacture of stretchers for umbrellas, and cut in pieces not exceeding the length therefor......................35 "
Wire, binding, for saddlery (iron rolled and flattened,) and other not specified......................35 "
Wire, tinned, (see iron wire tinned.)
Woad, or pastal......................free.
Women's bonnets or hats, of silk....60 ⅌ cent.
————————, of straw, chip, or grass......................40 "
Women's caps......................35 "
———— caps, of silk......................60 "
———— gowns and dresses, if no wool......................35 "
Wood, awl hafts......................35 "
—— balls, gilt or not......................35 "
—— backgammon men......................35 "
——, bar......................free.
——, box......................free.
——, Brazil......................free.
——, Brazilletto......................free.
—— chess men......................35 "
——, camwood......................free.
——, carmaguey......................free.
—— castors, with rivets......................35 ⅌ cent.
—— castors, if otherwise......................35 "
——, dye, all in sticks......................free.
——, fire......................20 ⅌ cent.
——, fustic......................free.
——, goncallo......................20 ⅌ cent.
—— jacks......................35 "
——, lignumvitæ......................free.
——, lance......................free.
——, lake......................25 ⅌ cent.
——, log......................free.
—— ornaments, gilt......................35 ⅌ cent.
——, Nicaragua......................free.

DUTY.

Wood, Pernambuco......................free.
——, queen's......................free.
——, red sanders......................free.
——, red......................free.
——, Rio de la Hache......................free.
—— rules......................35 ⅌ cent.
——, Santa Martha and other dyewoods......................free.
Wood, sandal, in sticks......................free.
——, ebony and granadilla......................free.
——, ebony green, (a dye)......................free.
——, unmanufactured, of any kind not enumerated......................20 ⅌ cent.
Wood, Jacaranda, or rose......................free.
——, rose, satin, cedar and mahogany......................free.
Wood, quassia, crude (drug)......................20 ⅌ cent.
——, all cabinet......................free.
——, manufactures of, not otherwise specified......................35 ⅌ cent.
Wood screws, so called (see iron screws.)
Wool, unmanufactured, the value at the last port of export is 12c. per pound or less, exclusive of charges in such port......................3 cts. ⅌ lb.
Wool, unmanufactured, the value at the last port of export, exclusive of charges in such ports, is more than 12c. and not over 24c. per pound. 6 c. ⅌ lb.
Wool, unmanufactured, the value at the last port of export, exclusive of charges in such ports, is over 24c. and not over 32 cts. ⅌ lb.
10 cts. per pound and 10 ⅌ cent.
Wool, as above, value over 32 cts. ⅌ lb......................12 cts. ⅌ lb. and 10 "
Wool, unmanufactured, imported in such a state, by mixture of dirt, etc., as to reduce to 12c. per pound, 10 "
Wool, mixed in same bale, if appraised over 24 cts. ⅌ lb.
10 cts. ⅌ lb. and 10 "
Wool of different qualities, in same

DUTY.

invoice, all charged at same price, so the average price shall be reduced more than 10 per cent., the whole to pay duty on finest wool in lot.

Wool, imported, scoured, shall pay, in lieu of the above duties, three times the amount of such duties.

Wool, all manufactures of, or of which wool shall be a component material, not otherwise provided for, 24 cts. ℔ lb. and 40 ℔ cent.

As above, if value over $2 ℔ sq. yd. . . . . 24 c. ℔ lb. and 45 "

Woolen bags. . . . . 24 cts. ℔ lb. and 40 "

——— cloth, not otherwise provided for. . . . . 24 cts. ℔ lb. and 40 "

Woolen cassimere, not otherwise provided for. . . . . 24 cts. ℔ lb. and 40 "

Woolen cloths and cassimeres, if value over two dollars per sq. yd. 24 cts. ℔ lb. and 45 "

Provided, that goods of like description, composed of worsted, the hair of the alpaca, goat, or other like animals, and weighing over 8 oz. per square yd., shall pay the same duty as on woolen cloths.

Woolen hosiery, all. . 20 cts. ℔ lb. & 30 "

——— flocks . . . . . 3 cts. ℔ lb.

——— listings . . . . . 30 ℔ cent.

Woolen shawls, not otherwise provided for. . . . . 24 cts. ℔ lb. and 40 "

Woolen shawls, if valued over $2 per sq. yd. . . . . 24 cts. ℔ lb. and 45 "

Woolen clothing, ready-made, and wearing apparel of every description, in whole or in part of wool, made up in whole or part by tailors, seamstresses, or manufacturers . . . . . 24 cts. ℔ lb. and 40 "

Woolen endless belts, for paper machines. . . . . 20 cts. ℔ lb. and 35 "

DUTY.

Woolen blanketing, for printing machines. . . . . 20 cts. ℔ lb. and 35 ℔ cent.

Wool, on the skin, raw . . . . . 20 "

Woolen tippets, wove. . 20 c. ℔ lb. & 30 "

Worms for stills . . . . . 35 "

Wormwood, oil of . . . . . 50 "

Worsted shawls, hemmed, not otherwise provided for. . . . . 35 "

Worsted, manufactures of, or combed wool, not otherwise provided for. . 50 "

Worsted bags. . . . . 50 "

——— caps (not wove). . . . . 50 "

——— table covers. . . . . 50 "

——— bindings. . . . . 50 "

——— hose. . . . . 35 "

——— drawers . . . . . 35 "

——— plains . . . . . 50 "

——— gloves . . . . . 35 "

——— mitts . . . . . 35 "

——— toilinets . . . . . 50 "

——— twist . . . . . 50 "

——— wove pantaloons. . . . . 35 "

——— shirts. . . . . 35 "

Y.

YAMS . . . . . 10 ℔ cent.

Yarn, coir . . . . . $1\frac{1}{2}$ c. ℔ lb.

——, cotton . . . . . 35 ℔ cent.

——, flax or linen, for carpeting, not over No. 8 lea., and valued at 24 cts. or less per lb. . . . . 30 "

Yarn, as above, valued over 24 cts. per lb. . . . . 35 "

Yarn, Jute . . . . . 25 "

Yarns, hemp . . . . . 5 cts. ℔ lb.

——, woolen, valued at 50c. and not over $1 per pound. 20 cts. ℔ lb. and 25 ℔ cent.

Yarn, woolen, over $1 per pound, 24 cts. ℔ lb. and 30 "

——, ———, value under 50c. per pound, and not over No. 14 in fineness. . . . . 16 cts. ℔ lb. and 25 "

Yarn, woolen, for carpets, over No. 14 in fineness . . . . . 35 "

DUTY.

Yarn, worsted, valued at 50c. and not over $1 per pound, 20 cts. ꝑ ℔. and 25 ꝑ cent.

Yarn, worsted, value over $1 per pound.........24 cts. ꝑ ℔. and 30 "

Yarn, worsted, value under 50c. per pound and not over No. 14 in fineness ....16 cts. ꝑ ℔. and 25 "

Yarn, worsted, for carpets, over No. 14 in fineness ....35 "

Yarn, untarred, hemp............ 5 c. ꝑ ℔.

Yellow, king's patent.............25 ꝑ cent.

——— berries (for dyeing) ....free.

———, chromate of potash........ 3 c. ꝑ. ℔.

———, citric acid...............10 cts. ꝑ ℔.

——— ochre, dry............50 c. ꝑ 100 ℔.

DUTY.

Yellow ochre, in oil ....$1 50 ꝑ 100 ℔.

———, salt of chrome ....20 ꝑ cent.

———, spirits ....20 "

Z.

ZAFFRE ....20 ꝑ cent.

Zinc, nails ....35 "

——, in pigs, or otherwise unwrought.......................1½ c. ꝑ ℔.

——, in blocks...................1½ "

——, in sheets ....2¼ "

——, sulphate of ....20 ꝑ cent.

——, oxide of, dry, or ground in oil. 1¾ c. ꝑ ℔.

——, manufactures of.............35 ꝑ cent.

——, valerianate of, (chemical).....20 "

FOR GENERAL INFORMATION.

Brandy and Spirits may be imported in bottles 12 in each case, but cannot be imported in other smaller packages, under the capacity of 15 gallons for brandy, and 90 gallons for spirits, (except arrack and sweet cordials,) under penalty of forfeiture.

Extract from Act of July 14, 1862.

SEC. 14. *And be it further enacted*, That from and after the day and year aforesaid, there shall be levied, collected, and paid on all goods, wares, and merchandise of the growth or produce of countries beyond the Cape of Good Hope, when imported from places this side of the Cape of Good Hope, a duty of ten per centum ad valorem, and in addition to the duties imposed on any such articles when imported directly from the place or places of their growth or production.

APPENDIX.

WAREHOUSING BILL.

PASSED AUGUST 6, 1846.

AN ACT to amend an Act entitled "An Act to provide revenue from Imports, and to change and modify existing laws imposing duties on Imports, and for other purposes."

Be it enacted by the Senate and House of Representatives of the United States of America in Congress assembled, That the twelfth section of the act entitled "An Act to provide revenue from imports, and to change and modify existing laws imposing duties on imports, and for other purposes," approved the thirtieth day of August, one thousand eight hundred and forty-two, is hereby amended so as hereafter to read as follows:—[SEC. 12] And be it further enacted, That on and after the day this act goes into operation the duties on all imported goods, wares or merchandise shall be paid in cash: Provided, That, in all cases of failure or neglect to pay the duties within the period allowed by law to the importer to make entry thereof, or whenever the owner, importer or consignee shall make entry for warehousing the same in writing, in such form and supported by such proof as shall be prescribed by the Secretary of the Treasury, the said goods, wares or merchandise shall be taken possession of by the collector, and deposited in the public stores, or in other stores to be agreed on by the collector or chief revenue officer of the port and the importer, owner or consignee, the said stores to be secured in the manner provided for by the first section of the act of the twentieth day of April, one thousand eight hundred and eighteen, entitled "An Act providing for the deposite of wine and distilled spirits in public warehouses, and for other purposes," there to be kept with due and reasonable care, at the charge and risk of the owner, importer, consignee, or agent, and subject at all times to their order upon payment of the proper duties and expenses, to be ascertained on due entry thereof for warehousing, and to be secured by bond of the owner, importer, or consignee, with surety or sureties, to the satisfaction of the collector in double the amount of the said duties, and in such form as the Secretary of the Treasury shall prescribe; Provided, That no merchandise shall be withdrawn from any warehouse in which it may be deposited, in a less quantity than in an entire package, bale, cask, or box, unless in bulk; nor shall merchandise so imported in bulk be delivered, except in the whole quantity of each parcel, or in quantity not less than one ton weight, unless by special authority of the Secretary of the Treasury. And in case the owner, importer, consignee, or agent of any goods on which the duties have not been paid, shall give to the collector satisfactory security that the said goods shall be landed out of the jurisdiction of the United States, in the manner now required by existing laws relating to exportations for the benefit of drawback, the collector and naval officer, if any, on an entry to re-export the same, shall, upon payment of the appropriate expenses, permit the said goods, under the inspection of the proper officers, to be shipped without the payment of any duties thereon. And in case any goods wares, or merchandise, deposited as aforesaid, shall remain in public store beyond one year, without payment of the duties and charges thereon, then said goods, wares or merchandise shall be appraised by the appraisers of the United States, if there be any at such port, and if none, then by two merchants to be designated and sworn by the collector for that purpose, and sold by the collector at public auction, on due public notice thereof being first given, in the manner and for the time to be prescribed by a general regulation of the Treasury Department; and at said public sale distinct printed catalogues, descriptive of said goods, with the appraised value affixed thereto, shall be distributed among the persons present at said sale; and a reasonable opportunity shall be given before such sale, to persons desirous of purchasing, to inspect the quality of such goods; and the proceeds of said sale, after deducting the usual rate of storage at the port in question, with all other charges and expenses, including duties, shall be paid over to the owner, importer, consignee, or agent, and proper receipts taken for the same; Provided, That the overplus, if any there be, of the proceeds of such sales, after the payment of storage, charges, expenses, and duties as aforesaid, remaining unclaimed for the space of ten days after such sales, shall be paid by the collector into the treasury of the United States; and the said collector shall transmit to the Treasury Department, with the said overplus, a copy of the inventory, appraisement, and account of sales, specifying the marks, numbers, and description of the packages sold, their contents and appraised value, the name of the vessel and master in which and of the port or place whence they were imported, and the time when and the name of the person or persons to whom said goods were consigned in the manifest, and the duties and charges to which the several consignments were respectively subject; and the receipt or certificate of the collector shall exonerate the master or person having charge or command of any ship or vessel in which said goods, wares or merchandise were imported, from all claim of the owner or owners thereof, who shall, nevertheless, on due proof of their interest, be entitled to receive from the treasury the amount of any overplus paid into the same under the provisions of this act; Provided, That so much of the fifty-sixth section of the general collection law of the second of March, seventeen hundred and ninety-nine, and the thirteenth section of the act of the thirtieth of August, eighteen hundred and forty-two, to provide revenue from imports, and to change and modify existing laws imposing duties on imports, and for other purposes, as conflicts with the provisions of this act, shall be, and is hereby repealed, excepting that nothing contained in this act shall be construed to extend the time now prescribed by law for selling unclaimed goods; Provided, also, That all goods of a perishable nature, and all gunpowder, fire-crackers, and explosive substances, deposited as aforesaid, shall be sold forthwith.

Sec. 2. And be it further enacted, That any goods, when deposited in the public stores in the manner provided for in the foregoing section, may be withdrawn therefrom and transported to any other port of entry, under the restriction provided for in the act of second of March, seventeen hundred and ninety-nine, in respect to the transportation of goods, wares and merchandise from one collection district to another, to be exported with the benefit of drawback; and the owner of such goods so to be withdrawn for transportation, shall give his bond with sufficient sureties, in double the amount of the duties chargeable on them, for the deposite of such goods in store in the port of entry to which they shall be destined, such bond to be cancelled when the goods shall be re-deposited in store in collection district to which they shall be transported; Provided, That nothing contained in this section shall be construed to extend the time during which goods may be kept in store, after their original importation and entry, beyond the term of one year.

Sec. 3. And be it further enacted, That if any warehoused goods shall be fraudulently concealed or removed from any public or private warehouse, the same shall be forfeited to the United States; and all persons convicted of fraudulently concealing or removing such goods, or of aiding or abetting such concealment or removal, shall be liable to the same penalties which are now imposed for the fraudulent introduction of goods into the United States; and if any importer or proprietor of any warehoused goods, or any person in his employ, shall by any contrivance fraudulently open the warehouse, or shall gain access to the goods, except in the presence of the proper officer of the customs acting in the execution of his duty, such importer or proprietor shall forfeit and pay for every such offence one thousand dollars. And any person convicted of altering, defacing, or obliterating any mark or marks which have been placed by any officer of the revenue on any package or packages of warehoused goods, shall forfeit and pay for every such offence five hundred dollars.

Sec. 4. And be it further enacted, That the collectors of the several ports of the United States shall make quarterly reports to the Secretary of the Treasury, according to such general instructions as the said Secretary may give, of all goods which remain in the warehouses of their respective ports specifying the quantity and description of the same; which returns or tables formed thereon, the Secretary of the Treasury shall forthwith cause to be published in the principal papers of the city of Washington.

Sec. 5. And be it further enacted, That the Secretary of the Treasury be and he is hereby authorized to make, from time to time, such regulations, not inconsistent with the laws of the United States, as may be necessary to give full effect to the provisions of this act, and secure a just accountability under the same. And it shall be the duty of the Secretary to report such regulations to each succeeding session of Congress

AN ACT

To extend the warehousing system by establishing private bonded warehouses, and for other purposes.

Be it enacted by the Senate and House of Representatives of the United States of America in Congress assembled, That from and after the passage of this act, any goods, wares or merchandise subject to duty, with the exception of perishable articles, also gunpowder, fire-crackers, and other explosive substances, which shall have been duly entered and bonded for warehousing, in conformity with existing laws, may be deposited at the option of the owner, importer, consignee, or agent, at his expense and risk, in any public warehouse owned or leased by the United States, or in the private warehouse of the importer, the same being used exclusively for the storage of warehoused goods of his own importation or to his consignment, or in a private warehouse used by the owner, occupant, or lessee, as a general warehouse for the storage of warehoused goods, such place of storage to be designated on the warehouse entry at the time of entering such merchandise at the custom-house: Provided, That such private warehouse shall be used solely for the purpose of storing warehoused goods, and shall have been previously approved by the Secretary of the Treasury, and have been placed in charge of a proper officer of the customs, who, together with the owner and proprietor of the warehouse, shall have the joint custody of all the merchandise stored in said warehouse, and all the labor on the goods so stored must be performed by the owner or proprietor of the warehouse, under the supervision of the officer of the customs in charge of the same, at the expense of the aforesaid owner or proprietor: And provided, further, That cellars and vaults of stores for the storage of wines and distilled spirits only, and yards for the storage of coal, mahogany, and other woods and lumber, may, at the discretion of the Secretary of the Treasury, be constituted bonded warehouses for the storage of such articles, under the same regulations and conditions as required in the storage of other merchandise; the cellars or vaults aforesaid shall be exclusively appropriated to the storage of wines or distilled spirits, and shall have no opening or entrance except the one from the street, on which separate and different locks of the custom house and the owner or proprietor of the cellars or vaults shall be placed.

Sec. 2. And be it further enacted, That unclaimed goods, wares or merchandise required by existing laws to be taken possession of by collectors of the customs, may be stored in any public warehouse owned or leased by the United States, or in any private bonded warehouse authorized by this act, and all charges for storage, labor, and other expenses accruing on any such goods, wares, or merchandise, not to exceed in any case the regular rates for such objects at the port in question, must be paid before delivery of the goods on due entry thereof by the claimant or owner; or if sold as unclaimed goods to realize the import duties, the aforesaid charges shall be paid by the collector out of the proceeds of the sale thereof, before paying such proceeds into the Treasury, as required by existing laws. And any collector of the customs is hereby authorized, under such directions and regulations as may be prescribed by the Secretary of the Treasury, to sell upon due notice, at public auction, any unclaimed goods, wares or merchandise deposited in public warehouse, whenever the same may, from depreciation in value, damage, leakage, or other cause, in the opinion of such collector, be likely to prove insufficient on a sale thereof to pay the duties, storage, and other charges if suffered to remain in public store for the period now allowed by law in the case of unclaimed goods.

Sec. 3. And be it further enacted, That before any of the stores or cellars aforesaid, owned or occupied by private individuals, shall be used as a warehouse for merchandise imported by other merchants or importers, the owner, occupant or lessee thereof shall enter into bond, in such sums and with such sureties as may be approved by the Secretary of the Treasury, exonerating and holding the United States and its officers harmless from or on account of any risk, loss or expense of any kind or description, connected with or arising from the deposit or keeping of the merchandise in the warehouse aforesaid; and all imports deposited in any public or private warehouse authorized by this act, shall be at the sole and exclusive risk and expense of the owner or importer.

Sec. 4. And be it further enacted, That all goods, wares and merchandise which may be hereafter duly entered for warehousing under bond, and likewise all merchandise now remaining in warehouse under bond, may continue in warehouse, without payment of duties thereupon, for a period of three years from the date of original importation, and may be withdrawn for consumption on due entry and payment of the duties and charges, or upon entry for exportation, without the payment of duties, at any time within the period aforesaid; in the latter case, the goods to be subject only to the payment of such storage and charges as may be due thereon: Provided, however, That where the duties shall have been paid upon any goods, wares or merchandise entered for consumption, said duties shall not be refunded on exportation of any such goods, wares, or merchandise, without the limits of the United States: And provided, further, That there shall be no abatement of the duties or allowance made for any injury, damage, deterioration, loss, or leakage sustained by any goods, wares, or merchandise, whilst deposited in any public or private bonded warehouse established or recognized by this act.

Sec. 5. And be it further enacted, That any goods, wares, or merchandise, duly entered for warehousing, may be withdrawn under bond, without payment of the duties, from a bonded warehouse in any collection district of the United States, and be transported to a bonded warehouse in any other collection district within the same, and re-warehoused thereat; and any such goods, wares, or merchandise, may be so transported to their destination wholly by land, or wholly by water, or partly by land and partly by water, over such routes as the Secretary of the Treasury may prescribe, and may likewise be conveyed over any foreign territory, the government of which may have, or shall by treaty stipulations grant, a free right of way over such territory; and for the purpose of better guarding against frauds upon the revenue on foreign goods transported between the ports of the Atlantic and those of the Pacific overland through any foreign territory, the Secretary of the Treasury be, and is hereby authorized to appoint special sworn agents as inspectors of the customs, to reside in said foreign territory where such goods may be landed or embarked, with power to superintend the landing or shipping of all goods passing coastwise between the ports of the United States on the Pacific and Atlantic, and whose duty it shall be, under such regulations and instructions as the Secretary of the Treasury may prescribe, to guard against the perpetration of any frauds upon the revenue: Provided, That the compensation paid to said inspector shall not in the aggregate exceed five thousand dollars per annum.

Sec. 6. And be it further enacted, That the Secretary of the Treasury shall prescribe the form of the bond to be given for the transportation of goods, wares, and merchandise, from a port in one collection district to a port in another collection district in the United States, as provided in the preceding section; also the time for such delivery; and for a failure to transport and deliver, within the time limited, any such bonded goods, wares, and merchandise, to the collector at the designated port, an additional duty of one hundred per cent. shall be levied and collected, which additional duty shall be secured by such bond, or said goods, wares, and merchandise may be seized and forfeited for such failure, and any steam or other vessel, or vehicle, transporting such bonded goods, wares, and merchandise, the master, owner, or conductor of which shall fail to deliver the same to the collector at the designated port, shall be liable to seizure and forfeiture.

Sec. 7. And be it further enacted, That all leases of stores now held by the United States for the purpose of storing warehoused or unclaimed goods, shall on the shortest period of termination named in said leases, be cancelled, and no leases shall be entered into by the United States for any stores for the storage of warehoused or unclaimed goods at any port where there may exist any private bonded warehouses, after the first day of July, eighteen hundred and fifty-five: Provided, That nothing herein contained shall be construed to prevent the leasing or hiring of such buildings or accommodation as may be required for the use of the United States' appraisers for the due examination and appraisal of imported merchandise at the ports where such officers are provided by law, nor to prohibit the leasing or hiring by collectors of the customs, for short periods, with the approval of the Secretary of the Treasury, of such stores as may be required for custom-house purposes, at any of the smaller revenue ports of the United States: Provided, That no collector or other officer of the customs shall enter into any contract or agreement for the use of any building to be thereafter erected as a public store or warehouse, and no lease of any building to be so used shall be taken for a longer period than three years, nor shall rent be paid, in whole or in part, in any case, in advance.

Sec. 8. And be it further enacted, That the Secretary of the Treasury be, and he is hereby authorized, upon production of satisfactory proof to him of the actual injury or destruction in whole or in part of any goods, wares, or merchandise, by accidental fire, or other casualty, while the same remained in the custody of the officers of the customs in any public or private warehouse under bond, or in the appraiser's stores, undergoing appraisal, in pursuance of law or regulations of the Treasury Department, or while in transportation under bond from the port of entry to any other port in the United States, to abate or refund, as the case may be, out of any moneys in the treasury not otherwise appropriated, the amount of impost duties paid or accruing thereupon ; and likewise to cancel any warehouse bond or bonds, or enter satisfaction thereon in whole or in part, as the case may be.

Sec. 9. And be it further enacted, That the Secretary of the Treasury be and is hereby authorized from time to time to establish such rules and regulations, not inconsistent with the laws of the United States, for the due execution of this act, as he may deem to be expedient and necessary ; and all acts and parts of acts conflicting with this are hereby repealed.

Approved March 28, 1854.

TO COLLECTORS AND OTHER OFFICERS OF THE CUSTOMS.

Treasury Department, *March* 30, 1854.

The annexed copy of an act of Congress, entitled "An act to extend the warehousing system by establishing private bonded warehouses, and for other purposes," approved the 28th instant, is herewith transmitted for the information and government of collectors and other officers of the customs.

There are several important provisions of this act which require a modification of the warehousing regulations of the 17th February, 1849. These regulations, however, in other respects will continue in force until modified or revoked by further instructions.

It will be perceived that by the provisions of the 4th section of this act, imported merchandise duly entered after its date for warehousing under bond may continue in warehouse without payment of duties thereupon for a period of three years from the date of original importation. It may be withdrawn at any time within that period, either for consumption on due entry therefor and payment of duties and charges, or for exportation without the payment of duties. When withdrawn for exportation, however, the storage and charges due on the merchandise so withdrawn must be paid.

When duties shall have been paid on merchandise entered for consumption, they cannot be refunded on the exportation of the merchandise without the limits of the United States ; nor can any abatement of duties be granted or allowance made for or on account of any injury, damage, deterioration, loss, or leakage, sustained by merchandise while in deposite in any public or private bonded warehouse established or recognized by the act.

In pursuance of the provisions of the same section, the bond given on the entry of the merchandise for warehousing will be according to the annexed form A

The extension of the warehousing period to three years, it will be perceived, is made applicable to merchandise bonded before the passage of the act and still remaining in warehouse. Any goods, wares, and merchandise, therefore, which may be in warehouse under bond on the receipt of these instructions, will be permitted to remain therein for the period of three years from the date of original importation, and may, at any time within that period, be withdrawn for consumption on payment of duties and charges, or for exportation on payment of such storage and charges as may be due thereon.

It must be distinctly understood, however, that when any bond given before the passage of this law for any merchandise still remaining in warehouse reaches maturity, the owner or importer, if he desires to avail himself of the warehousing period as now extended, must give a new and satisfactory bond according to form A, when the former bond will be cancelled.

The particular attention of collectors and other officers of the customs is called to the very important provisions of the 5th and 6th sections of the act which regulates the transportation of merchandise in bond.

The following routes for the transportation of merchandise in bond from one port of entry to another port of entry or delivery, have been authorized by the Secretary of the Treasury, to wit:

From the ports of Boston, New-York, Philadelphia, and Baltimore, to Pittsburg, Wheeling, Cincinnati, Louisville, St. Louis, Nashville, Natchez, Evansville, New Albany, Burlington, Vt., Sackett's Harbor, Rochester, Oswego Lewiston, Buffalo, Ogdensburg, Plattsburg, Cape Vincent, Erie, Toledo, Sandusky, Cleveland, Detroit, Michilimackinac, Chicago, Milwaukie, by canal, railroad, river, or lake, wholly or in part, as the party may select in his entry.

Also, from a port or ports on the Atlantic to any other port on the Atlantic, Gulf of Mexico, or the Pacific, or vice versa, by such route and conveyance as the party in his entry may select.

Also, from the port of New-Orleans to any port of entry or delivery on the Mississippi and its tributaries, and by such conveyance and route as the party in his entry shall select.

Also, from the ports of Charleston and Savannah to the ports of Knoxville Nashville, and Memphis.

Whatever mode of transportation may be adopted, whether by land or water, or partly by land and partly by water, if the port to which the merchandise is to be transported in bond be not more than three hundred miles distant, by the route proposed, from the port at which it is entered for transportation, thirty days will be allowed, but if the distance be more than three hundred miles, sixty days will be allowed for the transportation and delivery of the merchandise at its port of destination. But six months will be allowed for the transportation of merchandise in bond between the Atlantic and Pacific ports of the United States around Cape Horn, and three months by other routes between those points.

The period thus prescribed will be carefully inserted in each case in the transportation bond, which will be according to the annexed form B.

Each entry for transportation of bonded merchandise must contain a designation of the route by which it is to be transported.

Collectors of the customs will report weekly to the Department all the entries for transportation of merchandise in bond which have been made at their respective ports during the week, of merchandise transported thither in bond from other ports, according to the annexed forms C and D.

On the entry for re-warehousing of the merchandise on arrival at its destined port under transportation bond, the bond will be according to form E ; and the collector will immediately transmit the notice prescribed per form 17, in the regulations of the 17th February, 1849, to the collector at the port of with drawal, in order that the transportation bond may be duly cancelled.

When warehousing and transportation are combined in one entry, as prescribed in the 22d section of those regulations, the bond will be taken according to the annexed form F.

Care must be taken promptly to forward to the collector of the port to which merchandise entered for transportation in bond is destined, the triplicate copy of the entry for withdrawal and transportation, as prescribed in the regulations of the 17th February, 1849, on which will be distinctly noted the time limited in the bond for the transportation and delivery of the merchandise; and should there be no delivery within the time thus prescribed and limited, the collector at the port to which the merchandise was entered for transportation, will promptly notify the collector at the port of withdrawal of the non-delivery, who will at once demand payment, or upon failure thereof, pass over the transportation bond to the United States District Attorney for suit, and the proper proceedings will be taken to enforce the forfeitures prescribed in the 6th section of the annexed act.

JAMES GUTHRIE,
Secretary of the Treasury.

EXTRACTS

FROM REGULATIONS UNDER THE PROVISIONS OF THE WAREHOUSE LAWS.

GENERAL STORAGE OF BONDED GOODS.

Stores in the occupancy of persons desiring to engage in the business of storing dutiable merchandise under the warehouse acts, and of performing the labor on such goods, in what is usually termed the storage business.

Stores of this class shall be used solely for the storage of warehouse goods, and of unclaimed and seized goods, when ordered by the collector, and shall have been previously approved by the Secretary of the Treasury.

All the labor on the goods deposited in these stores must be performed by the owner or occupant of the warehouse; and the store shall be subject to such further rules as this Department may deem necessary, from time to time, for the safe-keeping of the goods and protection of the revenue, and to be discontinued as a bonded warehouse when the public interest may require. All arrangements, as regards the rates of storage and the price of labor on bonded goods in these stores, must be made between the importer and the owner, or occupant, of the store; and all amounts due for storage and labor must be collected by the latter, the collector looking only to the safe custody of the merchandise for the security of the revenue.

Charges for storage and labor.

Bond.

Before any goods can be deposited in a store of this description, the owner or occupant of such store shall enter into bond according to the following form, in such sum and with such sureties, as may be approved by the collector and this Department.

Seized and unclaimed goods may be stored in this class.

Unclaimed and seized goods may be stored in private bonded warehouse for general storing of claimable merchandise on the order of the collector, and the proprietor or owner thereof shall be liable for the safekeeping of the merchandise as for other goods; and all charges for labor, storage, and other expenses, shall not exceed, in any case, the regular rates for such objects at the port in question. In cases where differences of opinion shall arise as to the correctness of the charges so made, the decision of the president of the chamber of commerce, or the board of trade, in ports where such bodies exist, or if there be no such officers, the decision of the collector or chief revenue officer of the port, shall be binding on both parties. The collector shall give no permit to withdraw such goods without payment of the legal duties and charges so assessed, and if sold, shall cause the storage and charges to be paid out of the proceeds of the sale.

Duties and charges to be paid out of proceeds.

430. Merchandise duly deposited in a warehouse under bond, and entitled to remain therein, may be transferred to another warehouse, on the request of the importer or owner thereof; or when an importer may obtain the privilege of using a store or cellar of class 2, and may desire to transfer thereto such merchandise imported by or consigned to him, it may be done on his written request to the collector; but such transfers shall, in all cases, be at the risk and expense of the party requesting it, and under the supervision of an officer of the customs.

Transfer of merchandise from one warehouse to another.

SECTION II.

ENTRY FOR WAREHOUSING.

431. The entry of goods for warehousing shall be in the following form, and must be verified by oath or affirmation as in an entry of merchandise for immediate payment of duties:

FORM NO. 104.

Warehouse Entry.

Form of entry.

CUSTOM-HOUSE, ——,
Port of ——, 186

Entry of merchandise imported on the —— by ——, in the ——, —— —— master, from ——.

Marks.	Numbers.	Packages & contents.	Quantity.	Per cent.	Per cent.	Per cent.	Per cent.	Per cent.	Total.	Dutiable val. of each package.

432. The dutiable value of each package of dry goods, hardware, or other package goods, must in all cases be stated on this entry, when the invoice will permit its being done; and in case of deduction for damage or other causes, it must be adjusted on each package separately, that this entry may always be a true basis for withdrawal entries, either for consumption, trans-

portation, or exportation, and also for the warehouse accounts.

Store to be designated.

The owner or importer will exercise the option given him by law by designating, upon the entry, the warehouse in which he desires the merchandise shall be deposited.

WAREHOUSE BOND.

FORM No. 105.

Know all men by these presents, that we ——, ——, as principals, and ——, ——, as sureties, are held and firmly bound unto the United States of America in the sum of —— dollars, to be paid to the United States; for the payment whereof, we bind ourselves, our heirs, executors, administrators, and assigns, jointly and severally, firmly by these presents; as witness our hands and seals this —— day of ——, eighteen hundred and ——.

The condition of this obligation is such, that if the above bounden principals, or either of them, or either of their heirs, executors, adminstrators, or assigns, shall, on or before the expiration of three years, to be computed from the date of the importation of the goods, wares, and merchandise hereinafter mentioned, well and truly pay, or cause to be paid, unto the collector of the customs for the port of —— the sum of —— dollars, or the amount of duties to be ascertained as due and owing on goods, wares, and merchandise imported by —— ——, in the ——, —— master, from ——, consisting of ——, or shall, in the mode prescribed by law, on or before the expiration of the three years aforesaid, withdraw the said goods from the bonded store or public warehouse where they may be deposited at the port of ——, then this obligation is to be void; otherwise to remain in full force and virtue.

—— ——, [SEAL.]
—— ——, [SEAL.]
—— ——, [SEAL.]

Sealed and delivered in presence of—

May pay duty on whole or part before going into store.

437. On completion of entry for warehouse. should the importer desire to take the whole or any portion of his property from the vessel, and pay the duties at any time before final liquidation he shall be at liberty to do so by paying the duty on withdrawal entry for consumption, and one half storage for one month, and giving penal bond as required by 4th section of act of 28th May, 1830; but in no case shall any property remain on any wharf or pier after the inspector shall make the return of the cargo of his vessel, but his entire cargo shall be accounted for by warehouse receipts or landing permits.

Goods cannot remain on wharf.

hen the packages designated by the collector on the invoice and ordered to the appraisers' stores, shall have been reported, is examined, the collector shall direct the storekeeper to cause such packages to be removed from the appraisers' stores to the warehouse where the remainder of the goods described in the entry shall have been deposited. The expense of such removal shall be borne by the importer, and the order for removal shall be in the form following:

Transfer from appraisers' stores of examined goods.

FORM No. 107.

CUSTOM-HOUSE, ——
Collector's Office, ——, 186

To the Storekeeper at Appraisers' Stores:

You will transfer from appraisers' stores to bonded warehouse, —— street, the following examined packages:

[Here describe the merchandise.]

imported by —— ——, in the ——, from ——.

—— ——, *Collector.*

—— ——, *Naval Officer.*

438. The appraisers having reported on the invoice, the weigher, gauger, or measurer, having made his return of the the quantity, the damage, if any, having been ascertained, and the dutiable value of the merchandise and duties finally determined, the importer, consignee, or agent, may, at any time within three years from the date of importation, withdraw from warehouse any quantity of the same, not less than an entire case or package, or not less than one ton in weight, if the merchandise be in bulk; but it is to be distinctly understood that no merchandise can be entered for exportation or for transportation from one port to another in the United States, and withdrawn from warehouse on such entry, until all the examinations and returns have been made, and the dutiable value and duties definitely fixed.

Entry to be adjusted before withdrawal.

439. If, on examination by the appraisers, the merchandise be found to be undervalued in the entry, and additional duty incurred, such additional duty must be paid before any withdrawal entry of the merchandise from warehouse for consumption, transportation, or export, can be allowed.

Penalty to be paid before withdrawal.

440. Claims for damage on the voyage of importation must be made within ten working days after date of landing, in conformity with the general regulations on that subject; whereupon the appraisers will forthwith make the requisite examinations, determine the allowance to be made, and transmit their report to the collector without delay.

Damage.

SECTION III.

ENTRY FOR WITHDRAWAL FROM WAREHOUSE.

Entry for withdrawal for consumption.

ART. 442. The entry for withdrawal of merchandise from warehouse for *consumption* at port of original importation shall be made by the party in whose name the merchandise was warehoused, or by some person duly authorized for the purpose by him, and in either case shall be signed by the party making the withdrawal. This entry shall exhibit the marks and numbers of the packages, the description and quantity of the goods, aud the dutiable value of the same. On presentation to the proper officer in the collector's office, it shall be compared with the record on the warehouse books of the original warehouse entry, and if found correct, be properly entered therein, the warehouse bond number endorsed thereon, and the amount of duties payable estimated. From the collector's office it shall then be taken by the importer to the naval office, where a similar comparison shall be made with the warehouse records of that office, and the estimate of duties verified and endorsed upon the duplicate entry. The amount of duties thus ascertained having been paid, a permit will be issued for the delivery of the goods. The entry shall be in the following form, and shall be made in duplicate:

To be certified by naval officer.

FORM 109.

Withdrawal entry for consumption at port of original importation.

Entry of merchandise intended to be withdrawn from warehouse by —— ——, which was imported into this district on the ——, 186 , by —— ——, in the——, —— master, from ——.

Marks.	Numbers.	Packages & contents.	Quantity.	Per cent.	Per cent.	Per cent.	Per cent.	Per cent.	Total.	Dutiable val. of each package.

[To be signed by importer.]

No oath will be required on this entry. If merchandise be withdrawn by any other than original importer, the following certificate must be placed thereon:

Form No. 110.

I authorize ——— to withdraw from warehouse the goods described in this entry.

[To be signed by the importer.]

443. Merchandise in bulk, liquors, sugars, molasses, cocoa, pepper, and other articles bought and sold by weight, when withdrawn for export or transportation, must be entered for such destination at the actual quantities on which duties were estimated at the time of arrival in the United States; and to secure this, weighers, measurers, and guagers will be required to mark on each package its contents as determined by them on its entry for warehouse. On these quantities the duties on export and transportation entries will be estimated. Goods withdrawn for consumption may be taken at average valuations —care being had that on the last withdrawal the entire balance of duty be collected.

Withdrawals for transportation & export at actual quantities.

Withdrawals for consumption at average valuation.

444. Should the final withdrawal entry be for export or transportation, and there be any difference between the actual duty and the amount to close the sum due on the warehouse entry, the excess if any, shall be refunded on the last witdrawal for consumption, and the deficiency, if any, collected on amendment to said entry.

Form No. 112.

Transportation entry from one port to another in the United States.

Entry of merchandise intended to be withdrawn from warehouse by ——— ———, for transportation to ———, which was imported into this district on the ———, 186 , by ——— ———, in the ———, ——— ——— master, from ———.

Custom House, 186 .

Marks.	Numbers.	Packages & contents.	Quantity.	Per cent.	Per cent.	Per cent.	Per cent.	Per cent.	Total.	Dutiable val. of each package.

446. This entry shall be made in triplicate, and when withdrawn by other than the original importer, the same authority must be required as in case of entry for consumption. And in additions to the particulars required in that case, this entry shall

exhibit the name of the consignee, and the name of vessels by which the goods are to be transported ; or if the transportation be by land, or partly by land and partly by water, the particular railroad or other route shall be designated, which route shall be in accordance with the regulations hereinafter provided. The party making the entry shall also present a copy of so much of the original invoice as relates to the merchandise, if package goods, described in such entry, or if other than package goods, a copy of the whole invoice. This copy must be a literal copy of the original, and if in a foreign language, must be a translated copy, and contain all the particulars set forth in that document. The entry having been compared with the record of the original warehouse entry, as provided in case of entry for consumption, entered in the appropriate column in the warehouse account, and the warehouse bond number endorsed thereon, and having also been compared and entered in the books of the naval officer and the duties payable estimated, and the following oath taken by the party making entry, the collector will take a bond in the following form, in a penal sum equal to double the invoice or appraised value of the goods, with sufficient surety or sureties :

Designation of route to be on entry.

Copy of invoice to be attached.

FORM NO. 113.

Oath.

I do solemnly, sincerely, and truly swear that the goods, wares, and merchandise described in the within entry now delivered by me to the collector of the customs for the port of ———, are truly intended to be transported in bond by me to the port of ———, and delivered to the collector of said port, according to the provisions of the warehousing laws, and the regulations of the Secretary of Treasury : So help me God.

Sworn to this —— day of ———, 186 , before me,

—— ———, *Collector.*

Time of Transportation Bond.

447. If the port to which the merchandise is to be transported be not more than one hundred miles distant by the route proposed, the time inserted in the bond shall be twenty days ; if over one hundred, and less than two hundred and fifty miles, thirty days ; if over two hundred and fifty miles, and less than five hundred miles, sixty days ; and if over five hundred miles, ninety days ; but if the distance be over two hundred and fifty miles, the collector may, at the instance of the party, allow thirty additional days.

Collector may receive goods over time in certain cases.

Nine months will be allowed for transportation of merchandise in bond between the Atlantic and Pacific ports of the United States around Cape Horn, and four months by other routes between those ports. If the transportation within the time prescribed is retarded by accident or other unavoidable cause, on regular protest and due proof of the accident or other unavoidable cause, the collector may receive said goods, or any part thereof, within a reasonable time thereafter.

450. Wines and distilled spirits, in casks of all sizes, must have the number of bung and other holes legibly branded on the exterior, and sealed, to prevent alteration or adulteration in the transit. Goods to be sealed, &c.

Goods in bulk, and other articles which cannot be sealed, must be examined before delivery for transportation by the collector, and the weight, gauge, or measure specified on the entry and on the triplicate copy thereof. Before delivery from warehouse, whenever practicable, each package will also be legibly marked, "Port of ——, in bond for —— ——;" and samples will be taken of each package of liquors, except when in bottles, not exceeding eight ounces in quantity, and will be so marked as to injure the identity, be deposited with the storekeeper of the store, subject to the order of the collector. To be marked. Samples.

452. When merchandise is entered, and bond given for transportation between the Atlantic and Pacific ports of the United States, by way of the isthmus of Panama, or other inter-oceanic route over foreign territory, the collector will, before the delivery of the merchandise from warehouse, and at the expense of the transporter, cause each box, bale, case, or other package, to be corded, and a lead seal attached thereto; and segars in small boxes to be packed in cases and so sealed. Transportation across Isthmus of Panama.

All the foregoing provisions regarding branding, sealing, sampling, and casing of segars must be complied with in the case of all articles crossing the isthmus of Panama, or by other inter-oceanic routes over a foreign territory.

On arrival at the port on the isthmus from which the goods are to be shipped to the United States, the same examination and comparison shall be made by the United States revenue agent, if there be one residing there; if none, then by the United States consul; and the result certified by him on the copy of the entry, and the same delivered to the owner or his agent in charge of the goods.

453. Should the merchandise be transported in bond over the isthmus of Tehuantepec, or by the route of San Juan de Nicaragua, the same examinations and certificates will be required by the consul and revenue agent to test and insure an identification of the goods. Examination and certificates must in all cases be made by the United States revenue agent, if there be one, either at the port of arrival or departure on the route, and by the United States consul also, if there be one, at the other Nicaragua route

terminus of the route. If there be no United States revenue agent on the route, the examination and certificate will be made by the United States consul at the port of arrival or departure, if there be but one, and by both if there be one at each port.

Examination.

Examination at port of destination.

454. On arrival of the goods at the port of destination in the United States, the copy of the entry, with the official certificates thereon, shall be delivered at once to the collector of the customs, who, if satisfied of the identity of the goods, will admit the same to entry for rewarehousing; but if not so satisfied, will keep them in custody and report the case to the Department for instructions.

Manifest to accompany goods.

455. Masters of vessels, or conductors of railroad cars or other vehicles, by which goods are conveyed from one port of the United States to another over the routes above indicated, will be required to have and exhibit a manifest of the merchandise, particularizing the goods so transported in bond.

Entry for rewarehousing.

456. On the arrival of any goods, transported in bond, at the port of destination, they must be immediately entered for rewarehousing, the entry for which purpose shall be in the form following; such entry in all cases being a copy of the withdrawal entry at the port of last withdrawal:

Form No. 116.

Rewarehousing Entry.

Entry of merchandise intended to be rewarehoused by ——, which was imported into the port of ———, on the —— day of ———, 186 , and withdrawn from warehouse at port of ———, on the —— day of ———, 186 , for transportation to this district. ———, 186 .

Marks.	Numbers.	Packages & contents.	Quantity.	Per cent.	Per cent.	Per cent.	Per cent.	Per cent.	Total.	Dutiable val. of each package.

(To be signed.)

457. This entry shall be verified by the oath or affirmation of the party to whom the goods are consigned, in the form following, viz:

FORM No. 117.

Oath.

DISTRICT OF ——.

I, —— ——, do solemnly, sincerely, and truly swear, that the goods described in the entry now delivered by me to the collector of this district are the identical goods mentioned in a transportation entry made at the custom-house at —— ——, by ——, on the —— day of ——, 186 , and that said goods are the same in quality, quantity, value, and package, wastage and damage excepted, as at the time of original importation; So help me God.

Sworn to this —— day of ——, 186 , before me.

—— ——, *Collector.*

458. This oath or affirmation having been taken, and the place of deposit designated, a bond, with satisfactory security, in a penal sum equal to double the amount of the duties, shall be executed by the party.

461. Goods transported under bond from one port of the United States to another, and arriving in advance of the transportation papers, are to be treated as unclaimed goods, and sent to the bonded warehouses provided for the reception of that class of merchandise, until entry is made, when the goods may be transferred to such bonded store as the consignee may designate.

462. If, however, the consignee should desire to pay the duties and get possession of his goods immediately on arrival, an entry may be made in the following form, to be verified by oath or affirmation:

FORM No. 121.

Rewarehousing and withdrawal entry for consumption.

Entry of merchandise to be rewarehoused and withdrawn by ——, which was brought into this district by —— from the port of ——, on the —— day of ——, 186 , having been originally imported into —— by ——, in the —— form —— on the — day of ——, 186 .

Marks.	Numbers.	Packages & contents.	Quantity.	Per cent.	Per cent.	Per cent.	Per cent.	Per cent.	Total.	Dutiable val. of each package.

(To be signed.)

The oath or affirmation on this entry shall be as follows:

FORM No. 122.

Oath.

I do solemnly, sincerely, truly swear, that the goods described in this entry now delivered by me to the collector of this district, are the identical goods mentioned in transportation entry made at ——— by ———, on the ——— day of ———, 186 , and that the said goods are the same in quantity, value, and package (wastage and damage excepted), as at the time of orignal importation: So help me God.

Sworn to this ——— day of ———, before me, ———,

——— ———, *Collector.*

No rewarehouse bond required.

Penal bond.

In this case, no rewarehouse bond will be required; but the duties, which shall be the amount certified as payable on the triplicate entry, having been paid, and a penal bond taken, as provided in the 4th section, act 28th May, 1830, the collector will issue a permit for the delivery of the goods:

Rewarehouse withdrawal for export.

464. Should the consignee of any merchandise transported under bond desire to export the same immediately on arrival at the port of destination, he will give notice of the same to the collector, in writing, who will direct the storekeeper to assume the custody of the goods, wherever they may be, until the necessary entry is completed, and permit issues. Should there be any delay in the preparation of those papers, the goods will be sent by the collector to such warehouse as he may select. The entry will be made in the form annexed:

FORM No. 124.

Rewarehouse entry for immediate exportation.

Entry of merchandise brought into this district by ——— ——— from ———, and now to be exported by ——— ———, on board the ———, for ———, which was imported into the port of ———, on ———, 186 , having been originally imported into ———, by ——— ———, in the ———, from ———, on the ——— day of———,186 .

Marks.	Numbers.	Packages & contents.	Quantity.	Per cent.	Per cent.	Per cent.	Per cent.	Per cent.	Total.	Dutiable val. of each package.

(To be signed by the exporter.)

The entry having been verified by the oath or affirmation of the consignee, as provided in case of entry for rewarehousing, and also by the oath or affirmation of the exporter, in the following form, viz: **Oath.**

FORM No. 125.

DISTRICT OF ———.

I do solemnly, sincerely, and truly swear, that the goods, wares, and merchandise described in the within entry, now delivered by me to the collector of the customs for the port of ———, are truly intended to be exported by me to the port of ———, without the limits of the United States, and are not intended to be relanded within the limits of the United States. I further swear that, to the best of my knowledge and belief, the said goods, wares, and merchandise are the same in quality, quantity, value, and package, (wastage and damage excepted), as at the time of importation: So help me God.

Sworn to this —— day of ———, before me,

—— —— *Collector.*

And the export bond, hereinafter prescribed, having been executed, the collector will issue a permit, to be countersigned by the naval officer, in the annexed form, viz: **Bond.**

FORM No. 126.

DISTRICT OF ———,
Port of ———, 186

To the Storekeeper of the Port:

You are directed to deliver to the surveyor for exportation on board the ——, for ——, [here describe the merchandise,] brought into this district by ——, from ——.

—— ——, *Collector.*

—— ——, *Naval Officer.*

At the same time that this order is given to the storekeeper, a copy of the entry shall also be transmitted to the surveyor for the due shipment or lading of the goods. **Copy of entry to surveyor.**

The direction to the surveyor upon this entry shall be as follows:

FORM No. 127.

PORT OF ———, 186

To the Surveyor:

You will direct an inspector to examine the goods described in this entry, and, if found to agree exactly therewith, to superintend the lading thereof on board the ———, for ———, of which, when completed, you will grant a certificate.

—— ——, *Collector.*

—— ——, *Naval Officer.*

The return of the inspector upon this entry shall be as follows:

FORM No. 128.

PORT OF ——, 186 .

I, —— ——, have examined the goods described in the within entry, and, finding them to agree therewith, they were laden under my supervision on board the ——, for ——,

—— ——, *Inspector.*

Bond.

No bond other than the export bond will be required; and in this case, as well as in that of payment of duties, the certificate already prescribed for the cancellation of the transportation bond will be furnished to the party making entry, immediately on the receipt of the necessary evidence that the merchandise described in the transportation entry has been delivered; and a duplicate of the same will also be forwarded to the collector, or other proper officer, at the port of withdrawal

Certificate to cancel bond.

This entry to apply only to certain articles.

This form of entry will only be allowed on articles in bulk; woods, liquors that are branded and sealed, cases corded and sealed, sugar, molasses, coal, iron, and other heavy and bulky goods, when the identification can be readily made by the inspecting officer. All other articles must be rewarehoused, as previously provided for, and examined by the appraisers, before an export entry can be allowed.

An actual delivery to be made to Collector at port of transportation.

465. The merchandise must in all cases be actually delivered to the officer of the customs at the port where landed or unladen, whether entered for rewarehousing, payment of duties, or immediate exportation.

Rewarehouse withdrawals from

466. Should merchandise, after having been rewarehoused, be withdrawn for consumption, transportation, or exportation, the entries shall be according to the forms annexed—all the regulations as to oaths, bonds, examinations, &c., to be complied with, as provided for entries at first and second ports.

FORM No. 129.

Rewarehouse withdrawal entry for consumption.

Entry of merchandise intended to be withdrawn from warehouse for consumption by —— ——, which was brought into this district on the —— day of ——, 186 , by —— ——, from the port of ——, having been originally imported into ——, by —— ——, in the ——, from ——, on the —— day of ——, 186 .

Marks.	Numbers.	Packages & contents.	Quantity.	Per cent.	Per cent.	Per cent.	Per cent.	Per cent.	Total.	Dutiable val. of each package.

(To be signed.)

FORM No. 130.

Rewarehouse withdrawal entry for transportation in the United States.

Entry of merchandise intended to be withdrawn from warehouse by —— ——, for transportation to ———, which was brought into this district on the ———, 186 , by ——— ———, from the port of ———, the same having been originally imported into the district of ———, on the ——— day of ———, 186 , in the ———, from ———.

Marks.	Numbers.	Packages & contents.	Quantity.	Per cent.	Per cent.	Per cent.	Per cent.	Per cent.	Total.	Dutiable val. of each package.

(To be signed.)

FORM No. 131.

Rewarehouse withdrawal entry for exportation.

Entry of merchandise withdrawn from warehouse by —— ——, and to be exported by ——— ———, in the ———, ——— ——— master, for ———, which was brought into this district on the ———, 186 , from the port of ———, the same having been originally imported into the district of ———, on the ——— day of ———, 186 , in the ———, from ———.

Marks.	Numbers.	Packages & contents.	Quantity.	Per cent.	Per cent.	Per cent.	Per cent.	Per cent.	Total.	Dutiable val. of each package.

(To be signed.)

If withdrawn by any other than original party.

If the merchandise be withdrawn in either of these cases by any other than the party by whom brought into the district, the same authority is required as in case of withdrawal at port of original importation.

Warehouse and transportation entry.

467. On the arrival from any foreign port of any goods destined for immediate transportation to other ports in the United States, the warehousing and transportation may be combined in one entry, the oaths to be the same as prescribed in the warehouse entry. The forms of entry and bond shall be as follows, the regulations as to examinations being in all respects complied, with:

FORM NO. 132.

Warehouse entry and transportation in the United States.

Entry of merchandise imported by ——— ———, in ship ——— ——— ——— master, from ———, for warehouse and for transportation in bond to ———, 186 .

Marks.	Numbers.	Packages & contents.	Quantity.	Per cent.	Per cent.	Per cent.	Per cent.	Per cent.	Total.	Dutiable val. of each package

Oath.

468. This entry must be made in triplicate, in accordance with the rules already prescribed, stating, in addition, the date and time of transportation bond, and the triplicate forwarded to place of destination as in case of withdrawal from warehouse for transportation in the United States. The entry having been verified by the oath or affirmation of the importer, and the

transportation route having been designated, and all other requirements complied with, the collector will take a bond in the following form :

FORM No. 133.

Bond.

Know all men by these presents, that we, —— ——, —— ——, as principals, and —— ——, —— ——, as sureties, are held and firmly bound unto the United States of America in the sum of ——— dollars; for the payment whereof to the United States we firmly bind ourselves, our heirs, executors, administrators, and assigns, jointly and severally: as witness our hands and seals this —— day of ———, eighteen hundred and ————. **Bond.**

The condition of this obligation is such, that if the above bounden principals, or either of them, or either of their heirs executors, administrators, or assigns, shall, within ——— from the date hereof, or within such further time as the Secretary of the Treasury may, on application of any of them before said day, allow, or, in case of delay from unavoidable accident, within a reasonable time thereafter, transport in the ——— [here name vessel, railroad, &c., and route, as designated in the entry] the merchandise described in an entry made at the custom-house at ——— for warehouse and transportation in bond to the port of ———, as per margin, [describe on the margin the merchandise,] and shall deliver the same to the collector at said port, and produce to, and deposit with, the collector of the customs at the port of ———[here insert port of withdrawal] the certificate of the collector of the port of ——— [here insert port of destination] that the said merchandise has been delivered to him according to law, or, failing so to do, shall pay to the proper collecting officer of the United States at the port of ——— [here name the port of withdrawal] the amount of duties, endorsed on this bond as due and owing on the merchandise aforesaid, and an additional duty of one hundred per cent. imposed by the act of Congress of the 28th day of March, 1854, then this obligation is to be void; otherwise it shall remain in full force, and be forthwith enforced by due process of law. Here describe merchandise.

—— ——, [SEAL.]
—— ——, [SEAL.]

Sealed and delivered in the presence of—

—— ——.

In case of warehouse and transportation entries, the importing vessel may be considered the warehouse, without charge, during the time the examination is being made by the appraisers, and from which deliveries may be made for transportation; but should the examination be delayed beyond the time allowed by law for the goods to remain on board, they must be sent to such bonded warehouse as the importer may select, until the ex; amination is completed, under the usual warehouse permit; and when delivered for transportation, the delivery to take place under the permit as delivery for transportation. It shall be the duty, and it is required of the appraisers, whenever practicable that the goods so entered shall be examined on board the vessel in which imported, in order to save to the importer the charges for sending the same to store.

Route must be on entry.

Whatever mode of transportation may be adopted, whether by land or water, or partly by land and partly by water, the route must be set forth and particularly described in the entry.

Exp. from warehouse at port of importation.

473. When goods are withdrawn from warehouse for exportation at port of original importation, the entry shall be in the form following:

FORM No. 134.

Export entry from port of original importation.

Entry of merchandise intended to be withdrawn from warehouse by —— ——, and to be exported by him in the ——, —— —— master, for ——, which was imported into this district by —— ——, in the ——, —— —— master, from ——, on the —— day of ——, 186 .

Marks.	Numbers.	Packages & contents.	Quantity.	Per cent.	Per cent.	Per cent.	Per cent.	Per cent.	Total.	Dutiable val. of each package.

(To be signed by exporter.)

If exported by other than the original importer, the same authority will be required as in case of withdrawal for consumption, and the oath to be taken by the exporter shall be in the following form, viz.:

FORM No. 135.

Oath.

DISTRICT OF ——.

I do solemnly, sincerely, and truly swear, that the goods,

wares, and merchandise described in the within entry, now delivered by me to the collector of the customs for the port of ——— are truly intended to be exported by me to the port of ———, without the limits of the United States, and are not intended to be relanded within the limits of the United States. I further swear that, to the best of my knowledge and belief, the said goods, wares, and merchandise are the same in quality, quantity, value, and package, wastage and damage excepted, as at the time of importation : So help me God.

Sworn to this —— day of ———, 186 , before me.

—— ——, *Collector.*

474. The entry having been duly entered in the warehouse accounts, and the oath, as above prescribed, having been taken, the exporter shall enter into a bond with satisfactory security, in a penal sum equal to double the amount of the estimated duties on the goods, to produce the proofs required by the 81st section of the act of March 2d, 1799, of the landing of the same beyond the limits of the United States. **Bond.**

477. When any goods, wares, or merchandise, are imported into any port in the United States, and the intent is shown by invoice and manifest, bill of lading, or other evidence, that the same are to be exported immediately by sea beyond the limits of the United States, an entry for warehouse and exportation may be made in the following form: **Warehouse an exportation en try.**

FORM No. 140.

Warehouse and Exportation Entry.

Entry of merchandise imported for warehouse by —— ——, in the ———, —— —— master, from ———, on the —— day of ———, 186 , and to be immediately exported by —— ——, in the ———, —— ——, master, for ———.

Date.	Import vessel.	Where from.	Export vessel.	To what place exported.	Description of goods.	Per cent.	Per cent.	Per cent.	Per cent.	Per cent.	Total.

This entry for warehouse and exportation will only be permitted when an opportunity exists for immediate export. If the goods cannot be reshipped immediately on arrival, they **Restrictions as to using this form of entry.**

must go to a bonded warehouse as unclaimed, and remain until an opportunity offers, when entry in this form can be made.

Export bond how cancelled.

478. For the discharge of export bonds, the exporter must produce, within one year, if the shipment be to any port of Europe or America, and within two years, if to any port of Asia or Africa, a certificate under the hand of the consignee at the foreign port, describing the articles exported, and declaring that the same have been received by him from on board the vessel, specifying the name and nation of the vessel from which they were so received; which certificate shall be authenticated by the consul or agent of the United States residing at said port; or, in the absence of such officer, by two American merchants residing at such port; or, if there be no American merchants resident there, then by two respectable foreign merchants; which certificate shall be confirmed by the oaths or affirmations of the master and mate or other principal officers of the vessel, to be taken before the consul or commercial agent of the United States, if there be one; and if not, before some other person authorized by the laws of the country to administer the same. The forms of these certificates shall be as follows:

Form No. 142.

Certificate of a consignee, declaring the delivery of merchandise at a foreign port.

I, —— ——, of the (town or city) of ——, merchant, do hereby certify that the goods or merchandise hereinafter described have been landed in this (city, town, or port,) between the —— and —— days of ——, from on board the ——, of ——, whereof —— —— is at present master, viz.: [here describe the merchandise,] which, according to the bills of lading for the same, were shipped on board the ——, at the port of ——, in the United States of America, on or about the —— day of ——, and consigned to (me, or to us,) by —— ——, of —— aforesaid, merchant, (or by the master of said ——).

Given under (my or our) hands, at the (city) of ——, this —— day of ——, 186 .

—— ——

Form No 143.

Oath, or affirmation, of the principal officers of a vessel, confirming the landing of merchandise at a foreign port.

Port of ——

We —— ——, master, and —— ——, mate of ——, lately arrived from the port of ——, in the United States of America, do solemnly (swear, or affirm) that the goods or merchandise enumerated and described in the preceding certificate, dated the —— day of ——, and signed by —— ——, of the city of ——, merchant, were actually delivered at the said port from on board the ———, within the time specified in the said certificate.

Sworn (or affirmed) at the city of ———, before me, this —— day of ———, in the year ——.

——— ———.

Form No. 144.

Verification of the delivery of merchandise at a foreign port to be executed by a consul or agent of the United States.

I, ——— ———, (consul or agent) of the United States of America, at the city of ———, do declare that the facts set forth in the preceding certificate, subscribed by —— ——, of the said city, merchant, and dated the —— day of ——, are, (to my knowledge just and true; or, are in my opinion just and true, and deserving full faith and credit).

In testimony whereof, I have hereunto subscribed my name, [SEAL.] and affixed the seal of my office, at ——, this —— day of ——, 186

——— ———, *Consul.*

Form No. 145.

Verification of the delivery of merchandise, to be executed by American or foreign merchants, as the case may require.

We, —— ——, residing in the city of ———, do declare that the facts stated in the preceding certificate, signed by —— ——, of the said city, merchant, on the —— day of ———, are (to our knowledge just and true; or, are in our opinion just and true, and worthy of full faith and credit). We also declare that there is (no consul or other public agent for the United States of America, or American merchants, as the case may require,) now residing at this place.

Dated this —— day of ———, at the city of ———.

(Signatures.)

SECTION IV.

PRINTING OF SILKS IN BOND—PONGEES AND OTHER PLAIN WHITE.

Withdrawal of silks for printing.

Art. 479. Silks in bond may be withdrawn from warehouse to be colored, printed, stained, dyed, painted, or stamped, the collector taking a deposit in money equal to the amount of duties ascertained to be payable; which deposit shall be refunded if the goods aforesaid shall be returned to the warehouse repacked in the original condition, and according to original marks and numbers, within sixty days from date of delivery thereof. Each package shall, before the same be delivered from ware-

To be examined, sampled, &c.

house, be opened and examined by the proper officer of the customs, and the contents thereof measured or weighed, and the quality thereof ascertained, and a sample of each piece thereof reserved at the custom-house, and a particular account or registry of such examination shall be entered on the books of the custom-house. On the return of said goods, if the collector shall be satisfied that the contents of each package are the identical goods imported and registered as aforesaid, and not changed or altered, except by being colored, dyed, stamped, stained, painted, or printed, as aforesaid, he shall thereupon refund the deposit as aforesaid, and said goods shall be entitled to the same privileges as if in original condition, as per 4th section, act 22d May, 1824.

480. The form of entry for delivery of silks for this purpose shall be as follows :

Entry.

FORM No. 146

Withdrawal of silks for dyeing, &c.

Entry of silks intended to be withdrawn from warehouse for dyeing, coloring, printing, painting, or stamping, under the provisions of act 22d May, 1824, and Treasury instructions which were imported into this district on the —— day of ——, 18 , in the ——, —— —— master, from ——

Date.	Description of merchandise.	Duty, 25 per ct.	Duty, 30 per ct.	Total.	Dutiable val. of each package.

(To be signed.)

Deposit for duty.

On the same estimate of duties being made as required in withdrawal entries for payment of duties, and the goods being duly entered on the books as withdrawn for printing, &c., the party making entry will deposit with the collector a sum equivalent to the duties thus estimated.

To be examined when returned.

On the return of the goods within the time specified, they shall be examined by the warehouse superintendent, and if found to agree with the samples retained, he shall issue a certificate in the following form :

FORM No. 148.

DISTRICT OF ———,
Custom-house, ———.

I do hereby certify that the following described goods, returned to warehouse by ———, are the same goods as withdrawn by ———, on the —— day of ———, 18 , to be printed, painted, stamped, dyed or colored.

[Here describe the merchandise.]

I also certify the said goods are in the same condition as when withdrawn, except by being printed, painted, stamped, dyed or colored.

——— ———, *Warehouse Superintendent.*

Certificate of return to store.

On the presentation of this certificate, the deposit shall be refunded and the withdrawal entry cancelled.

Deposit when refunded.

If the goods are not returned within the period specified in the entry, the same will pass into the accounts as a regular withdrawal entry for consumption, and the deposit will go into the accounts as duties received.

If not returned in sixty days, to be considered as withdrawn for consumption.

SECTION V.

OF THE TRANSPORTATION AND EXPORTATION OF GOODS TO THE ADJACENT BRITISH PROVINCES.

ART. 482. On the arrival from foreign ports of any goods intended for immediate transportation and exportation to the adjacent British provinces of Canada and New-Brunswick, and which shall appear, by the invoices, bills of lading, and manifest, or other satisfactory evidence, to have been shipped to a port in the United States in transit and for exportation as aforesaid, the consignee or agent may make entry in triplicate, setting forth particularly in such entry the route by which the goods are to be forwarded, whether by land or by water, or partly by land and partly by water, and designating the last port in the United States from which the actual exportation is to be made, and the port or place in the adjacent province for which the goods are destined. The form of the entry shall be as follows:

Wareh'se, transportation and export to Canada.

Entry.

FORM No. 149.

Entry for exportation in bond to Canada.

CUSTOM-HOUSE, ———, 186 .

Entry of merchandise imported into this district by ——— ———, on the —— day of ———, 186 , in the ———, ——— ——— master, from ———, to be exported in bond to ———, in Canada, by way of ———.

Marks.	Numbers.	Packages & contents.	Quantity.	Per cent.	Per cent.	Per cent.	Per cent.	Per cent.	Total.	Dutiable val. of each package.

(To be signed.)

Oath.

483. This entry shall be verified by the oath or affirmation of the consignee or agent in the form prescribed by the 107th section of the act of March 2, 1799, in the form following:

Form No. 150.

I, —— ——, do solemnly, sincerely, and truly swear (or affirm) that the entry now subscribed with my name, and delivered by me to the collector of the district of ——, contains a just and true account of all the goods, wares, and merchandise contained in the several packages therein mentioned; that they are brought into this district solely for the purpose of being carried and transported by way of ——, with the intention of being immediately re-embarked, and carried without the limits of the United States, and are not intended, directly or indirectly, to be sold, exchanged, or consumed within the limits of the United States; and I do further swear (or affirm) that if I shall hereafter know that the whole or any part of said goods, wares, or merchandise, shall have been sold, alienated, exchanged, or consumed within the limits of the United States, I will immediately report the same, with the circumstances thereof, truly, to the collector of this district: So help me God.

Sworn before me this —— day of ——, 186 .

—— ——, *Collector.*

To be examined by invoice.

484. The entry having been compared with the invoice, and the duties estimated on the value of the invoice and duly sworn to, the consignee or agent shall enter into bond, in a penal sum equal to double the value of the goods.

Restrictions on this form of entry.

488. This form of entry will only be allowed when it shall appear by the invoice, bill of lading and manifest, or other satisfactory evidence, that the merchandise was destined, henw shipped at the foreign port, for exportation to a port in the adjacent British provinces, and consequently is not to be considered

an importation into the United States within the meaning and intention of the law. In this view, it is not deemed necessary that the invoice should be accompanied by the oath of the owner and the consular certificate, or that the examinations required in other cases should be made by the appraisers. Nor is it necessary that a copy of the invoice should be transmitted with such entry to the frontier port.

Owner's oath and consular certificate waived.

Not to be examined by appraisers.

489. All merchandise entered and exported to the adjacent British provinces under this form and the other forms of entry given in these instructions when the transportation is made wholly by land, or partly by land and partly by water, must be secured in the following manner: The collector before delivery will have all goods in boxes, cases, bales, or casks corded, and a lead seal attached thereto; all cigars in small boxes packed in cases and corded and sealed as above. Wines and distilled spirits in casks or other packages must have the number of bung or other holes in each package legibly branded on the exterior, and all such holes must be sealed to prevent adulteration or alteration in transit; he will also take a sample of each package of liquors, except when in bottles, not exceeding in quantity eight ounces, all of which samples must be immediately deposited with the storekeeperof the store where sampled, who will hold them subject to the orders of the collector. The expense of sealing, branding, encasing, and sampling must be paid by the owners before delivery. The triplicate entry and manifest forwarded as herein provided for, will specify particulars of sealing and branding.

Must be corded and sealed, or brand'd and sealed.

Sampled.

At owners' expense.

If the exportation to the adjacent British provinces be entirely by sea, the cording, sealing, casing, and branding will not be required; but in all cases of exportation by land, or partly by water, a strict adherence to the regulations will be required.

If by sea, the cording, sealing, &c., may be dispensed with.

Form No. 157.

Withdrawal entry from warehouse for exportation in bond to Canada.

Entry of merchandise to be withdrawn from warehouse by —— ——, which was imported by —— —— into this district on the —— day of ——, 186 , in the ——, —— —— master, from ——, and to be exported to ——, in Canada, by way of ——.

Marks.	Numbers.	Packages & contents	Quantity.	Per cent.	Per cent.	Per cent.	Per cent.	Per cent.	Total.	Dutiable val. of each package.

If withdrawn by other than the party who warehoused the goods, the same authority will be required as in other cases. The entry must be made in triplicate, and verified by the oath or affirmation of the exporter, in the following form, viz:

FORM NO. 158.

DISTRICT OF ——,

Port of ——.

Oath.

I, —— ——, solemnly, sincerely, and truly swear that the goods, wares, and merchandise described in the within entry now delivered by me to the collector of the customs for the port of ——, are truly intended to be transported and exported in bond by me to the port of ——, in Canada, by wav of ——, and are not intended to be relanded within the limits of the United States. I further swear, that to the best of my knowledge and belief, the said goods, wares, and merchandise are the same in quality, quantity, value, and packages, wastage and damage excepted, as at the time of importation: So help me God.

Sworn to this —— day of ——, before me.

—— ——, *Collector.*

Conductor of railroad car, to have manifest.

495. In all cases of exportation in the manner herein provided, the master or conductor of the vessel, railroad carriage, or other vehicle, shall be provided with a manifest of the goods laden on board such conveyance, particularly describing the same, the route, frontier port of exportation and foreign port of destination; which manifest shall be duly certified by the officer of the customs under whose supervision such goods were laden, and shall be forthwith delivered on arrival to the collector or other chief revenue officer of the frontier port.

Routes to Canada and other provinces.

496. Merchandise intended for exportation to the adjacent British provinces may be forwarded from the ports of importation in the United States by way of any of the following designated ports, viz.:

Rouse's Point, New-York. Detroit, Michigan.

Ogdensburg, New-York	Dunkirk, New-York.
Cnpe Vincent. do.	Eastport, Maine.
Suspension Bridge, do.	Pembina, Minnesota.
Lewiston, do.	Toledo, Ohio.
Buffalo, do.	Sandusky, Ohio.
Oswego, do.	Cleveland, Ohio.
Rochester, do.	Chicago, Illinois.
Plattsburg, do.	Milwaukie, Wisconsin.
Burlington, Vermont.	Sackett's Harbor, N. Y.
Swanton, do.	Erie, Pennsylvania.
Alburgh, do.	Whitehall, New-York.
Island Pond, do.	Michilimackinac,Michigan

SECTION VI.

INLAND EXPORTATION OF GOODS IN BOND TO PORTS AND PLACES IN MEXICO.

Entry for inland route to Mexico.

ART. 500. Merchandise in the original packages, duly entered and bonded, may be withdrawn at any time within three years from the date of importation, for immediate exportation to Chihuahua in Mexico, either by the route of the Arkansas river, through Van Buren, or by the route of the Missouri river, through Independence.

Routes.

501. Merchandise duly entered and bonded, or rewarehoused under bond at Point Isabel, in the collection district of Brazos de Santiago, may be withdrawn from warehouse at any time within three years from the date of importation, for immediate exportation to ports and places in Mexico, by land or water, or partly by land and partly by water, by the following routes, viz.: 1st, directly by water, to ports and places in Mexico lying on the sea-coast or Rio Grande; 2d, by land or water, under warehouse transportation bond, to Brownsville, Rio Grande City, Roma, and Loredo; thence by water to places in Mexico lying on the Rio Grande. Merchandise transported in bond from Point Isabel to Brownsville, Rio Grande City, Roma, and Loredo, may be rewarehoused thereat, only in first-class, fire-proof stores, according to the classification of the insurance companies at these places, previously approved by the Department and bonded.

Entries at Point Isabel.

502. Entries of goods in bond at Point Isabel may be made for transporting to and rewarehousing at Brownsville, Rio Grande City, Roma, and Loredo, on like bonds as are provided in the regulations for the transportation and rewarehousing at interior ports of delivery. Merchandise entered for exportation in bond at Point Isabel for Mexico may, at the option of the owner, be withdrawn at Rio Grande City, Roma, Loredo, or

Brownsville, for consumption, on due entry theref and payment of the proper duties and charges to the deputy collectors, at either of those points at which the merchandise may be; prompt returns of such entries and duties collected to be made by the deputy to the collector at Point Isabel, that the proper endorsements may be made on the entries and bonds at that port.

Via Lavaca.

503. Merchandise duly entered and bonded at any port of the United States may be withdrawn for immediate exportation in bond to San Fernando, Paso del Norte, and Chihuahua, and be transported by water to the port of Lavaca, in the collection district of Saluria, Texas, and be transhipped thence Inland to San Antonio, and from the latter place to the before-mentioned destinations in Mexico, either by way of Eagle Pass, the Presidio del Norte, and San Elizario, all on the Rio Grande. On the arrival of such goods at the port of Lavaca, they need not be rewarehoused, but must be landed by permission and under inspection of the surveyor of that port.

Goods to be corded and sealed.

504. In consideration of the long inland transportation and the risk of injury and defacing of the marks on the packages, thereby rendering the identification difficult, if not impossible *the packages must be corded, and a lead seal attached thereto*, as required for goods destined for Canada, at the expense of the exporter, under the direction of the storekeeper, before leaving the warehouse.

Marked.

505. Each package shall also be marked, under direction of the storekeeper, and before the goods are delivered from the warehouse, with these words: "Port of ———, in bond for ———." [naming the port or place of destination in Mexico.]

Entry.

506. The entry for withdrawal from warehouse for exportation inland to ports and places in Mexico, by land or water, or partly by land and partly by water, shall be in the following form, and shall set forth particularly the route and mode of conveyance by which the merchandise is to be exported—naming always the last customs station at which inspection is to be made, and from which the goods are to be exported:

Form No. 163.

Withdrawal entry for transportation and exportation in bond to Mexico.

Entry of merchandise to be withdrawn from warehouse by ——— ———, which was imported by ——— ———, into this district in the ———, ——— ——— master, from ———, and to be transported to ———, and thence exported to ———, in Mexico, by way of ———.

Marks.	Numbers.	Packages & contents.	Quantity.	Per cent.	Per cent.	Per cent.	Per cent.	Per cent.	Total.	Dutiable val. of each package.

This entre shall be verified by the oath or affirmation of the exporter, in the following form :

FORM No. 164.

DISTRICT OF ———,
Port of ———.

I, ——— ———, do solemnly, sincerely, and truly swear, that the goods, wares, and merchandise, described in the within entry, now delivered by me to the collector of the customs for the port of ———, are truly intended to be exported in bond by me to the port of ——, in Mexico, by way of ——, and are not intended to be relanded within the limits of the United States. I further swear, that to the best of my knowledge and belief, the said goods, wares, and merchandise, are the same in quality, quantity, value, and package, wastage and damage excepted, as at the time of importation : So help me God. Oath.

Sworn to this —— day of ———, before me.

—— ——, *Collector.*

The exporter shall enter into bond, in a penal sum equal to double the value of the goods, with security satisfactory to the collector. Bond.

510. The proof of due landing at the port of destination in Mexico will be a certificate of the United States consul or agent, which will be in the following form : Proof to cancel bond.

FORM No. 170.

I, ——— ———, consul or agent of theUnited States of America, residing at ———, in ———, do hereby certify that I have duly examined the packages of merchandise described in the within entry and invoice, and am fully satisfied that the goods have arrived at this place in the original packages as imported, without any change or alteration, and have been exported from the United States in good faith, to be disposed of and consumed in a foreign country.

In testimony whereof, I have hereunto set my hand, and affixed my official seal, this —— day of ——— A. D.
[L. S.] 186 , and of the independence of the United States of America the ——.

—— ——, *Consul of U. S.*

If there be no consul or agent of the United States residing at the place, then the certificate may be made by the consul of a nation in amity with the United States; and if there be no such consul there, then by two reputable merchants at said place.

SECTION X.

RELIEF FROM DUTIES ON GOODS INJURED OR DESTROYED WHILE IN BOND.

ART. 524. The 8th section of the warehousing law of the 28th March, 1854, providing for relief from duties in case of the destruction, in whole or in part, of bonded goods, while in warehouse, or in transitu, under warehouse transportation bond, from one port to another, or in the appraisers' store undergoing appraisal, it is deemed proper to state that the law proposes relief where actual injury is incurred, or the property is destroyed, in whole or in part, by accidental fire, shipwreck, or other like casualty; but does not provide for deterioration from dampness or other like cause, in the warehouse or in transitu under bond.

Application in case of loss in warehouse

525. Application for relief under the 8th section of the act of 28th March, 1854, must be made in writing, under oath or affirmation, by the claimant, to the collector of the port where the alleged injury or destruction, in whole or in part, of the goods, wares, and merchandise, by accidental fire, or other like casualty, occurred, setting forth that the same happened while the goods remained in the custody of the officers of the customs, in public or private warehouse under bond, or in the appraisers' stores undergoing appraisal, or while in transportation under bond, describing the place and manner of the accident, together with the extent of the injury, loss, or destruction, and the precise time when sustained.

Proof.

526. This statement must be accompanied by affidavits of two or more credible and disinterested persons, as to the injury, loss or destruction aforesaid.

527. On receipt of the forgoing application and statement, the collector will subjoin thereto an official statement of the officers of the customs connected with the custody of the goods, as to the facts stated by the claimant, together with a statement

whether the store or building in question was, at the time of the occurrence, a duly constituted bonded warehouse under the law, or appraisers' store, as the case may be.

528. The collector will report the foregoing to the Department, giving his views as to the character of the proof and the validity of the claim, stating the date of maturity, and parties to each bond, the amount due on each, the amount of duties, if any, paid together with any views or facts connected with the case he may deem useful in enabling the Department to discharge its duty under the law.

To be reported on by collector.

529. When total loss or damage is alleged to have occurred in the course of transportation from one port to another under bond, in pursuance of law and the regulations of the Department, applications for relief must be made in the following form. In cases of total loss of the vessel or vehicle in which transported, the application must be sustained by the protest of the master or conductor of such vessel or vehicle, the affidavit of the applicant, setting forth that the goods so alleged to be lost were actually on board such vessel or vehicle, and have been totally lost, and no reasonable expectation exists of saving any part thereof, together with the bill of lading, or other receipt for the transportation of said goods. In cases of damage when the goods have arrived at the port of destination, the application of the party must be sustained by evidence as hereinbefore prescribed in cases of loss in warehouse, and must be lodged with the collector within ten days after the landing of the merchandise, and while the goods are in the possession of the officers of the customs, and due appraisement will be made of the goods so alleged to be damaged, as in case of damage occurring on voyages of direct importation from foreign ports.

Damage or loss in transportation.

530. It will be borne in mind, however, that no abatement of duties, satisfaction or cancellation of the bond will be made under the eighth section of the act of the 28th March, 1854, without the previous sanction of the Department.

No abatement of duty without the sanction of Department.

RECIPROCAL TREATY.

IN REFERENCE TO COMMERCIAL INTERCOURSE WITH FOREIGN NATIONS, UNDER TREATY STIPULATIONS AND LAWS OF THE UNITED STATES.

SECTION I.

OF VESSELS OF NATIONS WITH WHOM THE UNITED STATES HAVE COMMERCIAL RELATIONS.

First Class.

ART. 911. Vessels belonging to the following nations are admitted, under the provisions of law, treaties of commerce and navigation, or conventions, into the ports of the United States, on the same terms as vessels of the United States, with the produce or manufactures of their own or any other country.

Argentine Confederation, under treaties of July 10 and 27, 1853; proclaimed April 9, 1855.

Austria.—Treaty August 27, 1829; proclaimed February 10, 1831; treaty May 8, 1848; proclaimed February 25, 1850.

Belgium.—Treaty, November 10, 1825; proclaimed March 31, 1846.

Act May 24, 1828. *Brazil.*—Under act of Congress of 24th May, 1828; proclaimed November 4, 1847.

Vessels of Brazil, therefore, with their cargoes, from Brazil, or any other foreign country whatever, are to be admitted without the payment of discriminating duties of tonnage or impost, it appearing from an official communication of the government of Brazil, that vessels of the United States and their cargoes are admitted to like privileges at the ports of Brazil.

Coffee or tea of Brazil. *Coffee or Tea*, the production of Brazil, imported direct from that country in Brazilian vessels, is exempt from duty under the tariff act of 1846, schedule I, and proclamation of the President, November 4, 1847.

Tariff Act, July 30, 1846.

Act May 24, 1828. *Chili.*—Under act of 24th May, 1828, and proclamation of the President, November 1, 1850.

Denmark.—By treaty of April 26, 1826 : proclaimed October 14, 1826.

Danish vessels from Danish islands. Act May 31, 1830.

Danish vessels, arriving from the Danish islands of Santa Cruz and St. Thomas, are not chargeable with tonnage duties in the ports of the United States; the vessels of Denmark and the United States, being placed on the same footing, in that respect, under the provisions of the act of Congress of the 31st May, 1830, and the treaty of April 26, 1826.

Ecuador.—By treaty of June 13, 1839; proclaimed September 23, 1842.

Act of Parliament, 12, 13 Victoria. Act Congress, May 24, 1828.

912. Great Britain and her possessions.—From and after January 1, 1850 (on which day the act of Parliament of 1849, altering her navigation laws, went into effect), British vessels are admitted into the ports of the United States, on the same terms as vessels of the United States with the produce and manufacture of her own or any other country. By operation of acts of Congress, the convention with Great Britain, of July 3, 1815, continued by conventions of October 20, 1818, and August 6, 1827, and the general instructions for the information of the officers of the customs and others interested, issued by the Department under date of October 19, 1849, to the effect that, in consequence of the alterations of the British navigation laws, British vessels, from British or other foreign ports, will, under existing laws, be allowed to enter in ports of the United States with cargoes of the growth, manufacture, or production of any part of the world; and that such vessels and their cargoes will be admitted on the same terms, as to duties, imposts, and charges, as vessels of the United States and their cargoes.

Instructions of Treasury Department of October 19, 1849.

Navigation act of March 1, 1817; United States vs. Ship Recorder, July 2, 1847. Blackford, 1,218

By decision of the Circuit Court of the United States, it has been determined that British vessels, bringing from British ports in Europe articles of the growth, produce, or manufacture of the British possessions in India, were not liable to the penalties provided in the navigation act of March 1, 1817.

Coffee from British India possessions.

Coffee of the growth of the coast of Malabar, or island of Ceylon, being the possession of Great Britain in India, will be entitled to free entry if imported from Calcutta, or other port of the British East Indies, in vessels of the United States, or in vessels put on the footing of national vessels by reciprocal treaties.

Coffee or tea from China via Singapore.

Coffee or tea, the production of China, imported via *Singapore*, a possession of Great Britain, may be admitted to free entry, if it be satisfactorily shown at the time of entry that it was laden on board the American importing vessel, or foreign vessel entitled by reciprocal treaty, from Chinese boats or junks in Chinese waters, intended in good faith to be conveyed therein direct to a specified port in the United States as its ultimate destination.

913. *Greece.*—Treaty December 10–22, 1837 ; proclaimed August 30, 1838

New-Granada.—Treaty December 12, 1846, and President's proclamation, June 12, 1848 ; consular convention May 4, 1850 ; proclamation December 5, 1851.

Guatemala.—Treaty March 3, 1849 ; proclaimed July 28, 1852.

Hanover.—Treaty June 10, 1846; proclaimed April 24, 1847.

Dukedom of Oldenburg, accession to the above treaty, under its 12th article, March 10, 1847.

Dukedom of Mechlenburg Schwerin, accession to same, December 9, 1847.

Coffee or tea in Hanseatic vessels. Tariff act, July 30, 1846; act August 3, 1846.

Hanseatic Towns—Hamburg, Lubec, Bremen.—Treaty December 20, 1827 ; proclaimed June 2, 1828 ; additional articles to above treaty, June 4, 1828 ; proclaimed January 14, 1829.

Coffee or tea, imported direct from the place of its production, in vessels of the Hanseatic Republics of Hamburg, Bremen, and Lubec, to be placed on the same footing with that in vessels of the United States or Dutch vessels.

Netherlands.—Treaty August 26, 1852 ; proclaimed February 26, 1853.

Coffee in vessels of the Netherlands. Tariff act July 30, 1846.

Coffee, the product of a possession of the Netherlands, imported into the United States in a vessel of the Netherlands direct from such possession, or from the Netherlands, may be admitted free of duty, under schedule 1 of the tariff law of 1846, and the first article of the treaty between the United States and the Netherlands, of August 26, 1852.

Norway.—Treaty July 4, 1827; proclaimed January 19, 1828

Peru, Republic of.—Treaty July 26, 1851; President's proclamation July 19, 1852.

Prussia.—Treaty May 1, 1828; proclaimed March 14, 1829.

Coffee or tea in vessels of Russia. Tariff act July 30, 1846; act Aug. 3, 1846.

Coffee or tea, imported direct from the place of its production, in vessels of the kingdom of Prussia, to be placed on the same footing with that in vessels of the United States or Dutch vessels.

Russia.—Treaty April 5–17, 1824; proclaimed January 12, 1826. Treaty December 6–18, 1832 ; proclaimed May 11, 1833. Convention July 22, 1854 (rights of neutrals at sea); proclaimed November 1, 1854.

San Salvador.—Treaty at Leon, January 2, 1850; proclamation of President, April 18, 1853.

Sardinia and Genoa.—Treaty November 26, 1838; pro claimed March 18, 1839.

Two Sicilies.—Treaty October 1, 1855; proclaimed December 10, 1856.

Sweden and Norway.—Treaty July 4, 1827; proclaimed January 19, 1828; act of May 31, 1830.

Swedish vessels from the island of St. Bartholomew are placed on an equal footing with those of the United States, by the treaty with Sweden and Norway of July 4, 1827; and become equally exempt from tonnage duty under the act of 31st May, 1830.

Tuscany.—Act of 24th May, 1828, and President's proclamation, September 1, 1836.

Venezuela.—Treaty January 20, 1836, proclaimed June 20, 1836.

SECTION II.

SECOND CLASS.

ART. 914. Vessels belonging to the following nations, with whom we have reciprocal treaties on the footing of "*the most favored nations*," or with which reciprocity exists by virtue of acts of Congress of the United States, are admitted into the ports of the United States, as respects tonnage or navigation duties, on the same terms as vessels of the United States, with the produce or manufactures of their own or any other country.

Bolivia.—Treaty with Peru-Bolivian Confederation, November 30, 1836; proclaimed May 28, 1836.

Costa Rica.—Treaty July 10, 1851; proclaimed May 26, 1852.

Mexico.—Treaty April 5, 1831; revived by 17th article of the treaty of February 2, 1848; treaty of December 30, 1853; President's proclamation, June 30, 1854.

Muscat.—Treaty September 21, 1833; proclaimed 24th June, 1837.

Ottoman Empire.—Treaty May 7, 1830; proclaimed February 4, 1832.

Uruguay, Oriental Republic.—Decree of Uraguayan government of October 11, 1853; and laws of the same, of June 17, 1854.

SECTION III.

THIRD CLASS.

Art. 915. Vessels belonging to the following nations are admitted into ports of the United States on the same terms as vessels of the United States, *only* when laden with the product or manufactures of the country to which the vessel belongs:

French vessels from ports in France liable to tonnage duty.

France.—Treaty June 24, 1822; act March 3, 1823; treaty proclaimed February 12, 1823. Tonnage duty, 94 cents per ton in both countries; consuls to certify to the origin of the cargo.

Exempt when from Martinique and Guadaloupe. French ordinance of Feb. 5, 1826; acts of Congress, May 9, 1828. July 13, 1832.

French vessels laden with the produce of *Martinique* and *Guadaloupe* are admitted on equal terms with vessels of the United States, as to duty and tonnage, when direct from said islands in ballast, or with articles the growth or manufacture of either of said islands, so long as the French ordinance o February 5, 1826, shall continue in force.

Exempt when from Cayenne. Acts May 9, 1828; June 1, 1842.

rench vessels from *Cayenne*, in French Guiana, are admitted with the same privileges, granted under act of May 9, 1828, to vessels from Martinique and Guadaloupe.

Exempt when from St. Pierre and Miquelon. Acts May 9, 1828; July 13, 1832; March 3, 1845; Pres. Proc. April 20, 1847.

French vessels from *St. Pierre* and *Miquelon* are admitted on the same footing as vessels from Martinique and Guadaloupe, under acts of May 9, 1828, and July 13, 1823.

Liable to tonnage duty when from the banks of Newfoundland, with fish.

A French vessel bringing fish from the banks of the British colony of Newfoundland, being the product of the waters of that colony, is not exempt from tonnage duties; the act of 3d March, 1845, exempting from such duties only French vessels *coming directly from the islands of Miquelon and St. Pierre*, either in ballast or laden with articles the growth or manufacture of either of said islands, and there being no other provision of law or treaty authorizing an exemption.

Liable when with fish from Les Petites Oies.

A French vessel arriving in the United States with a cargo of fish from the islands of Les Petites Oies, is chargeable with tonnage duties. The islands Les Petites Oies, not being appur tenant to either Miquelon or St. Pierre, but belonging to the colony of Newfoundland, are not within the provisions of the act of 3d March, 1845, which exempt from tonnage duties French vessels arriving direct from St. Pierre and Miquelon, with productions or manufactures of those islands; nor are they brought within the provisions of that law by the fact that, by a treaty between France and England, Les Petites Oies are constituted a French fishing station.

Hawaiian Islands.—Treaty at Honolulu, December 20, 1849, and President's proclamation, November 9, 1850.

Pontifical States.—Act of January 7, 1824, and proclamation of the President, June 7, 1827.

Act January 7 1824.

916. *Portugal and Colonies.*—Treaty August 26, 1840; proclaimed April 24, 1841. Under treaty stipulations with Portugal, the vessels of that country are not subject to tonnage duty on arriving in the United States from any port or country; nor when bringing articles the growth, production or manufacture of countries other than Portugal or her dependencies, liable to the penalties provided by the navigation act of 1st March, 1817, the articles so brought being entitled to entry on the payment of the duties imposed by the laws of the United States on the value of the cargo, including the discriminating duty of ten per cent. on the rate of the regular duty levied on the articles so imported, there being no provision in the existing treaty, as decided by the Supreme Court of the United States relieving a cargo, so imported, from the discriminating duty. Tea or coffee, therefore, imported in a Portuguese vessel directly from the place of its growth, is not exempt from duty under the tariff act of 1846, and the treaty with Portugal of August 26, 1840.

Portuguese vessels coming from any country not liable to tonnage duty.

Not liable to penalties under navigation Act of Mch. 1, 1817.

Cargo entitled to entry, but liable to discriminating duties.

Oldfield vs. Marriott, 10 Howard, 146.

Tea or coffee in Portuguese vessels from place of production not exempt from duty.

Coffee imported in vessels of Portugal into the United States, either from the Netherlands or from the place of its production, not coming within the exemption provided in schedule I of the tariff of 1846, becomes liable to the duty of twenty per cent. ad valorem, as an unenumerated article, under the provisions of the 3d section of the act, and to the further payment of the discriminating duty of ten per cent. of the said rate of regular duty.

Coffee in Portuguese vessels from Netherlands or elsewhere, liable to duty.

Spanish vessels from the Canary Islands.—It appearing from a communicaion of the Charge de Affaires of Spain, dated 23d August, 1853, as well as from the certificate of the consul of he United States at Teneriffe, dated 19th April, 1853, that, by a royal Spanish decree, dated 11th July, 1852, and proclaimed in said island on the 10th October, 1852, vessels of the United States, and their cargoes, arriving in said island, or other of the Canary islands, namely, Orotana, Ciudad Real de los Palmas, Anecife de Langarole, Puerto de Cabras, and San Sebastian, also declared free by said royal decree, no discriminating duty, therefore, is to be levied on Spanish vessels or their cargoes from those ports arriving in ports of the United States, provided that on each such arrival there be filed with the collector of the port in which the vessel arrives a certificate of the consul of the United States, at said island, showing that the said Spanish decree remains in full force.

No discriminating duties on vessels of Spain or their cargoes coming from the Canary Islands. Spanish decrees, August 23, 1852. Act May 24, 1828.

Vessels belonging to the nations enumerated in the foregoing class, may import the produce and manufactures of other coun-

Privileges to vessels of nations enumerated in this class.

tries, subject to the payment of discriminating duty, and (except Portugal) to the payment of tonnage duty.

SECTION IV.

FOURTH CLASS.

917. Vessels belonging to the following nations, having no reciprocal treaties with the United States, are subject to tonnage and discriminating duty on their cargoes as foreign vessels, whether laden with the produce or manufactures of their own or any other country.

Duties on Spanish vessels coming from Spain or her adjacent islands.
Acts July 13,1832; August 3, 1846; and sec. 11, act August 30, 1842.

Spain.—Vessels of Spain arriving at ports of the United States from ports of Spain, or her adjacent islands, are to pay, besides the additional or discriminating duty of ten per cent. on the cargo, imposed by the 11th section of the tariff act of 1842, a tonnage duty of five cents per ton, that being the rate of tonnage duty levied on vessels of the United States arriving in the ports of Spain or her said *European* islands.

Duties on such vessels coming from the islands of Cuba and Porto Rico.
Acts July 13 1832; June 30 1834.

The laws of 13th July, 1832, and 30th June, 1834, contemplate and require Spanish vessels coming from any port or place in the islands of Cuba or Porto Rico, to pay in the ports of the United States the same rate of duty on tonnage that shall be levied on vessels of the United States at the port in said islands from whence such Spanish vessels shall have last departed; and likewise such further tonnage duty as shall be equivalent to the amount of discriminating duty that would have been imposed on the cargoes imported in the same vessels, respectively, if the same had been exported from the port of Havana in vessels of the United States. It consequently follows, that where no tonnage duty or discriminating duty on the cargoes of vessels of the United States, entering and departing from ports or places in the island of Cuba is imposed and collected thereat, Spanish vessels, coming from such ports or places, are to be similarly treated, as regards tonnage duty, in ports of the United States.

It has been ascertained by this Department, from authentic sources, that vessels of the United States entering the ports in the islands of Cuba and Porto Rico, *in ballast*, are not subjected to the payment of any tonnage duty whatever; and that vessels of the United States entering the ports in the islands of Cuba and Porto Rico, with cargoes of any description of merchandise whatsoever, are exempted from any charge of tonnage duty, if such vessels export or convey therefrom cargoes of molasses taken in at said ports.

Exemption, therefore, from the liability to tonnage duty of Spanish vessels coming from the ports in the islands of Cuba and Porto Rico, is to be extended to such vessels arriving in ports of the United States, either in ballast or laden with molasses taken in at any of the said ports, together with such quantity of fresh fruit, the production of said islands, as may be deemed by the collector and naval officer, under the provisions of the 45th section of the act of 2d March, 1799, to be admissible as surplus stores; in case the said vessels depart from the United States in ballast, or with cargoes of molasses, or of the staple productions of the United States, under the restrictions contained in the 3d section of the act of 30th June, 1834, and the master of such vessel produce to the collector, at the time of entry, a certificate from the chief officer of the customs at the port in the islands of Cuba or Porto Rico from which the vessel last departed, certified by the consul of the United States, showing the continuance in said island of the exemption from tonnage duties of vessels of the United States under the circumstances above stated: likewise, what discriminating or other duty is charged on such vessels when departing from said port with cargoes of molasses.

The cargoes of such Spanish vessels, on entry, must, of course, be subjected to the duties levied on the article by the tariff act of 30th July, 1846, together with the additional duty imposed by the 11th section of the tariff act of 30th August, 1842.

Cargoes liable on entry to discriminating duty

Spanish vessels from Cuba and Porto Rico (except as above) are subject to tonnage duty (if from Cuba $1 50 per ton; if from Porto Rico, 87½ cents per ton), and ten per cent. additional duty on their cargoes; also a discriminating duty equal to the export duty to which a vessel of the United States would have been liable in those islands over a Spanish vessel; and, before clearing directly or indirectly for either of those islands, such further duty as a vessel of the United States with a similar cargo would be liable to over a Spanish vessel in the ports of those islands.

Rates of tonnage duty (when chargeable) on Spanish vessels from Cuba and Porto Rico. Acts July 13, 1832, and June 30, 1834.

A Spanish vessel leaving a port of Spain for a port in Cuba, but not finding there a satisfactory market, proceeding, without breaking bulk or taking in any goods at said island, to a port in the United States, would not (nor her cargo) on entry be subject to any other or higher duties of tonnage or imposts than she would be if direct from a port of Spain to the United States; the voyage, under the circumstances, being regarded as continuous.

Spanish vessels from Spain via Cuba.

Where Spanish vessels are about to depart from a port of the United States with any goods, wares, or merchandise, for any destination other than some port or place in the islands of Cuba or Porto Rico, the bond and security required by the 3d

On departure of Spanish vessels from ports of United States for ports other than Cuba or Port-

Rico, bond to be given. Act June 30, 1834, sec. 3.

section of the act of 30th June, 1834, must be exacted before allowing clearance or departure of the vessels.

Discriminating duty levied on Spanish vessel clearing from Un'd States port for Cuba or Porto Rico cannot be refunded. Sec. 2, act June 30, 1834.

Discriminating duty exacted on a *Spanish vessel* clearing from a port of the United States *for Cuba or Porto Rico*, under the 2d section of the act of 30th June, 1834, "concerning tonnage duty on Spanish vessels," cannot be refunded, although the vessel may never arrive at her destination, having been wrecked on the voyage. By the express terms of the law, "the duties accrued on the clearing and departing" of the vessel, whatever accidents may attend her passage.

Vessels of Spain from Canary islands.

As it regards certain privileges granted, under the laws of the United States, to Spanish vessels arriving from the Canary islands, reference will be had to article 916 of these Regulations.

SECTION V.

FIFTH CLASS.

Art. 918. Vessels belonging to the following nations with which the United States have commercial relations, are not referable to either of the preceding classes:

Borneo.—Convention June 23, 1850; proclaimed July 12, 1854.

Vessels of Borneo liable to tonnage duty.

Under the existing treaty, no duty exceeding *one dollar per registered ton* is levied on vessels of the United States entering the port of his highness the Sultan of Borneo, the said tonnage duty being in lieu of all other charges or duties whatsoever.

China.—Commerce with the five ports: Kwangchow, Amoy, Fuchow, Nangpo, Shanghai.—Treaty July 3, 1844; proclaimed April 18, 1846.

Vessels of China liable to tonnage duty.

A tonnage duty of five *mace* (equal to 72½ cents) per ton is levied in the ports of China on vessels of the United States.

Dominican vessels liable to tonnage duty.

A Dominican vessel arriving *from* that part of the island of Hayti in possession of the Dominican republic, is liable to a tonnage duty of one dollar per ton; that being the duty imposed on the tonnage of vessels of the United States arriving in Dominica; but their cargoes are not liable to a discriminating duty of ten per cent., no such duty being levied by the Dominican republic on the cargoes of vessels of the United States arriving in the ports of that republic.

Vessels of Hayti liable to tonnage duty.

Hayti.—A tonnage duty of one dollar per ton is to be levied on vessels of Hayti. The discriminating duty formerly levied in Hayti upon the cargo of vessels of nations having no treaties with her having been abolished, as to the United States, May 9, 1850.

Japan.—Treaty March 31, 1854; proclaimed June 22, 1855.

Vessels of the United States are permitted to enter the ports of Simoda and Hakodade in Japan, where they can be supplied with wood, water, coal, provisions, and other articles required by their necessities; such articles to be procured only through the agency of Japanese officers appointed for that purpose. Goods furnished by the Japanese are to be paid for in gold or silver, or received in exchange for other goods, under such regulations as may be temporarily established by the Japanese government. Any privilege or advantage granted, *in future*, by the government of Japan, to any other nation, to be extended also to the United States and the citizens thereof.

No tonnage duty charged on vessels of the United States in the ports of Japan.

Lew-Chew, royal government of.—Compact July 11, 1854; proclaimed March 9, 1855.

Vessels of the United States may be admitted into any of the ports of Lew-Chew, and purchases may be freely made, from either the officers or people of the island, of wood, water, or any other articles. At the harbor of Napa, wood is to be furnished by the officers at the rate of three thousand six hundred copper cash for one thousand catties; and water, at the rate of six hundred copper cash (43 cents) for one thousand catties, or six barrels full, each containing thirty gallons of the United States.

Trade with Lew-Chew.

Skilful pilots will be provided, to conduct the vessels of the United States into the port of Napa, at a compensation of five dollars, to be paid to the pilot, by the captain of the vessel, for such service.

Pilotage to be paid by captain of vessel.

Siam.—Treaty March 20, 1833; proclaimed June 24, 1837.

Trade with Siam.

Under the treaty of March 20, 1833, vessels of the United States entering any port of his Majesty's dominions, and selling or purchasing cargoes of merchandise, are required to pay, in lieu of import and export duties, tonnage, license to trade, or any other charge whatsoever, a *measurement duty only, as follows*: The measurement to be made from side to side, in the middle of the vessel's length; and if a single-decked vessel, on such single deck; if otherwise, on the lower deck. On every vessel selling merchandise, the sum of one thousand seven hundred *ticals* or *bats* shall be paid for every Siamese fathom in breadth, so measured; the said fathom being computed to contain seventy-eight American inches, United States measure, corresponding to ninety-six Siamese inches; but if the said vessel should come without merchandise, and purchase a cargo with specie only, she shall then pay the sum of fifteen hundred *ticals* or *bats* for each and every fathom before described. Neither the aforesaid *measurement duty*, nor any other charge whatsoever, shall be paid by any vessel of the United States entering a Siamese port for the purpose of refitting, or for refreshments, or to inquire the state of the market.

Measurem't duty in lieu of all other duties, tonnage, or license.

If hereafter the duties payable by foreign vessels be diminished in favor of any other nation, the same diminution shall be made in favor of the United States.

The *tical* is a Siamese coin, about equal in value to 61 cents money of the United States.

919. *Swiss Confederation.*—Convention November 25, 1850—proclaimed November 9, 1855.

Commercial relations with Switzerland.

By this convention it is stipulated in the eighth, ninth, tenth, and eleventh articles, that in all that relates to the importation, exportation, and transit of their respective products, the United States and the said Confederation shall treat each other, reciprocally, as the most favored nation, union of nations, state or society. Neither of the contracting parties to impose any higher or other duties upon the importation, exportation, or transit of the natural or industrial productions of the other, than are or shall be payable upon the like articles, being the produce of any other country, not embraced within its present limits. Each of the contracting parties engaging itself not to grant any favor in commerce to any nation, union of nations, or society, which shall not immediately be enjoyed by the other party; and should one of the contracting parties impose differential duties upon the products of any nation, the other party to be at liberty to determine the manner of establishing the origin of its own produce, destined to enter the country by which the differential duties are imposed.

Swiss goods in vessels of other countries.

By the 12th article of the convention, it is provided that no port of the United States shall be closed to articles arriving from Switzerland, when conveyed in vessels of the United States, or in vessels of any country having free access to the ports of said States. Swiss merchandise, therefore, arriving under the flag of the United States, or under that of one of the nations most favored by them, is to pay the same duties as the merchandise of such nation. Under any other flag it is to be treated as the merchandise of the country to which the vessel belongs.

Swiss goods when imported in vessels of France.

In accordance with these stipulations, it has been decided by this Department that Swiss goods imported in French vessels are not liable to discriminating duty, no such duty being chargeable on the products or manufactures of France, when directly imported from that country.

CALCULATION

OF

STERLING MONEY,

REDUCED INTO DOLLARS AND CENTS, AT THE CUSTOM-HOUSE VALUE OF

$4.84 THE POUND STERLING,

AS FIXED BY LAW.

s. d.	$ *cts.*	£	$ *cts.*	£	$ *cts.*	£	$ *cts.*	£	$ *cts.*
2 6	61	9	43 56	52	251 68	95	459 80	138	667 92
3 0	73	10	48 40	53	256 52	96	464 64	139	672 76
3 6	85	11	53 24	54	261 36	97	469 48	140	677 60
4 0	97	12	58 08	55	266 20	98	474 32	141	682 44
4 6	1 09	13	62 92	56	271 04	99	479 16	142	687 28
5 0	1 21	14	67 76	57	275 88	100	484 00	143	692 12
5 6	1 33	15	72 60	58	280 72	101	488 84	144	696 96
6 0	1 45	16	77 44	59	285 56	102	493 68	145	701 80
6 6	1 57	17	82 28	60	290 40	103	498 52	146	706 64
7 0	1 69	18	87 12	61	295 24	104	503 36	147	711 48
7 6	1 82	19	91 96	62	300 08	105	508 20	148	716 32
8 0	1 94	20	96 80	63	304 92	106	513 04	149	721 16
8 6	2 06	21	101 64	64	309 76	107	517 88	150	726 00
9 0	2 18	22	106 48	65	314 60	108	522 72	151	730 84
9 6	2 30	23	111 32	66	319 44	109	527 56	152	735 68
10 0	2 42	24	116 16	67	324 28	110	532 40	153	740 52
10 6	2 54	25	121 00	68	329 12	111	537 24	154	745 36
11 0	2 66	26	125 84	69	333 96	112	542 08	155	750 20
11 6	2 78	27	130 68	70	338 80	113	546 92	156	755 04
12 0	2 90	28	135 52	71	343 64	114	551 76	157	759 88
12 6	3 03	29	140 36	72	348 48	115	556 60	158	764 72
13 0	3 15	30	145 20	73	353 32	116	561 44	159	769 56
13 6	3 27	31	150 04	74	358 16	117	566 28	160	774 40
14 0	3 39	32	154 88	75	363 00	118	571 12	161	779 24
14 6	3 51	33	159 72	76	367 84	119	575 96	162	784 08
15 0	3 63	34	164 56	77	372 68	120	580 80	163	788 92
15 6	3 75	35	169 40	78	377 52	121	585 64	164	793 76
16 0	3 87	36	174 24	79	382 36	122	590 48	165	798 60
16 6	3 99	37	179 08	80	387 20	123	595 32	166	803 44
17 0	4 11	38	183 92	81	392 04	124	600 16	167	808 28
17 6	4 24	39	188 76	82	396 88	125	605 00	168	813 12
18 0	4 36	40	193 60	83	401 72	126	609 84	169	817 96
18 6	4 48	41	198 44	84	406 56	127	614 68	170	822 80
19 0	4 60	42	203 28	85	411 40	128	619 52	171	827 64
19 6	4 72	43	208 12	86	416 24	129	624 36	172	832 48
£ 1	4 84	44	212 96	87	421 08	130	629 20	173	837 32
2	9 68	45	217 80	88	425 92	131	634 04	174	842 16
3	14 52	46	222 64	89	430 76	132	638 88	175	847 00
4	19 36	47	227 48	90	435 60	133	643 72	176	851 84
5	24 20	48	232 32	91	440 44	134	648 56	177	856 68
6	29 04	49	237 16	92	445 28	135	653 40	178	861 52
7	33 88	50	242 00	93	450 12	136	658 24	179	866 36
8	38 72	51	246 84	94	454 96	137	663 08	180	871 20

STERLING MONEY.

[CONTINUED.]

£	$ cts.	£	$ cts.	£	$ cts.	£	$ cts.	£	$ cts.
181	876 04	232	1122 88	283	1369 72	334	1616 56	385	1863 40
182	880 88	233	1127 72	284	1374 56	335	1621 40	386	1868 24
183	885 72	234	1132 56	285	1379 40	336	1626 24	387	1873 08
184	890 56	235	1137 40	286	1384 24	337	1631 08	388	1877 92
185	895 40	236	1142 24	287	1389 08	338	1635 92	389	1882 76
186	900 24	237	1147 08	288	1393 92	339	1640 76	390	1887 60
187	905 08	238	1151 92	289	1398 76	340	1645 60	391	1892 44
188	909 92	239	1156 76	290	1403 60	341	1650 44	392	1897 28
189	914 76	240	1161 60	291	1408 44	342	1655 28	393	1902 12
190	919 60	241	1166 44	292	1413 28	343	1660 12	394	1906 96
191	924 44	242	1171 28	293	1418 12	344	1664 96	395	1911 80
192	929 28	243	1176 12	294	1422 96	345	1669 80	396	1916 64
193	934 12	244	1180 96	295	1427 80	346	1674 64	397	1921 48
194	938 96	245	1185 80	296	1432 64	347	1679 48	398	1926 32
195	943 80	246	1190 64	297	1437 48	348	1684 32	399	1931 16
196	948 64	247	1195 48	298	1442 32	349	1689 16	400	1936 00
197	953 48	248	1200 32	299	1447 16	350	1694 00	401	1940 84
198	958 32	249	1205 16	300	1452 00	351	1698 84	402	1945 68
199	963 16	250	1210 00	301	1456 84	352	1703 68	403	1950 52
200	968 00	251	1214 84	302	1461 68	353	1708 52	404	1955 36
201	972 84	252	1219 68	303	1466 52	354	1713 36	405	1960 20
202	977 68	253	1224 52	304	1471 36	355	1718 20	406	1965 04
203	982 52	254	1229 36	305	1476 20	356	1723 04	407	1969 88
204	987 36	255	1234 20	306	1481 04	357	1727 88	408	1974 72
205	992 20	256	1239 04	307	1485 88	358	1732 72	409	1979 56
206	997 04	257	1243 88	308	1490 72	359	1737 56	410	1984 40
207	1001 88	258	1248 72	309	1495 56	360	1742 40	411	1989 24
208	1006 72	259	1253 56	310	1500 40	361	1747 24	412	1994 08
209	1011 56	260	1258 40	311	1505 24	362	1752 08	413	1998 92
210	1016 40	261	1263 24	312	1510 08	363	1756 92	414	2003 76
211	1021 24	262	1268 08	313	1514 92	364	1761 76	415	2008 60
212	1026 08	263	1272 92	314	1519 76	365	1766 60	416	2013 44
213	1030 92	264	1277 76	315	1524 60	366	1771 44	417	2018 28
214	1035 76	265	1282 60	316	1529 44	367	1776 28	418	2023 12
215	1040 60	266	1287 44	317	1534 28	368	1781 12	419	2027 96
216	1045 44	267	1292 28	318	1539 12	369	1785 96	420	2032 80
217	1050 28	268	1297 21	319	1543 96	370	1790 80	421	2037 64
218	1055 12	269	1301 96	320	1548 80	371	1795 64	422	2042 48
219	1059 96	270	1306 80	321	1553 64	372	1800 48	423	2047 32
220	1064 80	271	1311 64	322	1558 48	373	1805 32	424	2052 16
221	1069 64	272	1316 48	323	1563 32	374	1810 16	425	2057 00
222	1074 48	273	1321 32	324	1568 16	375	1815 00	426	2061 84
223	1079 32	274	1326 16	325	1573 00	376	1819 84	427	2066 68
224	1084 16	275	1331 00	326	1577 84	377	1824 68	428	2071 52
225	1089 00	276	1335 84	327	1582 68	378	1829 52	429	2076 36
226	1093 84	277	1340 68	328	1587 52	379	1834 36	430	2081 20
227	1098 68	278	1345 52	329	1592 36	380	1839 20	431	2086 04
228	1103 52	279	1350 36	330	1597 20	381	1844 04	432	2090 88
229	1108 36	280	1355 20	331	1602 04	382	1848 88	433	2095 72
230	1113 20	281	1360 04	332	1606 88	383	1853 72	434	2100 56
231	1118 04	282	1364 88	333	1611 72	384	1858 56	435	2105 40

STERLING MONEY.

[CONTINUED.]

£	$	cts.	£	$	cts.	£	$	cts.	£	$	cts.	£	$	cts.
436	2110	24	487	2357	08	538	2603	92	589	2850	76	640	3097	60
437	2115	08	488	2361	92	539	2608	76	590	2855	60	641	3102	44
438	2119	92	489	2366	76	540	2613	60	591	2860	44	642	3107	28
439	2124	76	490	2371	60	541	2618	44	592	2865	28	643	3112	12
440	2129	60	491	2376	44	542	2623	28	593	2870	12	644	3116	96
441	2134	44	492	2381	28	543	2628	12	594	2874	96	645	3121	80
442	2139	28	493	2386	12	544	2632	96	595	2879	80	646	3126	64
443	2144	12	494	2390	96	545	2637	80	596	2884	64	647	3131	48
444	2148	96	495	2395	80	546	2642	64	597	2889	48	648	3136	32
445	2153	80	496	2400	64	547	2647	48	598	2894	32	649	3141	16
446	2158	64	497	2405	48	548	2652	32	599	2899	16	650	3146	00
447	2163	48	498	2410	32	549	2657	16	600	2904	00	651	3150	84
448	2168	32	499	2415	16	550	2662	00	601	2908	84	652	3155	68
449	2173	16	500	2420	00	551	2666	84	602	2913	68	653	3160	52
450	2178	00	501	2424	84	552	2671	68	603	2918	52	654	3165	36
451	2182	84	502	2429	68	553	2676	52	604	2923	36	655	3170	20
452	2187	68	503	2434	52	554	2681	36	605	2928	20	656	3175	04
553	2192	52	504	2439	36	555	2686	20	606	2933	04	657	3179	88
454	2197	36	505	2444	20	556	2691	04	607	2937	88	658	3184	72
455	2202	20	506	2449	04	557	2695	88	608	2942	72	659	3189	56
456	2207	04	507	2453	88	558	2700	72	609	2947	56	660	3194	40
457	2211	88	508	2458	72	559	2705	56	610	2952	40	661	3199	24
458	2216	72	509	2463	56	560	2710	40	611	2957	24	662	3204	08
459	2221	56	510	2468	40	561	2715	24	612	2962	08	663	3208	92
460	2226	40	511	2473	24	562	2720	08	613	2966	92	664	3213	76
461	2231	24	512	2478	08	563	2724	92	614	2971	76	665	3218	60
462	2236	08	513	2482	92	564	2729	76	615	2976	60	666	3223	44
463	2240	92	514	2487	76	565	2734	60	616	2981	44	667	3228	28
464	2245	76	515	2492	60	566	2739	44	617	2986	28	668	3233	12
465	2250	60	516	2497	44	567	2744	28	618	2991	12	669	3237	96
466	2255	44	517	2502	28	568	2749	12	619	2995	96	670	3242	80
467	2260	28	518	2507	12	569	2753	96	620	3000	80	671	3247	64
468	2265	12	519	2511	96	570	2758	80	621	3005	64	672	3252	48
469	2269	96	520	2516	80	571	2763	64	622	3010	48	673	3257	32
470	2274	80	521	2521	64	572	2768	48	623	3015	32	674	3262	16
471	2279	64	522	2526	48	573	2773	32	624	3020	16	675	3267	00
472	2284	48	523	2531	32	574	2778	16	625	3025	00	676	3271	84
473	2289	32	524	2536	16	575	2783	00	626	3029	84	677	3276	68
474	2294	16	525	2541	00	576	2787	84	627	3034	68	678	3281	52
475	2299	00	526	2545	84	577	2792	68	628	3039	52	679	3286	36
476	2303	84	527	2550	68	578	2797	52	629	3044	36	680	3291	20
477	2308	68	528	2555	52	579	2802	36	630	3049	20	681	3296	04
478	2313	52	529	2560	36	580	2807	20	631	3054	04	682	3300	88
479	2318	36	530	2565	20	581	2812	04	632	3058	88	683	3305	72
480	2323	20	531	2570	04	582	2816	88	633	3063	72	684	3310	56
481	2328	04	532	2574	88	583	2821	72	634	3068	56	685	3315	40
482	2332	88	533	2579	72	584	2826	56	635	3073	40	686	3320	24
483	2337	72	534	2584	56	585	2831	40	636	3078	24	687	3325	08
484	2342	56	535	2589	40	586	2836	24	637	3083	08	688	3329	92
485	2347	40	536	2594	24	587	2841	08	638	3087	92	689	3334	76
486	2352	24	537	2599	08	588	2845	92	639	3092	76	690	3339	60

STERLING MONEY.

[CONTINUED.]

£	$ cts.	£	$ cts.	£	$ cts.	£	$ cts.	£	$ cts.
691	3344 44	742	3591 28	793	3838 12	844	4084 96	895	4331 80
692	3349 28	743	3596 12	794	3842 96	845	4089 80	896	4336 64
693	3354 12	744	3600 96	795	3847 80	846	4094 64	897	4341 48
694	3358 96	745	3605 80	796	3852 64	847	4099 48	898	4346 32
695	3363 80	746	3610 64	797	3857 48	848	4104 32	899	4351 16
696	3368 64	747	3615 48	798	3862 32	849	4109 16	900	4356 00
697	3373 48	748	3620 32	799	3867 16	850	4114 00	901	4360 84
698	3378 32	749	3625 16	800	3872 00	851	4118 84	902	4365 68
699	3383 16	750	3630 00	801	3876 84	852	4123 68	903	4370 52
700	3388 00	751	3634 84	802	3881 68	853	4128 52	904	4375 36
701	3392 84	752	3639 68	803	3886 52	854	4133 36	905	4380 20
702	3397 68	753	3644 52	804	3891 36	855	4138 20	906	4385 04
703	3402 52	754	3649 36	805	3896 20	856	4143 04	907	4389 88
704	3407 36	755	3654 20	806	3901 04	857	4147 88	908	4394 72
705	3412 20	756	3659 04	807	3905 88	858	4152 72	909	4399 56
706	3417 04	757	3663 88	808	3910 72	859	4157 56	910	4404 40
707	3421 88	758	3668 72	809	3915 56	860	4162 40	911	4409 24
708	3426 72	759	3673 56	810	3920 40	861	4167 24	912	4414 08
709	3431 56	760	3678 40	811	3925 24	862	4172 08	913	4418 92
710	3436 40	761	3683 24	812	3930 08	863	4176 92	914	4423 76
711	3441 24	762	3688 08	813	3934 92	864	4181 76	915	4428 60
712	3446 08	763	3692 92	814	3939 76	865	4186 60	916	4433 44
713	3450 92	764	3697 76	815	3944 60	866	4191 44	917	4438 28
714	3455 76	765	3702 60	816	3949 44	867	4196 28	918	4443 12
715	3460 60	766	3707 44	817	3954 28	868	4201 12	919	4447 96
716	3465 44	767	3712 28	818	3959 12	869	4205 96	920	4452 80
717	3470 28	768	3717 12	819	3963 96	870	4210 80	921	4457 64
718	3475 12	769	3721 96	820	3968 80	871	4215 64	922	4462 48
719	3479 96	770	3726 80	821	3973 64	872	4220 48	923	4467 32
720	3484 80	771	3731 64	822	3978 48	873	4225 32	924	4472 16
721	3489 64	772	3736 48	823	3983 32	874	4230 16	925	4477 00
722	3494 48	773	3741 32	824	3988 16	875	4235 00	926	4481 84
723	3499 32	774	3746 16	825	3993 00	876	4239 84	927	4486 68
724	3504 16	775	3751 00	826	3997 84	877	4244 68	928	4491 52
725	3509 00	776	3755 84	827	4002 68	878	4249 52	929	4496 36
726	3513 84	777	3760 68	828	4007 52	879	4254 36	930	4501 20
727	3518 68	778	3765 52	829	4012 36	880	4259 20	931	4506 04
728	3523 52	779	3770 36	830	4017 20	881	4264 04	932	4510 88
729	3528 36	780	3775 20	831	4022 04	882	4268 88	933	4515 72
730	3533 20	781	3780 04	832	4026 88	883	4273 72	934	4520 56
731	3538 04	782	3784 88	833	4031 72	884	4278 56	935	4525 40
732	3542 88	783	3789 72	834	4036 56	885	4283 40	936	4530 24
733	3547 72	784	3794 56	835	4041 40	886	4288 24	937	4535 08
734	3552 56	785	3799 40	836	4046 24	887	4293 08	938	4539 92
735	3557 40	786	3804 24	837	4051 08	888	4297 92	939	4544 76
736	3562 24	787	3809 08	838	4055 92	889	4302 76	940	4549 60
737	3567 08	788	3813 92	839	4060 76	890	4307 60	941	4554 44
738	3571 92	789	3818 76	840	4065 60	891	4312 44	942	4559 28
739	3576 76	790	3823 60	841	4070 44	892	4317 28	943	4564 12
740	3581 60	791	3828 44	842	4075 28	893	4322 12	944	4568 96
741	3586 44	792	3833 28	843	4080 12	894	4326 96	945	4573 80

STERLING MONEY.

[CONTINUED.]

£	$ cts.	£	$ cts.	£	$	£	$	£	$
946	4578 64	975	4719 00	1400	6776	4300	20812	7200	34848
947	4583 48	976	4723 84	1500	7260	4400	21296	7300	35332
948	4588 32	977	4728 68	1600	7744	4500	21780	7400	35816
949	4593 16	978	4733 52	1700	8228	4600	22264	7500	36300
950	4598 00	979	4738 36	1800	8712	4700	22748	7600	36784
951	4602 84	980	4743 20	1900	9196	4800	23232	7700	37268
952	4607 68	981	4748 04	2000	9680	4900	23716	7800	37752
953	4612 52	982	4752 88	2100	10164	5000	24200	7900	38236
954	4617 36	983	4757 72	2200	10648	5100	24684	8000	38720
955	4622 20	984	4762 56	2300	11132	5200	25168	8100	39204
956	4627 04	985	4767 40	2400	11616	5300	25652	8200	39688
957	4631 88	986	4772 24	2500	12100	5400	26136	8300	40172
958	4636 72	987	4777 08	2600	12584	5500	26620	8400	40656
959	4641 56	988	4781 92	2700	13068	5600	27104	8500	41140
960	4646 40	989	4786 76	2800	13552	5700	27588	8600	41624
961	4651 24	990	4791 60	2900	14036	5800	28072	8700	42108
962	4656 08	991	4796 44	3000	14520	5900	28556	8800	42592
963	4660 92	992	4801 28	3100	15004	6000	29040	8900	43076
964	4665 76	993	4806 12	3200	15488	6100	29524	9000	43560
965	4670 60	994	4810 96	3300	15972	6200	30008	9100	44044
966	4675 44	995	4815 80	3400	16456	6300	30492	9200	44528
967	4680 28	996	4820 64	3500	16940	6400	30976	9300	45012
968	4685 12	997	4825 48	3600	17424	6500	31460	9400	45496
969	4689 96	998	4830 32	3700	17908	6600	31944	9500	45980
970	4694 80	999	4835 16	3800	18392	6700	32428	9600	46464
971	4699 64	1000	4840 00	3900	18876	6800	32912	9700	46948
972	4704 48	1100	5324 00	4000	19360	6900	33396	9800	47432
973	4709 32	1200	5808 00	4100	19844	7000	33880	9900	47916
974	4714 16	1300	6292 00	4200	20328	7100	34364	10000	48400

CALCULATION

OF

FRANCS,

REDUCED INTO DOLLARS AND CENTS, AT THE CUSTOM-HOUSE VALUE OF

$18\frac{6}{10}$ CENTS PER FRANC,

AS FIXED BY LAW.

Francs.	$ *cts.*	*Francs.*	$ *cts.*	*Francs.*	$ *cts.*	*Francs.*	$ *cts.*
1	19	39	7 25	77	14 32	1600	297 60
2	37	40	7 44	78	14 51	1700	316 20
3	56	41	7 63	79	14 69	1800	334 80
4	74	42	7 81	80	14 88	1900	353 40
5	93	43	8 00	81	15 07	2000	372 00
6	1 12	44	8 18	82	15 25	2100	390 60
7	1 30	45	8 37	83	15 44	2200	409 20
8	1 49	46	8 56	84	15 62	2300	427 80
9	1 67	47	8 74	85	15 81	2400	446 40
10	1 86	48	8 93	86	16 00	2500	465 00
11	2 05	49	9 11	87	16 18	2600	483 60
12	2 23	50	9 30	88	16 37	2700	502 20
13	2 42	51	9 49	89	16 55	2800	520 80
14	2 60	52	9 67	90	16 74	2900	539 40
15	2 79	53	9 86	91	16 93	3000	558 00
16	2 98	54	10 04	92	17 11	3100	576 60
17	3 16	55	10 23	93	17 30	3200	595 20
18	3 35	56	10 42	94	17 48	3300	613 80
19	3 53	57	10 60	95	17 67	3400	632 40
20	3 72	58	10 79	96	17 86	3500	651 00
21	3 91	59	10 97	97	18 04	3600	669 60
22	4 09	60	11 16	98	18 23	3700	688 20
23	4 28	61	11 35	99	18 41	3800	706 80
24	4 46	62	11 53	100	18 60	3900	725 40
25	4 65	63	11 72	200	37 20	4000	744 00
26	4 84	64	11 90	300	55 80	4100	762 60
27	5 02	65	12 09	400	74 40	4200	781 20
28	5 21	66	12 28	500	93 00	4300	799 80
29	5 39	67	12 46	600	111 60	4400	818 40
30	5 58	68	12 65	700	130 20	4500	837 00
31	5 77	69	12 83	800	148 80	4600	855 60
32	5 95	70	13 02	900	167 40	4700	874 20
33	6 14	71	13 21	1000	186 00	4800	892 80
34	6 32	72	13 39	1100	204 60	4900	911 40
35	6 51	73	13 58	1200	223 20	5000	930 00
36	6 70	74	13 76	1300	241 80	5100	948 60
37	6 88	75	13 95	1400	260 40	5200	967 20
38	7 07	76	14 14	1500	279 00	5300	985 80

FRENCH MONEY.

[CONTINUED.]

Francs.	$ cts.	*Francs.*	$ cts.	*Francs.*	$ cts.	*Francs*	$ cts.
5400	1004 40	8900	1655 40	33000	6138 00	67000	12462 00
5500	1023 00	9000	1674 00	34000	6324 00	68000	12648 00
5600	1041 60	9100	1692 60	35000	6510 00	69000	12834 00
5700	1060 20	9200	1711 20	36000	6696 00	70000	13020 00
5800	1078 80	9300	1729 80	37000	6882 00	71000	13206 00
5900	1097 40	9400	1748 40	38000	7068 00	72000	13392 00
6000	1116 00	9500	1767 00	39000	7254 00	73000	13578 00
6100	1134 60	9600	1785 60	40000	7440 00	74000	13764 00
6200	1153 20	9700	1804 20	41000	7626 00	75000	13950 00
6300	1171 80	9800	1822 80	42000	7812 00	76000	14136 00
6400	1190 40	9900	1841 40	43000	7998 00	77000	14322 00
6500	1209 00	10000	1860 00	44000	8184 00	78000	14508 00
6600	1227 60	11000	2046 00	45000	8370 00	79000	14694 00
6700	1246 20	12000	2232 00	46000	8556 00	80000	14880 00
6800	1264 80	13000	2418 00	47000	8742 00	81000	15066 00
6900	1283 40	14000	2604 00	48000	8928 00	82000	15252 00
7000	1302 00	15000	2790 00	49000	9114 00	83000	15438 00
7100	1320 60	16000	2976 00	50000	9300 00	84000	15624 00
7200	1339 20	17000	3162 00	51000	9486 00	85000	15810 00
7300	1357 80	18000	3348 00	52000	9672 00	86000	15996 00
7400	1376 40	19000	3534 00	53000	9858 00	87000	16182 00
7500	1395 00	20000	3720 00	54000	10044 00	88000	16368 00
7600	1413 60	21000	3906 00	55000	10230 00	89000	16554 00
7700	1432 20	22000	4092 00	56000	10416 00	90000	16740 00
7800	1450 80	23000	4278 00	57000	10602 00	91000	16926 00
7900	1469 40	24000	4464 00	58000	10788 00	92000	17112 00
8000	1488 00	25000	4650 00	59000	10974 00	93000	17298 00
8100	1506 60	26000	4836 00	60000	11160 00	94000	17484 00
8200	1525 20	27000	5022 00	61000	11346 00	95000	17670 00
8300	1543 80	28000	5208 00	62000	11532 00	96000	17856 00
8400	1562 40	29000	5394 00	63000	11718 00	97000	18042 00
8500	1581 00	30000	5580 00	64000	11904 00	98000	18228 00
8600	1599 60	31000	5766 00	65000	12090 00	99000	18414 00
8700	1618 20	32000	5952 00	66000	12276 00	100000	18600 00
8800	1636 80						

CALCULATION

OF

BREMEN RIX DOLLARS,

REDUCED INTO DOLLARS AND CENTS AT THE CUSTOM-HOUSE VALUE OF

78¾ CENTS PER RIX DOLLAR,

AS FIXED BY LAW.

R. Dol.	*$ cts.*	*R. Dol.*	*$ cts.*	*R. Dol.*	*$ cts.*	*R. Dol.*	*$ cts.*
1	78¾	39	30 71	77	60 64	1600	1260 00
2	1 58	40	31 50	78	61 43	1700	1338 75
3	2 36	41	32 29	79	62 21	1800	1417 50
4	3 15	42	33 08	80	63 00	1900	1496 25
5	3 94	43	33 86	81	63 79	2000	1575 00
6	4 73	44	34 65	82	64 58	2100	1653 75
7	5 51	45	35 44	83	65 36	2200	1732 50
8	6 30	46	36 23	84	66 15	2300	1811 25
9	7 09	47	37 01	85	66 94	2400	1890 00
10	7 88	48	37 80	86	67 73	2500	1968 75
11	8 66	49	38 59	87	68 51	2600	2047 50
12	9 45	50	39 38	88	69 30	2700	2126 25
13	10 24	51	40 16	89	70 09	2800	2205 00
14	11 03	52	40 95	90	70 88	2900	2283 75
15	11 81	53	41 74	91	71 66	3000	2362 50
16	12 60	54	42 53	92	72 45	3100	2441 25
17	13 39	55	43 31	93	73 24	3200	2520 00
18	14 18	56	44 10	94	74 03	3300	2598 75
19	14 96	57	44 89	95	74 81	3400	2677 50
20	15 75	58	45 68	96	75 60	3500	2756 25
21	16 54	59	46 46	97	76 39	3600	2835 00
22	17 33	60	47 25	98	77 18	3700	2913 75
23	18 11	61	48 04	99	77 96	3800	2992 50
24	18 90	62	48 83	100	78 75	3900	3071 25
25	19 69	63	49 61	200	157 50	4000	3150 00
26	20 48	64	50 40	300	236 25	4100	3228 75
27	21 26	65	51 19	400	315 00	4200	3307 50
28	22 05	66	51 98	500	393 75	4300	3386 25
29	22 84	67	52 76	600	472 50	4400	3465 00
30	23 63	68	53 55	700	551 25	4500	3543 75
31	24 41	69	54 34	800	630 00	4600	3622 50
32	25 20	70	55 13	900	708 75	4700	3701 25
33	25 99	71	55 91	1000	787 50	4800	3780 00
34	26 78	72	56 70	1100	866 25	4900	3858 75
35	27 56	73	57 49	1200	945 00	5000	3937 50
36	28 35	74	58 28	1300	1023 75	5100	4016 25
37	29 14	75	59 06	1400	1102 50	5200	4095 00
38	29 93	76	59 85	1500	1181 25	5300	4173 75

BREMEN RIX DOLLARS.

R. Dol.	$	cts.	R. Dol.	$	cts.	R. Dol.	$	cts.	R. Dol.	$	cts.
5400	4252	50	8700	6851	25	12000	9450	00	18000	14175	00
5500	4331	25	8800	6930	00	12100	9528	75	19000	14962	50
5600	4410	00	8900	7008	75	12200	9607	50	20000	15750	00
5700	4488	75	9000	7087	50	12300	9686	25	21000	16537	50
5800	4567	50	9100	7166	25	12400	9765	00	22000	17325	00
5900	4646	25	9200	7245	00	12500	9843	75	23000	18112	50
6000	4725	00	9300	7323	75	12600	9922	50	24000	18900	00
6100	4803	75	9400	7402	50	12700	10001	25	25000	19687	50
6200	4882	50	9500	7481	25	12800	10080	00	26000	20475	00
6300	4961	25	9600	7560	00	12900	10158	75	27000	21262	50
6400	5040	00	9700	7638	75	13000	10237	50	28000	22050	00
6500	5118	75	9800	7717	50	13100	10316	25	29000	22837	50
6600	5197	50	9900	7796	25	13200	10395	00	30000	23625	00
6700	5276	25	10000	7875	00	13300	10473	75	31000	24412	50
6800	5355	00	10100	7953	75	13400	10552	50	32000	25200	00
6900	5433	75	10200	8032	50	13500	10631	25	33000	25987	50
7000	5512	50	10300	8111	25	13600	10710	00	34000	26775	00
7100	5591	25	10400	8190	00	13700	10788	75	35000	27562	50
7200	5670	00	10500	8268	75	13800	10867	50	36000	28350	00
7300	5748	75	10600	8347	50	13900	10946	25	37000	29137	50
7400	5827	50	10700	8426	25	14000	11025	00	38000	29925	00
7500	5906	25	10800	8505	00	14100	11103	75	39000	30712	50
7600	5985	00	10900	8583	75	14200	11182	50	40000	31500	00
7700	6063	75	11000	8662	50	14300	11261	25	41000	32287	50
7800	6142	50	11100	8741	25	14400	11340	00	42000	33075	00
7900	6221	25	11200	8820	00	14500	11418	75	43000	33862	50
8000	6300	00	11300	8898	75	14600	11497	50	44000	34650	00
8100	6378	75	11400	8977	50	14700	11576	25	45000	35437	50
8200	6457	50	11500	9056	25	14800	11655	00	46000	36225	00
8300	6536	25	11600	9135	00	14900	11733	75	47000	37012	50
8400	6615	00	11700	9213	75	15000	11812	50	48000	37800	00
8500	6693	75	11800	9292	50	16000	12600	00	49000	38587	50
8600	6772	50	11900	9371	25	17000	12387	50	50000	39375	00

CALCULATION

OF

PRUSSIAN RIX DOLLARS,

REDUCED INTO DOLLARS AND CENTS, AT THE CUSTOM-HOUSE VALUE OF

69 CENTS PER RIX DOLLAR,

AS FIXED BY LAW.

Thalers.	$ *cts.*	*Thalers.*	$ *cts.*	*Thalers.*	$
1	0 69	60	41 40	1100	759
2	1 38	70	48 30	1200	828
3	2 07	80	55 20	1300	897
4	2 76	90	62 10	1400	966
5	3 45	100	69 00	1500	1035
6	4 14	110	75 90	1600	1104
7	4 83	120	82 80	1700	1173
8	5 52	130	89 70	1800	1242
9	6 21	140	96 60	1900	1311
10	6 90	150	103 50	2000	1380
11	7 59	160	110 40	3000	2070
12	8 28	170	117 30	4000	2760
13	8 97	180	124 20	5000	3450
14	9 66	190	131 10	6000	4140
15	10 35	200	138 00	7000	4830
16	11 04	300	207 00	8000	5520
17	11 73	400	276 00	9000	6210
18	12 42	500	345 00	10000	6900
19	13 11	600	414 00	20000	13800
20	13 80	700	483 00	30000	20700
30	20 70	800	552 00	40000	27600
40	27 60	900	621 00	50000	34500
50	34 50	1000	690 00	100000	69000

POUNDS SPANISH,

REDUCED TO POUNDS AVOIRDUPOIS.

lb. S	*lb. Av'd.*	*lb. S.*	*lb. Av'd.*	*lb. S.*	*lb. Av'd.*	*lb. S.*	*lb. Av'd.*	*lb. S.*	*lb. Av'd.*
1	1 01	43	43 62	85	86 22	19000	19273 60	61000	61878 40
2	2 03	44	44 63	86	87 24	20000	20288 00	62000	62892 80
3	3 04	45	45 65	87	88 25	21000	21302 40	63000	63907 20
4	4 06	46	46 66	88	89 27	22000	22316 80	64000	64921 60
5	5 07	47	47 68	89	90 28	23000	23331 20	65000	65936 00
6	6 09	48	48 69	90	91 30	24000	24345 60	66000	66950 40
7	7 10	49	49 71	91	92 31	25000	25360 00	67000	67964 80
8	8 12	50	50 72	92	93 32	26000	26374 40	68000	68979 20
9	9 13	51	51 73	93	94 34	27000	27388 80	69000	69993 60
10	10 14	52	52 75	94	95 35	28000	28403 20	70000	71008 00
11	11 16	53	53 76	95	96 37	29000	29417 60	71000	72022 40
12	12 17	54	54 78	96	97 38	30000	30432 00	72000	73036 80
13	13 19	55	55 79	97	98 40	31000	31446 40	73000	74051 20
14	14 20	56	56 81	98	99 41	32000	32460 80	74000	75065 60
15	15 22	57	57 82	99	100 43	33000	33475 20	75000	76080 00
16	16 23	58	58 84	100	101 44	34000	34489 60	76000	77094 40
17	17 24	59	59 85	200	202 88	35000	35504 00	77000	78108 80
18	18 26	60	60 86	300	304 32	36000	36518 40	78000	79123 20
19	19 27	61	61 88	400	405 76	37000	37532 80	79000	80137 60
20	20 29	62	62 89	500	507 20	38000	38547 20	80000	81152 00
21	21 30	63	63 91	600	608 64	39000	39561 60	81000	82166 40
22	22 32	64	64 92	700	710 08	40000	40576 00	82000	83180 80
23	23 33	65	65 94	800	811 52	41000	41590 40	83000	84195 20
24	24 35	66	66 95	900	912 96	42000	42604 80	84000	85209 60
25	25 36	67	67 96	1000	1014 40	43000	43619 20	85000	86224 00
26	26 37	68	68 98	2000	2028 80	44000	44633 60	86000	87238 40
27	27 39	69	69 99	3000	3043 26	45000	45648 00	87000	88252 80
28	28 40	70	71 01	4000	4057 60	46000	46662 40	88000	89267 20
29	29 42	71	72 02	5000	5072 00	47000	47676 80	89000	90281 60
30	30 43	72	73 04	6000	6086 40	48000	48691 20	90000	91296 00
31	31 45	73	74 05	7000	7100 80	49000	49705 60	91000	92310 40
32	32 46	74	75 07	8000	8115 20	50000	50720 00	92000	93324 80
33	33 48	75	76 08	9000	9129 60	51000	51734 40	93000	94339 20
34	34 49	76	77 09	10000	10144 00	52000	52748 80	94000	95353 60
35	35 50	77	78 11	11000	11158 40	53000	53763 20	95000	96368 00
36	36 52	78	79 12	12000	12172 80	54000	54777 60	96000	97382 40
37	37 53	79	80 14	13000	13187 20	55000	55792 00	97000	98396 80
38	38 55	80	81 15	14000	14201 60	56000	56806 40	98000	99411 20
39	39 56	81	82 17	15000	15216 00	57000	57820 80	99000	100425 60
40	40 58	82	83 18	16000	16230 40	58000	58835 20	100000	101440 00
41	41 59	83	84 20	17000	17244 80	59000	59849 60	200000	202880 00
42	42 60	84	85 21	18000	18259 20	60000	60864 00	300000	304320 00

100 lbs. Spanish equal to 101$\frac{44}{100}$ lbs. Avoirdupois.

AUSTRIAN POUNDS,

REDUCED TO UNITED STATES POUNDS.

A. P.	U. S. Pounds.	A. P.	U. S. P.	A. P.	U. S. P.	A. P.	U. S. P.
1	1 23.60	20	24.72	300	370.80	4000	4944
2	2 47.20	30	37.08	400	494.40	5000	6180
3	3 70.80	40	49.44	500	618.00	6000	7416
4	4 94.40	50	61.80	600	741.60	7000	8650
5	6 18.00	60	74.16	700	865.20	8000	9888
6	7 41.60	70	86.52	800	988.80	9000	11124
7	8 65.20	80	98.88	900	1112.40	10000	12360
8	9 88.80	90	111.24	1000	1236.00	20000	24720
9	11 12.40	100	123.60	2000	2472 00	30000	37080
10	12 36.00	200	247.20	3000	3708.00	50000	61800

POUNDS OF ANTWERP.

ALSO,

BELGIUM, BRUSSELS, GHENT, LIEGE, BRUGES, MONS, NAMUR,

TOURNAY, LOUVAIN, MALINES, COURTRAY,

ST. NICHOLAS, AND OSTEND,

REDUCED TO UNITED STATES POUNDS.

A. P.	U. S. P.	A. P.	U. S. P.	A. P.	U. S. P.	A. P.	U. S. P.
1	1 03.35	20	20 67.00	300	310.05	4000	4134.00
2	2 06.70	30	31 00.50	400	413.40	5000	5167.50
3	3 10.05	40	41 34.00	500	516.75	6000	6201.00
4	4 13.40	50	51 67.50	600	620.10	7000	7234.50
5	5 16.75	60	62 01.00	700	723.45	8000	8268.00
6	6 20.10	70	72 34.50	800	826.80	9000	9301 50
7	7 23.45	80	82 68.00	900	930.15	10000	10335.00
8	8 26.80	90	93 01.50	1000	1033.50	20000	20670 00
9	9 30.15	100	103 35.00	2000	2067.00	30000	31005.00
10	10 33.50	200	206 70.00	3000	3100.50	50000	51675.00

TONS REDUCED TO POUNDS.

TONS.	POUNDS.	TONS.	POUNDS.	TONS.	POUNDS.	TONS.	POUNDS.
1	2240	44	98560	87	194880	130	291200
2	4480	45	100800	88	197120	131	293440
3	6720	46	103040	89	199360	132	295680
4	8960	47	105280	90	201600	133	297920
5	11200	48	107520	91	203840	134	300160
6	13440	49	109760	92	206080	135	302400
7	15680	50	112000	93	208320	136	304640
8	17920	51	114240	94	210560	137	307880
9	20160	52	116480	95	212800	138	309120
10	22400	53	118720	96	215040	139	311360
11	24640	54	120960	97	217280	140	313600
12	26880	55	123200	98	219520	141	315840
13	29120	56	125440	99	221760	142	318080
14	31360	57	127680	100	224000	143	320320
15	33600	58	129920	101	226230	144	322560
16	35840	59	132160	102	228480	145	324800
17	38080	60	134400	103	230720	146	327040
18	40320	61	136640	104	232960	147	329280
19	42560	62	138880	105	235200	148	331520
20	44800	63	141120	106	237440	149	333760
21	47040	64	143360	107	239680	150	336000
22	49280	65	145600	108	241920	151	338240
23	51520	66	147840	109	244160	152	340480
24	53760	67	150080	110	246400	153	342720
25	56000	68	152320	111	248640	154	344960
26	58240	69	154560	112	250880	155	347200
27	60480	70	156800	113	253120	156	349440
28	62720	71	159040	114	255360	157	351680
29	64960	72	161280	115	257600	158	353920
30	67200	73	163520	116	259840	159	356160
31	69440	74	165760	117	262080	160	358400
32	71680	75	168000	118	264320	200	448000
33	73920	76	170240	119	266560	300	672000
34	76160	77	172480	120	268800	400	896000
35	78400	78	174720	121	271040	500	1120000
36	80640	79	176960	122	273280	600	1344000
37	82880	80	179200	123	275520	700	1568000
38	85120	81	181440	124	277760	800	1792000
39	87360	82	183680	125	280000	900	2016000
40	89600	83	185920	126	282240	1000	2240000
41	91840	84	188160	127	284480	2000	4480000
42	94080	85	190400	128	286720	3000	6720000
43	96320	86	192640	129	288960	5000	11200000

CWTS. REDUCED TO POUNDS.

CWTS.	POUNDS.	CWTS.	POUNDS.	CWTS.	POUNDS.	CWTS.	POUNDS.	CWTS.	POUNDS.
1	112	53	5936	105	11760	157	17584	209	23408
2	224	54	6048	106	11872	158	17696	210	23520
3	336	55	6160	107	11984	159	17808	211	23632
4	448	56	6272	108	12096	160	17920	212	23744
5	560	57	6384	109	12208	161	18032	213	23856
6	672	58	6496	110	12320	162	18144	214	23968
7	784	59	6608	111	12432	163	18256	215	24080
8	896	60	6720	112	12544	164	18368	216	24192
9	1008	61	6832	113	12656	165	18480	217	24304
10	1120	62	6944	114	12768	166	18592	218	24416
11	1232	63	7056	115	12880	167	18704	219	24528
12	1344	64	7168	116	12992	168	18816	220	24640
13	1456	65	7280	117	13104	169	18928	221	24752
14	1568	66	7392	118	13216	170	19040	222	24864
15	1680	67	7504	119	13328	171	19152	223	24976
16	1792	68	7616	120	13440	172	19264	224	25088
17	1904	69	7728	121	13552	173	19376	225	25200
18	2016	70	7840	122	13664	174	19488	226	25312
19	2128	71	7952	123	13776	175	19600	227	25424
20	2240	72	8064	124	13888	176	19712	228	25536
21	2352	73	8172	125	14000	177	19824	229	25648
22	2464	74	8288	126	14112	178	19936	230	25760
23	2576	75	8400	127	14224	179	20048	231	25872
24	2688	76	8512	128	14336	180	20160	232	25984
25	2800	77	8524	129	14448	181	20272	233	26096
26	2912	78	8736	130	14560	182	20384	234	26208
27	3024	79	8848	131	14672	183	20496	235	26320
28	3136	80	8960	132	14784	184	20608	236	26432
29	3248	81	9072	133	14896	185	20720	237	26544
30	3360	82	9184	134	15008	186	20832	238	26653
31	3472	83	9296	135	15120	187	20944	239	26768
32	3584	84	9408	136	15232	188	21056	240	26880
33	3696	85	9520	137	15344	189	21168	241	26992
34	3808	86	9632	138	15456	190	21280	242	27104
35	3920	87	9744	139	15568	191	21392	243	27216
36	4032	88	9856	140	15680	192	21504	244	27328
37	4144	89	9968	141	15792	193	21616	245	27440
38	4256	90	10080	142	15904	194	21728	246	27552
39	4368	91	10192	143	16016	195	21840	247	27664
40	4480	92	10304	144	16128	196	21952	248	27776
41	4592	93	10416	145	16240	197	22064	249	27888
42	4704	94	10528	146	16352	198	22176	250	28000
43	4816	95	10640	147	16464	199	22288	251	28112
44	4928	96	10752	148	16576	200	22400	252	28224
45	5040	97	10864	149	16688	201	22512	253	28336
46	5152	98	10976	150	16800	202	22624	254	28448
47	5264	99	11088	151	16912	203	22736	255	28560
48	5376	100	11200	152	17024	204	22848	256	28672
49	5488	101	11312	153	17136	205	22960	257	28784
50	5600	102	11424	154	17248	206	23072	258	28896
51	5712	103	11536	155	17360	207	23184	259	29008
52	5824	104	11648	156	17472	208	23296	260	29120

CWTS. REDUCED TO POUNDS.

[CONTINUED.]

CWTS.	POUNDS.	CWTS.	POUNDS.	CWTS.	POUNDS.	CWTS.	POUNDS.	CWTS.	POUNDS.
261	29232	293	32816	324	36288	355	39760	386	43232
262	29344	294	32928	325	36400	356	39872	387	43344
263	29456	295	33040	326	36512	357	39984	388	43456
264	29568	296	33152	327	36624	358	40096	389	43568
265	29680	297	33264	328	36736	359	40208	390	43680
266	29792	298	33276	329	36848	360	40320	391	43792
267	29904	299	33488	330	36960	361	40432	392	43904
268	30016	300	33600	331	37072	362	40544	493	44016
269	30128	301	33712	332	37184	363	40656	994	44128
270	30240	302	33824	333	37296	364	40768	395	44240
271	30352	303	33936	334	37408	365	40880	396	44352
272	30464	304	34048	335	37520	366	40992	397	44464
273	30576	305	34160	336	37632	367	41104	398	44576
274	30688	306	34272	337	37744	368	41216	399	44688
275	30800	307	34384	338	37856	369	41328	400	44800
276	30912	308	34496	339	37968	370	41440	450	50400
277	31024	309	34608	340	38080	371	41552	500	56000
278	31136	310	34720	341	38192	372	41664	550	61600
279	31248	311	34832	342	38304	373	41776	600	67200
280	31360	312	34944	343	38416	374	41888	650	72800
281	31472	313	35056	344	38528	375	42000	700	78400
282	31584	314	35168	345	38640	376	42112	750	84000
283	31696	315	35280	346	38752	377	42224	800	89600
284	31808	316	35392	347	38864	378	42336	850	95200
285	31920	317	35504	348	38976	379	42448	900	100800
286	32032	318	35616	349	39088	380	42560	950	106400
287	32144	319	35728	350	39200	381	42672	1000	112000
288	32256	320	35840	351	39312	382	42784	2000	224000
289	32368	321	35952	352	39424	383	42896	3000	336000
290	32480	322	36064	353	39536	384	43008	4000	448000
291	32592	323	37176	354	39648	385	43120	5000	560000
292	32704								

QRS. REDUCED TO POUNDS.

QRS.	POUNDS.	QRS.	POUNDS.	QRS.	POUNDS.	QRS.	POUNDS.	QRS.	POUNDS.
1	28	14	392	27	756	40	1120	53	1484
2	56	15	420	28	784	41	1148	54	1512
3	84	16	448	29	812	42	1176	55	1540
4	112	17	476	30	840	43	1204	56	1568
5	14	18	504	31	868	44	1232	57	1596
6	168	19	532	32	896	45	1260	58	1624
7	196	20	560	33	924	46	1288	59	1652
8	224	21	588	34	952	47	1316	60	1680
9	252	22	616	35	980	48	1344	61	1708
10	280	23	644	36	1008	49	1372	62	1736
11	308	24	672	37	1036	50	1400	63	1764
12	336	25	700	38	1064	51	1428	64	1792
13	364	26	728	39	1092	52	1456	65	1820

POUNDS OF AMSTERDAM AND THE NETHERLANDS.

ALSO,

CURACOA, FLANDERS, HOLLAND, SURINAM, ROTTERDAM, THE HAGUE, UTRECHT, LEYDEN, GRONINGEN, LEUWARDEN, HAARLEM, DORT, MAESTRICHT, NIMEGUEN, DELFT, ZEVOLLE,

REDUCED TO UNITED STATES POUNDS.

A. P.	U. S. P.	A. P.	U. S. P.	A. P.	U. S. P.	A. P.	U. S. P.
1	1 08.93	20	21 78.60	300	326.79	4000	4357.20
2	2 17.86	30	32 67.90	400	435.72	5000	5446.50
3	3 26.79	40	43 57.20	500	544.65	6000	6535.80
4	4 35.72	50	54 46.50	600	653.58	7000	7625.10
5	5 44.65	60	65 35.80	700	762.51	8000	8714.40
6	6 53.58	70	76 25.10	800	871.44	9000	9803.70
7	7 62.51	80	87 14.40	900	980.37	10000	10893.00
8	8 71.44	90	98 03.70	1000	1089.30	20000	21786.00
9	9 80.37	100	108 93.00	2000	2178.60	30000	32679.00
10	10 89.30	200	217 86.00	3000	3267.90	40000	43572.00

SPANISH ARROBAS

REDUCED TO UNITED STATES POUNDS.

S. A.	U. S. P.	S. A.	U. S. P.	S. A.	U. S. P.	S. A.	U. S P.
1	25.36	20	507.20	300	7608	4000	101440
2	50.72	30	760.80	400	10144	5000	126800
3	76.08	40	1014.40	500	12680	6000	152160
4	101.44	50	1268.00	600	15216	7000	177520
5	126.80	60	1521.60	700	17752	8000	202880
6	152.16	70	1775.20	800	20288	9000	228240
7	177.52	80	2028.80	900	22824	10000	253600
8	202.88	90	2282.40	1000	25360	11000	278960
9	228.24	100	2536 00	1100	27896	12000	304320
10	253.60	110	2789.60	1200	30432	13000	329680
11	278.96	120	3043.20	1300	32968	14000	355040
12	304.32	130	3296.80	1400	35504	15000	380400
13	329.68	140	3550.40	1500	38040	16000	405760
14	355.04	150	3804.00	1600	40576	17000	431120
15	380.40	160	4057.60	1700	43112	18000	456480
16	405.76	170	4311.20	1800	45648	19000	481840
17	431.12	180	4564.80	1900	48184	20000	507200
18	456.48	190	4818.40	2000	50720	30000	760800
19	481.84	200	5072.00	3000	76080	50000	1268000

FRENCH KILLOGRAMMES

REDUCED TO UNITED STATES POUNDS.

F. K.	U. S. P.	F. K.	U. S. P.	F. K.	U. S. P.	F. K.	U. S. P.	F. K.	U. S. P.
1	2.21	20	44.20	300	663	3000	6630	30000	66300
2	4.42	30	66.30	400	884	4000	8840	40000	88400
3	6.63	40	88.40	500	1105	5000	11050	50000	110500
4	8.84	50	110.50	600	1326	6000	13260	60000	132600
5	11.05	60	132.60	700	1547	7000	15470	70000	154700
6	13.26	70	154.70	800	1768	8000	17680	80000	176800
7	15.47	80	176.80	900	1989	9000	19890	90000	198900
8	17.68	90	198.90	1000	2210	10000	22100	100000	221000
9	19.89	100	221.00	1100	2431	11000	24310	110000	243100
10	22.10	110	243.10	1200	2652	12000	26520	120000	265200
11	24.31	120	265.20	1300	2[illegible]73	13000	28730	130000	287300
12	26.52	130	287.30	1400	3094	14000	30940	140000	309400
13	28.73	140	309.40	1500	3315	15000	33150	150000	331500
14	30 94	150	331.50	1600	3536	16000	35360	160000	353600
15	33.15	160	353 60	1700	3757	17000	37570	170000	375700
16	35.36	170	375.70	1800	3978	18000	39780	180000	397800
17	37.57	180	397.80	1900	4199	19000	41990	190000	419900
18	39.78	190	419.90	2000	4420	20000	44200	200000	442000
19	41.99	200	442.00						

FRENCH LITRES

REDUCED TO UNITED STATES PINTS.

LITRES	U. S. PINTS.	LITRES.	U. S. PINTS.	LITRES.	U. S. P.	LITRES.	U. S. P.
1	2.11	20	42.20	300	633	3000	6330
2	4.22	30	63.30	400	844	4000	8440
3	6.33	40	84.40	500	1055	5000	10550
4	8.44	50	105.50	600	1266	6000	12660
5	10.55	60	126.60	700	1477	7000	14770
6	12.66	70	147.70	800	1688	8000	16880
7	14.77	80	168.80	900	1899	9000	18990
8	16.88	90	189.90	1000	2110	10000	21100
9	18.99	100	211.00	1100	2321	11000	23210
10	21.10	110	232.10	1200	2532	12000	25320
11	23.21	120	253.20	1300	2743	13000	27430
12	25.32	130	274.30	1400	2954	14000	29540
13	27.43	140	295.40	1500	3165	15000	31650
14	29.54	150	316.50	1600	3376	16000	33760
15	31.65	160	337.60	1700	3587	17000	3[illegible]870
16	33.76	170	358.70	1800	3798	18000	37980
17	35.87	180	379.80	1900	4009	19000	40090
18	37.98	190	400.90	2000	4220	20000	42200
19	40.09	200	422.00				

PORTUGUESE ARROBAS

REDUCED TO UNITED STATES POUNDS.

P. A.	U. S. P.	P. A.	U. S. P.	P. A.	U. S. P.	P. A.	U. S. P.
1	32.38	20	647.60	300	9714	3000	97140
2	64.76	30	971.40	400	12952	4000	129520
3	97.14	40	1295.20	500	16190	5000	161900
4	129.52	50	1619.00	600	19428	6000	194280
5	161.90	60	1942.80	700	22666	7000	226660
6	194.28	70	2266.60	800	25904	8000	259040
7	226.66	80	2590.40	900	29142	9000	291420
8	259.04	90	2914.20	1000	32380	10000	323800
9	291.42	100	3238.00	1100	35618	11000	356180
10	323.80	110	3561.80	1200	38856	12000	388560
11	356.18	120	3885.60	1300	42094	13000	420940
12	388.56	130	4209.40	1400	45332	14000	453320
13	420.94	140	4533.20	1500	48570	15000	485700
14	453.32	150	4857.00	1600	51808	16000	518080
15	485.70	160	5180.80	1700	55046	17000	550460
16	518.08	170	5504.60	1800	58284	18000	582840
17	550.46	180	5828.40	1900	61522	19000	615220
18	582.84	190	6152.20	2000	64760	20000	647600
19	615.22	200	6476.00				

FRENCH FEET

REDUCED TO UNITED STATES FEET.

F. F.	U. S. F.	F. F.	U. S. F.	F. F.	U. S. F.	F. F.	U. S. F.	F. F.	U. S. P.
1	1 06.6	21	22 38.6	180	191 88	1500	1599.00	12000	12792
2	2 13.2	22	23 45.2	190	202 54	1600	1705.60	13000	13858
3	3 19.8	23	24 51.8	200	213 20	1700	1812.20	14000	14924
4	4 26.4	24	25 58.4	210	223 86	1800	1918.80	15000	15990
5	5 33.0	25	26 65.0	220	234 52	1900	2025.40	16000	17056
6	6 39.6	30	31 98	230	245 18	2000	2132.00	17000	18129
7	7 46.2	40	42 64	240	255 84	2100	2238.60	18000	19188
8	8 52.8	50	53 30	250	266 50	2200	2345.20	19000	20254
9	9 59.4	60	63 96	300	319 80	2300	2451.80	20000	21320
10	10 66.0	70	74 62	400	426 40	2400	2558.40	30000	31980
11	11 72.6	80	85 28	500	533 00	2500	2665.00	40000	42640
12	12 79.2	90	95 94	600	639 60	3000	3198	50000	53300
13	13 85.8	100	106 60	700	746 20	4000	4264	60000	63960
14	14 92.4	110	117 26	800	852 80	5000	5330	70000	74620
15	15 99.0	120	127 92	900	959 40	6000	6396	75000	79950
16	17 05.6	130	138 58	1000	1066 00	7000	7462	80000	85280
17	18 12.2	140	149 24	1100	1172 60	8000	8528	85000	90610
18	19 18.8	150	159 90	1200	1279 20	9000	9594	90000	95940
19	20 25.4	160	170 56	1300	1385 80	10000	10660	95000	101270
20	21 32.0	170	181 22	1400	1492 40	11000	11726	100000	106600

RATES OF FOREIGN MONEY OR CURRENCY.

FIXED BY LAW.

	$ cts.	Fractional parts of the Currency.		Act passed.	
Ducat of Naples........	80	100 grani		May	22, 1846
Franc of France and Belgium..............	0 18$\frac{6}{10}$	100 centimes		do	22, do
Florin of the Netherlands	40	100 do		do	22, do
Florin of the Southern States of Germany....	40	60 kreutzers	4 pfennings	do	22, do
Florin of Austria.......	48½	60 do	4 do	do	22, do
Florin of Trieste........	48½	60 do	4 do	do	22, do
Florin of Nuremburg...	40	60 do	4 do	do	22, do
Florin of Frankfort.....	40	60 do	4 do	do	22, do
Florin of Bohemia......	48½	60 do	4 do	do	22, do
Florin of the city of Augsburgh...............	48½	60 do	4 do	do	22, do
Guilder of Netherlands and other places—same as Florins............					
Lira of the Lombardo and Venetian Kingdom....	16	100 centisimi	100 millessemi	do	22, do
Livre of Leghorn.......	16	20 soldi	12 denair	do	22, do
Livre Tournois of France	18½			March	2, 1799
Lira of Tuscany........	16	20 soldi	12 do	May	22, 1846
Lira of Sardinia........	18$\frac{6}{10}$	4 reali	20 soldi	do	22, do
Livre of Genoa..........	18$\frac{6}{10}$	20 soldi	12 denair	do	22, do
Milrea of Portugal.....	1 12	1000 reas		March	3, 1843
Milrea of Madeira......	1 00	1000 do		do	3, do
Milrea of Azores.......	83½	1000 do		do	3, do
Marc Banco of Hamburg	35	16 shillings	12 pfennings	do	3, do
Ounce of Sicily.........	2 40	30 tari	20 grani	May	22, 1846
Pound Stl. of G. Britain	4 84	20 shillings.	12 pence	July	27, 1842
Pound Stl. of Jamaica...	4 84				
Pound Sterling of British Provinces of Nova Scotia, New Brunswick, Newfoundland, & Canada.................	4 00	20 do	12 do	May	22, 1846
Pagoda of India........	1 94	36 fanams	48 jittas	March	3, 1801
Pagoda Star of Madras..	1 84	36 fanams	48 jittas	do	2, do
Real Vellum of Spain...	5	34 Maravedis		do	2, 1799
Real Plate of Spain	10	34 do		do	2, do
Rupee Company........	44½	16 annas	12 pice	do.	3, 1843
Rupee British India.....	44½	16 do	12 do	do	3, do
Rix dollar (or Thaler) of Prussia and the Northern States ef Germany	69	30 groschen	12 pfennings	May	22, 1846
Rix Dollar of Bremen...	78¾	72 grotes	5 swares	March	3, 1842
Dollar Thaler of Bremen of 72 grotes..........	71	72 grotes	5 swares	do	3, 1843
Rix Dollar (or Thaler) of Berlin...............	69	30 groschen	12 pfennings	May	22, 1846
Rix Dollar (or Thaler) of Saxony..............	69	30 do	12 do	do	22, do
Rix Dollar (or Thaler) of Leipsic...............	69	30 do	12 do	do	22, do

RATES OF FOREIGN MONEY OR CURRENCY.—(CONTINUED.)

	$ cts.	Fractional parts of the Currency.		Act passed.
Rouble, silver, of Russia	75	100 kopecks		March 3, 1843
Specie Dollar of Denmark	1 05	6 marks	16 skillings	May 22, 1846
Specie Dollar of Norway	1 06	6 do	16 do	do 22, do
Specie Dollar of Sweden	1 06	48 skillings	12 'ore	do 22, do
Tale of China..........	1 48	10 mace	100 candarems	March 2, 1799

CURRENCIES BY USAGE.

When a Consular Certificate of the real value of Exchange is not attached to the Invoice

	$ cts.	Fractional parts of the Currency.	
Banco Rix dollar, Sweden..........	39¾		
" " Norway.........	39¾		
" " Denmark........	53		
Guilder, Brabant.................	33¾		
Crown of Tuscany...............	1 05	20 soldi	12 denari
Curacoa Guilder................	40	20 stivers	12 pfennings
Francisconi.....................	1 06		
Kobang of Japan...............	1 38	4 Itzebou	1600 seni
Leghorn Dollar or Pezzo..........	90$\frac{76}{100}$	20 soldi	12 denari
Livre of Catalonia...............	53½	20 sueldos.	12 dineros
Livre of Neufchatel..............	26½	20 sols	12 deniers
Rix Mynth Dollar of Sweden.......	26½		
Rix ral Thaler of Gottenburg......	27¾		
Swiss Livre.....................	27	100 centimes	
Scudi of Malta..................	40	12 tair	20 grani
Scudi, Roman...................	99 *a* 99½		
St. Gall Guilder.................	40$\frac{36}{100}$	60 kreutzers	4 pfennings
Rix Dollar of Batavia............	75	48 stivers	
Roman Dollar..................	1 05		
Rouble, paper of Russia..........	....	100 kopecks	Varies from 4 roubles 65 copecks to 4 roubles 84 copecks to the dollar.
Tical of Siam....................	61		
Turkish Piastre..................	5	100 aspers	
Current Mark....................	28		
Florin of Prussia................	22¾		
Florin of Basle..................	41		
Genoa Livre....................	21		
Livre Tournois of France.........	18½		

In all cases where the Consul's Certificate is not attached to the Invoice, a Bond for the production of one will be required.

69–73

THE FOLLOWING RATES OF TARE

Were adopted, under Act of Congress, July 14th, 1862.

Article	Packing	Tare	
Almonds	in bales	2½	per cent.
do.	in bags	2	do.
do.	in frails	8	do.
Alum	in casks	10	do.
Alum, coarse or ground	in sacks	2	pounds per sack.
Barytes		3	per cent.
Cheese	in casks or tubs	10	do.
Cassia	in mats	9	do.
Coffee, Rio	in single bags	1	do.
do.	in double bags	2	do.
do. All other, actual tare			
Cinnamon	in bales	6	do.
Cocoa	in bags	2	do.
do.	in ceroons	8	do.
Chicory	in bags	2	do.
Copperas	in casks	10	do.
Currants	in casks	10	do.
Hemp, Manilla	in bales	4	pounds per bale.
do. Hamburg, Leghorn, Trieste		5	do.
Indigo	in ceroons	10	per cent.
Melado		11	do.
Nails	in bags	2	do.
do.	in casks	8	do.
Ochre, dry	in casks	8	do.
do. oil	in casks	12	do.
Peruvian Bark	in ceroons	10	do.
Paris White	in casks	10	do.
Pepper	in bags	2	do.
do.	in double bags	4	do.
Pimento	in bags	2	do.
Raisins	in casks	12	do.
do.	in boxes	25	do.
do.	in half boxes	27	do.
do.	in quarter boxes	29	do.
do.	in frails	4	do.
Rice	in bags	2	do.
Spanish Brown, dry	in casks	10	do.
do. do. oil	in casks	12	do.
Sugar	in hhds.	12½	do.
do.	in tierces	12	do.
do.	in bbls.	10	do.
do.	in boxes	14	do.
do.	in bags	2	do.
do.	in mats	2½	do.
Salt, fine	in sacks	3	pounds per sack.
Teas, China or Japan	invoice weight		
do. all others, actual tare			
Tobacco, Leaf	in bales	10	pounds per bale.
do. do.	in bales, ex. covers	12	do.
Whiting	in casks	10	per cent.

EXTRACTS FROM ACT 14th JULY, 1862.

Sec. 16. *And be it further enacted*, That from and after the passage of this act, in estimating the allowance for tare on all chests, boxes, cases, casks, bags, or other envelope or covering of all articles imported liable to pay any duty, where the original invoice is produced at the time of making entry thereof, and the tare shall be specified therein, it shall be lawful for the collector, if he shall see fit, or for the collector and naval officer, if such officer there be, if they shall see fit, with the consent of the consignees, to estimate the said tare according to such invoice; but in all other cases the real tare shall be allowed, and may be ascertained under such regulations as the Secretary of the Treasury may from time to time prescribe; but in no case shall there be any allowance for draft.

MISCELLANEOUS TABLE

OF

FOREIGN WEIGHTS AND MEASURES.

Arroba of Brazil		equal to	32.38 pounds	United States
Arroba of Buenos Ayres		do	25.36 do	do
Amir, or Emir, of Stuttgard		do	78 gallons	do
Ahm of Hanover		do	41.43 do	do
Ahm of Leipsic		do	40 do	do
Balsam Copavia, 8 lbs		do	1 do	do
Butt of wine		do	130 do	do
Canado of Balsam Copavia		do	30 pounds	do
Chaldron of Coal, British Provinces.		do	36 bushels	do
do do Cumberland		do	53 do	do
Coal, last of Hamburg		do	5100 pounds	do
Cheki of opium (from Smyrna)		do	1 66-100 do.	do
Coal, a railway wagon load, Pictou		do	62 cwt.	do
Flax, a head of, about		do	6 3-4 pounds	do
Foot, 100 cubic, of St. Domingo		do	121-13 feet	do
Honey, 1 gallon weighs			12 pounds	do
Imperial gallon		equal to	1-20 gallons	do
do quarter		do	8.25 bushels	do
do bushel		do	1.03 do.	do
do yard		do	36 inches	do
Linseed, one bushel		do	47 pounds	do
Mudd, or Maud, of Rotterdam		do	148 do	do
Mudde, of Augsburg		do	14.92 gallons	do
Moyo of salt (Spain)		do	70 bushels	do
Modius of salt (from Ivica, Spain)		do	40 do	do
do do (Oporto and St. Ubes)		do	23 do	do
Mass (of Antwerp) ¼th of ohm		do	10 gallons	do
Ohm do		do	40 do	do
Pesado of Buenos Ayres		do	35 pounds	do
do of dry hides of Montevideo		do	40 do	do
do of dry salt hides of do		do	40 do	do
do of wet salt hides of do		do	60 do	do
Picul of hemp, of Manilla		do	139-50 pounds	do
Picul of Siam		do	133 1-3 pounds	do
Cajar do		do	20 piculs	do
Pounds of Austria	100 lb.	do	123 50-100	do
do Antwerp	do	do	103 35-100	do
do Bavaria	do	do	123 50-100	do
do Belgium	do	do	103 35-100	do
do Brussels	do	do	103 35-100	do
do Bremen	do	do	110 12-100	do
do Berlin	do	do	103 11-100	do
do Hamburg	do	do	110 4-10,000	do
do Malaga	do	do	101 44-100	do
do Netherlands	do	do	108 93-100	do
do German Zol. States	do	do	110 25-100	do

Pounds of Portugal	100 lb.	equal to	101 19-100 pounds		U. States
do Prussia	do	do	110 25-100		do
do Rotterdam	do	do	108 93-100		do
do Spain	do	do	101 44-100		do
do St. Domingo	do	do	107 93-100		do
do Trieste	do	do	123 60-100		do
do Vienna	do	do	123 50-100		do

The palm of Marble from Carrara $5\frac{57}{100}$ cubic or $9\frac{6}{100}$ im inches by actual measurement.

Quintal of France	do	220 54-100		do
Salma of oil	do	42.16 gallons		do
Skippond of Gottonburg	do	300 pounds		do
do of Gefle	do	$314\frac{1}{10}$ do		do
Salt, one barrel	do	$3\frac{1}{2}$ bushels		do
Vara, Spanish	do	8 feet		do
Vara of Baracoa	do	20 feet		do
Oils, Linseed, 1 gallon	do	7 pounds	12 oz.	do
" Rapeseed, do	do	7 "	12 "	do
" Cocoanut, do	do	7 "	8 "	do
" Olive, do	do	7 "	9 "	do
" Groundnut, do	do	7 "	9 "	do
" Palm, do	do	7 "	8 "	do

TABLE OF WEIGHTS AND MEASURES,

REDUCED TO THE STANDARD OF THE UNITED STATES.

ALEXANDRIA, (EGYPT.)

Cantaro of 100 rottoli farforo of 15 oz. (avoirdupois) .... $93\frac{1}{2}$ lbs.
100 rottoli zaydino $21\frac{1}{2}$ oz. .... $133\frac{1}{2}$ "
100 " zaura of 33 oz. .... 207 "
100 " mina $26\frac{2}{3}$ oz. .... 167 "
1 oke 400 drams of 16 carats each .. $43\frac{2}{3}$ oz.

ALICANT, (SPAIN.)

Arroba .... 27.39 lbs. av.
Quintal .... $109\frac{1}{2}$ lbs.
100 varas .... 83.22 im. yds.

AMSTERDAM.

100 lbs. 1 centner .... 108.93 lbs.
Last of grain .... 85.25 bush.
Ahm of wine .... 41.00 gall.
Amsterdam foot .... 0.93 ft.
Antwerp foot .... 0.94 ft.
Rhinland foot .... 1.03 ft.
Amsterdam ell .... 2.26 ft.
Ell of Hague .... 2.28 ft.
Ell of the Brabant .... 2.30 ft.
Medden or measure of coal .... $2\frac{3}{4}$ bus.

Ahm, or Ohm, a German wine measure varies in different places

Of Dantzic .... 33.00 im. galls.
" Hamburg .... 31.75 " "
" Hanover .... 34.25 " "
" Rotterdam .... 33.25 " "

ANCONA, (ITALY.)

100 lbs. Roman equal ...... 102.75 Ancona.
100 lbs. Ancona .... 73.75 lbs.
The braccio .... 25.33 in.
" wine soma, 2 barili 24 boccali, 18.90 im. galls.
The rubbio of corn, 8 coppi .. 7.87 im. bush.

ARRAGON, (SPAIN.)

Libras of 100 lbs. .... 77.01 lbs.
Quintal, 4 arrobas of 36 lbs. .... 112.00 "

AUSTRIA.

The ell of Vienna .... 30.6 im. in.
" klafter, 6 Vienna feet ..... 6.23 " "
" Vienna wine eimas of 70 klofpen, 40 maases, or 4 viertels ..... 12.46 im. galls.
The fuder .... 32 eimers.
" dreyling .... 30 "
" corn metzen of 4 viertels, or 8 achtels, 1.69 im. bush,
100 metzen .... $21\frac{1}{6}$ im. qrs.
30 mutzen .... 1 mutti
The Vienna lb. 4 qu. 16 oz., or 32 loths, 8645 Troy grains.
100 lbs. 1 centner .... $123\frac{1}{2}$ lbs.
20 lbs .... 1 stone.
The oil oma, 107 Vienna lbs., 14.17 im. galls.
" woollen ell of Trieste ..... 26.6 im. in.
" silk " " .... 25.22 " "
" wine oma or eimer .... 12.45 im. galls.
" barile .... $144\frac{1}{2}$ " "
100 staii of corn .... $28\frac{3}{8}$ im. qrs.

BASSORA, (PERSIAN GULF.)

Maund attary, 25 vakias tary....28.05 lbs.
One vakia........................19 oz.

BATAVIA, (E. INDIES.)

Large Bahar..................$4\frac{1}{2}$ peculs.
Small Bahar..................3 "
1 pecul......................100 catties.
1 catty......................16 tales.
1 pecul................135 lbs. 10 oz.

BAVARIA.

The ell......................$32\frac{4}{5}$ im. in.
" Wine eimer of 60 maas..8.12 im. galls.
" Scheffel of 6 metzen or 12 viertels, 9.98 im. bush.
" centner, or quintal, of 5 stones, or 100 lbs., 56 kilos, or..........$123\frac{1}{2}$ lbs. av.
" traders', or long ell......24.00 im. in.
" fustian, or short ell.......23.32 " "
" muid of 48 maas......15.08 im. galls.
" schaff of 8 metzen......5.65 im bush.
100 lbs. heavy weight......108.30 lbs. av.
100 lbs. light " ....104.23 " "
The Augsburg mark, 16 loths, 64 quintins, or 3,643 grains troy.

BELGIUM.

The Antwerp silk ell.........27.32 im. in.
" woollen ell..............26.97 " "
" Brabant ell..............27.58 " "
" oam of 50 stoops.......$32\frac{2}{7}$ im. galls.
" velte..................4.1 " "
" last of $37\frac{1}{2}$ viertels.......$10\frac{1}{4}$ im qrs.
100 lbs. Brabant weight....103.35 lbs. av.

BERGEN, (NORWAY.)

Shippond, 20 lisponds............320 lbs.
Centner, $6\frac{1}{4}$ lisponds..............100 "
Lispond.........................16 "
Waag, 3 bismar pounds............36 "
1 lb. 2 marcs, 16 oz. 32 loths.
100 Norway pounds...........110.23 "

CHRISTIANA, (NORWAY.)

Shippond.........................352 lbs.

LAURWIG, (NORWAY.)

Shippond.........................352 lbs.

BOMBAY.

Candy equal to...................560 lbs.
Maund " ....28 "
Seer " ....$11\frac{1}{5}$ oz.
Candy " ....20 maunds.
Maund " ....40 seers.
Seer " ....30 pice.

BRAZIL.

5 varas.........................6 im. yds.
4 cavados......................3 " "
99 Brazilian lbs..................100 av.

AT RIO JANEIRO.

100 medidas, $61\frac{1}{10}$ im. galls., or $73\frac{1}{3}$ U. S. galls.
12 alqueires...................$13\frac{1}{4}$ bush.

AT MARANHAM.

1 alqueire......................$1\frac{1}{4}$ bush.

AT BAHIA.

1 canada....................$1\frac{2}{3}$ im. galls.
7 alqueires......................6 bush.

BREMEN.

Shipfund...................$2\frac{1}{2}$ centners.
Centner......................127.44 av.
Waag of iron....................120 "
Stone of flax....................20 "
Stone of wool....................10 "
Lispund..........................14 "
100 lbs.....................$110\frac{12}{100}$ "
The ell of 2 feet............22.76 im. in.
100 ells..................63.25 im. yds.
The ahm of 20 viertels, 45 stubchen, or 180 quarts...................$31\frac{1}{2}$ im. galls.
1 fuder Rheinish wine............6 ahms.
1 ahm French wine.........44 stubchens.
1 tonne of beer..............45 "
10 lbs. Bremen..........nearly 11 lbs av.
Last of corn...............9.77 im. bush.

CADIZ, (SPAIN.)

Quintal of 4 arrobas..............100 lbs.
1 lb. 2 marcs 16 oz., or........256 adarms.
100 lbs. equal to...............101.43 lbs.

CAIRO, (EGYPT.)

Cantaro, 100 rottoli...............95 lbs.
One rottoli is...............144 drachms.
Occa equal to 400 drams, or.....26.39 lbs.
36 occas equal to..............1 cantaro.

CHINA.

Tail............................$1\frac{1}{3}$ oz.
16 tails, 1 catty..................$1\frac{1}{3}$ lbs.
100 catties, 1 picul..............$133\frac{1}{3}$ "
The covid of 10 punts.......14.625 im. in.
32 covids....................13 im. yds.
The li of 180 fathoms.........632 " "
200 lis........................1 degree

Liquids and grain are sold by weight.

3 peculs.....................400 lbs. av

84 catties........................1 cwt.
12 taels..........................1 lb.

CHILI.

100 varas..................100 im. yds.
96 Chilian, 100 lbs. Spanish..101.44 lbs. av.

In all other respects same as Spain.

CALCUTTA.

Maund equal to..................40 seers.
Seer " ....16 chattacks.
English factory maund.......74 lbs. 10 oz.
Seer.......................1 lb. 13 oz.
Chattack........................1 oz.
Bengal bezar maund is 10 per cent. heavier than the factory maund.
Bezar maund equal to 82 lbs. 2 oz. 2.1–13 drams.
Seer equal to.........2 lbs. 13.2–3 drams.
Chattock................2 oz. 5–6 drams.

CONSTANTINOPLE.

Quintal equal to............100 rottolis.
" " ....45 okes.
" " ....176 cheques.
" " ....127 lbs.
1 " oke, " ......2 lbs. 13 oz. 4 drams.

CUBA.

Measures and Weights.—The standards of Spain are those generally in use.

In trade the following proportions are commonly observed:

108 varas...................100 im. yds.
1 vara......................$33\frac{1}{3}$ im. in.
The fanega................2.90 im. bush.
" arroba of wine or spirits, 3.42 im. gals. or......................4.10 gals. U. S.
The quintal of 4 arrobas each 25 lbs. or $101\frac{3}{4}$ lbs. av.
1 arroba....................25 lbs. 7 oz.
The varas of Neuvitas...81 superficial feet.
" ton of wood estimated at 20 Spanish ....quintals.

DENMARK.

100 lbs. 1 centner.............110.28 lbs.
Barrel or toende of corn........3.95 bush.
Viertel of wine................2.04 galls.
Copenhagen, or Rhineland foot...1.03 foot.
Centner or 100 lbs. Denmark equal to 110.28 lbs.
1 lispund.........................16 ".
1 bismerpund....................12 "
1 waag, 3 bismerpunds or.........36 lbs.
The ell of 2 Rhineland feet...24.75 im. in.
" viertel of 4 kans or 8 pots, 1.70 im. galls.
" hhd of 30 viertels..........51 " "
100 viertels...............170.08 " "
The ahm of 4 ankers........33.14 " "
60 bbls.....................29 im. qurs.
The toende or bbl..........3.83 im. bush
" last of corn, 12 toendes, 45.91 " "
" shippond of 20 lisponds, or 320 lbs. Danish, $3\frac{1}{7}$ cwt............352 lbs. av.
The ship last 4000 lbs. Dan, or 4400 " "

ENGLAND.

Old ale gallon.................1.22 galls.
Imperial gallon...............1.20 "
Old wine " ....1.00 "
Quarter of grain, or 8 imperial bushels, 8-25 bush.
Imperial corn bushel, or 8 imperial gallons 1.03 bush.
Old Winchester do............1.00 "
Imperial yard.................36.00 in.
Troy lb..............$\frac{144}{175}$ths of a lb. av.
Newcastle chaldron..............53 cwt.
Stone.............................16 lbs..
Tun of wine...............256 im. galls.

The Wine Measure is

the gal., 4 qts., 8 pints, or 32 gills, and contains 231 cubic inches. Of these gallons.

The anker contains.............10 galls.
" rundlet " ....18 "
" tierce " ....42 "
" hhd " ....63 "
" puncheon " ....84 "
" pipe " ....126 "
" butt " ....126 "
" ton " ....252 "

The wine gallon is $\frac{1}{6}$ less than the imperial, or 5 imperial gallons equal to 6 wine gallons.

The standard gauges of wine recognised in the trade are:

The pipe of port...........115 im. galls.
" " of Lisbon..........117 " "
" " of Cape or Maderia..92 " "
" " of Teneriffe........100 " "
" butt of sherry..........108 " "
" hhd of claret............46 " "
" aume of hock............30 " "

Ale and Beer Measure.

The gallon divided in the same manner as the wine gallon, equal to 282 cubic inches Of these gallons.

The firkin.......................9 galls.
" kilderkin.....................18 "
" barrel........................36 "
" hhd...........................54 "
" puncheon......................72 "
" butt..........................108 "
" tun...........................216 "
59 galls. of ale are equal to....60 im. "

The Fodder of Lead.

At London and Hull.............$19\frac{1}{2}$ cwt.
" Newcastle....................21 "
" Chester......................20 "
" Stocton......................22 "
" Derby........................$22\frac{1}{2}$ "
The London chaldron coal........$25\frac{1}{2}$ "

FRANCE.

Metre.........................3.28 feet.
Decimetre (1-10th metre).....3.94 inches.
Velt..........................2.00 galls.
Hectolitre....................26.42 "
Decalitre.....................2.64 "
Litre.........................2.11 pints.
Kilolitre.....................35.32 feet.
Hectolitre....................2.84 bush.
Decalitre.....................9.08 quarts.
Millier.......................2.205 lbs.
Quintal.......................220.54 "
Killogramme...................2.21 "
100 pounds....................107.93 "
100 feet......................106.60 feet.
Tun (of wine).................240 galls.

FLORENCE AND LEGHORN.

100 lbs. or 1 cantaro............74.86 lbs.
Moggio of grain.............16.59 bush.
Barile of wine..............12.04 galls.

GENOA.

100 lbs. peso grosso............76.86 lbs.
100 lbs. or peso sotile............68.89 "
Mina of grain...................3.43 bush.
Mezzarola of wine............39.22 galls.
The oil barile of 4 quarti or 64 quarteroni..................14.23 im. galls.
The barile of wine........16.34 " "
100 Rottoli of $1\frac{1}{2}$ lbs.....104.83 lbs. avoir.
The palmas, a measure for marble. $\frac{1}{2}$ cubic ft.
The braccio...................$2\frac{1}{3}$ palmi.

GIBRALTER.

British weights and measures are employed; also the following Spanish:

The pipe of 117 galls.—105 im. galls, or 126 U. S. galls.
The arroba (l'q'd meas.) 2.77 im. g.. $3\frac{1}{3}$ "
The arroba (weight)..........26 lb. avoir.
" quintal of 100 lbs.... $101\frac{3}{4}$ " "
" 5 fanegas of grain...........3 bush.
" 2 " " maize or beans..$4\frac{1}{8}$ "

GUIANA, (BRITISH), includes Berbice, Demerara, and Esequibo.

Measures and weights chiefly British.

The Dutch ell of 26 inches..27 inches U. S.

GUIANA, OR SURINAM.

Partly the property of the city of Amsterdam. Measures and weights, chiefly those of Holland under the old system.

GUIANA (FRENCH), OR CAYENNE.

Measures, weights, and money, same as France.

HAYTI, OR ST. DOMINGO.

The measures and weights are chiefly those of the old French system.
The old English wine gallon is used.

The quintal of 100 livres.107.928 lbs. U. S.
toise (of 6 peids de roi)..19490 metres.
2. 1315 im yards, or 6 feet $4\frac{3}{4}$ inches.
100 peids................106 60 feet.
100 lbs Haytien.........107 93 lbs. avoir.

HAMBURG.

Last of grain.................89.64 bush
Ahm. of wine..................38.25 galls.
Hamburg foot..................0.96 feet.
Ell...........................1.22 "
Shipfund, $2\frac{1}{2}$ centners or..........280 lbs.
Hamburg, equal to.............299 lbs.
1 centner equal to 8 lispunds, or 112 lbs. Hamburg.
1 lispund equal to............14 lbs. do.
1 stone of flax equal..........20 lbs. do.
1 stone of wool equal to.......10 lbs. do.
1 stone of feathers equal to....10 lbs. do.
100 lbs of Hamburg equal to..$110\frac{4}{1000}$ lbs
The ell of 2 feet, or 6 palms..22.58 im. in.
" Brabant ell.............27.58 " "
4 ankers, 5 eimers, 20 viertels 40 stubgen, or 160 quarters...................1 ahm.
6 ahms........................1 Fuder
The faas of wine is 4 oxhofts or 6 tierces.
The wispel, corn measure, of 10 scheffels.
20 faas, or 40 himstens........29 im. bush.
3 wispels=1 last of wheat or rye—1 stock of barley or oats=$10\frac{7}{8}$ im. qrs. 89.61 bus.
The centner of 112 Hamburg lbs., or 8 lispunds..............119.64 lbs. avoirds

A small tonne of butter . 224 lbs. Hamburg.
A great " " . 280 " "
A quatrel of train oil, of 2 tonnes or 64 stubgen, is 4 centners, or 448 Hamburg lbs., or................478.56 lbs. U. S.
A pipe of oil is........820 lbs. Hamburg.

ITALY.

100 rottoli of 31⅞ oz. each, equal to 196½ lbs.
1 cantaro grosso, equal to........196½ lbs.

LUBECK, (HANSEATIC STATES.)

The ell of 2 feet..........22.70 im. inches
The ahm 20 viertels, 40 stubgen, or 80 kannes. 31.87 im. gals, or 38.25 U. S. gls.
The last of wheat or rye.....11.04 im. qrs.
The last of oats.............11.95 " "
1 centner, 8 lispunds, 112 lbs....119.67 lbs. U. S.
100 Lubec lbs...........106.85 lbs. U. S.

MADRAS.

Candy, equal to.................500 lbs.
Candy, equal to..............20 maunds.
Maund, equal to...................8 bis.
Bis, equal to.....................8 seers.

MALACCA.

Pecul, equal to..................135 lbs.
A pecul, equal to 100 catties, or 1600 tales.

MALTA.

100 lbs. 1 cantaro.............174.50 lbs.
Salma of grain................8.22 bush.
Cantaro, equal to.............100 rottoli.
Rottoli, equal to..................30 oz.
One cantaro equal to (mercantile usage) 175 lbs.
The barile of wine.........9.35 im. galls.
" caffiso of oil...........4.50 " "
" canna of 8 palmi........82 40 inches.
3½ palmi........................1 yard.
64 rottoli.................1 cwt. 112 lbs.

MAURITIUS, (OR, ISLE OF FRANCE.)

The quintal of 100 lbs. French poids de marc....................108 lbs. U. S.
20 quintals—1 French ton...2160 lbs. U. S.
1 velt....................2 galls. "
30 velts...................1 cask. "

NAPLES.

Cantaro grosso...............196.50 lbs.
Cantaro Picolo...............106.00 "
Carro of grain...............52.24 bush.
Carro of wine...............264.00 galls.
The canna, or ell, of 8 palmi..83.05 inches.
The passo is 7½ palmi.
" barile (wine or brandy measure) of 60 Caraffi................9.60 im. galls.
The carro is 2 botte or 24 barile
" pipe is 14 barile.
" salma (oil measure of 16 staja, or 256 quarti) weighs 324½ lbs...34.91 im. galls.
At Gallipoli,
The oil salma of 10 staja, or 320 piquatte 34.11 im. galls.
At Bari,
The salma. ....36.42 im. galls.
The tomolo (corn measure) of 2 mezzette, or 4 quarti. is...........1,519 im bush.
The 100 tomoli............19 im. quartes.
" carro of 36 tomoli.......6,84 im qurs.

NETHERLANDS.

Ell..........................3.28 feet.
Mudde of Zak.................2.84 bush.
Vat hectolitre................26.42 galls.
Kan litre....................2.11 pints.
Pond killogramme..............2.21 lbs.
100 pounds..................108. 93 "

Measures and weights.

The modern system, introduced in 1820, is the same as France, but with the old Dutch nomenclature.

The ell or metre of 10 palms.
100 elles.
The vat or hectolitre of 100 kans or litres.
The kan is divided into 10 maatjes or 100 vingerhords.
The mudde, zak, or hectolitre (dry measure) of 10 schepels, or 100 kops or litres, 100 mudden.
The pond or killogramme,
100 ponden.

The old measures and weights, still retained in many places, are as follows:

The Amsterdam foot.
" Rhineland foot.
" Amsterdam ell.
" Brabant or Flemish ell.
" wine stekan of 8 stoops..4.27 im. galls.
" brandy " " " ..4.13 " "
" beer " " " ..4.32 " "
" Amsterdam ahm of 4 ankers, 8 wine stekans, 64 stoops, 128 mingels, 256 pintes, 512 mutjes.......34.16 im. galls.
The velt contains 3 stoops.
" oxhoft " 96 "
" legger " 240 "
" vat, 6 ahms, or 384 stoops.
" Amsterdam corn last, 27 mudden, 36 sacks, or 108 schepels....82 62 im. bush.
The Rotterdam ahm.......33.32 im. galls

The centner of 100 lbs....108.93 lbs. U. S.
A last for freight is estimated at 4,000 lbs.

NICE, (SARDINIA.)

The ell....................46.77 inches.
" charge (liquid measure), of 12 rubbi 20.75 im. galls.
The charge (corn measure), of 4 setiers 4.40 im. bush.
The quintal of 6 rubbi or 150 lbs. 103.14 lbs. U. S.

PORTUGAL.

100 lbs......................101.19 lbs.
32 lbs. (1 arroba)..............32.38 "
4 arrobas of 32 lbs. (1 quintal)..129.52 "
Alquiere......................4.75 bush.
Mojo of grain................23.06 "
Last of salt..................70.00 "
Almude of wine..............4.37 galls.
The moyo (dry measure), of 15 fanegas, 60 Lisbon alquieres, or 240 quartos 22.39 im. bush., or 23.06 U. S. bush.
100 Lisbon alquieres.......37.32 im. bush.
100 Oporto " ....46.50 " "
The tonelada.................54 arrobas.
" palmo of 8 inches........8.62 inches.
" pe, or foot................1½ palmos.
" vara, 5 palmos..........43.11 inches.
" covado—3 palmos—is 24¾ Portuguese, or 26.67 im. inches.
The braca....................10 palmos
" Lisbon almude (liquid meas.) of 2 pots, 12 canadas, or 48 quartillos 3.64 im. galls., or 4.37 galls. U. S.
The barile..................18 almudes.
" pipe.....................26 "
" tonelado.................52 "
" Oporto almude is 5.61 im. galls. or 6.73 galls. U. S.

On March 8, 1850, the U. S. consul reports the almude of Portugal at 7½ galls. U. S.

PRUSSIA.

100 lbs. of 2 Cologne marks each.103.11 lbs.
Quintal, 110 lbs...............113.42 "
Sheffel of grain................1.56 bush.
Eimar of wine...............18.14 galls.
Ell of cloth....................2.19 feet.
Foot......................12.356 inches.
The ell of 25½ Prussian inches..26.26 "
100 ells.....................72.94 yards.
The ohm of 2 eimers, 4 ankers, or 120 qts. 30.23 im. galls., or 36.28 galls. U. S.
The ohm of Dantzic......39.60 " "
The oxhoft....................3 meriso
" tun (beer meas.) 100 qts., or 25.19 im. galls.
The scheffel (corn measure) of 16 metzen, or 48 qts..................1.512 im. bush.
5¼ scheffels......................1 im. qr.
100 " ....18.89 im. qrs.
60 " ....1 last.
The ship last...........4000 Prussian lbs.
" last of timber..........80 cubic feet.

ROME.

Rubbio of grain...............8.36 bush.
Barile of wine................15.41 galls.
100 Roman lbs. equal to.........74.77 lbs.
The foot....................11.72 inches.
" Mercantile canna of 8 palmi..78.35 in.
" tavola censuale, 1000 square metres 11.96 square yards.
The rubbio................18.484 tavoli.
" wine barile, 32 boccali, 128 fogliette, 12.84 im. galls., or 15.41 U. S. galls.
16 barile.......................1 botte
The soma of oil, 80 boccali.36.14 im. galls.
" oil barile of 28 " .12.65 " "
" rubbio of corn, 4 quarts, 22 scorzi, or 88 quartucci.8.10 im. bu. or 8.34 U. S. bu

RUSSIA.

100 lbs. of 32 loths each........90.26 lbs.
Chertwert of grain............5.95 bush.
Vedro of wine...... ....3.25 galls.
Pood............................36 lbs.
The Russian foot.........13.75 im. inches.
" Moscow " ....13.17 " "
" archine (cloth meas.)...28,00 " "
100 archines " " ......77.77 yards.
The sagene or fathom.............7 feet.
" anker..........2 stekars or 3 vedros.
" oxhoft.....................6 ankers.
10 poods...................1 berkovitz.

SICILY.

Cantaro grosso..........192.53 lbs. U. S.
Cantaro sottile..........175.03 " "
100 lbs..................70.01 " "
Salma grossa of grain.....9.77 bush. "
Salma generale.......... 7.84 " "
Salma of wine..........23.06 galls. "
The canna, 8 palmi, 96 inches, or 81.35 in.
" tonna, 4 barile, or.....31.24 im. galls.
" pipe 12 " .....93.72 " "
" caffiso of oil, in Messina.2.58 " "
Or by weight..............24 lbs. avoir.

In Palermo, oil is sold by the cantaro grosso.

SPAIN.

Quintal, or 4 arrobas............101.44 lbs.
Arroba.........................25.36 "
Arroba of wine...............4.43 galls.
Fanega of grain................1.60 bush.
The fanega (corn meas.) of 12 celemines or 48 quartillos..............1.55 im. bush.
100 fanegas..................19⅜ im. qrs.
The cahiz, 12 fanegas,........18⅗ im. bush.
" burgos foot of 12 pulgados or 16 dedos......................11.128 inches.
The vara or Castile ell, 3 feet or 4 palmos......................33.38 inches.
100 varas...................92.73 yards.
The cantara, or quarter arroba (wine meas.) of 8 azumbres, 32 quartillos.3.54 im. gls.
16 wine arrobas, 1 moyo....56.64 " "
The lesser arroba (oil meas.) of 4 quartillos, or 100 quarterones.......2.77 im. galls.
The botta.30 wine arrobas, or 38½ oil ar'bs.
" pipe..27 " " " 34½ " "
The botta.................95½ im. galls.

The preceding are the Castilian standards, which are the general or official standards of Spain, but the local variations are numerous, viz.:

ALICANT.

100 varas.................83.22 im yards.
The tonelado, 2 pipes, 80 arrobas, 100 cantars...................254⅓ im. galls.
The caffise..................6¾ im. bush.
" arroba of 24 great lbs.27.39 lbs. avoir.
" " " 36 small " .27.39 " "
" quintal...................4 arrobas.
" carga....................10 "

BARCELONA.

The canna, 2 varas..........62.25 inches.
" carga, 16 cortanes, 12 arrobas 27¼ im. galls.
The pipe......................4 cargas
" oil carga is divided into 11 arrobas.
" salma, 4 quartuas......7.53 im. bush.
" carga of corn..........2⅓ quartuas.
" arroba of 26 lbs., each 12 oz. 21.37 lbs. avoir.
The quintal...................4 arrobas.

BILBOA.

The fanega (corn meas.)......1.65 im. bush.
" quintal of 100 lbs......108 lbs. avoir.
" quintal macho, used in weighing iron, is 146 lbs., or............157⅗lbs. avoir.

MALAGA.

The arroba (weight.).........36 lbs. U. S.
The cantara, or arroba, of 8 azumbres, 3.49 im. galls.
The pipe of wine..........118½ " "
" botta of oil.........43 Castilian arrobas.
" carga of raisins. 7 ar'bs, or 177½ lbs. av.

VALENCIA.

The varra...............36.16 im. inches.
" arroba (liquid meas.)...2.59 im. galls.
" carga of wine............15 arrobas.
" " " oil..............12 "
" cahiz.................5.65 im. bush.
" arroba (weight)........28¼ lbs. avoir.
4 arrobas.......................1 quintal.
3 quintals......................1 carga.

SAXONY.

The ell....................22.30 inches.
100 ells....................61.96 yards.
The eimer of 72 kannes...17.81 galls. U. S.
" ahm, 2 eimers.......35.62 " "
" oxhoft. 3 " ....53.43 " "
" fass, 5 " ....89.05 " "
" fuder, 12 " ......213.72 " "
" corn scheffel is 2.859 im. bush., or 2.945 bush., U. S.
The wispel..2 mattus, 24 scheffels, 8.58 im.qs.
" last of wheat or rye contains.6 wispels.
" last of barley or oats.......2 "
" centner of 110 lbs...113.23 lbs. avoir.

ST. GALL.

100 heavy pounds equal to........128 lbs.
100 light pounds equal to.........102 "

SURAT.

20 Surat maunds or 10 Bengal factory maunds......................1 candy.
One candy................746 lbs. 10 oz.

SWEDEN.

The aln or ell of 2 feet....23.38 im. inches.
100 ells....................64.94 yards.
The fathom.......................3 ells.
" kann (liquid measure) 2 stoops, or 8 quarters...............2.76 pints, U. S.
100 kannes...........69.0720 galls. U. S.
Anker, 15 kannes, or....10.3608 " "
Eimer, 30 " ....20.7216 " "
Tunna, 48 " ....33.1545 " "
Ahm, 60 " ....41.4432 " "
Oxhufond 90 " ...62.1648 " "
Pipe 180 " ..124.3296 " "
Fuder 360 " ..248.6592 " "

The tunna (corn measure), of 2 spann, 8 fjerdingar, 32 kappar or 56 kannes—4.029 im. bush.; but, as 4 kappar are allowed to each tunna of wheat, oats, barley or rye, for good measure, the tunna of corn is 4 1-2 im. bushs.
The commercial weight is termed victualie weight.
100 lbs. victualie.........93.76 lbs. avoir.
The lispund...........20 lbs. vict. weight.
" sten..............32 " "
" centner..........120 " "
" waag...........165 " "
" skeppund of 20 lispunds is 400 lbs. vict. wt., or 375.04 lbs. avoir.
The iron or metal is $\frac{4}{5}$ of the victualie wt.
" skeppund for metal....300 lbs. avoir.

The Gefle weight exceeds Stockholm wt. 5 per cent.

TRIESTE.

100..........................123.60 lbs.
Stajo of grain...................2.34 bush.
Orna or eimer of wine.........14.94 galls.
Ell for woollens.................2.22 feet.
Ell for silk.......................2.10 "

TUSCANY.

(Grand Duchy of Florence and Leghorn.)
The quintal of 100 Tuscan lbs. 74.86 lbs. avoir.
The cantaro, 100 rotoli of 30 oz. each, 175 lbs. avoir.
16 cantars........36 bush., or 1 chaldron.
The pisata, 330 rottoli.....577½ lbs. avoir.
12.80 rottoli.................1 ton British.
The braccio of 20 soldi.....22.979 inches.
100 braccia.................63.83 yards.
The passetto...................2 braccia.
" canna...................5 "
" Tuscan mile...........28.33 "
" barril (wine meas.) of 20 fiasci 12.04 galls. U. S.
" oil barril..............7.36 im. galls.
" soma....................2 barrili.
" cogna...................10 "
" stajo (corn measure) 2 mine, 2.676 im. pecks.
100 staja.............66 9-100 im. bushs.
The sacca of 3 staja..........2 " "
" moggio of 24 staja, 2 im. qrs., or 16.50 bush. U. S.

TURKEY.

The pik or ell is of two kinds: the quarter pik, called halebi or archim, used in the measurement of silks and woolens, is 27.90 inches.
The lesser pik, termed endasse, used in the measurement of cottons and carpets, is 27.06 inches.
The pik in trade is reckoned at. .27 inches.
The almude (liquid meas.)....1⅐ im. galls.
100 almudes..............115.10 " "
The almude of oil weighs..........8 okes.
" oke of 4 chequers, or 400 drams, 2 lbs. 13 oz., 4⅓ drams avoir.
The fortin (corn measure), 4 killows, 3.84 im. bush.
100 killows...................12 im. qrs.
The cantar or quintal of 44 okes, or 100 rotoli...................125 lbs. avoir.

The preceding are Constantinople weights. In Smyrna.

100 killows..................17¾ im. qrs.
2 killows of Smyrna equal to 3 of Constantinople.
The cantar..............127.29 lbs. avoir.
One cantar..................7½ batmans.
" " ....45 okes.
" " ....100 rotoli.
The batman of Persian silk........6 okes.
" cantar of cotton yarn........45 "
" taffee of busa silk.........610 drams.
" cheque of goat wool......800 "
" " " opium..........250 "
" tchekis of Smyrna..........1⅝ avoir.

SERVIA.—A Province of European Turkey.

The rottoli of 180 drams...1.27 lbs. avoir.
" oke of 400 drams......2.83 " "
" almude (liquid meas)...1.15 im. galls.
" killow of corn..........96 im. bush.
" pike....................26⅝ inches.

TURIN (SARDINIA.)

The rasso or ell.............23.60 inches.
" mile of 800 trabucchi.....2697 yards.
" Piedmontese mile.........2771 "
" brenta of 6 rubbi.....14.41 im. galls.
" carso of oil is.............10 breuti.
" corn sacco of 3 staja is. .3.17 im. bush.
" pound of 1½ marks is...5693 troy grs.
4 rubby or 100 lbs........81.33 lbs. avoir.

VENICE.

100 libbre peso groso.....105.17 lbs. avoir
100 " " sottile....66.41 "
100 secchi..............236.19 "
100 staji..................29.19 im. qrs.
Moggio of grain..............9.08 bush.
100 braccia, woolen measure,.74.47 yards.
100 " silk measure......69.81 "
Aufora, liquid measure, 114 im. gals., or 136.80 galls. U. S.

LIST OF THE COLLECTION DISTRICTS

OF THE

CUSTOMS OF THE UNITED STATES.

ALABAMA.

Mobile.

CALIFORNIA.

San Francisco.

Ports of Delivery :

San Diego, Monterey, and junction of the Gila and Colorado, at head of Gulf of California.

CONNECTICUT.

Fairfield,
Middletown,
New-London,
New-Haven,
Stonington.

DELAWARE.

Wilmington.

DIST. OF COLUMBIA.

Alexandria,
Georgetown.

FLORIDA.

Apalachicola,
Key West,
Pensacola,
St. Augustine,
St. Marks,
St. Johns.

GEORGIA.

Brunswick,
Hardwick,
Savannah,
Sunbury,
St. Marys.

ILLINOIS.

Chicago.

KENTUCKY.

Louisville.

LOUISIANA.

New-Orleans,
Teche.

MASSACHUSETTS.

Barnstable,
Boston and Charlestown,
Edgartown,
Fall River,
Gloucester,
Marblehead,
Newburyport,
New-Bedford,
Nantucket,
Salem and Beverly,
Plymouth,

MARYLAND

Annapolis,
Baltimore,
Oxford,
Town Creek,
Vienna.

MAINE.

Bangor,
Belfast,
Bath,
Frenchman's Bay,
Kennebunk,
Machias,
Passamaquoddy,
Penobscot,
Portland,
Saco,
Waldsborough,
Wiscasset,
York.

MISSISSIPPI.

Natchez,
Pearl River,
Ship Island,
Vicksburg.

MISSOURI.

St. Louis.

MICHIGAN.

Detroit,
Michilimackinac.

NEW-YORK.

Albany,
Buffalo Creek,
Cold Spring,
Champlain,
Cape Vincent,
Genesee,
Greenport,
New-York City,
Niagara,
Oswegatchee,
Oswego,
Sackett's Harbor,
Sag Harbor,
Troy.

NEW-JERSEY.

Bridgetown,
Burlington,
Camden,
Great Egg Harbor,
Little Egg Harbor,
Newark,
Perth Amboy.

NORTH CAROLINA.

Beaufort,
Camden,
Edenton,
Newbern,
Ocracoke,
Plymouth,
Washington,
Wilmington.

NEW-HAMPSHIRE.

Portsmouth.

OHIO.

Cuyahoga,
Cincinnati,
Miami,
Sandusky.

OREGON.

Astoria.

PENNSYLVANIA.

Philadelphia,
Presqu' Isle,
Pittsburg.

RHODE ISLAND.

Bristol and Warren,
Newport,
Providence.

SOUTH CAROLINA.

Beaufort,
Charleston,
Georgetown.

TENNESSEE.

Nashville.

TEXAS.

Galveston, to which is annexed Sabine, Velasco, Matagorda, Cavall, La Vaca, and Corpus Christi, as *Ports of Delivery only.* — Act of January 12, 1846.

For that part of the State southwest of the counties of Matagorda and Warters, and including said counties, that Saluvia shall be the Collecting District, and Matagorda, Aransas, Copano, and Corpus Christi, are *Ports of Delivery only.*

VIRGINIA.

Cherry Stone,
East River,
Norfolk and Portsmouth,
Petersburg,
Richmond,
Tappahannock,
Wheeling,
Yorktown,
Yeocomico.

VERMONT.

Burlington

INFORMATION FOR SHIPMASTERS.

ENTRY OF VESSELS FROM FOREIGN PORTS.

It is necessary that the manifests (three copies) of vessels from foreign ports should be made out before arrival, in order to be presented to the boarding-officer *upon* arrival. They should include *everything* on board; and, after stating the cargo laden at the port of departure, if there should be any return cargo, it should then be added under that head. If there are any surplus stores, these should then be particularized; and, finally, the passengers' names, individually, with the numbers of packages of baggage belonging to *each*—the whole to be signed by the master.

Where there are passengers, a separate list, (besides the names on each manifest,) including the names, age, sex, occupation, country to which they severally belong, and of which they intend to become inhabitants, and if any have died on the passage, will also be necessary.

Another list of passengers, similar to the last, is required by the mayor of the city.

If any part of the cargo is to be landed at a different port than the first one of entry, *it must be so stated in the manifest, as otherwise that privilege will be lost*, and the cargo required to be landed at the first port of entry.

The captain will be particular in having his crew mustered by the boarding-officer, upon arrival, in order to the cancelling of the bond given for their safe return.

Vessels must report at the custom-house, within twelve hours, and enter within forty-eight hours, after arrival.

If the captain is not an owner of the vessel, and there should be a resident owner at the port of entry, such owner is required to accompany the captain, in order to swear to the register.

ENTRY OF VESSELS COASTWISE.

Nothing further is required than the clearance from the custom-house at the port of departure, and the register, if she is a registered vessel.

CLEARANCE OF VESSELS FOR FOREIGN PORTS.

Every shipper must clear his goods at the custom-house *before* the vessel can clear. From these shippers' clearances, the vessel's manifest is to be made, after the same form, and including all the particulars therein contained.

A notarial crew-list and duplicate shipping articles are also required. If there is any change of owner or master, notice thereof should be given, at least the day previous, in order that the register may be endorsed or a new one issued.

Inquiry should also be made, a day or two previous to clearing, (in case of vessels last from foreign ports,) whether the return of the inward cargo corresponds with the manifest, as delays may otherwise occur in settling discrepancies, which to adjust may and does frequently detain vessels from clearing, when the hurry is great, and consignees are anxious to get their vessels to sea.

If there is any cargo brought in the vessel, not to be landed, a permit must be obtained to retain the same on board, several days before clearing, as the officer discharging the vessel cannot make his return without it; and, without *his* return, the vessel cannot be cleared. When cleared, the captain will re ceive his register, crew-list, clearance, bill of health, and shipping articles; *or*, in case of a *foreign* vessel, all that he requires is a clearance and bill of health, upon presenting which to the consul of his nation, he will receive all other necessary papers.

CLEARANCE OF VESSELS COASTWISE.

Duplicate manifests, made out from the bills of lading (number of packages in each bill of lading being stated *in writing*,) with the shippers and consignees, and places of residence, is all that is required.

☞ It is deemed unnecessary to state the different desks to which application must be made in entering and clearing, as these are liable to be changed and as full information on this head can easily be obtained at the time, by simply asking, when leaving one desk, where to proceed; and so on, until the entry or clearance is completed.

THE NEW PASSENGER LAW.

AN ACT

To regulate the Carriage of Passengers in Steamships and other Vessels.

SEC. 1. Be it enacted by the Senate and House of Representatives of the United States of America in Congress assembled, That no master of any vessel owned in whole or in part by a citizen of the United States, or by a citizen of any foreign country, shall take on board such vessel, at any foreign port or place, other than foreign contiguous territory of the United States, a greater number of passengers than in proportion of one to every two tons of such vessel, not including children under the age of one year in the computation, and computing two children over one and under eight years of age as one passenger. That the spaces appropriated for the use of such passengers, and which shall not be occupied by stores or other goods not the personal baggage of such passengers, shall be in the following proportions, viz.: On the main and poop decks or platforms and in the deck-houses, if there be any, one passenger for each sixteen clear superficial feet of deck, if the height or distance between the decks or platforms shall not be less than six feet; and on the lower deck, (not being an orlop deck,) if any, one passenger for eighteen such clear superficial feet, if the height or distance between the decks or platforms shall not be less than six feet, but so as that no passenger shall be carried on any other deck or platform, nor upon any deck where the height or distance between decks is less than six feet, with intent to bring such passenger to the United States, and shall leave such port or place and bring the same, or any number thereof, within the jurisdiction of the United States; or if any such master of any vessel shall take on board his vessel, at any port or place within the jurisdiction of the United States, any greater number of passengers than in the proportion aforesaid to the space aforesaid, or to the tonnage aforesaid, with intent to carry the same to any foreign port or place other than foreign contiguous territory as aforesaid, every such master shall be deemed guilty of a misdemeanor, and upon conviction thereof, before any circuit or district court of the United States, shall for each passenger taken on board beyond the limit aforesaid, or the space aforesaid, be fined in the sum of fifty dollars, and may also be imprisoned, at the discretion of the judge before whom the penalty shall be recovered, not exceeding six months; but should it be necessary for the safety or convenience of the vessel, that any portion of her cargo, or any other articles, or article, should be placed on, or stored in, any of the decks, cabins, or other places appropriated to the use of passengers, the same may be placed in lockers or enclosures prepared for the purpose, on an exterior sarface impervious to the wave, capable of being cleansed in like manner as the decks or platforms of the vessel. In no case, however, shall the places thus provided be deemed to be a part of the space allowable for the use of passengers, but the same shall be deducted therefrom, and in all cases where prepared or used, the upper surface of said lockers on enclosed spaces shall be deemed and taken to be the deck or platform from which measurement shall be made for all the purposes of this act. It is also provided that one hospital in the spaces appropriated to passengers, and separate therefrom by an appropriate partition, and furnished as its purposes require, may be prepared, and when used, may be included in the space allowable for passengers, but the same shall not occupy more than one hundred superficial feet of deck or platform. *Provided*, That on board two-deck ships, where the height between the decks is seven and one-half feet or more, fourteen clear superficial feet of deck shall be the proportion required for each passenger.

Sec. 2. And be it further enacted, That no such vessel shall have more than two tiers of berths, and the interval between the lowest part thereof and the deck or platform beneath, shall not be less than nine inches, and the berths shall be well constructed, parallel with the sides of the vessel, and separated from each other by partitions, as berths ordinarily are separated, and shall be at least six feet in length and at least two feet in width, and each berth shall be occupied by no more than one passenger; but double berths of twice the above width may be constructed, each berth to be occupied by no more, and by no other, than two women, or by one women and two children under the age of eight years, or by husband and wife, or by a man and two of his own children under the age of eight years, or by two members of the same family; and if there shall be any violation of this section in any of its provisions, then the master of the vessel and the owners thereof shall severally forfeit and pay the sum of five dollars for each passenger on board of said vessel on such voyage, to be recovered by the United States in any port where such vessel may arrive or depart.

Sec. 3. And be it further enacted, That all vessels, whether of the United States or any foreign country, having sufficient capacity or space according to law for fifty or more passengers (other than cabin passengers) shall, when employed in transporting such passengers between the United States and Europe, have, on the upper deck, for the use of such passengers, a house over the passage-way leading to the apartments allotted to such passengers, below deck, firmly secured to the deck or combings of the hatch, with two doors, the sills of which shall be at least one foot above the deck, so constructed that one door or window in such house may at all times be left open for ventilation; and all vessels so employed, and having the capacity to carry one hundred and fifty such passengers, or more, shall have two such houses; and the stairs or ladder leading down to the aforesaid apartment shall be furnished with a hand-rail of wood or strong rope; but booby hatches may be substituted for such houses.

Sec. 4. And be it further enacted, That every such vessel so employed, and having the legal capacity for more than one hundred such passengers, shall have at least two ventilators to purify the apartment or apartments occupied by such passengers; one of which shall be inserted in the after part of the apartment or apartments, and the other shall be placed in the forward portion of the apartment or apartments, and one of them shall have an exhausting cap to carry off the foul air, and the other a receiving cap to carry down the fresh air; which said ventilators shall have a capacity proportioned to the size of the apartment or apartments to be purified; namely, if the apartment or apartments will lawfully authorize the reception of two hundred such passengers, the capacity of such ventilators shall each be equal to a tube of twelve inches diameter in the clear, and in proportion for larger or smaller apartments; and all said ventilators shall rise at least four feet six inches above the upper deck of any such vessel, and be of the most approved form and construction; but if it shall appear, from the report to be made and approved, as hereinafter provided, that such vessel is equally well ventilated by any other means, such other means of ventilation shall be deemed and held to be a compliance with the provisions of this section.

Sec. 5. And be it further enacted, That every vessel carrying more than fifty such passengers, shall have for their use on deck, housed and conveniently arranged, at least one caboose or cooking range, the dimensions of which shall be equal to four feet long and one foot six inches wide for every two hundred passengers; and provision shall be made in the manner aforesaid, in this ratio, for a greater or less number of passengers; but nothing herein contained shall take away the right to make such arrangements for cooking between decks, if that shall be deemed desirable.

Sec. 6. And be it further enacted, That all vessels employed as aforesaid shall have on board, for the use of such passengers, at the time of leaving the last port whence such vessel shall sail, well secured under deck, for each passenger, at least twenty pounds of good navy bread, fifteen pounds of rice, fifteen pounds of oatmeal, ten pounds of wheat flour, fifteen pounds of peas and beans, twenty pounds of potatoes, one pint of vinegar, sixty-gallons of fresh water, ten pounds of salt beef, free of bone, all to be of good quality; but at places where either rice, oatmeal, wheat flour, or peas and beans cannot be procured, of good quality and on reasonable terms, the quantity of either or any of the other last named articles may be increased and substituted therefor; and, in case potatoes cannot be procured on reasonable terms, one pound of either of said articles may be substituted in lieu of five pounds of potatoes; and the captains of such vessels shall deliver to each passenger at least one-tenth part of the aforesaid provisions weekly, commencing on the day of sailing, and at least three quarts of water, daily; and if the passengers on board of any such vessel in which the provisions and water herein required shall not have been provided as aforesaid shall at any time be put on short allowance during any voyage, the master or owner of any such vessel shall pay to each and every passenger who shall have been put on short allowance, the sum of three dollars for each and every day they may have been put on short allowance, to be recovered in the Circuit or District Court of the United States; and it shall be the duty of the captain or master of every such ship or vessel to cause the food and provisions of all the passengers to be well and properly cooked, daily, and to be served out and distributed to them, at regular and stated hours, by messes, or in such other manner as shall be deemed best and most conducive to the health and comfort of such passengers, of which hours and manner of distribution due and sufficient notice shall be given. If the captain or master of any such ship or vessel shall wilfully fail to furnish and distribute such provisions, cooked as aforesaid, he shall be deemed guilty of a misdemeanor, and upon conviction thereof, before any Circuit or District Court of the United States, shall be fined not more than one thousand dollars, and snall be imprisoned for a term not exceeding one year: Provided, That the enforcement of this penalty shall not affect the civil responsibility of the captain or master and owners, to such passengers as may have suffered from said default.

SEC. 7. And be it further enacted, That the captain of any such vessel so employed is hereby authorized to maintain good discipline, and such habits of cleanliness among such passengers as will tend to the preservation and promotion of health; and to that end he shall cause such regulations as he may adopt for this purpose to be posted up, before sailing, on board such vessel, in a place accessible to such passengers, and shall keep the same so posted up during the voyage; and it is hereby made the duty of said captain to cause the apartments occupied by such passengers to be kept at all times in a clean, healthy state; and the owners of every such vessel so employed are required to construct the decks, and all parts of said apartment, so that it can be thoroughly cleansed; and they shall also provide a safe, convenient privy or water closet for the exclusive use of every one hundred such passengers. And when the weather is such that said passengers cannot be mustered on deck with their bedding, it shall be the duty of the captain of every such vessel to cause the deck occupied by such passengers to be cleansed with chloride of lime, or some other equally efficient disinfecting agent, and also at such other times as said captain may deem necessary.

SEC. 8. And be it further enacted, That the master and owner or owners of any such vessel so employed, which shall not be provided with the house or houses over the passage ways, as prescribed in the third section of this chapter, or with ventilators, as prescribed in the fourth section of this chapter or with the cambooses or cooking-ranges, with the houses over them, as prescribed in the fifth section of this chapter, shall severally forfeit and pay to the United States the sum of two hundred dollars for each and every violation of, or neglect to conform to, the provisions of each of said sections; and fifty dollars for each and every neglect or violation of any of the provisions of the seventh section of this chapter, to be recovered by suit in any Circuit or District Court of the United States within the jurisdiction of which the said vessel may arrive, or from which she may be about to depart, or at any place within the jurisdiction of such courts, wherever the owner or owners or captain of such vessel may be found.

SEC. 9. And be it further enacted, That the collector of the customs at any port of the United States at which any vessel so employed shall arrive, or from which any such vessel shall be about to depart, shall appoint and direct one or more of the inspectors of the customs for such port to examine such vessel, and report, in writing, to such collector, whether the requirements of law have been complied with in respect to such vessel; and if such report shall state such compliance, and shall be approved by such collector, it shall be deemed and held as *prima facie* evidence thereof.

SEC. 10. And be it further enacted, That the provisions, requisitions, penalties, and liens of this act, relating to the space in vessels appropriated to the use of passengers, are hereby extended and made applicable to all spaces appropriated to the use of steerage passengers in vessels propelled in whole or in part by steam, and navigating from, to, and between the ports, and in manner as in this act named, and to such vessels and to the masters thereof; and so much of the act entitled, "An act to amend an act entitled, 'An act to provide for the better security of the lives of passengers on board of vessels propelled in whole or in part by steam, and for other purposes,'" approved August thirtieth, eighteen hundred and fifty-two, as conflicts with this act, is hereby repealed; and the space appropriated to the use of steerage passengers in vessels so as above propelled and navigated, is hereby subject to the supervision and inspection of the collector of the customs at any port of the United States at which any such vessel shall arrive, or from which she shall be about to depart; and the same shall be examined and reported in the same manner, and by the same officers, by the next preceding section directed to examine and report.

SEC. 11. And be it further enacted, That the vessels bound from any port in the United States to any port or place in the Pacific ocean, or on its tributaries, or from any such port or place to any port in the United States on the Atlantic or its tributaries, shall be subject to the foregoing provisions regulating the carriage of passengers in merchant vessels, except so much as relates to provisions and water; but the owners and masters of all such vessels shall in all cases furnish to each passenger the daily supply of water therein mentioned; and they shall furnish a sufficient supply of good and wholesome food, properly cooked; and in case they shall fail so to do, or shall provide unwholesome or unsuitable provisions, they shall be subject to the penalty provided in the sixth section of this chapter, in case the passengers are put on short allowance of water or provisions.

Sec. 12. And be it further enacted, That the captain or master of any ship or vessel arriving in the United States, or any of the Territories thereof, from any foreign place whatever, at the same time that he delivers a manifest of the cargo, and if there be no cargo, then at the time of making report or entry of the ship or vessel, pursuant to law, shall also deliver and report to the collector of the district in which such ship or vessel shall arrive, a list or manifest of all the passengers taken on board of the said ship or vessel at any foreign port or place; in which list or manifest it shall be the duty of the said master to designate, particularly, the age, sex, and occupation of the said passengers, respectively, the part of the vessel occupied by each during the voyage, the country to which they severally belong, and that of which it is their intention to become inhabitants; and shall further set forth whether any and what number have died on the voyage; which list or manifest shall be sworn to by the said master, in the same manner as directed by law in relation to the manifest of the cargo, and the refusal or neglect of the master aforesaid to comply with the provisions of this section, or part thereof, shall incur the same penalties, disabilities, and forfeitures as are provided for a refusal or neglect to report and deliver a manifest of the cargo aforesaid.

Sec. 13. And be it further enacted, That each and every collector of the customs, to whom such manifest or list of passengers as aforesaid shall be delivered, shall quarter-yearly return copies thereof to the Secretary of State of the United States, by whom statements of the same shall be laid before Congress at each and every session.

Sec. 14. And be it further enacted, That in case there shall have occurred on board any ship or vessel arriving at any port or place within the United States or its Territories, any death or deaths among the passengers, (other than cabin passengers,) the master or captain or owner or consignee of such ship or vessel shall, within twenty-four hours after the time within which the report and list or manifest of passengers mentioned in section twelve of this act is required to be delivered to the collector of the customs, pay to the said collector the sum of ten dollars for each and every passenger above the age of eight years who shall have died on the voyage by natural disease; and the said collector shall pay the money thus received at such times and in such manner as the Secretary of the Treasury by general rules shall direct, to any board or commission appointed by and acting under the authority of the State within which the port where such ship or vessel arrived is situated, for the care and protection of sick, indigent, or destitute emigrants, to be applied to the objects of their appointment; and if there be more than one board or commission who shall claim such payment, the Secretary of the Treasury, for the time being, shall determine which is entitled to receive the same, and his decision in the premises shall be final and without appeal. Provided, That the payment shall in no case be awarded or made to any board or commission or association formed for the protection or advancement of any particular class of immigrants or emigrants of any particular nation or creed; and if the master, captain, owner or consignee of any ship or vessel, refuse or neglect to pay to the collector the sum and sums of money required, and within the time prescribed by this section, he or they shall severally forfeit and pay the sum of fifty dollars, in addition to such sum of ten dollars for each and every passenger upon whose death the same has become payable, to be recovered by the United States in any circuit or district court of the United States where such vessel may arrive, or such master, captain, owner or consignee may reside, and when recovered, the said money shall be disposed of in the same manner as is directed with respect to the sum and sums required to be paid to the collector of customs.

Sec. 15. And be it further enacted, That the amount of the several penalties imposed by the foregoing provisions regulating the carriage of passengers in merchant vessels, shall be liens on the vessel or vessels violating those provisions, and such vessel or vessels shall be libelled therefor in any Circuit or District Court of the United States where such vessel or vessels shall arrive.

Sec. 16. And be it further enacted, That all and every vessel or vessels which shall or may be employed by the American Colonization Society, or the Colonization Society of any State, to transport, and which shall actually transport, from any port or ports of the United States to any colony or colonies on the west coast of Africa, colored emigrants to reside there, shall be, and the same are hereby, subject to the operation of the foregoing provisions regulating the carriage of passengers in merchant vessels.

Sec. 17. And be it further enacted, That the collector of customs shall examine each emigrant ship or vessel on its arrival at this port, and ascertain and report to the Secretary of the Treasury at the time of sailing, the length of the voyage, the ventilation, the number of passengers, their space on board, their food, the native country of the emigrants, the number of deaths, the age and sex of those who died during the voyage; together with his opinion of the cause of the mortality, if any, on board; and if none, what precautionary measures, arrangements, or habits, are supposed to have had any, and what, agency in causing the exemption.

Sec. 18. And be it further enacted, That this act shall take effect, with respect to vessels sailing from ports in the United States, on the eastern side of the continent, within thirty days from the time of its approval: and with respect to vessels sailing from ports in the United States on the western side of the continent, and from ports in Europe, within sixty days from the time of its approval; and with respect to vessels sailing from ports in other parts of the world, within six months from the time of its approval.

And it is hereby made the duty of the Secretary of State to give notice in the ports of Europe and elsewhere, of this act, in such manner as he shall deem proper.

Sec. 19. And be it further enacted, That from and after the time that this act shall take effect with respect to any vessels, then in respect to such vessels the act of second March, eighteen hundred and nineteen, entitled "An act regulating passenger ships and vessels," the act of twenty-second February, eighteen hundred and forty-seven, entitled "An act to regulate the carriage of passengers in merchant vessels," the act of second March, eighteen hundred and forty-seven, entitled "An act to amend an act entitled 'An act to regulate the carriage of passengers in merchant vessels," and to determine the time when said act shall take effect," the act of thirty-first January, eighteen hundred and forty-eight, entitled "An act exempting vessels employed by the American Colonization Society in transporting colored emigrants from the United States to the coast of Africa, from the provisions of the acts of the twenty-second February and second of March, eighteen hundred and forty-seven, regulating the carriage of passengers in merchant vessels," the act of seventeenth May, eighteen hundred and forty-eight, entitled "An act to provide for the ventilation of passenger vessels, and for other purposes," and the act of third March, eighteen hundred and forty-nine, entitled "An act to extend the provisions of all laws now in force relating to the carriage of passengers in merchant vessels, and the regulations thereof," are hereby repealed. But nothing in this act contained shall in any wise obstruct or prevent the prosecution, recovery, distribution, or remission of any fines, penalties, or forfeitures which may have been incurred, in respect to any vessels, prior to the day this act goes into effect, in respect to such vessels, under the laws hereby repealed, for which purpose the said laws shall continue in force.

But the Secretary of the Treasury may, in his discretion, and upon such conditions as he shall think proper, discontinue any such prosecutions, or remit or modify such penalties.

Approved March 3, 1855.

CIRCULAR.

Treasury Department, Oct. 15, 1849.

In consequence of questions submitted by merchants and others, asking, in consideration of the recent alteration of the British Navigation Laws, on what footing the commercial relations between the United States and Great Britain will be placed, on and after the first day of January next—the day on which the recent act of the British Parliament goes into operation—the Department deems it expedient, at this time, to issue the following general instructions for the information of the officers of the customs and others interested:

First. In consequence of the alterations of the British Navigation Laws, above referred to, British vessels, from British or other foreign ports, will, (under our existing laws,) after the first of January next, be allowed to enter in our ports with cargoes of the growth, manufacture, or production of any part of the world.

Second. Such vessels and their cargoes will be admitted, from and after the date before mentioned, on the same terms, as to duties, imposts, and charges, as vessels of the United States and their cargoes.

W. M. MEREDITH, *Secretary of the Treasury.*

EXTRACTS

Of Laws Regulating Vessels engaged in Foreign Trade.

Vessels built in the United States, wholly owned and commanded by citizens of the United States, and no other, can be registered and entitled to the privileges of a vessel of the United States; but such vessel cannot be so entitled if owned in whole or in part by any citizen residing in a foreign country unless he be a consul of the United States, or partner in a house of trade within the United States.

No registered vessels can be entitled to the privileges of an American vessel, if owned wholly or in part by a naturalized citizen, residing for more than one year in his native country, or more than two years in any foreign country, except he be a consul or agent of the United States; but she may be so entitled, in case of a bona fide sale to a resident citizen of the United States.

Oath of ownership to be taken by every owner of a registered vessel, and transmitted, within 90 days, to the collector granting the register.

Previous to the registering of any vessel, the resident owner or master must give bond that the register shall be solely used for the vessel; and in case of her being lost, sold to foreigners, or broken up, the register to be surrendered within eight days after the arrival of the master within the United States.

In order to the registering of a vessel built within the United States a certificate of the master carpenter who built her must be produced, setting forth her description, and for whom built.

In cases of steam vessels owned by a company, the oath of the president or secretary is sufficient, without designating the names of the persons composing the company.

Vessels to be registered in the port where the owner, or if there be more than one, the managing owner, resides.

Her name, and the port to which she belongs, to be painted on her stern white letters on a black ground, not less than three inches in length, under a penalty of fifty dollars.

In case a registered vessel should be transferred, in whole or in part, to a foreigner, her register must be surrendered within seven days, or the bond will be forfeited.

No vessel which has been registered, and thereafter seized or captured, and condemned, by any foreign power, or shall, by sale, become the property of a foreigner, shall be entitled to a new register, (unless claimed by her former owners, at the time of her seizure or capture), but shall be deemed a foreign vessel.

Change of master to be reported by new master, or owner, and oath of citizenship to be endorsed on register, or the register shall be void, and the master forfeit 100 dollars.

Upon the entry of a registered vessel, from a foreign port, at the port where an owner resides, he must make oath that the register contains the names of all the owners, and that no foreign citizen has any share in such vessel, by way of trust, confidence, or otherwise.

If any register shall be fraudulently used for any vessel not entitled to the benefit thereof, she shall be forfeited.

If any vessel, enrolled or licensed, proceeds on a foreign voyage without surrendering her enrollment or license, and being registered, she shall be liable to forfeiture.

In case a register is lost, destroyed, or mislaid, the master, on oath, and in compliance with the requisitions of the law, may receive a new one.

On satisfactory proof to the secretary of the treasury that a vessel has been sold, by process of law, and her register retained by her former owners, he may direct a new one to be issued.

No sea letter, or other document, certifying a vessel to be the property of a citizen of the United States, can be issued, except to vessels duly registered or enrolled, and licensed as vessels of the United States.

When a registered vessel is transferred, in whole or in part, to a citizen, or altered in form, burthen or rig, she must be registered anew, by her former name, or lose the benefits of an American vessel.

Every case of transfer, in whole or in part, must be by bill of sale, reciting the certificate of registry at length, and the certificate surrendered.

Vessels arriving from a foreign port must enter at an established port of entry, and no cargo can be unladen except at a port of entry or delivery.

Every American vessel arriving from a foreign port, must be provided with a manifest of her whole cargo, or the master forfeits a sum equal to the value of all goods not included therein; all goods not included, belonging to the master, officers, or crew, to be forfeited. The manifest to be delivered to the first officer of the customs who shall board her. Neglect, or refusal to produce manifest, subjects the master to a penalty of $500.

Merchandise destined for delivery at different districts must be distinctly set forth on the manifest.

Merchandise unladen without permit from the proper officers of the customs, to be forfeited: and the master and mate, each, forfeit one thousand dollars—except by an unavoidable necessity, to be satisfactorily proved to the collector

The register and crew list to be deposited with the collector, on entry of vessel, within 48 hours of arrival, and arrival reported to collector, within 24 hours.

Foreign vessels, on entry, to produce manifest of cargo, and certificate of consul of nation to which they belong, of the deposit of their papers with him.

No vessel permitted to an entry, until the master shall have delivered to the post-master all letters directed to persons within the United States.

Before departure for a foreign port, the master of every vessel must deliver to the collector a manifest of his whole cargo, and the value thereof, and obtain a clearance, under penalty of $500.

In case any part of the cargo consists of goods subject to inspection, by the laws of the States, a certificate of inspections must be produced, previous to clearance.

Before clearance, the shippers or consignors of the cargo must deliver a manifest of their portion of the cargo, under oath, setting forth the kind, quantity, and value of each article, and the foreign port where intended to be landed.

Vessels licensed for the fisheries, intending to trade at any foreign place, must obtain permission from the collector of the port whence she departs, deliver a manifest, and comply with all the requisitions of the laws applying to vessels engaged in foreign trade. If found within three leagues of the coast with foreign goods on board of the value of $500, without such permission, will be forfeited.

AN ACT

To provide for Recording the Conveyances of Vessels, and for other purposes.

Be it enacted by the Senate and House of Representatives of the United States of America, in Congress assembled, That no bill of sale, mortgage, hypothecation, or conveyance of any vessel, or part of any vessel of the United States, shall be valid against any person other than the grantor or mortgagor, his heirs and devisees, and persons having actual notice thereof; unless such bill of sale, mortgage, hypothecation, or conveyance be recorded in the office of the Collector of the Customs where such vessel is registered or enrolled: Provided, That the lien by bottomry on any vessel, created during her voyage, by a loan of money or materials necessary to repair or enable such vessel to prosecute a voyage, shall not lose its priority or be in any way affected by the provisions of this Act.

Sec. 2. And be it further enacted, That the Collectors of the Customs shall record all such bills of sale, mortgages, hypothecations, or conveyances, and also, all certificates for discharging and cancelling any such conveyances, in a book or books to be kept for that purpose, in the order of their reception, noting in said book or books, and also on the bill of sale, mortgage, hypothecation, or conveyance, the time when the same was received, and shall certify on the bill of sale, mortgage, hypothecation, or conveyance, or certificate of discharge or cancellation, the number of the book and page where recorded, and shall receive for so recording such instrument of conveyance or certificate of discharge, fifty cents.

Sec. 3. And be it further enacted, That the Collectors of the Customs shall keep an index of such records, inserting alphabetically the names of the vender or mortgagor, and the vendee or mortgagee, and shall permit said index and books of records to be inspected during office hours, under such reasonable regulations as they may establish, and shall, when required, furnish to any person a certificate, setting forth the names of the owners of any vessel registered or enrolled, the part or proportions owned by each, (if inserted in the register or enrollment,) and also the material facts of any existing bill of sale, mortgage, hypothecation, or other incumbrance upon such vessel, recorded since the issuing of the last register or enrollment, viz.: the date, amount of such encumbrance, and from and to whom, or in whose favor made; the Collectors shall receive for each such certificate, one dollar.

Sec. 4. And be it further enacted, That the Collectors of the Customs shall furnish certified copies of such records on the receipt of fifty cents for each bill of sale, mortgage, or other conveyance.

Sec. 5. And be it further enacted, That the owner or agent of the owner of any vessel of the United States, applying to a Collector of the Customs for a register or enrollment of a vessel, shall, in addition to the oath now prescribed by law, set forth in the oath of ownership the part or proportion of such vessel belonging to each owner, and the same shall be inserted in the register or enrollment; and that all bills of sale of vessels registered or enrolled shall set forth the part of the vessel owned by each person selling, and the part conveyed to each person purchasing.

Sec. 6. And be it further enacted, That the twelfth clause or section of the act, entitled "An Act in addition to the several Acts regulating the shipment and discharge of seamen and the duties of consuls," approved July twentieth, eighteen hundred and forty, be so amended, as that all complaints in writing, to the consuls or commercial agents as therein provided, that a vessel is unseaworthy, shall be signed by the first, or the second and third officers, and a majority of the crew, before the consul or commercial agent shall be authorized to notice such complaint, or proceed to appoint inspectors, as therein provided,

Sec. 7. And be it further enacted, That any person, not being an owner. who shall on the high seas, wilfully, with intent to burn or destroy, set fire to any ship or other vessel, or otherwise attempt the destruction of such ship or other vessel, being the property of any citizen or citizens of the United States, or procure the same to be done, with the intent aforesaid, and being thereof lawfully convicted, shall suffer imprisonment to hard labor, for a term not exceeding ten years, nor less than three years, according to the aggravation of the offence.

Sec. 8. And be it further enacted, That this Act shall be in force from and after the first day of October next ensuing.

Approved, July 29, 1840.

I certify that the foregoing is a true copy of the original roll on file in the Department of State.

W. S. DERRICK, *C. C.*

CIRCULAR.

INSTRUCTIONS TO COLLECTORS AND OTHER OFFICERS OF THE CUSTOMS RELATING TO MANIFESTS.

TREASURY DEPARTMENT, *May*, 1851.

The existing laws of the United States require that all vessels, whether American or foreign, coming from a foreign port, and bound to a port of the United States, shall, upon arriving within four leagues of the coast thereof, or within the limits of any collection district, produce to the proper officer of the revenue who may first board any such vessel, a full manifest of the cargo on board, detailing all the items thereof, the port or ports where the same may have been shipped, the names of the consignees thereof, and the different ports, if more than one, where the same is consigned or intended to be entered.

But the Department has ascertained that the execution of the salutary provision of the law on this subject has, in latter years, been in many ports greatly relaxed or entirely neglected, and masters of vessels are constantly permitted to make out and deliver their manifests after they have actually arrived at their port of entry.

The obvious protection to the revenue which this provision of law was intended to afford is thus greatly lessened; and, in cases of vessels bound to inland ports, great facilities are thus afforded for illegally landing portions of their cargo while passing up the great estuaries or rivers of the country, which portions thus landed, under the present practice of making out their manifests after reaching their port of entry, they can omit to report, but which otherwise would have to be accounted for, if the return of it had been included upon a manifest delivered agreeably to law, on their first entering the waters of the United States.

Independent, however, of these circumstances, and of the manifest necessity of throwing around the collection of the revenue all the guards against fraud which the law has provided and enjoined, the Department cannot, in a faithful discharge of its duties, allow so explicit a provision of the law to be relaxed, and still less to fall into disuse; and the Collectors of the Customs, the commanders of the revenue vessels, and all the boarding officers in the revenue service, are therefore required to carry the same into effect in future. The commanders of the revenue cutters are instructed to board *all vessels from foreign ports* arriving within the limits before referred to, and to demand and retain, *one copy* of their manifest, to be forwarded to the Collector of the port to which said vessels may respectively be bound, *and to make, as provided by law, the needed endorsement on another copy*, to remain on board the vessel thus boarded; and if the masters of any such vessels should not have their manifests ready for delivery, the officer, if practicable, and if not attended with too great delay and inconvenience, should remain on board until such manifest can be prepared and delivered to him. In all cases where the masters of such vessels from a foreign port have no manifests of their cargo ready for delivery when thus boarded, or who shall neglect or refuse to deliver them when demanded by such boarding officer, the latter is instructed to report the same to the Collector of the port to which such vessel may be bound; and said Collector will, prior to enforcing the penalty prescribed by law, make report to the Department, accompanied by an affidavit of the master of the vessel, setting forth the causes for neglecting to comply with the law and regulations, together with any extenuating facts or circumstances involved in the case, for the consideration and action of the Department. The commanders of the cutters, and the boarding officers, are further instructed to transmit direct to this Department, monthly abstracts of all vessels thus boarded, and reported to the Collectors.

Although the Department is precluded from suspending or omitting to enforce the provisions of the law on this subject, yet, for the reasons before stated, and until proper notification of these instructions can be given, it will, in the exercise of the remitting power vested in it by law, extend such leniency and indulgence as the peculiar circumstances of the cases respectively may admit of, without hazarding the interests of the public revenue. But whatever leniency it may thus exercise, in such cases, in consequence of the erroneous practice which has existed for such a length of time in not properly enforcing the law on this subject, the penalty will be rigidly enforced in all cases where the masters of vessels were aware of the change in that respect, and of the existence of the present circular, previous to their leaving a foreign port for the United States.

The consuls and commercial agents of the United States abroad will be requested to take proper measures to give publicity to these regulations for the government of masters and owners of foreign vessels bound to the United States.

WM. L. HODGE,
Acting Secretary of the Treasury.

Reciprocity Treaty between the United States of America and her Britannic Majesty; concluded fifth June, 1854; *ratified by the United States ninth August,* 1854; *exchanged ninth September,* 1854; *and proclaimed eleventh September,* 1854.

BY THE PRESIDENT OF THE UNITED STATES OF AMERICA.

A PROCLAMATION.

Whereas a treaty between the United States of America and her Majesty the Queen of the United Kingdom of Great Britain and Ireland, was concluded and signed by their respective plenipotentiaries at Washington, on the 5th day of June last, which treaty is, word for word, as follows:

The Government of the United States being equally desirous with her Majesty, the Queen of Great Britain, to avoid further misunderstanding between their respective citizens and subjects in regard to the extent of the right of fishing on the coasts of British North America, secured to each by article 1 of a Convention between the United States and Great Britain, signed at London on the 20th day of October, 1818; and being also desirous to regulate the commerce and navigation between their respective territories and people, and more especially between her Majesty's possessions in North America and the United States, in such manner as to render the same reciprocally beneficial and satisfactory, have, respectively, named plenipotentiaries to confer and agree thereupon—that is to say, the President of the United States of America, William L. Marcy, Secretary of State of the United States; and her Majesty, the Queen of the United Kingdom of Great Britain and Ireland, James, Earl of Elgin and Kincardine, Lord Bruce and Elgin, a peer of the United Kingdom, Knight of the most ancient and most noble Order of the Thistle, and Governor-General in and over all her Britannic Majesty's Provinces on the Continent of North America, and in and over the Island of Prince Edward; who, after having communicated to each other their respective full powers, found in good and due form, have agreed upon the following articles:

ARTICLE 1. It is agreed by the high contracting parties, that, in addition to the liberties secured to the United States fishermen by the above-mentioned Convention of October 20, 1818, of taking, curing and drying fish on certain coasts of the British North American Colonies, therein defined, the inhabitants of the United States shall have, in common with the subjects of her Britannic Majesty, the liberty to take fish of every kind, except shell-fish, on the sea-coasts and shores, and in the bays, harbors, and creeks of Canada, New-Brunswick, Nova-Scotia, Prince Edward's Island, and of the several islands there unto adjacent, without being restricted to any distance from the shore, with permission to land upon the coasts and shores of those colonies and the islands thereof, and also upon the Magdalen Islands, for the purpose of drying their nets and curing their fish: provided that, in so doing, they do not interfere with the rights of private property, or with British fishermen, in the peaceable use of any part of the said coast, in their occupancy for the same purpose.

It is understood that the above-mentioned liberty applies solely to the sea fishery, and that the salmon and shad fisheries, and all fisheries in rivers, and the mouths of rivers, are hereby reserved, exclusively, for British fishermen.

And it is further agreed, that, in order to prevent or settle any disputes as to the places to which the reservation of exclusive right to British fishermen, contained in this article, and that of fishermen of the United States, contained in the next succeeding article, apply, each of the high contracting parties on the application of either to the other, shall, within six months thereafter, appoint a commissioner. The said commissioners, before proceeding to any business, shall make and subscribe a solemn declaration that they will impartially and carefully examine and decide, to the best of their judgment, and according to justice and equity, without fear, favor, or affection to their own country, upon all such places as are intended to be reserved and excluded from the common liberty of fishing under this and the next succeeding article and such declaration shall be entered on the record of their proceedings.

The commissioners shall name some third person to act as an arbitrator or umpire in any case or cases on which they may themselves differ in opinion If they should not be able to agree upon the name of such third person, they shall each name a person, and it shall be determined by lot which of the two persons so named shall be the arbitrator or umpire in cases of difference or disagreement between the two commissioners. The person so to be chosen to be arbitrator or umpire shall, before proceeding to act as such in any case, make and subscribe a solemn declaration in a form similar to that which shall already have been made and subscribed by the commissioners, which shall be entered on the record of their proceedings. In the event of the death, absence, or incapacity of either of the commissioners, or of the arbitrator or umpire, or of their or his omitting, declining, or ceasing to act as such commissioner, arbitrator or umpire, another and different person shall be appointed or named as aforesaid to act as such commissioner, arbitrator or umpire, in the place and stead of the person so originally appointed or named as aforesaid, and shall make and subscribe such declaration as aforesaid.

Such commissioners shall proceed to examine the coasts of the North American Provinces, and of the United States embraced within the provisions of the first and second article of this treaty, and shall designate the places reserved by the said articles from the common right of fishing therein.

The decision of the commissioners and of the arbitrator or umpire shall be given in writing in each case, and shall be signed by them respectively.

The high contracting parties hereby solemnly engage to consider the decision of the commissioners conjointly, or of the arbitrator or umpire, as the case may be, as absolutely final and conclusive in each case decided upon by them or him respectively.

Article 2. It is agreed by the high contracting parties that British subjects shall have, in common with the citizens of the United States, the liberty to take fish of every kind, except shell-fish, on the Eastern seacoasts and shores of the United States north of the 36th parallel of north latitude, and on the shores of the several islands thereunto adjacent, and in the bays, harbors, and creeks of the said seacoasts and shores of the United States and of the said islands, without being restricted to any distance from the shore, with permission to land upon the said coasts of the United States and of the islands aforesaid, for the purpose of drying their nets and curing their fish: provided that, in so doing, they do not interfere with the rights of private property, or with the fishermen of the United States in the peaceable use of any part of the said coasts in their occupancy for the same purpose.

It is understood that the above-mentioned liberty applies solely to the sea fishery, and that salmon and shad fisheries, and all fisheries in rivers and mouths of rivers, are hereby reserved, exclusively, for fishermen of the United States

Article 3. It is agreed that the articles enumerated in the schedule hereunto annexed, being the growth and produce of the aforesaid British colonies or of the United States, shall be admitted into each country respectively, free of duty.

Schedule of Articles free of Duty by Reciprocity Treaty with the British Provinces of N. A. and the United States.

GRAIN, FLOUR, and BREADSTUFFS OF all kinds.
ANIMALS of all kinds.
FRESH, SMOKED, and SALTED MEATS.
COTTON-WOOL, SEEDS, and VEGETABLES.
UNDRIED FRUITS, DRIED FRUITS.
FISH of all kinds.
PRODUCTS of FISH, and of all other creatures living in the water.
POULTRY, EGGS.
HIDES, FURS, SKINS, or TAILS, undressed.
STONE or MARBLE, in its crude or unwrought state.
SLATE.
BUTTER, CHEESE, TALLOW.
LARD, HORNS, MANURES.
ORES of METALS, of all kinds.
COAL.
PITCH, TAR, TURPENTINE, ASHES.
TIMBER and LUMBER of all kinds, round, hewed, and sawed, unmanufactured in whole or in part.
FIRE-WOOD.
PLANTS, SHRUBS, and TREES.
PELTS, WOOL.
FISH OIL.
RICE, BROOM-CORN, and BARK.
GYPSUM, ground or unground.
Hewn or wrought, or unwrought, BURR or GRINDSTONES.
DYE-STUFFS.
FLAX, HEMP, and TOW, unmanufactured.
UNMANUFACTURED TOBACCO.
RAGS.

ARTICLE 4. It is agreed that the citizens and inhabitants of the United States shall have the right to navigate the river St. Lawrence, and the canals in Canada used as the means of communicating between the great lakes and the Atlantic Ocean, with their vessels, boats, and crafts, as fully and freely as the subjects of her Britannic Majesty, subject only to the same tolls and other assessments as now are, or may hereafter be, exacted of her Majesty's said subjects; it being understood, however, that the British Government retains the right of suspending this privilege on giving due notice thereof to the Government of the United States.

It is further agreed, that if at any time the British Government should exercise the said reserved right, the Government of the United States shall have the right of suspending, if it think fit, the operation of article 3 of the present treaty, in so far as the province of Canada is affected thereby, for so long as the suspension of the free navigation of the river St. Lawrence or the canals may continue.

It is further agreed, that British subjects shall have the right freely to navigate Lake Michigan with their vessels, boats, and crafts, so long as the privilege of navigating the river St. Lawrence, secured to American citizens by the above clause of the present article, shall continue; and the Government of the United States further engages to urge upon the State Governments to secure to the subjects of her Britannic Majesty the use of the several State canals, on terms of equality with the inhabitants of the United States.

And it is further agreed, that no export duty, or other duty, shall be levied on lumber or timber of any kind cut on that portion of the American territory in the State of Maine watered by the river St. John and its tributaries, and floated down that river to the sea, when the same is shipped to the United States from the province of New Brunswick.

ARTICLE 5. The present treaty shall take effect as soon as the laws required to carry it into operation shall have been passed by the Imperial Parliament of Great Britain and by the Provincial Parliaments of those of the British North American colonies which are affected by this treaty on the one hand and by the Congress of the United States on the other. Such assent having been given, the treaty shall remain in force for ten years from the date at which it may come into operation, and further, until the expiration of twelve months after either of the high contracting parties shall give notice to the other of its wish to terminate the same; each of the high contracting parties being at liberty to give such notice to the other at the end of the said term of ten years, or at any time afterwards.

It is clearly understood, however, that this stipulation is not intended to affect the reservation made by article 4 of the present treaty, with regard to the right of temporarily suspending the operations of articles 3 and 4 thereof.

ARTICLE 6. And it is hereby further agreed, that the provisions and stipulations of the foregoing articles shall extend to the island of Newfoundland, so far as they are applicable to that colony. But if the Imperial Parliament, the Provincial Parliament of Newfoundland, or the Congress of the United States, shall not embrace in their laws, enacted for carrying this treaty into effect, the colony of Newfoundland, then this article shall be of no effect; but the omission to make provision by law to give it effect, by either of the legislative bodies aforesaid, shall not in any way impair the remaining articles of this treaty.

ARTICLE 7. The present treaty shall be duly ratified, and the mutual exchange of ratifications shall take place in Washington within six months from the date hereof, or earlier if possible.

In faith whereof, we, the respective plenipotentiaries, have signed this treaty, and have hereunto affixed our seals.

Done in triplicate, at Washington, the fifth day of June, Anno Domini one thousand eight hundred and fifty-four.

W. L. MARCY, [L. S.]
ELGIN AND KINCARDINE. [L. S.]

And whereas the said treaty has been duly ratified on both parts, and the respective ratifications of the same were exchanged in this city on the 9th instant, by William L. Marcy, Secretary of State of the United States, and John F. Crampton, Esq., her Britannic Majesty's Envoy Extraordinary and Minister Plenipotentiary to this Government, on the part of their respective Governments:

Now, therefore, be it known, that I, FRANKLIN PIERCE, President of the United States of America, have caused the said treaty to be made public, to the end that the same, and every clause and article thereof, may be observed and fulfilled with good faith by the United States and the citizens thereof.

In testimony whereof, I have hereunto set my hand and caused the seal of the United States to be affixed.

[L. S.] Done at the city of Washington, this eleventh day of September, in the year of our Lord one thousand eight hundred and fifty-four and of the independence of the United States the seventy-ninth
FRANKLIN PIERCE.

By the President:
W. L. MARCY, *Secretary of State.*

CHAPTER X.

REGULATIONS UNDER THE RECIPROCITY TREATY BETWEEN THE UNITED STATES AND GREAT BRITAIN, CONCLUDED JUNE 5, 1854.

SECTION I.

ARTICLES ENTITLED TO FREE ENTRY.

ART. 920. Under the treaty of reciprocity with Great Britain, concluded the 5th June, 1854, and promulgated by proclamation of the President on the 11th September, 1854, and 16th March, 1855, the following decisions in regard to the articles enumerated, imported from the British provinces of *Canada, New Brunswick, Nova Scotia, Prince Edward's Island,* and *Newfoundland* and its dependencies, will govern in the practice of the several ports of the United States, in view of the provisions of said treaty, and the acts of Congress to carry it into effect, namely: in regard to fish of all kinds from any one of the enumerated provinces, imported after the 11th September, 1854, the date of the President's first proclamation; and in respect to all the other articles contained in the list appended to the treaty, imported subsequently to the date of the acceptance of said treaty by each of the provinces respectively, viz.:

By Canada, from and after October 18, 1854.
New Brunswick, from and after November 11, 1854.
Prince Edward's Island, from and after November 17, 1854.
Nova Scotia, from and after December 15, 1854.
Newfoundland, from and after November 14, 1855.

Hudson's Bay Company or Prince Rupert's Land is not comprehended among the provinces or colonies referred to in the treaty.

Articles entitled to free entry.

Animals of all kinds.
Ashes, comprehending pot and pearl ashes, black salts and salts of ley.
Bags, barrels, or other original packages, containing flour, wheat, or other

free products; provided the article so contained is not usually imported in bulk, and the envelope is appropriate and ordinarily used in the conveyance of such articles. In cases where the character of the package may induce reasonable suspicion of an intent to evade the payment of the duties imposed by law, the collector will make seizure of the same, and report the facts to this department.

Barley.
Bark of hemlock or trees.
Beams, when rough hewn, or sawed only.
Beans.
Boards, when rough hewn or sawed only.
Bran.
Breadstuffs, of all kinds, not further manufactured than flour or meal.
Broom corn.
Burr stones, hewn or wrought, or unwrought.
Butter.
Canada Balsam, collected from a species of the pine tree, as turpentine.
Castoreum, a product of the beaver.
Cattle tails, if undressed.
Cheese.
Clap boards, if rough hewn or sawed only.
Coal.
Corn, Indian, or maize.
Cotton wool.
Dried fruits.
Dye Stuffs.
Fish, of all kinds, products of fish, and of all other creatures living in the water; the exemption from duty to extend to the fisheries of Newfoundland and Labrador.
Fish, wholly or partly cooked, in cans hermetically sealed.
Fire-wood.
Flax, unmanufactured.
Flour, of all kinds.
Fresh meats.
Fruits, dried or undried.
Fruits, preserved, in cans, hermetically sealed.
Furs, undressed.
Grain, of all kinds.
Grindstones, hewn or wrought, or unwrought.
Gypsum, ground, or unground.
Hair, on the hide or skin, or tail thereof, undressed.
Hemp, unmanufactured.
Hides, undressed.
Horns.
Horn tips

Hubs, for wheels, if rough hewn or sawed only.
Knees for vessels, do. do. do.
Lasts for vessels, do. do. do.
Last blocks, do. do. do.
Laths, do. do. do.
Lard.
Linseed.
Lumber, of all kinds, round, rough hewn, or sawed only.
Manures.
Marble, in its crude or unwrought state.
Meal, of all kinds.
Meats, fresh, smoked, or salted.
Meats, wholly or partly cooked, preserved without oil or spirits, in cans hermetically sealed.
Middlings (as flour.)
Mill feed (as flour.)
Nuts.
Oats.
Oat meal.
Oil, from fish.
Ores, of metals, of all kinds.
Palings, pickets, posts, &c., if rough hewn or sawed only.
Pates, or scraps of raw hides or skins.
Pearl and pot ash.
aPes.
Pelts.
Pitch.
Plants.
Potatoes.
Poultry.
Poultry, cooked wholly or partly, preserved in cans hermetically sealed.
Products of fish, and all other creatures living in the water.
Provender, from wheat or other grain.
Rags.
Railroad ties, rough hewn or sawed only.
Raw hides and skins, or parts thereof.
Rice.
Rotten wood.
Salted meats.
Salts of ley and black salts, (see Ashes.)
Sausages and sausage meat.
Saw-logs.
Scantling, rough hewn or sawed only.
Screenings from grain.
Seeds.

Shingles, rough hewn or sawed only.
Shingle bolts, do. do.
Shingle wood, do. do.
Shipstuffs, as breadstuffs.
Shrubs.
Skins, or tails, undressed.
Skins, or parts thereof, undressed.
Slate.
Spars, round and sawed only.
Spokes of wheels, if rough hewn or sawed only.
Stone, in its crude, or unmanufactured state.
Tails, undressed.
Tallow.
Tar.
Timber, of all kinds, round, rough hewn, or sawed only.
Tobacco, unmanufactured.
Tow, do.
Trees.
Turpentine.
Vegetables.
Vegetables, wholly or partly cooked, preserved in cans hermetically sealed.
Venison.
Wool, unmanufactured.

SECTION II.

Art. 921.—ARTICLES LIABLE TO DUTY UNDER THE EXISTING REVENUE LAWS.

Axle trees, for carriages, (see Timber and Lumber.)
Beams, (see Timber and Lumber.)
Bears' grease.
Beeswax.
Boards, (see Timber and Lumber.)
Biscuit.
Bread.
Cakes.
Clapboards, (see Timber and Lumber.)
Felloes for wheels, (see Timber and Lumber.)
Grease, of all kinds, except butter, tallow and lard.
Gunpowder.
Gypsum, calcined.
Hay.
Hops.
Iron, in pigs and blooms.

Hubs for wheels,
Knees for vessels,
Laths,
Lasts,
Last blocks,
(See Timber and Lumber.)

Lime.
Malt.
Milk.
Mineral water of St. Catherine's
Oil cake.
Plaster of Paris, calcined.

Palings,
Pickets,
Posts,
Railroad ties,
Scantlings,
Shingles,
Shingle bolts,
Shingle wood,
Spars,
Spokes for wheels,
(See Timber and Lumber.

Spirits of turpentine.

Timber and lumber.—Articles of wood entered under these or any other designations, remain liable to duty under the existing tariff, if manufactured in whole or in part by planing, shaving, turning, splitting, or riving, or any process of manufacture other than rough hewing or sawing.

GENERAL INFORMATION.

ADDITIONAL, OR PENAL DUTY, of 20 per cent. ad valorem, provided, in certain cases, by the 8th section of the Tariff Act of 1846, to be exacted and paid before the delivery of goods for consumption, or their being withdrawn from the warehouse for transportation or exportation. In no case to be returned as debenture.

ADDITIONS TO ENTRIES of purchased goods, under the 8th section of the Tariff Act of 30th July, 1846. Where goods have been actually purchased, the law requires the invoice to state the true *cost*, and not the market value abroad; on which value, with certain added charges, the duties are to be assessed. The privilege, therefore, given in the 8th section of the act referred to, is to enable importers of any goods that have been actually purchased, on making entry of the same, to add to the cost given in the invoice, to bring it up to the *true market value abroad*, and by so doing, exempt the goods from the additional duty imposed by said section. The additions contemplated by the law in such cases must take place at the time of making entry, and cannot be allowed at any subsequent period.—*Circular, October* 12, 1849.

ALLOWANCE.—Under the provisions of the 52d section of the general collection law of 2d March, 1799, *allowance for damage* may still be made on the articles mentioned in the 58th and 59th sections of that act, now subject to ad valorem rates of duty, under the tariff of 1846; the *deficiency, leakage* or *breakage*, being taken into consideration by the appraisers, as among the elements of *actual damage* to be ascertained by them, in the manner prescribed in *Circular instructions of* 25*th November*, 1846.

Where claims are made for damage on certain liquors *in bottles*, under the 59th section of the Act of March, 1799—unless the importer at the time of entry, shall in the exercise of the option given by said section, prefer that the actual quantity be ascertained by tale—the allowance for breakage shall in no case exceed the per centage provided by said section, in such cases, namely, of *ten per cent.* on beer, ale, and porter, and *five per cent.* on all other liquors.—*Circular, December* 31*st*, 1847.

ALLOWANCE ON ABATEMENT OF DUTIES, under the last *proviso* of the 21st section of the Tariff Act of 30th August, 1842, for *deficiency of articles in packages*, can only take place where it shall satisfactorily appear to the appraisers that the packages had not been opened *after their shipment.*

Such *allowance or abatement*, on separate articles or packages, included in the manifest, but not found on board the vessel at the time of unlading the same in the United States, cannot be made, unless satisfactory proof be adduced, that, by accident or other cause, such articles or packages had never been actually shipped; or that being shipped, they had been actually lost or destroyed by accident or other cause during the voyage, *and before the arrival of the vessel within the limits of any collection district of the United States.—Circular, December* 31, 1847.

Applications for allowance for damage must be sworn to before a Deputy Collector, and lodged in Liquidating Department, Custom House, within ten working days from landing of the merchandise.

DAMAGE incurred in lading merchandise on board the vessel at a foreign port of shipment, not to be considered as having occurred "during the voyage."

Damage must be ascertained at the port of the United States where the vessel originally enters, and cannot be certified from any other port to which the goods may be conveyed.—*See Circular*, 25*th November*, 1846.

Damage—The proof required before appraisement will be a certificate under oath of owner, consignee, agent, or other reliable person, after personal inspection of the vessel and cargo, of their belief of the existence of damage.—*Circular, February* 1, 1849.

DISCOUNT.—Never to be allowed in any case, except on articles where its has been the uniform and established usage heretofore; and never more than the actual discount, positively known to the appraisers.—*Circular*, 25*th November*, 1846.

Not to be allowed unless exhibited on the invoice; but if appearing on the invoice, although not deducted from the foot of the same, to be allowed.

DRUGS.—Essential oils and medicinal preparations found on examination by the appraisers, to be *deteriorated, adulterated, or inferior in strength and purity,* to be exported within six months, or the collector to cause them to be destroyed. —*Circular, July* 8, 1848.

ENTRY cannot be made for warehouse, when no invoice accompanies the importation.—*Circular, October* 12*th*, 1849.

FEES.—When goods are withdrawn from warehouse in quantities less than the entire importation, the expense of weighing, gauging, or measuring must be paid by the owner, importer, or agent, if it be necessary to weigh, gauge or measure such portion, in order to ascertain the dutiable value.—*Circular, October* 30*th*, 1846.

INVOICE or entry to contain the weight, quantity or measure of goods, or the same to be weighed, gauged or measured at the expense of the importer.—*Act* 30*th July*, 1846, *Sec.* 4.

Fire Insurance on goods for any period prior to their shipment for the United States, is to be included in such charges.—*Circular, December* 31*st*, 1847.

No REFINED LUMP OR LOAF SUGAR can be imported into the United States except in ships or vessels of at least 120 tons burthen, and in packages containing at least 600 lbs., under the penalty of forfeiting the same, together with the ship or vessel.—*Act of* 2*d March*, 1799, *Section* 103.

DRAWBACK ON REFINED SUGARS exported, 1½ cent per pound.—*Circular, September* 29*th*, 1848.

No DISTILLED SPIRITS, except arrack, brandy in casks of no less capacity than fifteen gallons, and sweet cordial, can be imported in casks or vessels of less capacity than ninety gallons, wine measure, nor in casks which have been marked pursuant to any law of the United States, on pain of forfeiture of the same, together with the ship or vessel in which they were imported.—*Act of* 2*d March*, 1799, *Section* 103.

Brandies and spirituous liquors may be imported in bottles, if in packages containing not less than one dozen each.

No drawback allowed on Pickled Fish, of the fisheries of the United States, except the value of the foreign salt with which the same is cured.—*Act* 30*th July*, 1846, *Section* 5.

No BEER, ALE, or PORTER, can be imported in casks or vessels of less capacity than forty gallons, beer measure; or if in bottles, in packages containing less than six dozen, under the penalty of forfeiting the same, together with the ship or vessel in which they were imported.—*Act of* 2*d March*, 1799, *Section* 103.

No goods, wares, or merchandise, subject to duty, can be imported into the United States, on the seaboard, in vessels of less than 30 tons burthen, under the penalty of the forfeiture of vessel and cargo.—*Act of* 2*d March*, 1799, 92*d Section*

In all cases where there are more goods found on board a vessel than the master thereof has reported in his manifest, he shall, with the consent of the officers of customs, make a post entry for the same, and pay two dollars therefor; and for every disagreement between his manifest and cargo he is liable to a fine of five hundred dollars.—*Act of 2d March*, 1799, *Section* 57.

The number of bushels of wheat is to be ascertained by actual *measuremen* by the standard bushel, and not by weight.

COAL, Pictou measure, 20 per cent. excess allowed.

Within *twenty* days after the clearance of a vessel, the exporter of goods by said vessel must swear to the export entry, and give a bond that they shall not be landed in any place or port within the limits of the United States, *or forfeit the drawback.—Act of March* 2*d*, 1823.

REGISTER ACT.

Every owner of a vessel, residing within the limits of the United States, to swear (or affirm) to the register within ninety days after its being granted, or it becomes void, and the vessel and cargo pays foreign tonnage and duty.

AN ACT

For the allowance of drawback on foreign merchandise imported into certain districts of the United States from the British North American Provinces, and exported to foreign countries.

Be it enacted by the Senate and House of Representatives of the United States of America, in Congress assembled, That any merchandise imported from the British North American Provinces adjoining the United States, which shall have been duly entered, and the duties thereon paid or secured according to law, at either of the ports of entry in the collection districts situated in the northern, north-eastern, and north-western frontiers of the United States, may be transported by land or by water, or partly by land and partly by water, to any port or ports from which merchandise may, under existing laws, be exported for the benefit of drawback, and be thence exported with such privilege to any foreign country: Provided, That such exportations shall be made within one year from the date of importation of said merchandise, and that existing laws relating to the transportation of merchandise entitled to drawback, from one district to another, or to two other districts, and the due exportation and proof of landing thereof, and all regulations which the Secretary of the Treasury may prescribe for the security of the revenue, shall be complied with.

Approved August 8th, 1846.

List of the States at present composing the German Zoll-Verein.

The kingdom of..........................Prussia.
The kingdom of..........................Bavaria.
The kingdom of..........................Hanover.
The kingdom of..........................Saxony.
The kingdom of..........................Wirtemberg.
The Grand Duchy of......................Baden.
The Grand Duchy of......................Oldenburg.

The Grand Duchy of........................Luxemburg.
The Grand Duchy of........................Saxe-Weimar-Eisenach.
The Grand Duchy of........................Hesse (Darmstadt.)
The Electorate of (Curfürstenthum) of........Hesse (Cassel.)
The Duchy of.............................Brunswick.
The Duchy of.............................Nassau.
The Duchy of.............................Saxe Meiningen.
The Duchy of.............................Saxe Altenburg.
The Duchy of.............................Saxe Coburg-Gotha.
The Duchy of.............................Anhalt-Bernburg-Cöthen and Dessau.
The Principality (Landgrafschaft) of..........Hesse Homburg.
The Principality (Türstenthum) of............Schwartzburg-Rudolstadt.
The Principality of.........................Schwartzburg-Sondershausen.
The Principality of.........................Reuss-Griez.
The Principality of.........................Reuss-Schleiz-Lobenstein.
The Principality of.........................Ebersdorf
The Principality of.........................Waldeck.
The free town of............................Frankfort (on the Mayn.)

AN ACT

To authorize the importation of brandy in casks of a capacity not less than fifteen gallons, and the exportation of the same for the benefit of a drawback of the duties.

Be it enacted by the Senate and House of Representatives of the United States of America, in Congress assembled, That from and after the passage of this act, brandy may be imported into the United States in casks of a capacity of not less than fifteen gallons, anything in any law to the contrary notwithstanding: *Provided,* however, that all the provisions of existing laws, not inconsistent with this act, relating to the importation of foreign spirits, be complied with: *And provided further,* That all brandy imported in casks, of a capacity less than 90 gallons, shall be deposited, at the expense and risk of the importer, in such public or other warehouses, as shall be designated by the collector or surveyor for the port, where the same shall be landed; and shall be removed therefrom in the manner prescribed by an act entitled "An act providing for the deposit of wines and distilled spirits in public warehouses, and for other purposes."

Approved 2d March, 1827.

EXTRACTS FROM LAWS RELATIVE TO INVOICES.

Act of March 3, 1801. § 2.—Invoices must be made out in the currency of the country from whence the goods are imported.

Treasury Instructions, April 4, 1840.—When the value of such currency is not fixed by law, the invoice must be accompanied by a consular certificate, stating the true value of such currency in Spanish or United States silver dollars, and in default thereof bond for the production of such certificates is to be given.

Act of 1st *of March*, 1823, § 2.—If no invoice of goods has been received by the consignee or owner, they may be entered by appraisement, the owner or consignee first taking oath that no invoice has been received, and giving bond to produce invoice.

§ 6.—Goods belonging to persons residing in the United States, but absent from place of importation, may be admitted to entry, the importer or agent first giving bond to produce invoice duly verified by the oath of the owner, administered by a collector of the customs, or by a public officer duly authorized to administer oaths.

§ 7.—Goods belonging to a person not residing at the time in the United States, cannot be admitted to entry, unless accompanied by an invoice verified by the owner's oath, stating that the goods were actually purchased for his account, and that the invoice contains a true and faithful account of the *cost* of such goods.

§ 8.—If such goods have not been acquired in the usual mode, of bargain and sale; or if they belong in whole or in part to the manufacturer thereof, the oath annexed to invoice must specify that the invoice contains the actual *fair market value* at the time and place when and where the same were procured or manufactured.

The verification may be made before a consul or commercial agent of the United States; if there is no consul or commercial agent in the country, or place of purchase, the oath may be administered by any public officer authorized in such place to administer oaths, which authority must be authenticated by a consul or commercial agent of the United States; if there be no such consul or agent, then by the authentication of a consul of any nation at peace with the United States; if no such consul can be found, then the certificate of two respectable merchants will answer.

§ 10.—Goods owned by persons not residing in the United States, and not accompanied with an invoice verified as required above, *may be* admitted to entry by the *Secretary of the Treasury*, the collector first certifying that no fraud was intended; but before such entry shall be permitted, the importer shall give bonds to produce an invoice of such goods, duly verified by the owner, in the mode and to the effect before mentioned.

The owner, consignee, or agent of imports on entry of the same, to make such addition in the entry to the cost or value given in the invoice as in his opinion may raise the same to the true market value of such imports in the principal markets of the country whence the importation shall have been made, or in which the goods imported shall have been originally manufactured or produced, as the case may be.—*Act 30th July*, 1846, *Section* 8

AN ACT

Explanatory of an Act entitled "An Act making appropriations for the civil and diplomatic expenses of the Government for the year one thousand eight hun dred and thirty-nine."

SEC. 1. Be it enacted by the Senate and House of Representatives of the United States of America, in Congress assembled, That nothing contained in the second section of the act entitled "An Act making appropriations for the civil and diplomatic expenses of Government for the year one thousand eight hundred and thirty-nine," approved on the third day of March, one thousand eight hundred and thirty-nine, shall take away, or be construed to take away or impair, the right of any person or persons, who have paid or shall hereafter pay money, as and for duties, under protest, to any collector of the customs, or other persons acting as such, in order to obtain goods, wares and merchandise, imported by him or them, or on his or their account, which duties are not authorized or payable in part or in whole by law, to maintain any action at law against such collector, or other person acting as such, to ascertain and try the legality and validity of such demand and payment of duties, and to have a right to a trial by jury touching the same, according to the due course of law. Nor shall anything contained in the second section of the act aforesaid be construed to authorize the Secretary of the Treasury to refund any duties paid under protest, nor shall any action be maintained against any collector, to recover the amount of duties so paid under protest, unless the said protest was made in writing and signed by the claimant, at or before the payment of said duties, setting forth distinctly and specifically the grounds of objection to the payment thereof.

Approved, February 26, 1845.

Form of Protest.

To —— ——, COLLECTOR.

SIR: We do hereby protest against the payment of (state the rate) charged on (enumerate the article) contained in this entry, claiming, that under existing laws said goods are *only* liable to a duty of (state the rate claimed) be cause (state the reason), we pay the amount exacted in order to get possession of the goods, and claim to have the difference refunded.

New-York, 18 (Signed.)

Form of Consular Certificate of the Value of Currency.

I, A B, consul of the United States of America, do hereby certify that the true value of the currency of the kingdom of ———, in which currency the annexed invoice of merchandise is made out, is —— cents, estimated in United States or Spanish silver dollars.

(Signed.) A B.

Gunpowder and Fire-crackers, how to be Exported.

549. Gunpowder, fire-crackers, and other explosive substances, the deposit of which in any public or private bonded warehouse is prohibited by law, may be entered, on arrival from a foreign port, for immediate exportation in bond by sea, it being understood that the warehouse and export entries shall be made simultaneously, and the articles transferred directly from the vessels in which imported to the vessel in which the exportation is to be made. Fire-crackers, securely cased, may also be entered for immediate transportation from one port to another, either by sea or inland, for the purpose of being immediately exported under the rule before provided, from such second port, but in no case to be actually warehoused; and should entry for exportation not be made on arrival at second port, the collector will cause the same to be sold, as in case of failure to enter at port of original importation.

REGULATIONS IN REGARD TO MERCHANDISE IN TRANSIT FROM ONE PORT OF THE UNITED STATES TO ANOTHER, OVER FOR EIGN TERRITORY.

Routes and regulations for transportation of merchandise from one port to another in the United States through Canada.

ART. 953. Merchandise may be transported in bond from the Atlantic ports of the United States, by way of Ogdensburg, Oswego, and Buffalo, and the Collingwood railway between Toronto and Collingwood, in Canada, to the warehousing ports of the United States on Lakes Huron and Michigan, and, also, over the route by way of Ogdensburgh to Hamilton and Niagara, in Canada, connecting with the Great Western railway to Detroit, under the same conditions as those prescribed in Article 451 of these regulations in regard to merchandise passing through a portion of Canada over the Great Western railway.

Companies to give bond.

956. The companies owning the roads or lines must enter into bond, to be approved by the Department, for the safe custody of the merchandise shipped or transported by their lines and placed under customs lock, and two or more competent persons must be appointed and sworn as inspectors of the customs to retain the custody of the goods in transit, and see that they are properly delivered at the port of destination.

Inspector to have custody of goods on the route.

Penalty for Smuggling Goods Subject to Duty into the United States, or for attempting to Pass a Fraudulent Invoice. Sec. 19, Act August 30, 1842.

The 19th section of the tariff act of the 30th August, 1842, provides that if any person shall, knowingly and wilfully, with intent to defraud the revenue of the United States, smuggle or clandestinely introduce into the United States, any goods, wares, or merchandise, subject to duty by law, and which should have been invoiced, without paying or accounting for the duty, or shall make out or pass, or attempt to pass, through the customhouse, any false, forged, or fraudulent invoice, such person, and all aiders or abettors, shall be deemed guilty of a misdemeanor, and, on conviction thereof, shall be fined in any sum not exceeding five thousand dollars, or imprisoned for any term of time not exceeding two years, or both, at the discretion of the court.

Sampling, Packing, and Repacking.

646. All merchandise in public or private bonded warehouses, duly entered for warehousing, may be examined at any time during the business hours of the port by the importer, consignee, or agent, who shall have liberty to take samples of his goods in quantities according to the usage of the port; make all needful repairs of packages, and to repack the same, provided the original contents are placed in the new package, and the original marks and numbers placed thereon, in the mode prescribed in

the 75th section of the act of 2d March, 1799, and 32d section, act of 1st March, 1823; provided, that no samples shall be taken, nor shall any goods be exhibited or examined unless under the immediate supervision of an officer of the customs, and by order of the importer, owner, or consignee, at his expense; nor shall any package be repaired, or goods repacked, without a written order from the collector of the port.

Dutiable Value of Imports.

299. The value upon which duties are to be assessed is thus established to be: **Value of which duties are to be assessed.**

First. The actual market value or wholesale price of the merchandise in the principal markets of the country from which it was imported into the United States, at the date of exportation, to be ascertained by appraisement.

Second. All costs and charges, except insurance, and including, in every case, a charge for commissions at the usual rates, to be ascertained and added to the value found by appraisement, by the collector and naval officer, or the collector alone at ports where there is no naval officer.

300. The term "country," as used in the law, is to be regarded as embracing all the possessions of a nation, however widely separated, which are subject to the same supreme executive and legislative authority and control. Accordingly, where duties were assessed on merchandise imported from Halifax, on its general market value in Liverpool, at the date of its exportation from Halifax to the United States, the action of the Department was sustained by the Supreme Court of the United States; Liverpool being, in the opinion of the appraisers, a principal market of Great Britain for the merchandise in that case. **Definition of the term "country." Stairs and others vs. Peaslee, Howard's Reports, v. 18, p. 522.**

301. What are to be regarded as the "principal markets" of a country, in any given case, is for the determination of the appraisers. It is a question of fact, not of law; and the decision of the appraisers is conclusive upon the government and the importer. **Definition of the terms "principal markets." Stairs vs. Peaslee, 18 Howard's Reports, p. 522.**

302. The "period of exportation," where the merchandise is laden on board a vessel in the shipping port of the country of origin, or in which it was purchased or procured for shipment to an owner, consignee, or agent, residing in the United States, must be deemed and taken to be the date at which the vessel actually leaves the foreign port for her destination in the United States. **Definition of "period of exportation."**

That period may ordinarily be established by the production of the clearance granted to the vessel at the foreign port of departure, and the declaration of the master, under oath, at the time of entry, of the date when the vessel sailed. **How established**

303. Merchandise from an interior country, having no shipping **Date of exporta-**

tion of merchandise from countries having no shipping ports.

ports of her own, through the ports of another country, as from Switzerland, for example, destined for the United States by way of Havre, is considered as *exported*, within the meaning of the law, when it passes the frontier boundary between France and Switzerland, on such destination.

Foreign market value, and cost and charges in such cases.

The wholesale price or general market value of such merchandise in the principal markets of the interior country at the date when it passed the frontier for its destination in the United States, will, on importation and entry, be ascertained by the appraisers with a view to the assessment of duty; and to the value so ascertained will be added the cost of transportation, and other expenses, to the frontier, as dutiable charges.

"Date of exportation" from interior country to be proved.

Satisfactory proof of the date of exportation from such interior country must be exhibited on the entry.

Secondary evidence.

304. In the absence, satisfactorily explained, of the proofs above indicated, showing the date of exportation from the foreign country, or in addition thereto, other evidence of that fact, such as letters of advice, entries in the vessel's log-book or journal, or testimony of witnesses, may be taken into consideration by the appraisers.

Costs and charges to be added to foreign actual market value. Sec. 16, Act Aug. 30, 1842.

305. The law requires that there shall be added to the "actual market value or wholesale price" of imports, ascertained as above, in order to fix the dutiable value, "all costs and charges, except insurance, and including in every case a charge for commissions at the usual rates."

306. These charges are:

First. The expenses of putting up and packing, together with the value of the sack, package, box, crate, hogshead, barrel, bale, cask, can, bottles, jars, vessels, and demijohns, and coverings of all kinds.

Second. Commissions must in every case be made a dutiable charge at the usual rates, but never less than 2½ per cent., without the special sanction of the Department, nor less than is stated in the invoice. If it appear on the face of the invoice or entry at less than the usual rate, it must be advanced to that rate for the ascertainment of dutiable value. Where there is a distinct brokerage, or where brokerage is a usual charge at the place of shipment or purchase, that is to be added likewise. Commissions on the amount of *shipping charges* at the foreign port of exportation constitute one of the charges liable to duty under existing laws and instructions.

Third. Export duty, as on silks from China, storage at the foreign shipping ports, cost of putting cargoes on board ship including drayage, labor, bill of lading, lighterage, town dues, and shipping charges, dock or wharf dues, and all charges to place the articles on ship-board, and fire insurance, if effected for a period prior to the shipment of goods to the United States.

Marine insurance is not to be treated as a dutiable charge.

Marine insurance, and cost of transportation from port of exportation, to be excluded as dutiable charges.

Freight, or cost of transportation, from the foreign port of exportation, is not a dutiable charge.

Merchandise passing through ports of an intermediate country on a destination for the United States.

307. In the case of merchandise arriving in the United States, after having been transported from the country of its production, manufacture, or procurement, to another country, by land or water, and the collector of the customs at the port of importation, shall be satisfied by the evidence adduced, that the merchandise was originally exported with a *bona fide* intention of having it transported to a port in the United States as its final port of destination, no dutiable costs or charges will have accrued, either on the transportation from the first to the intermediate port, or while remaining in or leaving the latter, the voyage or transportation being regarded as continuous from the country whence originally exported in good faith, on a declared destination for a port and parties in the United States.

Illustrations of the regulation.

In illustration of this rule, it may be remarked, that the evidence of final destination being satisfactory, no duties would be chargeable in ports of the United States on the freight, or transportation, or charges in the intermediate ports, on goods originally from China to Liverpool, from Malaga to Valparaiso, from Dresden to Bremen, or from Basle to Havre, on the said goods being transhipped for the United States from the several intermediate ports enumerated.

Fees to be received.

593. The following is the list of fees required by law to be paid at the several custom-houses, and no other fees shall be received than those here specially enumerated

For admeasuring every vessel, in order to the enrolment, or licensing and recording the same, if of 5 tons and less than 20	$0 50
Of 20 and not over 70	75
Over 70 and not over 100	1 00
Over 100 tons	1 50
For certificate of enrolment	50
Endorsement on certificate of enrolment	20
License, and granting the same, including bond, if not over 20 tons	25
Above 20 and not over 100	50
Over 100 tons	1 00
Endorsement on a license	20
Certifying manifest, and granting permit for licensed vessels to go from district to district, under 50 tons	25
Over 50 tons	50

Receiving certified manifest, and granting permit on arrival of such vessel, if under 50 tons	$0 25
Over fifty tons	50
For certifying manifest, and granting permission to registered vessels to go from district to district	1 50
Receiving certified manifest, and granting permit on arrival of such registered vessel	1 50
Granting permit to a vessel, not belonging to a citizen of the United States, to go from district to district, and receiving manifest	2 00
Receiving manifest and granting permit to unload for last-mentioned vessel, on arrival at one district from another	2 00
Granting permit for vessel carrying on fishery to trade at a foreign port	25
Report and entry of foreign goods imported in such vessel	25
Entry of vessel of 100 tons and more	2 50
Clearance of vessel of 100 tons and more	2 50
Entry of vessel under 100 tons	1 50
Clearance of ditto	1 50
Post entry	2 00
Permit to land or deliver goods	20
Bond taken officially	40
Permit to load goods for exportation entitled to drawback	30
Debenture or other official certificate	20
Bill of health	20
Official documents, except register, required by any merchant, owner, or master of any vessel not before enumerated	20
Admeasurement, and certifying vessels of 100 tons and under	1 cent per ton.
Over 100 and not over 200	1 50
Over 200	2 00
Other services to be performed by the surveyor, in vessels of 100 tons and more, having on board merchandise subject to duty	3 00
For like services in vessels under 100 tons, having similar merchandise	1 50
All vessels not having merchandise subject to duty	66⅔
Protection	25
Crew list	5

Certificate of registry and bond.............	$2 25
Endorsement on register...................	1 00
General permit to ship, to land passengers' baggage...............................	20

Weighing: 1⅞ cent per 112 pounds. Gauging: Casks, 12 cents each; cases and baskets, 4½ cents each. Ale, porter, &c., 1½ cent per dozen bottles. Measuring: Coal, 90 cents per 100 bushels; chalk, brimstone, &c., 90 cents per 100 bushels; salt, 75 cents per 100 bushels; potatoes, seeds, grain, and all other measurable articles, 45 cents per 100 bushels. Marble, mahogany, cedar-wood, &c., the actual expense incurred.	When invoice does not contain the weight, measure, or gauge of merchandise, required to be weighed, measured or gauged, and when goods are withdrawn from warehouse in less quantity than the entire importation, as per article 541 of these regulations.

For licenses to steamers, as a compensation for the inspections and examinations made for the year, under the steamboat law approved August 30, 1852, in addition to the fees above mentioned for issuing enrolments and licenses to vessels:

For each vessel of a thousand tons and over..........	$35 00
For each of five hundred tons and over, but less than one thousand.....................................	30 00
For each under five hundred tons and over one hundred and twenty-five tons............................	25 00
For each under one hundred and twenty-five tons.....	20 00
For the first certificate granted by any inspector or inspectors to each engineer and pilot...............	1 00
For each subsequent certificate......................	1 00
For recording all bills of sale, mortgages, hypothecations, or conveyance of vessels, under act of July 29, 1850...	0 50
For recording all certificates for discharging and cancelling any such conveyances...................	50
For furnishing a certificate setting forth the names of the owners of any registered or enrolled vessel, the parts or proportions owned by each, and also the material facts of any existing bill of sale, mortgage, hypothecation, or other incumbrance, the date, amount of such incumbrance, and from and to whom made...	1 00
For furnishing copies of such records, for each bill of sale, mortgage, or other conveyance...............	50

AN ACT

To amend the Acts regulating the Appraisement of Imported Merchandise, and for other purposes.

Be it enacted by the Senate and House of Representatives of the United States of America, in Congress assembled, That in all cases where there is or shall be imposed any ad-valorem rate of duty on any goods, wares, or merchandise imported into the United States, it shall be the duty of the Collector within whose district the same shall be imported or entered, to cause the actual market value or wholesale price thereof, at the period of the exportation to the United States, in the principal markets of the country from which the same shall have been imported into the United States, to be appraised, estimated, and ascertained; and to such value or price shall be added all costs and charges, except insurance, and including, in every case, a charge for commissions at the usual rates, at the true value at the port where the same may be entered upon which duties shall be assessed.

Sec. 2. And be it further enacted, That the certificate of any one of the appraisers of the United States, of the dutiable value of any imported merchandise required to be appraised, shall be deemed and taken to be the appraisement of such merchandise required by existing laws to be made by such appraisers. And where merchandise shall be entered at ports where there are no appraisers, the certificate of the revenue officer to whom is committed the estimating and collection of duties, of the dutiable value of any merchandise required to be appraised, shall be deemed and taken to be the appraisement of such merchandise required by existing laws to be made by such revenue officer.

Sec. 3. And be it further enacted, That there shall be appointed by the President of the United States, by and with the advice and consent of the Senate, four appraisers of merchandise, to be allowed an annual salary each of two thousand five hundred dollars, together with their actual travelling expenses, to be regulated by the Secretary of the Treasury, who shall be employed in visiting such ports of entry in the United States, under the direction of the said Secretary, as may be deemed useful by him for the security of the revenue, and shall at such ports afford such aid and assistance in the appraisement of merchandise thereat as may be deemed necessary by the Secretary of the Treasury, to protect and insure uniformity in the collection of the revenue from Customs; and wherever practicable, in cases of appeal from the decision of the United States' appraisers, under the provisions of the seventeenth section of the Tariff Act of the thirtieth August, eighteen hundred and forty-two, the Collector shall select one discreet and experienced merchant, to be associated with one of the appraisers appointed under the provisions of this Act, who, together, shall appraise the goods in question; and if they shall disagree, the Collector shall decide between them; and the appraisement thus determined shall be final, and deemed and taken to be the true value of said goods, and the duties shall be levied thereon accordingly, any Act of Congress to the contrary notwithstanding.

SEC. 4. And be it further enacted, That this Act shall take effect on and after the first day of April next; and all Acts and parts of Acts inconsistent with the provisions of this Act, be and the same are hereby repealed.

Approved, March 3, 1851.

ACT OF MARCH 3, 1797.

An Act to provide for mitigating or remitting the Forfeitures, Penalties, and Disabilities, accruing in Certain Cases therein mentioned.

Persons subject to fine, forfeiture, or penalty, under law, relating to revenue, registering, recording, enrolling, or licensing vessels may apply for mitigation or remission to Secretary of the Treasury through the district courts. Manner of application. Secretary empowered to remit, &c.—when.

§ 1. Be it enacted, &c., That whenever any person, or persons who shall have incurred any fine, penalty, forfeiture, or disability, or shall have been interested in any vessel, goods, wares, or merchandise, which shall have been subject to any seizure, forfeiture, or disability, by force of any present or future law of the United States, for the laying, levying, or collecting, any duties or taxes, or by force of any present or future act, concerning the registering and recording of ships or vessels, or any act concerning the enrolling and licensing ships or vessels employed in the coasting trade or fisheries, and for regulating the same, shall prefer his petition to the judge of the district in which such fine, penalty, forfeiture, or disability, shall have accrued, truly and particularly setting forth the circumstances of his case, and shall pray that the same may be mitigated or remitted, the said judge shall inquire, in a summary manner, into the circumstances of the case; first causing reasonable notice to be given to the person or persons claiming such fine, penalty, or forfeiture, and to the attorney of the United States for such district, that each may have an opportunity of showing cause against the mitigation or remission thereof; and shall cause the facts, which shall appear upon such inquiry, to be stated and annexed to the petition, and direct their transmission to the Secretary of the Treasury of the United States, who shall thereupon have power to mitigate or remit such fine, forfeiture, or penalty, or remove such disability, or any part thereof, if, in his opinion, the same shall have been incurred without wilful negligence, or any intention of fraud, in the person or persons incurring the same; and to direct the prosecution, if any shall have been instituted for the recovery thereof, to cease and be discontinued, upon such terms or conditions as he may deem reasonable and just.

Certain State courts invested with like power as district judges.

§ 2. That the judicial courts of the several States, to whom by any of the said acts a jurisdiction is given, shall and may exercise all and every power in the cases cognizable before them for the purpose of obtaining a mitigation, or remission, of any fine, penalty, or forfeiture, which may be exercised by the judges of the district courts in cases depending before them.

Reservation of right of informer.

§ 3. That nothing herein contained shall be construed to affect the right or claim of any person to that part of any fine, penalty or forfeiture, incurred by the breach of any of the laws aforesaid which such person shall or may be entitled to by virtue of the said laws, in cases where a prosecution has been commenced, or information has been given, before the passing of this act, or any other act relative to the mitigation or remission of such fines, penalties, or forfeitures; the amount of which right and claim shall be assessed and valued by the proper judge, or court, in a summary manner.

Limitation of this act.

§ 4. That this act shall continue in force for the term of two years, and from thence to the end of the next session of Congress, and no longer.*

Power of Attorney.

Know all men by these presents, that we ———, ———, comprising the firm of ———, ———, doing business at ————, in the State of ————, do hereby make, constitute and appoint ——— ———, of ———, our true and lawful attorney for us and in our names, or in the name of said firm, to enter in the manner provided by law, and the rules and regulations of the treasury department at any custom-house of the United States, for consumption, warehouse, warehouse and transportation, or warehouse and exportation, all or any goods, wares, or merchandise, which may be imported into the United States, for us, or in our names, or in the names of said firm of ——— ———, or which may be transferred to us whilst in warehouse, or which may be consigned us, on warehouse and transportation entry.

And we do further authorize our said attorney to execute and deliver in our names and under our seals such bond or bonds as may be necessary to be executed to the United States, or to the Collector of the Customs for the time being, in making such entry or withdrawal as aforesaid, in such penalty and upon such conditions as may be required by law or by the rules and regulations of the treasury department. And we further authorize our said attorney on entering said goods, wares and merchandise as aforesaid to receive the same, and to execute such oath of ownership and control over the same as we or either of us might do if we or either of us were personally present, and to receive from the United States, or the Collector of Customs, all sums of money which may become due to us for refund duties by reason of over-payments, damage on merchandise on the voyage of importation or otherwise.

* This section repealed by act of 11th Feb., 1800; and the residue of the act continued in force without limitation of time.

And we do further authorize our said attorney, an attorney, or attorneys under him for that purpose, to make and substitute, with full power to do all that he might or could, under and by virtue of his power of attorney, hereby ratifying and confirming all that our said attorney, or his substitute or substitutes, shall do in his behalf.

In witness whereof we have hereunto set our names and seals, this —— day of ————, A. D., 186—,

Sealed and delivered }
in presence of }

[NOTE.—This power of attorney should be signed by every member of the firm, and be executed and acknowledged before a Notary Public.]

Power of Substitution.

Know all men by these presents, that I, ———— ————, by virtue of the power of attorney, executed by ———— ———— to me, bearing date the —— day of ————, 186—, do substitute and appoint ———— ———— to do, perform and execute every act or thing which I might or could do in, by, and under the aforesaid power.

In witness whereof I have hereunto set my hand and seal this —— day of ————, 186—.

In the presence of

TREASURY DEPARTMENT, *March 24th*, 1860.

The following regulation is in addition to those prescribed in article 451 of the General Regulations of the 1st of February, 1857, viz.:

Railroad iron, sugar and molasses in hogsheads, and all other goods in bulk which cannot be put into locked cars, may be transported in platform cars, which must be duly bonded and the merchandise so manifested that every rticle shall be particularly described.

Instead of article 954 of the General Regulations the following will be substituted·

Foreign merchandise duly entered free of duty, or duty paid, and merchandise of domestic origin, may be transported over these routes into Canada, and thence into the United States, in cars bonded and secured as provided in article 451; and to prevent detention of the goods and frauds on the public revenue, the owner or consignee shall, at the frontier port, before the merchandise is transported into Canada, present manifests thereof in triplicate, snbscribed by him, to the collector, in which shall be specified the description of the articles, the marks and numbers of the packages shipped by him, the ports of destination, to whom consigned, and the route over which the transportation is to be made.

www.ingramcontent.com/pod-product-compliance
Lightning Source LLC
LaVergne TN
LVHW010232110826
845151LV00004B/1269